TO CROWN THE WAVES

I0808962

TO CROWN THE WAVES

THE GREAT NAVIES OF THE FIRST WORLD WAR

EDITED BY
Vincent P. O'Hara
W. David Dickson
Richard Worth

NAVAL INSTITUTE PRESS
ANNAPOLIS, MARYLAND

Naval Institute Press
291 Wood Road
Annapolis, MD 21402

© 2013 by Vincent O'Hara
All rights reserved. No part of this book may be reproduced or utilized in any form or by any means, electronic or mechanical, including photocopying and recording, or by any information storage and retrieval system, without permission in writing from the publisher.

First Naval Institute Press paperback edition published in 2021.
ISBN: 978-1-68247-648-2 (paperback)
ISBN: 978-1-61251-269-3 (eBook)

The Library of Congress has cataloged the hardcover edition as follows:
To crown the waves : the great navies of the First World War / edited by Vincent P. O'Hara, W. David Dickson, and Richard Worth.
pages cm
Includes bibliographical references and index.
ISBN 978-1-61251-082-8 (hbk. : alk. paper) — ISBN 978-1-61251-269-3 (ebook) 1. World War, 1914–1918—Naval operations. 2. Navies—History—20th century. 3. Naval history, Modern—20th century. I. O'Hara, Vincent P., date II. Dickson, W. David, date III. Worth, Richard, date
D580.C83 2013
940.4'5—dc23

2013000611

♾ Print editions meet the requirements of ANSI/NISO z39.48-1992 (Permanence of Paper).
Printed in the United States of America.

29 28 27 26 25 24 23 22 21 9 8 7 6 5 4 3 2 1
First printing

CONTENTS

MAPS, TABLES, AND ILLUSTRATIONS

Maps

Tables

Illustrations

ACKNOWLEDGMENTS

To Crown the Waves is a collaborative effort and would not exist without the help and patience of many people. Richard Worth and W. David Dickson have worked with me four years on this project and its predecessor, *On Seas Contested*. They have recruited participants, read, reviewed, and revised the chapters and have written material. They have, however, been above all patient and willing, and I sincerely appreciate their belief and participation in this work. Dr. Zvonimir Freivogel, Jean Moulin, and John Roberts came to this project new, finding the time in their schedules to undertake what is basically a labor of love, and with their expertise they have made this a far better book. Trent Hone, Stephen McLaughlin, Axel Niestlé, Dr. Peter Schenk, and Dieter Thomaier knew what they were getting into and agreed to contribute anyway. My thanks to all of them. Dr. Enrico Cernuschi receives special thanks. Dr. Cernuschi has contributed far more than his share of the Italian chapter and has read and commented on the entire manuscript. I also want to give special thanks to Michael Yaklich, of Pittsburgh, Pennsylvania, who has been an astute reader and has contributed many, many corrections and improvements. Thanks to John Spencer for assisting in the translation of Mr. Moulin's chapter from French to English. Tom Cutler is my editor at Naval Institute, and I thank him for his constant and generous support. Finally, as I type these words I think of the time away from my family I have spent working on this and other books, and I thank my wife, Maria, and my children, Yunuen and Vincent, who stand by my side in all that I do.

VINCENT P. O'HARA

INTRODUCTION

It has been a century since a Serbian nationalist assassinated the Austrian archduke Franz Ferdinand in Bosnia and the continent of Europe descended into an orgy of savagery that today is called the First World War. The reason why such a relatively rich and self-confident community of nations, sharing for the most part a common culture, could turn upon itself in such barbaric fashion is perhaps the great question of the twentieth century. A short list of the war's tragic offspring includes the Great Depression, World War II, the Holocaust, and the Cold War. Even the political divisions of the Middle East that are at the roots of much twenty-first century unrest are a consequence of the Great War.

The veterans of the First World War are all gone. The picture of the conflict that lingers in the collective memory of their descendants is one of muddy trenches and young men, faces encased in gas masks, crouching in a blasted landscape. The land armies numbered almost seventy million, and the deaths eight million, so this perception is natural. However, it obscures that essential fact that the First World War was also fought at sea, and there, in the failed naval blockade of the United Kingdom and the successful blockade of the Central Powers, the war was eventually won.

The carnage inflicted at sea was tremendous. It included the loss of over 13 million tons of mercantile shipping and 756 major warships, including 27 Allied and 7 Central Power capital ships. More than 100,000 men died. From this turmoil the images that resonate are dreadnought battleships cutting through the waves in massive lines and predator submarines lurking in the oceanic wastes. The war at sea, however, was more, and these images might as well include a German cruiser bottled up an African river, or the kaiser's East Asian flotilla massacring a British squadron off Chile or being annihilated itself in the South Atlantic; more than 8,500 men died in a single North Sea clash of dreadnoughts; battleships dueled on the Black Sea; there were amphibious assaults against Baltic islands; and bi-wing bombers clustered on the decks of primitive aircraft carriers. The war at sea was global in its dimensions, and once the land war stalemated on the western front, it was on the waves that victory was determined.

The world's premier navy, Britain's Royal Navy, led the Triple Entente, or the Allies, with support from the French Marine Nationale and the Imperial Russian Navy. In opposition, the German Kaiserliche Marine teamed with the Austro-Hungarian Kaiserliche und Königliche Kriegsmarine, but a diplomatic twist sent the third member of this Triple Alliance, Italy's Regia Marina, to the Allied side. Two years later Germany's own naval efforts provoked the United States into joining the Allied camp as well.

At sea World War I was a time of new and rapidly evolving martial technologies and the collision of nineteenth-century concepts with twentieth-century weapons. Admiral Jacky Fisher, the creative genius behind the all-big-gun battleship, first served on board HMS *Victory,* which had been Admiral Nelson's flagship at Trafalgar. Within the span of Fisher's career, steel superseded wood, sail gave way to steam, and giant guns hurling one-ton shells a distance of ten miles replaced muzzle-loading smooth-bore cannons. Torpedoes appeared, launched now by the sinister submersible and the pesky airplane that transformed sea warfare to a three-dimensional affair. The challenges faced by men like Fisher and his near contemporaries Germany's Alfred Tirpitz, Italy's Paolo Thaon di Revel, Japan's Heihachiro Togo, and America's William Benson seem likely to be repeated as twentieth-century militaries struggle to incorporate twenty-first-century technologies.

To Crown the Waves is an examination of the war at sea and the seven major navies that fought this war. It pools the expertise of historians from five nations who examine not only ships and weaponry but also doctrines and traditions, industry and bases, training and goals—less tangible factors that gave each fleet a unique personality and influenced how it met the challenges it faced. Laid out to a common structure, the chapters allow for easy reference and comparison following this outline:

I. Backstory
   A. Pre-1914 history
   B. Mission/function (navy's prewar missions, intended enemy, construction philosophy)

- II. Organization
  - A. Command structure
    - 1. Administration
    - 2. Command and fleet organization
    - 3. Communications
    - 4. Intelligence
  - B. Infrastructure, logistics, and commerce
    - 1. Bases
    - 2. Industry
    - 3. Shipping
  - C. Personnel
    - 1. Demographics
    - 2. Training
    - 3. Culture
- III. The Ways of War
  - A. Surface warfare
    - 1. Doctrine
    - 2. Ships/weapons
  - B. Submarine warfare
    - 1. Offensive
      - a. Doctrine
      - b. Boats/weapons
    - 2. Antisubmarine
  - C. Mine warfare
    - 1. Doctrine
    - 2. Ships/weapons
  - D. Amphibious warfare
    - 1. Doctrine/capabilities
    - 2. Coastal defense
  - E. Aviation
- IV. War Experience and Evolution
  - A. Wartime evolution
    - 1. Surface warfare
    - 2. Submarines
    - 3. Aviation
  - B. Summary and assessment.

To Crown the Waves follows several conventions. Rather than wrestle the metric-measurement navies into the imperial system used by the U.S.

Navy and the Royal Navy (or vice versa), this work adheres to neither one system nor the other; the appendix provides a conversion table. All miles are nautical miles. Non-English terms are used sparingly, and ranks are expressed in English. The book is lightly footnoted, and a selected bibliography lists the more important works consulted by the authors as well as additional references in English.

Editors:
Vincent P. O'Hara, of Chula Vista, California, W. David Dickson of Hernando, Mississippi, and Richard Worth of Bolivar, Missouri, also edited *On Seas Contested: The Seven Great Navies of the Second World War*, published by Naval Institute Press (2010).

Contributing authors:
Chapter 1, the Austro-Hungarian Kaiserliche und Königliche Kriegsmarine, is the work of Zvonimir Freivogel, who is based in Germany. Dr. Freivogel has published books and articles in German, English, Italian, Polish, and Serbo-Croatian in periodicals including *Warship*, *STORIA Militare*, and *Okręty Wojenne*. Dr. Freivogel's most recent work is *Tauchgang um das K.u.K. Schlachtschiff Szent* Istvan (Marine Arsenal, 2008).

Chapter 2, on the French Marine Nationale, is authored by Jean Moulin of Blois, France. Mr. Moulin has written forty-seven books and more than a hundred articles on naval subjects, most recently *Les contre-torpilleurs de type* Aigle (Marine Editions, 2012).

Chapter 3, on the German Kaiserliche Marine, is a collaboration by the authors who also wrote the German chapter in *On Seas Contested*. It is led by Dr. Peter Schenk and includes Axel Niestlé, and Dieter Thomaier, all from Germany.

Chapter 4, on the British Royal Navy, is by John Roberts of England, whose recent credits include *Battleship Dreadnought* (Conway Maritime Press, 2003) and *British Warships of the Second World War* (Chatham, 2003).

Chapter 5, on the Italian Regia Marina, is the work of Enrico Cernuschi of Pavia Italy and Vincent P. O'Hara, the co-authors of the Italian chapter in *On Seas Contested*. Mr. Cernuschi has written more than twenty books and three hundred articles. Mr. O'Hara's most recent work is *In Passage Perilous: Malta and the Convoy Battles of June 1942* (Indiana University Press, 2012).

Chapter 6, on the Russian Imperial Navy, is authored by Stephen McLaughlin. Mr. McLaughlin's credits include the Soviet chapter in *On Seas Contested*, "Russian and Soviet Battleships" (Naval Institute Press, 2003), as well as many articles on the Russian navy in *Warship* and *Warship International*.

Trent Hone contributed chapter 7, on the U.S. Navy. Mr. Hone also wrote the U.S. Navy chapter in *On Seas Contested*. He is coauthor of *Battle Line: The United States Navy 1919–1939* (Naval Institute Press, 2006) and has written for the *Journal of Military History*, *Naval War College Review*, and *Warship*.

The introduction, chapter 8, and the conclusion are the work of the editors.

1

AUSTRIA-HUNGARY

Die Kaiserliche und Königliche Kriegsmarine

Zvonimir Freivogel

BACKSTORY

Pre-1914 History

The Austro-Hungarian Imperial and Royal (*kaiserliche und königliche*, or k.u.k.) Navy was a relatively recent naval force, despite the facts that the Austrian Empire was one Europe's oldest states and that as early as 1379 and 1382 the towns of Duino and Trieste on the northeastern Adriatic coast had sworn allegiance to the Habsburgs. Austria was, like Germany, a predominantly continental-oriented power, and over the next four hundred years few efforts were undertaken to develop a navy. Attempts by Emperors Charles VI (1685–1740) and Joseph II (1741–90) were thwarted by Venice, a regional naval power, and Austria commanded only several gunboats for trade protection along its short coastal stretch.

Austria's first real chance to develop a navy came in 1797, when Austria—in accordance with the peace treaty of Campo Formio and in exchange for its Dutch provinces—received from Napoleon all Venetian territories, including Istria and Dalmatia, and the naval arsenal at Venice as well. But this "gift horse" was toothless: French soldiers removed most of the materials from the arsenal, damaging warships being built or repaired there, and between 1798 and 1805 the Austro-Venetian navy had at its disposal only few frigates and smaller sailing vessels. In 1805 even these became French, but in 1814 Austria conquered Venice, Istria, and Dalmatia once again, acquiring the remnants of France's Venetian and Illyrian naval detachments. Thereafter the small Austrian navy patrolled the Adriatic and sent single ships into the Levant, and in 1840 a naval force operated with British and Turkish warships off the Syrian coast against Mehmed Ali's efforts to establish Egyptian independence from the Ottomans.

The Austrian navy's organizational structure became independent from the army in 1824, but the fleet—with Venetian (Italian) officers and crews from Venice, Croatia, Dalmatia, and Istria—remained a "foreign body" for continental Austrians. This was accentuated by the mutiny at Venice in 1848, during which most of the ships raised Italian flags. A small part of the navy operated from Trieste in the blockade of Venice put the mutiny down in 1849. Afterward the navy was reorganized: the officer corps, the command language, and the ship's names were Germanized, and the main naval base was transferred from Venice to Pola, where a new naval arsenal was established in 1856. In 1859, during the Franco-Sardinian war against Austria, a French naval detachment operated unmolested in the Adriatic, even using Lussin Island as a naval base, but after 1860 the imperial navy, under Archduke Ferdinand Max—the future and ill-fated Emperor Maximilian I of Mexico—made great progress, building its first ironclads and taking part in the Danish-German war in 1864. The war of 1866—with Prussia and Italy against Austria—forged the navy: under Rear Admiral Wilhelm v. Tegetthoff it defeated off Lissa a larger Italian fleet in the biggest naval action fought between Trafalgar and Tsushima. Nonetheless, defeated by Prussia on land, Austria was compelled to cede Venice to Italy, though it retained the eastern Adriatic coast.

After the glorious 1866 victory, the Austrian (from 1867 Austro-Hungarian) navy was neglected again. Its best commander, Admiral Tegetthoff, died prematurely in 1871, and the fleet fell into disrepair. Financial restrictions made shipbuilding almost impossible. In addition to four newly built center-battery ships, four Lissa veterans (including one wooden ship of the line) were similarly "modernized," built anew but using funds appropriated for refit and repair. The fleet commander, Admiral Maximilian von Sterneck, adapted the ideas of the Jeune École, and between 1880 and 1898 Austria built two ram-cruisers, called "Sterneck's tin cans," followed by one armored cruiser, five coastal-defense battleships, three torpedo cruisers, and scores of torpedo boats. In fact, the "fish torpedo" was invented in Fiume by the English businessman Robert Whitehead from an idea of the Croatian/Austrian naval officer J. Luppis. Torpedo units of the Austrian navy were seen as a "mobile line of defense" in the passages between the numerous islands along the eastern Adriatic coast.

Between 1898 and 1913 systematical building programs were possible for the first time under Admirals Hermann von Spaun and Count

Rudolf Montecuccoli di Polinago, officers who held in succession the post of commander in chief, leading the navy in accordance with Alfred Thayer Mahan's ideas. Three 8,000- and three 10,000-metric-ton battleships were built before 1907, together with two armored and three protected cruisers, twelve destroyers, and thirty-six torpedo boats. The Austrian navy was, at the beginning of the twentieth century, the world's eighth largest, climbing to the seventh after the Russian fleet was decimated during the Russo-Japanese war.

After 1907, there followed three 14,000-ton predreadnoughts and the first submarines. Two 20,000-ton dreadnoughts were ordered in 1910, followed by two more dreadnoughts, four scout cruisers, six destroyers, twenty-seven torpedo boats, and several smaller units. All these vessels were completed before or during the war, in contrast to the follow-on units of the 1914 program (four 24,000-ton dreadnoughts, three 4,900-ton cruisers, six destroyers, and five submarines), which were not laid down due to the outbreak of war.

Mission/Function

Austria ruled 370 miles of Adriatic coast but lacked a port on the open Mediterranean. Not surprisingly, the Austrian navy considered the Adriatic and its approaches as its most probable theater of war, and for strategic (and economical) reasons the fleet was configured for coastal defense. Nonetheless, naval operations between 1872 and 1914 included international "peacekeeping" missions in the eastern Mediterranean and numerous training and diplomatic missions around the world, like the participation of Austro-Hungarian cruisers and landing detachments in the Boxer Rebellion in China in 1900–1901. At the same time Austria pursued a policy of expansion to the east in the direction of Greece, coming into conflict with Serbia. Another rivalry existed between Austria-Hungary and Italy, which was trying to expand in the same area and saw the Adriatic as an Italian "lake." Czarist Russia, which sought free access to the Mediterranean and wished to conquer Constantinople, was another traditional Balkan rival. Great Britain opposed Russian aspirations, wishing to see the Ottoman Empire slowly fade away and thus to increase its influence in the Middle East and secure vital routes to India. France sought influence in Syria, and Germany in Asia Minor. Thanks to delicate British diplomacy (and to several blunders on the German and Austrian side), the Triple Alliance of Germany, Austria, and Italy was slowly encircled by the Entente Cordiale of France, Great Britain, and Russia. In the case of war against the French and British navies in the Mediterranean, the combined Italian and Austrian fleets, together with the German Mediterranean Squadron, were to operate from Sicilian bases under the overall command of the Austrian commander in chief, Admiral Anton Haus.

Because of rising tensions in Italian-Austrian affairs, the Austrian chief of the General Staff, General Conrad von Hötzendorf, developed from 1909 new "war scenarios": War Case I assumed war against Italy, with Germany and Russia remaining neutral; War Case B (for Balkans) assumed war against Serbia and Montenegro, with all other nations neutral; War Case R assumed a conflict in alliance with Germany and Romania against Russia, with other nations neutral, but included secondary actions against Serbia and Montenegro.

In the case of war with Italy military strategy envisaged an offensive thrust into Italian territory by the bulk of the army—supported by the navy, assuming command of the sea was acquired. Although the Italian navy was stronger than the Austrian, Austrian naval strategy was conceived in an offensive spirit, and the war at sea was to start with a massive surprise attack by a cruiser flotilla on large Italian bases, merchant shipping, and coastal targets. The strategic doctrine was based on belief in the need to seek a decisive battle with the enemy in order to obtain command of the sea, and it was thought that this decisive battle would take place immediately after the outbreak of war. Because the Austrian main battle fleet was based at Pola, this engagement could take place in the area between Pola and Trieste or, in case Italy was allied with Montenegro, off the Gulf of Cattaro. If the Italian navy obtained command of the sea, the principal mission of the Austrian fleet would be defense of the coast, with the battle fleet concentrated at Pola and the mobile defense resting largely on torpedo boats, augmented by scout cruisers and destroyers.

These plans came to nothing in the summer of 1914, when the chain reaction of alliances and treaties pulled almost all nations into the Great War. Italy remained neutral at first, which left the Imperial and Royal Navy locked in the Adriatic and the Germans at Constantinople. Austria's major opponent at sea during this period was the French Marine Nationale. The navy's task was to defend the Adriatic, but Admiral Haus did not react to the French battle fleet's initial probes into the Adriatic in 1914, trying to preserve his fleet for the decisive battle against the Italian archenemy. When Italy finally joined the Entente in May 1915 and declared war on Austria-Hungary, the k.u.k. main fleet shelled Italian Adriatic towns unopposed while the Italian dreadnoughts remained at Taranto. The Austrian battle fleet was afterward degraded to the role of a "fleet-in-being," and the war theater was left to light forces and submarines. At this point the navy's war tasks were to protect supply lines, support air attacks against Italian soil, and help Austrian and German submarines reach the Mediterranean. There were neither enough fast cruisers and destroyers for the all necessary tasks nor large enough submarines to wage a traffic war in the Mediterranean. Nonetheless, the Austrian navy was successful in defending the coast and in providing the logistical base for submarine operations in the Mediterranean.

ORGANIZATION

Command Structure

Administration

In the Dual Monarchy there were only three ministries: war, finance, and foreign affairs, with the navy represented by the Naval Section in the War Ministry. Austria-Hungary concentrated its main interest and resources on the army, and the navy was a stepchild in regard to financial allocations. Between 1866 and 1904 the naval share of the total defense budget rose from 7.7 to 15.7 percent. In 1867 the Austrian naval budget amounted to 7.625 million crowns, rising to only 17.4 million crowns in 1899, compared to an Italian naval budget of 90 million crowns and a British Royal Navy budget of 550 million crowns.[1] Another obstacle was the initial Hungarian opposition to increases in naval expenditure. Because of the dual status of the Austro-Hungarian Empire, the two independent parliament delegations of Austria and Hungary needed to mutually approve the defense budget, and the Hungarians were initially against naval programs, partially because the kingdom lacked significant ship- and ordnance-building facilities.

In 1904 the navy was required to cut its special budget requirements from 50 to 25 million crowns, while the army was asked to reduce its provision by only 5 million crowns; Admiral Spaun resigned in protest. No new construction was provided between 1905 and 1909. The 1910 budget included two installments to amortize old debts but again no funds for new ships. The heir to the throne, Archduke Franz Ferdinand, became in the meantime fond of the navy, supporting Admiral Montecuccoli in plans that included ordering two dreadnoughts in 1910 and taking a credit of 32 million crowns for this purpose.[2] In 1911 these funds were approved, and when Montecuccoli retired in 1913 on his seventieth birthday the Austro-Hungarian navy had 700 officers, 10,000 sailors and technicians, and 16,000 reservists. Montecuccoli's successor, Vice Admiral Haus, had more luck with his 1914 budget, but these funds had not been used when the war broke out.

Organization

Command Organization

The commander in chief of the Austro-Hungarian navy was at the same time head of the Naval Section in the War Ministry at Vienna and supervised several departments. His staff included two admirals, ten staff officers (i.e., in the rank of captain or commander), fourteen more junior officers and nine officers for local duties, five high-ranking engineers, one high-ranking legal and medical officer, fourteen supply officers, and several clerks. Having ministerial rank, the commander in chief was responsible for naval matters and funding and answered to delegations of both parliaments. In 1913 Admiral Haus transferred his seat of command from Vienna to Pola, but the Naval Section of the War Ministry, under his deputy, Rear Admiral Karl Kailer von Kaltenfels, remained at Vienna. Haus had with him at Pola only a small staff, led by his chief of staff, Captain Alfred Cicoli, who was succeeded in 1914 by Captain Joseph Rodler.

Haus—promoted to the rank of grand admiral—died in February 1917, and his successor, Admiral Maximilian Njegovan, remained responsible for operational control, but the position of the head of Naval Section was separated and given to Vice Admiral Kailer, partially to curtail the commander in chief's political influence in Vienna. Njegovan was retired in February 1918, after a sailors' mutiny in the Bays of Cattaro, to be replaced by young Rear Admiral Miklós Horthy de Nagybanya, popular after his dashing attack against the Otranto Barrage in May 1917. Local naval commanders on land were the:

a. Harbor Admiral of Pola (in 1914 Vice Admiral Eugen Ritter von Chmelarz), responsible for the defense of Pola and Istria, except the Trieste area
b. Naval coastal commander of the Trieste area (Rear Admiral Alfred Freiherr von Koudelka), responsible for shipbuilding at Trieste
c. Naval coastal commander of the Sebenico area (Rear Admiral Hugo Zaccaria from 1913, when this command was established)
d. Naval coastal commander at Castelnuovo in the Bocche di Cattaro (Captain Egon Klein).

Fleet Organization and Order of Battle

The Austro-Hungarian navy was organized after well-proven British and French principles. In peacetime one squadron under a vice admiral was operational year-round, with one division of the three newest battleships and the Cruiser Flotilla, which included one armored cruiser, one light cruiser, and a destroyer/torpedo-boat flotilla. In summer a second squadron, with another battleship division, additional cruisers, and more torpedo units reinforced the active squadron. In winter these vessels served at Pola as a reserve squadron, for training purposes with reduced crews but ready to be operational at short notice.

After mobilization, according to the order of battle for 27 July 1914, principal seagoing forces were the Battle Fleet at Pola, under the direct command of Admiral Haus, and the Cruiser Flotilla. The Battle Fleet included 1st and 2nd Heavy Squadrons. The 1st, under Vice Admiral Maximilian Njegovan, comprised the 1st Division, with three *Tegetthoff*-class dreadnoughts under Njegovan himself, and the 2nd, with three *Radetzky*-class battleships under Rear Admiral Anton Willenik. The 2nd Squadron, under Rear Admiral Franz Löfler, comprised the 3rd Division, with three *Erzherzog*-class battleships under Löfler, and the 4th, with three *Habsburg*-class battleships under Rear Admiral Karl Seidensacher.

The Cruiser Flotilla, under Rear Admiral Paul Fiedler, comprised the 1st Cruiser Division (with three armored cruisers, three light cruisers, *Szigetvár, Zenta,* and *Aspern*) and two torpedo flotillas. The 1st Torpedo Flotilla—led by the scout cruiser *Saida,* under Captain Heinrich Seitz—included the 1st, 2nd, and 3rd Torpedo Divisions, with six *Tátra-* and six *Huszár*-class destroyers and ten torpedo boats. The 2nd Torpedo Flotilla—led by the scout *Admiral Spaun,* under Captain Benno von Millenkovich—comprised the 4th, 5th, and 6th Torpedo Divisions, with six *Huszár*-class destroyers and eighteen torpedo boats. Attached to the torpedo flotillas were the torpedo depot ships *Gäa* and *Steamer IV.*

The fleet train included the repair ship *Cyclop,* the yacht *Lacroma,* oil tanker *Vesta,* water carrier *Najade,* tug *Gigant,* old destroyer *Meteor,* and several steamers for transport and storing of ammunitions, provisions, coals, fuel, and barrage equipment, like antisubmarine nets and booms. The 5th Heavy Division, with three coastal battleships of the *Monarch* class under Rear Admiral Richard Ritter von Barry, and the 2nd Cruiser Division, with the old cruisers *Kaiser Franz Joseph I* and *Panther,* were initially stationed in the Bocche di Cattaro for defense against Montenegro.

The local command at Pola was responsible for the inner harbor, the Fasana anchorage, and the areas between Cap Compare and Peneda and between Cap Compare and Promontore. It had at its disposal several hulks and harbor-defense vessels, including the old cruiser *Leopard,* two minelayers, some tugs and dispatch boats, and the 7th Torpedo Division, with three old destroyers and eight old torpedo boats. Attached to the Pola defenses were the Submarine Station, with the depot ship *Pelikan* under Lieutenant Commander Franz Ritter von Thierry (also commander of the Submarine

Station) and six submarines, and a detachment of seven minesweepers converted from torpedo boats. Defense of Lussin (part of the Pola Harbor Command) was provided by the old destroyer *Magnet,* four smaller torpedo boats, and several mine depot ships.

The Trieste Naval Command had at its disposal mine depot ships of Mining Command IV, with four older torpedo boats, four customs guard steamers, and two requisitioned vessels. Local defense of Sebenico included Mining Command III, with two mine depot ships, two minesweepers, old destroyer *Komet,* and eight older torpedo boats. Naval defenses of the Bocche di Cattaro comprised the Mining Command II, with the old ironclad *Kronprinz Erzherzog Rudolf* as harbor guard ship, under Commander Richard Florio, together with the minelayer *Dromedar* and the tug *Büffel,* two minesweepers, the old torpedo ship *Zara,* the stationary ship *Kaiser Max,* the old destroyer *Blitz,* and four old torpedo boats.

Communications

As early as during the 1866 war, telegraph lines from Lissa and Lessina had served to inform Tegetthoff at Pola about the activities of Italian fleet, enabling him to sail in time to defeat the enemy. Before 1914 communication lines along the coast were modernized to include wireless equipment.

Tactical

During peacetime the naval reconnaissance and communications service used signal stations along the coast. Before the war this service was upgraded by powerful wireless stations at Pola, Sebenico, and Klinci in the Bocche di Cattaro, new observation and signals stations, and the construction of the Central Information Collecting Station at Pola. There were sixteen peacetime signal stations—four in the Pola Section, nine in the Sebenico Section, and three in the Klinci Section—with another eleven installed after mobilization. Civilian postal installations at Trieste, Pola, Spalato, Zara, and Ragusa served as signals stations for the navy. After mobilization all regular stations received additional personnel, and new stations were established in shortest possible time. During the war their number grew again, with observation posts on Curzola, near Raguza, in the Trieste area, and between the Bocche and Durazzo.

In 1903 some Austro-Hungarian ships were equipped with experimental wireless stations of Siemens-Braun and Rochefort types, and from 1904 additional Siemens-Braun wireless stations were ordered. After 1907 the navy introduced a new wireless specialty for crewmen. Some ships received Telefunken or Poulsen wireless apparatus, but Telefunken-type stations were found to be of better quality, being also promoted for merchant ships by the Ministry of Commerce, in contrast to the Marconi apparatus carried by some merchant vessels. In 1914 there were fifty-five wireless stations on k.u.k. warships, and during the war their number rose to 219, all of Telefunken type and mostly delivered by the Siemens & Halske factory at Vienna.

Strategic

Long-range wireless stations at Pola (Radio-Pola, from 1916 called Radio-Tivoli, with a thousand-kilometer range), Sebenico, Castelnuovo, and Lussin enabled communications with fleet units on the Adriatic and in the Mediterranean. During the war a strong new wireless station was built east of Pola (Gross-Radio-Pola), to become operational on 5 September 1916. "Old" Radio-Pola served afterward as a reserve and "eavesdropping" station.

Intelligence

Admiral Haus upgraded the intelligence organization and modeled it after British naval intelligence. The Naval Evidence Bureau at Pola collected data on foreign navies and published reports and books for use of naval officers. Foreign wireless and telephone messages were intercepted even before the war and partially deciphered. "Collecting offices" (*Sammelstellen*) at Sebenico and Klinci sent data received from local signal stations—like visual and sound detections of ships or naval gunfire, sightings of airplanes, suspect movements of boats or people—to the Central Office (Zentrale Sammelstelle) at Pola, where all information, including items dispatched by secret agents, was collated, compared, and evaluated by naval officers to build a "plotting image" for use by naval commanders.

To protect Austrian wireless traffic, firm rules were followed and codes were completely changed each time it seemed they might have been compromised, such as after the losses of *U 12* off Venice, of destroyer *Lika* in shallow water off Durazzo, and of German *UC 12* off Taranto, and after the defection of torpedo boat *T 11* to the Italians. This was in contrast to German practice, where codes remained unchanged after the loss of the cruiser *Magdeburg*, enabling British cryptographers to read German wireless messages for the remainder of the war.

Regarding "special operations" of Austro-Hungarian agents, the Italian battleships *Benedetto Brin* and *Leonardo da Vinci* were sunk in harbor by Austrian saboteurs who smuggled explosive devices on board. Another action, to "kidnap" Italian MAS (motor torpedo) boats from Ancona in April 1918, went awry. Austrian sailors entered the city unhindered in uniforms similar to those of the Regia Marina, but the single MAS found in the harbor was not operational, and the Austrian agents all became prisoners of war.

Infrastructure, Logistics, and Commerce

Bases

The principal Austro-Hungarian naval base was the Central War Harbor (Zentralkriegshafen) at Pola, with an extensive naval arsenal. There were numerous workshops, four slipways, four large and several smaller floating docks, floating cranes, and a score of harbor tugs, with two thousand permanent and up to three thousand periodically employed workers. In June 1915 the number of workers in the Arsenal and the Building Establishment reached 8,130. All kinds of warships and even seaplanes were built and repaired there, machinery, artillery, and torpedoes were serviced, ship's boats produced, and so forth. Attached to the arsenal was the Ammunition Institute at Vallelunga. Pola was the seat of the Naval Technical Committee, responsible for technical research, ship design, and improvement of armament. Other institutions were the Building Establishment, Hydrographical Institute, Naval Hospital, Supply Institute, Naval Clothing Institute, and Naval Court. The whole k.u.k. fleet could be anchored in the main harbor or dispersed to the Fasana anchorage. Pola was located at the southern tip of the Istria Peninsula, and it dominated the northern Adriatic, including shipping routes to and from Venice—the main Italian harbor on the Adriatic—and to Ancona in the southwest. At the same time it shielded the principal Austrian merchant harbors of Trieste and Fiume. The harbor was protected by older and newer fortifications, as well as by fortified lines on land. The harbor of Lussin Piccolo on Lussin served as a base for torpedo boats and a dispersion anchorage for bigger vessels.

Because Pola was near Italy, the navy envisaged building another naval base. One of the locations considered was Sebenico, easy to protect because of its narrow entrance but even easier for a determined enemy to blockade, because the islands off Sebenico were not fortified. Another possible location was Trau, west of Spalato, but the cost of fortifying nearby islands was again prohibitive, and only Sebenico was developed, as a secondary base for torpedo flotillas.

In the south, the great natural harbor of Bocche di Cattaro encompassed several deep and well-protected bays, but they were within artillery range of Montenegrin positions. After the defeat of Montenegro in January 1916, the Bocche served as a permanent base for Austrian and German submarines operating in the Mediterranean and for the k.u.k. Cruiser Flotilla. The local arsenal at Teodo performed small-scale repairs. (See map 1.1.)

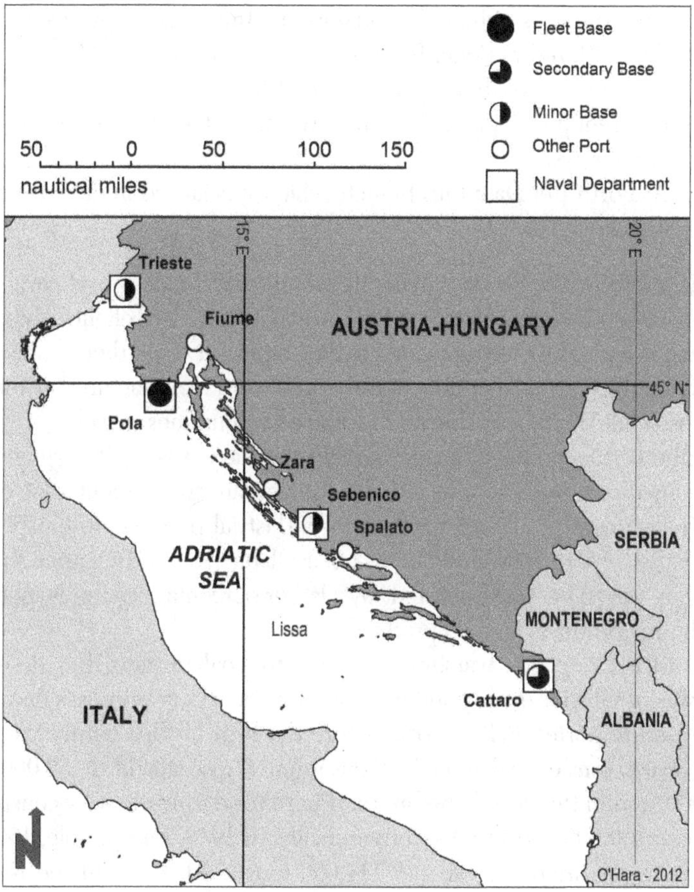

Map 1.1. Austro-Hungarian Naval Bases

Industry

Austria-Hungary had before 1914 an industrial base adequate to build and maintain the navy. In addition to the Pola Arsenal the major shipyards included:

- At Trieste: Stabilimento Tecnico Triestino/STT, where all modern battleships except one were built.
- At Monfalcone: Cantiere Navale Triestino/CNT, which constructed lighter units.
- At Fiume, on Hungary's coastal enclave: the new Ganz-Danubius shipyard, where one dreadnought, two scout cruisers, and several destroyers, torpedo boats, and submarines were built. One of the

consequences of building warships in Hungarian shipyards was that they differed in detail from the Austrian-built ships. Most extreme was the case of dreadnought *Szent István*, which had a completely different power plant, with only two, and not four, steam-turbine sets and screws.

- At Porto Re: Danubius branch, which specialized in destroyers and torpedo boats.

In addition, the Skoda armament factory at Plzen delivered naval guns of all calibers. The steel factory at Witkowitz fabricated excellent armor plating, and even in the Hungarian half of the empire, at Györ, there was a naval armament factory. As mentioned, torpedoes were manufactured at Fiume, and the small Whitehead shipyard produced submarines as well.

One of the problems in developing the navy was a 1904 agreement between the Naval Section and the Hungarian government that called for 34.4 percent of all expenditures for industrial products to be spent in Hungary. If a particular product was not available from a Hungarian source, Hungary was to be "compensated" by a larger percentage of funds spent for purchasing products it could produce.

Austro-Hungarian warships were mostly coal burners, but domestic coal was of inferior quality and was used for secondary purposes only. The fleet used imported British coal. Before the turn of the century the navy used 30,000 tons of coal annually. Consumption rose steadily to 50,000 tons in 1900, and in the decade before the First World War the navy consumed between 100,000 and 115,000 tons annually. In 1912, for example, 150,000 tons were procured abroad, and 117,000 tons used. By 1914 the reserve equaled 500,000 tons—a quantity insufficient for a long war, when imports would be cut by blockade. It was one of the reasons fleet movements were curtailed in the second half of the war. Some of the ships had partially oil-burning furnaces (new battleships, destroyers of the *Tátra* class, 250-ton torpedo boats) or used only oil (new coastal torpedo boats), and twelve big oil tanks were built at Pola.

Shipping (Sea Routes and Traffic)

The Austro-Hungarian merchant navy had a strong presence in the eastern Mediterranean and operated on the high seas as well. The oldest and biggest shipping company was the Austrian Lloyd of Trieste, with sixty-two steamers at the turn of the century transporting yearly 1.5 million tons of cargo, followed by Austro-Americana, founded in 1895, with thirty-five steamers and a million tons of cargo. The third significant company was the Hungarian

Adria firm, with thirty-five steamers and 0.95 million tons of cargo yearly. The main merchant harbors were Austrian Trieste, where two-thirds of the maritime cargo and passenger traffic of the Habsburg Empire took place, and Hungarian Fiume, with one-third. Other harbors along the coast were of local significance, with smaller coastal shipping lines connecting the towns and the islands. One of the reasons for their existence was the insufficient road and railroad net: only Trieste, Pola, and Fiume were connected to the hinterland with standard-gauge railroad lines. The lines to Spalato and Sebenico were narrow-gauge, similar to the railroad connecting Sarajevo in Bosnia with Metkovic and Ragusa. From there a line led along the coast to the Bocche di Cattaro.

After the outbreak of war, almost all merchantmen, except these needed for local traffic or set aside for the navy, were sent to protected anchorages in the Bay of Buccari, on the Novigrad Sea near Zara, and to Prukljan Lake near Sebenico. Ships outside home waters were captured by the enemy or interned in neutral harbors, to be requisitioned later by the adversaries. Other merchant vessels in protected anchorages were later chartered by the Austro-Hungarian navy or army as transport or accommodation ships, auxiliary escorts, or submarine chasers.

Shipping routes along the coast were shielded by outer islands and protected at critical points by minefields, but there were two exposed areas—off Cape Planka (between Sebenico and Spalato) and between Ragusa and Bocche di Cattaro. There French submarines waited for Austro-Hungarian maritime traffic, damaging and sinking several merchantmen; later, Italian submarines penetrated the inner passage to attack shipping there.

Personnel

Demographics

In 1913 there were nine hundred naval officers, and together with naval clerks their number eventually reached 1,630. Some 72 percent were embarked (including stationary, harbor accommodation, and training ships), and the rest were stationed on land.

Conscripts were recruited in commands at Trieste, Fiume, and Sebenico for a period of four years, remaining later in the 1st and 2nd Reserves. Initially mostly Croatian seamen and fishermen from the coast were recruited for the navy. Their number—some five thousand—remained always constant, even in 1900, when the navy was only ten thousand men strong. Because the demands for crewmen grew to 18,000 in 1913 and to 20,000 in 1914, it became necessary for the navy to recruit from all parts of the Dual Monarchy, and the number of Germans, Czechs, and Hungarians grew accordingly, while the number of Croatians fell to a third of the total.

In 1913 there were 401 chief petty officers and 3,776 junior petty officers, mostly graduates from the Machine School at Pola and the school for noncommissioned officers (NCOs) at Sebenico, with others coming from the ranks of reenlisted cadres. In 1913 there were 12,500 men from the 1st Reserve, 7,100 from the 2nd, 2,260 from the additional reserve, and 800 on permanent leave. Through mobilization on 31 July 1914 the numbers of personnel rose to 33,736 men, with 19,405 embarked on operational ships.

Training

The Naval Academy at Fiume trained officers. It usually had 180 pupils (*Seeaspiranten*) but accepted additional students in the last years before the war. Supply officers were trained on the hulk *Bellona* at Pola. There was another school for naval aspirants on the hulk *Feuerspeier* used by the Artillery School at Pola, and the midshipmen (*Kadetten*) from Fiume went together with those from Pola to complete their theoretical studies on the training hulk *Custozza* at Pola. Practical studies were undertaken on ships of the fleet. At the end of each school term a cruise was conducted on board a training ship. After leaving the academy in the grade of ensign (*Fähnrich*), naval officers were further trained in specialties, like artillery, mining, or torpedoes. The Artillery School at Pola instructed officers, together with ninety NCOs and 650 sailors each year. Mining and torpedo schools were organized on two hulks, with annual classes of fourteen NCOs and 130 sailors in the Torpedo School and two hundred sailors in the Mining School, together with twenty-five NCOs and a hundred sailors of the wireless branch. The Machine School at Pola instructed 650 students in three classes, with a further four to five hundred active personnel designated for the machine branch. The NCO school at Sibenik had at its disposal two harbor ships and a new building at Mandalina, where six hundred pupils were trained as future NCOs in all branches, except for machinery and electrical.

During the war the Naval Academy was moved from Fiume to Schloss Hof, near Vienna, and later to Braunau at Inn, in Austria, remaining there until 1918. The level of naval officer training remained high, but during the war it was necessary to mobilize former merchant marine officers as reserve second lieutenants, and their training and sense of duty was sometimes seen as inadequate.

Culture

From Tegetthoff's time on, the Austrian officer corps learned in the Naval Academy not only the nautical and warrior "trades" but general education and culture as well, including at least two foreign languages. The officers were to know German as the official language, with Italian or Croatian as "unofficial" languages and English and French for general studies. After 1882, Hungarian language instruction was mandatory for all students coming from this part of the empire, and these students afterward could learn either English or French, but not both.

Austria-Hungary was a multinational empire, with twenty different nationalities. In contrast to the separate national regiments and battalions of the Austro-Hungarian army, every naval ship was an ethnic microcosm of the Dual Monarchy. The naval officer corps—in contrast to that of the army—contributed to the navy's successful record as a multinational institution. High-ranking officers, like Admiral Spaun, spoke and wrote German, English, Italian, and French, which was necessary for political, military, and diplomatic missions. Sailors often selected their specialties in accordance with their national and social backgrounds: Croatians and Italians were mostly deckhands, Germans and Czechs gunners and machinists, Magyars machine-gun crews, and so forth.

Table 1.1 Nationalities of Austro-Hungarian Officers and Seamen, 1885 and 1910

	Officers (percent)		Seamen (percent)	
Nationality	1885	1910	1885	1910
Germans	44.9	51.0	7.9	24.5
Magyars	14.7	12.9	5.6	12.6
Czechs	12.3	9.2	4.5 (inc. Slovaks)	7.1
Slovaks	-		-	2.4
Poles	4.0	2.8	0.5	1.0
Ruthenes	-	-	-	0.2
Slovenes	4.0	4.2	4.6	3.6
Croatians	10.3	9.8	44.9	29.8
Romanians	-	0.3	-	0.4
Italians	9.7	9.8	32.0	18.3

Source: After Lawrence Sondhaus, *The Austro-Hungarian Naval Officer Corps, 1867–1918.*

Moreover, despite the emperor's title "His Most Catholic Majesty," the k.u.k. navy practiced religious freedom, and even the Chief Naval Constructor, General-Engineer Siegfried Popper (who designed all modern Austro-Hungarian battleships), was of the Jewish faith. (See table 1.1.) Social differences between officers (coming from the middle class, with some from aristocratic circles) and their men (originating from the working class) were typical for this era and were more distinct on larger warships. For example, the living quarters for the thousand enlisted men on a *Tegetthoff*-class dreadnought were no bigger than the quarters for a hundred officers, including the admiral's cabin and saloon. The differences escalated during the war, when victuals became rare and officer's messes were better supplied than those of the crew, with some officers sharing the provisions with their families. In combination with war weariness (many peacetime sailors

Photo 1.1. Taking care of the men: The executive officer of a *Tegetthoff*-class battleship samples the rations prepared for the crew. (Courtesy of Eng. René Greger)

had already seen seven years of service), this resulted in bad blood between hungry crewmen and their officers and led to the mutiny in the Bocche in February 1918. The riots exploded on bigger warships, lying idle in harbor. On scout cruisers, destroyers, and torpedo boats the differences were less pronounced and the sense of duty higher, even more so in submarines, where everybody was literally in the same boat.

The Austro-Hungarian navy was a highly professional and effective force, maintaining the tradition and the spirit of Lissa, but when Emperor Charles ceded the fleet to the South-Slav National Council on 31 October 1918 it dissolved almost overnight, like the empire it represented. All non-Slav officers and men were disembarked and sent home, but the remaining South Slav and Czech seamen were not able to retain the fleet after Italians occupied Pola and French units Bocche di Cattaro. The ships were divided between the victorious states in 1920, to be—with few exceptions—scrapped shortly thereafter.

THE WAYS OF WAR

Surface Warfare

Doctrine

In the Austrian navy much greater attention was always given to tactics than to strategy, and the Naval Section regularly issued tactical and tactical-operational instructions for the fleet. Three principal factors were regarded as crucial in bringing a decisive outcome in battle: superiority in speed over the enemy, simultaneous concentrated fire on the weakest part of the enemy's main body, and the spiritual strength of commanders in combination with high crew morale.

The battle fleet included the most modern and largest battleships, fast cruisers, destroyers, and high-seas torpedo boats. Each of the several fleet detachments was subdivided into smaller tactical units. To be capable of successfully engaging the enemy at both short and long ranges, each fleet detachment was intended to include no more than eight and no fewer than six battleships, to ensure effective control. The basic tactical unit was a battle division, composed of three units of the same class, with exception of the 1st Battle Division with four units (after 1915, when the fourth dreadnought was completed). Two battle divisions constituted a battle squadron.

By day the fleet's cruising formation was to include an antisubmarine screen of cruisers and destroyers, while some ten to twelve miles ahead of the main body an armored cruiser was placed as the lead ship. Three scouting groups, each comprising a scout cruiser and a destroyer, were spread out and positioned within ten nautical miles of the lead ship. Torpedo flotillas were to sail in the rear, to be out of the way during a daylight battle. Torpedo boats were to intervene in the daylight battle only if their own battleships were disabled or to attack damaged enemy battleships. During the night, the scouting vessels and the protective screen were positioned within signal distance from the main body. The cruisers and destroyers were separated within supporting distance, and a pair of cruisers reinforced each side of the protective screen. The naval staff believed that night torpedo attacks would be more effective than during daylight but generally doubted that opportunities for night attack would be offered.

The most favorable cruising formation of the main body was the squadron in line abreast, because by simply turning to one side ships could assume divisional column formation. Another formation was *en echelon*. After establishing contact with the enemy's main body, the Austrian main body was to deploy from cruising into single-line battle formation in the direction of the approaching enemy. Before 1914 it was considered that long-range artillery duels were those conducted at ranges in excess of nine thousand yards. According to the prevalent Austrian view, the ideal firing range was about 6,500 yards; the k.u.k. command believed that long-range battles were ineffective and led to too great an expenditure of ammunition. In the initial phase the fleet commander was to withhold his own fire while trying with successive changes in course to close the distance rapidly and then open fire at short range.

The final phase of the artillery duel was to follow after the fleet had broken up the enemy's battle fleet. The firing range was then to decrease rapidly until at under 3,300 yards torpedoes would be used against the enemy battle formation. Following the breakthrough, the end result would be the "melee," enabling the use of rams (!) and torpedoes. If the enemy tried to escape the Austrian cruiser flotilla was to give chase and execute a series of concentrated torpedo attacks.

The basic tactical unit for a torpedo attack in a fleet action was to comprise one scout cruiser, two destroyers, and four to six high-seas torpedo boats. The cruiser was to serve as a leader, and the destroyers would fend off attacks by enemy torpedo boats. The execution of the attack was to be left to the initiative of the torpedo-boat group commander.

Ships/Weapons

Battleships

Four 20,000-ton turbine-powered dreadnoughts of the *Tegetthoff* class, together with three semidreadnoughts of the *Radetzky* class (14,500 tons, driven by vertical triple-expansion steam engines), formed the backbone of the battle fleet. They were strongly armed and armored but lacked sufficient underwater protection, a defect they shared with most of the world's battleships. Austro-Hungarian dreadnoughts had four triple 305-mm (12-inch) centerline turrets, with the inner pair superimposed. In July 1914 only *Viribus Unitis* and *Tegetthoff* were commissioned, *Prinz Eugen* was in training, and *Szent István* still incomplete, joining the fleet only in December 1915. *Radetzky, Erzherzog Franz Ferdinand,* and *Zrinyi* were armed with six twin turrets in a hexagonal formation, with 305-mm guns forward and aft and 240-mm (9.4-inch) guns in side turrets. Of the older battleships the *Erzherzog*-class ships (*Erzherzog Karl, E. Friedrich, E. Ferdinand Max,* 10,600 tons) were of some value thanks to their 20.5-knot speed and a strong intermediate battery of twelve 190-mm guns, in addition to their (relatively weak) main battery of four 240-mm guns. Battleships of the *Habsburg* class (*Habsburg, Árpád,* and *Babenberg,* of 8,300 tons, with three 240-mm guns in two turrets and twelve 150-mm [5.9-inch] secondary guns, nominal speed of 19.5 knots) were better suited for coastal-defense duties. The *Habsburg* class was an evolution of the *Monarch* class (*Monarch, Wien,* and *Budapest,* 5,700 tons, four 240-mm and six 150-mm guns), built in accordance with restrictive financial politics and called "coast defense ships" to push their approval through. Projected dreadnoughts of an improved *Tegetthoff* type would have been more strongly armed (with ten 350-mm guns in two twin and two triple turrets), but if built on 24,500 tons' displacement as designed, they would have suffered from size limitations again, as well as from some of the *Tegetthoffs*' defects.

Cruisers

The armored cruiser *Kaiserin und Königin Maria Theresia* (5,247 tons) was, in spite of her reconstruction in 1909/10, obsolescent and of scant military value. *Kaiser Karl VI* (6,325 tons, two 240-mm and eight 150-mm guns) and *Sankt Georg* (7420 tons, two 240-mm, five 190-mm and four 150-mm guns) were useful as a support for scout cruisers but weaker than foreign ships of their type. Three old *Zenta*-class cruisers (2,350–2,456 tons) were slow and weakly armed (with eight 120-mm guns), and two older torpedo cruisers, *Panther* and *Leopard* (1,582 tons) were even worse, useful only for local defense against a weaker enemy. Two "tin cans" of the *Kaiser Franz Joseph I* class (4,031 and 4,064 tons) were reconstructed in 1905/1906, receiving 150-mm/40 (that is, 40-caliber) guns in place of a heavy, single 240-mm mount, in addition to their casemate 150-mm/35 guns. *Kaiserin Elisabeth* was at Qingdao in 1914, taking part in the defense of this German base against the Japanese, and was scuttled in the harbor after her ammunition was spent.

The cruisers best suited for the Adriatic naval war were four 3,500-ton scout cruisers of the *Admiral Spaun* and improved *Admiral Spaun* classes. *Admiral Spaun* was the first Austrian warship powered by steam turbines and was prone to teething problems, but the other three cruisers had more reliable machinery. Arsenal-built *Spaun* had a four-shaft arrangement with six Parsons turbine sets, CNT-built *Saida* had two shafts with two Melms-Pfenniger steam turbines, and Danubius-built *Helgoland* and *Novara* were similar but with two AEG steam turbines. The main deficiency of the ships of this class was their small-caliber main battery (seven single 100-mm/3.9-inch mounts in *Spaun*, nine in the other three); it was envisaged to partially rearm them, replacing some of the 100-mm with one or two 150-mm mounts, but this was never executed, because they were always needed for raids. During the war their torpedo armament was strengthened: instead of two single 450-mm tubes *Spaun* received four twin 533-mm torpedo mounts, and other three cruisers three 533-mm twins. Their high speed (officially twenty-seven knots) made them almost invulnerable when chased by Entente cruisers and destroyers.

On the stocks in the CNT shipyard at Monfalcone were four cruisers ordered for China. The "great China cruiser," displacing 4,900 tons, was to carry four 203-mm (8-inch) and twelve 120-mm (4.7-inch) guns, but in 1917/18 it was decided to complete her with eight 150- and two 90-mm guns and four 450-mm torpedo tubes. Because CNT was situated in the middle of the front line with Italy, no work was possible before the end of 1917, and the plans never materialized. Three smaller (1,860-ton) "China cruisers" made such scant progress that completion was never considered feasible.

Destroyers and Torpedo Boats

In naval Habsburg nomenclature destroyers were called "torpedo vessels" (*Torpedofahrzeuge*), to distinguish them from smaller "torpedo boats" and bigger "torpedo ships" and "torpedo cruisers." Older Austrian destroyers were useful for local and secondary tasks, like minelaying. Better suited for fleet and escort duties were twelve four-hundred-ton VTE-powered destroyers of the *Huszár* class, of which the Yarrow prototype was built in Great Britain and eleven in domestic shipyards. In 1912/13 all received five 66-mm/30 guns in place of seven 47-mm/44 guns, in addition to their single 66-mm/45 gun. Single 450-mm torpedo tubes were replaced by twins. There was an additional unit of this class, the former *Lung Tuan*, ordered by China and completed in 1914 as *Warasdiner*. Despite being already outmoded in 1914, the *Huszárs* served together with bigger turbine-powered *Tátra*-class destroyers as jacks-of-all-trades in the Adriatic. The *Tátras* were built at Porto Re and represented the type best suited for the Adriatic. Six more were envisaged in the 1914 program but were canceled when the war began. The *Tátras* had two 100-mm/50 and six 66-mm/45 guns and two twin 450-mm torpedo tubes. After two of original six were lost in December 1915, four more were built to a slightly modified design and completed in 1917.

Photo 1.2. Destroyer *Dukla* of the improved *Tátra* class, perfectly suited for the Adriatic war theater (Courtesy of Dr. Lothar Baumgartner)

There were many 200-ton *Kaiman* torpedo boats and older Schichau-, Yarrow-, and Pola-built boats. New "high-seas" turbine boats were designed in 1910, but because of chronic underfunding, these 250-ton boats were more coastal than high-seas vessels. Eight were built at Trieste, with Danubius to build sixteen and CNT three follow-ons. They were Austria's first smaller turbine-powered vessels. When completed between 1913 and 1916, they became useful escorts and patrol vessels and supported seaplane raids against the Italian coast.

Coastal Units

The Austro-Hungarian navy ignored at first the potential of small, fast boats powered by gasoline engines, but after initial Italian successes with their MAS boats work started on similar designs, including the world's very first "air-cushion" craft. After successful trials that boat was dismantled and the "borrowed" aircraft engines returned to the Arsenal. There followed armored motor torpedo boats, but only one of nine ordered was launched, and it was never used in anger. Another design was for a versatile motor torpedo/gunboat; *Gleitboot No. I* was tested in May and June 1918. A second unit of this class was probably launched, and four were in the early stages of construction when the war ended.

Weapons

All modern Austrian naval guns were quick-firing weapons, with simple operating breechblocks (mostly of the sliding type) and propellant charges in brass cases. The 305-mm guns in their cramped triple turrets achieved a rate of fire of one round every two minutes. It is interesting to note that 120-mm guns on the *Zenta*-class cruisers were followed on scout cruisers by lighter but more powerful 100-mm guns, with greater range and higher kinetic energy on target. They used fixed shells, enabling a high rate of fire, but contemporary 150-mm weapons used separate shell and propellant charges, because the fixed ammunition initially used was too heavy for manual handling. Most representative of the lighter Austrian guns was the so-called 7-cm gun (in fact a 66-mm-caliber weapon), with various types and marks, including antiaircraft guns, later replaced with heavier 90-mm antiaircraft guns.

Austro-Hungarian submarine, destroyer, and torpedo-boat torpedoes were of 450-mm caliber, but scout cruisers and battleships were armed with larger 533-mm weapons. (See tables 1.2 and 1.3.)

Submarine Warfare

Offensive

Doctrine

Initially Austro-Hungarian submarines were to provide harbor and coastal defense, but soon it became clear that their best role was strategic war against enemy trade routes. The k.u.k. submarine flotilla, however, was too weak for offensive high-seas operations; it could not send even one submarine to the Dardanelles in 1915, and Germany finally dispatched boats to the Mediterranean. German submarines initially operated there under the Austro-Hungarian and Turkish flags, because war between Italy and Germany was not declared until 28 August 1916. Some of the best-known German submarines (*U 35*, *U 38*, and *U 39*) retained the Austrian flag even after this date, to conceal earlier "misuse."

Admiral Haus was often criticized for not understanding the possibilities of the submarine, but the deficiencies of the small boats in Austrian service were well known to him. When better types were available, he became a major proponent of unrestricted U-boat warfare. The results achieved by Austrian boats operating on the Adriatic and on Mediterranean trade routes were small in comparison to German successes (220,421 gross registered tons, or GRT, of merchant ships sunk and captured by Austro-Hungarian submarines, versus 3.5 million GRT sunk by German boats in the Mediterranean theater during the war), but these figures were in direct relation to the strengths of both submarine flotillas in this theater.

Boats/Weapons

The Austro-Hungarian navy was late in forming a submarine flotilla, awaiting developments and finally ordered six experimental 240-ton boats of three different designs. The Lake boats *U 1* and *U 2*, assembled at Pola and armed with three torpedo tubes, were obsolete and unreliable when completed and suffered from problems even after modifications, being finally relegated to secondary duties. The German-built *U 3* and *U 4* had two forward torpedo tubes and were powered by kerosene engines. *U 3* was lost in 1915, but *U 4* remained in service to the end of the war. The Holland type boats *U 5* and *U 6* were built by Whitehead at Fiume, followed by *U 12*, built on speculation and bought by Vienna in 1914. They were armed with two bow torpedo tubes and were successful in attacking enemy warships. After trials were evaluated, five 695-ton submarines (*U 7–U 11*) were ordered from Germania in 1913, to be delivered in 1915. They were armed with six torpedo tubes and one 66-mm deck gun and designed for high speed on the surface and underwater (seventeen and eleven knots, respectively). The outbreak of war prompted the Austrian naval leadership to sell them uncompleted to Germany.

After German submarines started to arrive in the Adriatic in 1915, the Austro-Hungarian navy ordered three coastal 125-ton boats of the German UB I type and bought two completed, already in German service. These were renamed *U 10* and *U 11* (former *UB 1* and *UB 15*), and new construction was designated *U 15–17*. All had two torpedo tubes and two torpedoes, serving mostly in the Adriatic because of their short range. The Whitehead shipyard was building small submarines for Denmark, and the navy officially seized their construction plans, ordering four units (*U 20–23*) on 27 March 1915. The construction of these 173-tons boats, of limited military value, was divided between Austria and Hungary, but the modification of many details delayed completion. They were commissioned in 1917 and operated without success; two were lost during the war. Better was the idea to build modified German UB II–type coastal submarines of 264 tons on the surface and 301 tons submerged, armed with two torpedo tubes and four torpedoes. *U 27* and *28* were completed by CNT in the Pola Arsenal and *U 29–32* by Danubius. All were commissioned in 1917, with two more ordered from CNT being completed as *U 40* and *U 41* in 1917–18. The

Table 1.2 Principal Austro-Hungarian Naval Guns

Bore (in./mm)	Cal.	Model	Shell (kg)	MV (m/sec)	Range (m)	F/C (sec.)	Ship or classes
13.8/350	45	Skoda 1916, QF	635–710	820	25,000–31,500	.	*Improved Tegetthoff* class
12/305	45	Skoda 1908, QF	450	800	20,000	30	*Tegetthoff* & *Radetzky* classes
12/305	35	Krupp 1880, BL	455	.	10,000	.	*Kr. Erz. Rudolph*
9.4/240	45	Skoda 1909, QF	215	800	16,400	24	*Radetzky* class
9.4/240	40	Skoda 1901, QF	229	705	.	24	*Babenberg, Sankt Georg, Erzherzog* class
9.4/240	40	Krupp 1897, QF	215	725	.	.	*Habsburg, Árpád, Kaiser Karl VI*
9.4/240	40	Krupp 1894, BL	215	690	.	.	*Monarch* class
9.4/240	35	Krupp 1886, BL	190	.	.	.	*Maria Theresia, Franz Joseph* class (originally)
7.5/190	35	Skoda 1918, QF	.	.	.	.	*Ersatz Zenta* class
7.5/190	42	Skoda 1903, QF	97	800	15,500	10–15	*Erzherzog class, St. Georg, M. Theresia*
5.9/150	50	Skoda 1910, QF	45.5	880	15,000	.	*Tegetthoff* class
5.9/150	40	Skoda 1896, QF	45.5	725	.	6–7.5	*Habsburg, Monarch* classes
5.9/150	40	Krupp 1894	45.5	690		.	*Franz Joseph* class
5.9/150	35	Krupp 1886	32–39	650	7,400	.	*Franz Joseph* class
4.7/120	50	Skoda 1914, QF	23.8	800	.	.	*Ersatz Zenta* class
4.7/120	45	Skoda 1910 & 1914, QF	23.8	800	15,000	.	*Improved Tátra* & river monitors
4.7/120	40	Skoda 1896, BL	23.8	700	12,000	5	*Zenta* & river monitor *Körös*

4.7/120	35	Krupp 1880, 1894, Skoda 1894, BL	23.7		7,000	.	*Rudolph* & river monitors
4.7/120	35	Skoda 1918	.	.	.	.	For submarines
3.9/100	50	Skoda 1907, 1910, 1911, QF	13.8	900	15,200	5	*Radetzky, Tátra,* and *Spaun* classes
3.9/100	35	Skoda 1917, QF	.	.	.	.	For uncompleted submarines
3.5/90	35	Skoda 1918, QF	10.2		.	.	
3.5/90	45	Skoda 1912, QF	11.4	780–840	12,300	5–12	Anti-aircraft, on various ships
2.95/75	30	Skoda 1917	6.0	600	Ceiling 6,000	.	
2.95/75	15	Skoda ….	.	.	.	.	U 27 class submarines
2.6/66	50	7 cm Skoda BAG*, 1910, 1913	4.5	830	8,000, ceiling 5,000	3	Anti-aircraft on *Tegetthoff* class
2.6/66	45	7 cm Skoda BAG & TAG**, 1900, 1909	4.5	730/900	6,000 / 8,000	3	*Huszár* & *Tátra* classes
2.6/66	42	7 cm Skoda QF			6,000	4–5	Old destroyers
2.6/66	30	7 cm Skoda 1910, TAG & BAG	5.78	550	7,000	.	*Huszár* class & torpedo boats
2.6/66	26	Skoda 1915	5.3	480		.	River patrol boats
1.85/47	44	Skoda 1897, 1914 (Model Hotchkiss)	1.5	710/850	4,000	.	On various ships as light batteries
1.85/47	33	Hotchkiss 1890	1.1	560	.	.	

* BAG: *Ballonabwehrgeschütz* = anti-aircraft gun, TAG: *Torpedobootabwehrgeschütz* = anti-torpedo-boat gun

Table 1.3 Austro-Hungarian Torpedoes (in service 1898–1918, all built by Whitehead, Fiume)

Model & production year	Caliber & length (mm)	Torpedo & explosive charge weight (kg)		Range (m/kts)	Ship or classes armed
35 cm Type C (1886/87)	356 / 4500	Max. 275	45	600 / 24	Older torpedo boats, *Meteor*, *Panther* class
40 cm (1888–91)	406 / 5100	Max. 435	97	600 / 25–27	*Rudolph*, *F. Joseph*, *Planet*, *Trabant*
45 cm L/4 (1892)	450 / 4030	432	89	400 / 28 800 / 26	*M. Theresia*, *Satellit*
45 cm L/6 (1897)	450 / 6000	642	100	1000 / 28 2000 / 26	For coastal defense
35 cm Type D (1903–1907)	356 / 4550	350	45	800 / 27 1000 / 26	Replacement for Whitehead type C
45 cm L/5 (1898)	450 / 5000	520	150	400 / 30	–
45 cm L/5 (1902)	450 / 5100	560	100	400 / 30 1000 / 28	*Monarch*, *Zenta*, *Cobra* classes
45 cm L/5 (1903/1904)	450 / 5100	565	59	3000 / 30	*Habsburg class*, submerged tubes
45 cm L/5 (1905/1906)	450 / 5120	644	95	3000 / 32.5 6000 / 20	*Huszár*, *Kaiman* classes
45 cm L/5 (1905/1906)	450 / 5120	642	95	3000 / 32 6000 / 19.5	*St. Georg*, *Erzherzog* class, submerged tubes

45 cm L/5 (1909–15)	450 / 5200	654	110	5000 / 33.5 10.000 / 20.5	*Huszar, Kaiman*, torpedo boats
45 cm L/5 (1909)	450 / 5200	654	110	5,000 / 33.5 10,000 / 20.5	Submarines
45 cm L/5	–	–	–	–	*Radetzky* class, submerged tubes
45 cm L/5 (1916)	450 / 5,570	852	182	–	*Ersatz Triglav* class
53 cm L/6.3 (1909)	533 / 6,300	1336	180	1,000 / 41 10,000 / 29	*Tegetthoff* class, submerged tubes
53 cm L/7.18 (1914)	533 / 7,180	1590	180	1,000 / 41 10,000 / 36	*Adm. Spaun* & improved *Spaun* class

navy purchased two worn-out German UB II boats, *UB 43* and *UB 47*, and commissioned them in July 1917 as *U 43* and *47*. Austrian designers were in the meantime developing bigger submarines—the *U 48* class at Pola, *U 50* class at Fiume, and *U 52* class at Trieste—in fact wasting efforts and materials on several projects with similar characteristics (818–849 tons surface displacement, 1,100–1,200 tons submerged, six 450-mm torpedo tubes, and two 100-mm or 120-mm deck guns). Similar was the case with German UB III–type submarines, whose design was bought and modified by at least two shipyards (*U 101* class). Danubius was also designing the *U 107* class, similar to the original Germania 695-ton boats sold in 1914. Several boats of all these classes were laid down but never completed because of material and workforce shortages.

Austro-Hungarian submarines were armed with 450-mm torpedo tubes. The first submarines had no deck guns but later received 37- or 47-mm guns from old warships, as it was simpler and cheaper to sink coastal vessels with shells than with torpedoes. *U 14*, the ex-French boat *Curie*, received a German 88-mm gun, as did *U 43* and *U 47*. *U 20*–class boats were armed with 66-mm guns and the *U 27* class with 75-mm.

Photo 1.3. *U 12* damaged the French flagship *Jean Bart* in December 1914 but was lost in August 1915 in the Italian minefield off Venice. (Boris Lemachko collection)

Antisubmarine

Initially Austrian forces attacked enemy submarines—if sighted on the surface—by ramming and shelling, as happened to the French boat *Monge*, surprised on the surface off the Bocche and run over by the cruiser *Helgoland* in December 1915. Later, specialized weapons against submerged submarines were adopted, like a towed underwater explosive sweep called Drachen (Dragon). Carbonit depth charges of the C 15 type were of German origin, and there were also Austrian Schönthaler and Langen-Müller types. Detection was the main problem; submarines were attacked when sighted during or after their attack. Clear seawater on the eastern Adriatic coast enabled the spotting of submarines from prominent observation posts along the coast or from seaplanes patrolling overhead. This was one of the reasons the Austro-Hungarian navy neglected the development of acoustic search and detection systems. Austrian seaplanes scored two world antisubmarine firsts: a seaplane from Trieste heavily damaged the British *B 10* at Venice in August 1916, and the aircraft *L 132* and *L 135* sank the French submarine *Fresnel* in open waters on 15 September 1916. Killing enemy submarines was another specialty of Austrian and German submariners in the Adriatic. Other measures, like patrolling and escorting transports along the coast, were of less significance. Austro-Hungarian convoys included one or two merchantmen with single escorts; some ships sailed alone, with naval vessels patrolling in key areas. In 1918 the Habsburg navy established a Submarine Chaser Flotilla, using smaller steamers. It is not confirmed that these ships sunk anything, but one became a victim of an Italian submarine.

Passive antisubmarine measures included nets (in fact, steel ropes hanging free from boom barricades) and mines in front of Austrian bases, and at least one submarine—*Curie*—was trapped in the net at Pola. Large k.u.k. warships were initially equipped with Bullivant antitorpedo nets, but these were removed during the war, because of their effect on the ships' speed.

Mine Warfare

Doctrine

The Austro-Hungarian navy was interested in defensive mining to protect naval bases and coastal zones and in offensive operations using mines embarked on ships of the fleet. Four Pola mine barrages included 1,500 mines laid in "rays," with concentrations higher near the coast and thinner at the rims some ten nautical miles offshore. Coastal artillery covered the passages between the fields and the shore.

Mines envisaged for the defense of Trieste remained initially at Pola, to be laid after Italy declared war. Sebenico was defended by minefields between the outer islands and by barrages between the islands facing the harbor entrance, with two smaller fields east of the islands, extending to the coast. Off Bocche di Cattaro a twenty-one-mine barrage was laid in the Bay of Traste to prevent enemy landings there, with further barrages off Prevlaka and Cape Ostro (twenty-eight mines) and in front of the main entrance (thirty-three mines). Across the straits between Kobila and Kabala a controlled minefield was laid, supported by artillery batteries and by two torpedo-launching stations. These fields were later enlarged.

To defend Pola, Austria produced numerous mines of simple construction, but before 1914 these weapons lacked the autodestruction device required by the 1907 Hague naval conference. Because of the adverse weather during the winter of 1914/15, many active mines became loose (476 from Pola barrage and 107 from the Bocche barrages!) and posed a great danger for Austrian and neutral vessels. The first victim of the Pola mines was the Austrian passenger ship *Baron Gautsch,* which strayed into the field off Rovigno on 13 August 1914 and sank with great loss among her passengers, including the families of civil servants evacuated from Dalmatia. In the night of 23 August the old torpedo boat *Tb 26* sank after hitting a floating mine off Pola, and two more merchantmen were lost in the barrage, one of these a Greek three-masted schooner.

During the war Austro-Hungarian warships laid four thousand defensive and two thousand offensive mines along the Albanian coast between Medua (Shin-Gjen) and Durazzo (Dürres), as well as off Venice and Brindisi.

Ships/Weapons

There were three old minelayers—*Dromedar* (with a capacity of 50 mines), *Salamander* (90 mines), and *Basilisk* (145 mines)—and a newer vessel, *Chamaeleon* (240 to 300 mines). The old steamer *Carniolia* served as a mine depot, and mines could also be laid by numerous warships, such as cruisers, destroyers, and torpedo boats, together with special mining launches and lighters. Older torpedo boats were converted for minesweeping, together with five requisitioned steamers, eleven large motorboats, and some tugs and naval tenders. Between 1908 and 1918 a series of forty-seven-ton mine tenders/tugs was ordered and built. Austro-Hungarian mines were of the older A, B, and B1 electrical-contact types and of newer C type (in several variants), with a 250-kg and a 70-kg explosive charge. Because mines were costly, Italian mines of different types were also salvaged and used.

Amphibious Warfare

Doctrine/Capabilities

Being a coastal-defense force, the Austro-Hungarian navy envisaged landing operations and defense of threatened coastal zones, and it performed several related exercises before the war. The first combined exercise with army units was conducted in 1902, during the last visit of Emperor Franz Joseph I to the coast. This involved three *Monarch*-class battleships and three torpedo cruisers covering the landing of two infantry regiments, one light battery, and one cavalry squadron, transported by four merchant vessels. The troops landed on 3 September at three points on the eastern coast of Istria, out of range of Pola's coastal artillery. As the first wave, each of the battleships sent ashore a naval detachment. The landing of troops, guns, and horses lasted almost five hours, because small ship's boats were used and many crossings were needed. "Defending" troops were too weak to prevent the landing or halt the advance of the "attackers," and when the defenders retreated to the Pola fortress the exercise was terminated. The lessons learned were that a superior naval force could choose where and when to land and that Trieste, Pola, and Fiume could be threatened by enemy landings. Other lessons included that weather conditions in Quarnero Bay often prohibited landing operations and that the eastern Istria coast—stony, with scarce vegetation and water sources—was not an optimal landing area. Afterward it was decided to extend Pola's fortifications to the east, covering possible landing points with artillery fire.

The navy performed another large-scale exercise in the Gruz area in 1906, with a beachhead in brigade strength. Archduke Franz Ferdinand himself commanded the landing, General Conrad von Hötzendorf led the defense, and battleships operated with both the attacking and defending forces, demonstrating that the old days of the coastal-defense navy had ended.

The Austro-Hungarian navy had neither independent nor attached marine units, but all sailors were trained to participate in landing detachments. There were plenty of occasions for landings in the Balkans and in the Levant during the volatile years between 1878 (occupation of Bosnia-Herzegovina) and 1914 and in the Far East during the Boxer Rebellion. There were no dedicated landing craft built, and the infantry went ashore in ship's boats towed by steam pinnacles, while towed rafts were used for artillery and cavalry. During the First World War a naval battalion was formed at Trieste to operate on the southern wing of the Isonzo front, and some of its personnel manned the "Lagoon Flotilla" vessels.

The only real landing from Austro-Hungarian warships during the war was a raid against Italian-occupied Pelagosa Island on 28 July 1915, when four *Tátra*-class destroyers landed four officers and 104 men, thinking the Italian garrison was only thirty men strong. Because in fact there were ninety Italian marines with five guns, the Austrian detachment was (perhaps prematurely) recalled after losing two dead and eight wounded from infantry fire. There were numerous river crossings on the "lagoon front" in 1917 after the victory at Caporetto, but the landing at Grado of one strengthened company with four guns by motorboats of the lagoon flotilla, scheduled for 29 October 1917, was postponed because of heavy weather. It finally took place on 31 October, after the Italians retreated from this occupied township.

Coastal Defense

Before the war Pola was already the best protected of all the Dual Monarchy's coastal areas. On 15 May 1915 artillery on the naval front included one modern 420-mm howitzer, six 305-mm guns, two 305-mm mortars, sixteen 280-mm guns (four modern), three 240-mm guns, four-240-mm mortars, thirty-six 210-mm mortars, two 190-mm guns, and thirty-four 150-mm guns—in total, 104 heavy mountings, together with 157 lighter artillery pieces. On the land front there were 110 heavy- and intermediate-caliber guns, with 140 mostly obsolete lighter guns and 86 machine-guns. Naval guns on the coast and on the Brioni Islands were mounted in forts, some in armored turrets, protecting Fasana anchorage, the harbor entrance, and the southern approaches. On Monte Cope, south of Pola and dominating the Premantura Peninsula, there was a powerful and modern 150-mm battery, and a mobile 420-mm howitzer battery protected the southern flank. The fortifications were extended to the east, but the northern defense line was obsolete in 1914, and it was envisaged to move it farther north. The harbor of Lussin Piccolo was protected by old batteries, with the main position on Monte Asino modernized in 1907 with two 240-mm guns and several 210-mm mortars. The old ironclad *Mars* (ex-*Tegetthoff*) was initially part of the harbor defenses.

Troops defending Pola on 1 June 1915 totaled 1,410 officers and 51,840 men, with 3,500 horses and 1,200 oxen, and included Sea Battalions I, II, and III, the coastal-defense garrisons of Rovigno, Albona, and Fort Lussin. The naval contingent (excluding fleet personnel and the sea battalions) numbered 1,000 officers and 5,070 men.

Another important fortress was the Bocche di Cattaro in the south, where the maritime front included Fort Ostro, with four old 210-mm mortars and four old 90-mm and four newer 80-mm guns; Fort Mamula, with four 210-mm mortars and eighteen 80-mm guns; batteries on Prevlaka, with 80-mm guns; Lustica, with four 210-mm mortars and four 150-mm guns; Kabala and Kobila (the same as Lustica); and Fort Spanjol at Castelnuovo, with four 210-mm mortars and six 90-mm guns. The coastal Fort Radisevic, with two 150-mm coastal guns and four 210-mm mortars, covered mine barrages in the Bay of Traste. On the land front there were eighteen 120-mm guns, eight 100-mm howitzers in armored turrets, twenty 150-mm mobile howitzers, thirty-seven field guns, two mortars, and forty-one machine guns. The 47th Infantry Division was detached to defend the Bocche, but only five battalions were present, together with three batteries (comprising twelve guns) and one cavalry troop. The 14th Mountain Brigade, with five battalions, operated outside of the fortress.

Old fortifications at Spalato, Sebenico, Lessina, Zara, Fiume, Zengg, and Carlopago were abandoned or razed. Some fortifications modernized in the second half of the nineteenth century were obsolete in 1914 and likewise abandoned, like those of Ragusa and Sebenico, but the navy later restored the old Fort St. Nikola at Sebenico's harbor entrance to serve as the mine-defense center, with five antique 210-mm guns, five old 150-mm, and some 47-mm guns. Later six 120-mm guns from the old station ship *Donau* were added, but the value of all these batteries was minimal, and the navy intended to defend Sebenico actively using the cruiser *Maria Theresia* and the torpedo flotilla stationed there.

In spite or because of these measures, none of the Entente states during the war seriously contemplated landing on the Austro-Hungarian coast. There were never enough troops for this kind of enterprise (especially after bad experiences with the landing on Gallipoli in 1915), and neither the French-Montenegrin plans to occupy the Bocche in 1914 nor the Italian idea to land on Lagosta or Sabbioncello in 1915 were realized.

Aviation

The advantages of naval aircraft were recognized by Austro-Hungarian naval authorities as early as 1910. The navy's first aircraft were fragile and vulnerable, but better types were designed and built by domestic industry to operate in the relatively good weather of the Adriatic. Austro-Hungarian naval aircraft were flying boats, able to remain on the surface after forced landing to be towed away and repaired. Some early aircraft were ordered abroad, but most were produced by Phönix/Albatros and Lohner at Vienna, by Austro-Daimler at Wiener Neustadt, by the Austrian Oeffag, the Hungarian UFAG, and some other firms.

The first Austro-Hungarian seaplane base was founded in 1910 at Altura, near Pola, and was moved in 1912 to the small island of Sta. Catarina in Pola Harbor. The island was artificially enlarged for trials and training; after Puntisella was completed in 1916 Sta. Catarina served as a repair center and, from 1917, as the air arsenal. A station at Cosada, near Pola, served for schooling, and Puntisella became Pola's main seaplane station, being protected by wheeled fighters stationed at Valbandon. Another principal seaplane base was founded at Kumbor, in the Bocche di Cattaro, with numerous hangars and workshops. After Durazzo was occupied in 1916 a naval air station was established there, and smaller stations were organized at Gravosa near Ragusa, Sebenico, Spalato, Lagosta, Rogoznica (near Sebenico), Curzola, Zara, Lussin, Fiume, and Parenzo. Naval Air Station Trieste was founded in 1915. Another small air base was organized at Grado in 1917 and two auxiliary stations at Keszthely and in Odessa.

Austrian naval aviation never came under control of another service, and observers—with some of the pilots—were naval officers, trained in navigation and ship identification. Austro-Hungarian seaplanes performed reconnaissance, mine and submarine search, and fighter-interceptor and bombing over the sea but also over enemy territory, and the navy's seaplanes conducted numerous air attacks against Italian harbors. From 1917 onward, Austro-Hungarian naval aircraft were outnumbered by enemy air forces but tied up three times their numbers on the Italian-Austrian front.

In 1914 there were only 14 aircraft, but 570 flying boats entered service during the war. Of these 72 were lost in action, 163 by accident, and 94 were deleted as worn out. There were heavy losses among flying personnel, and despite replacements there were only 120 such personnel in January 1918, the same as a year earlier. In September 1918 the navy still had 230 operational seaplanes and wheeled fighters at its disposal, but only 48 pilots and 31 observers.

Riverine Forces

An important instrument of Austro-Hungarian power projection was the Danube Flotilla, centered in 1914 on a fleet of six river monitors, with four more building and completed during the war. Two "supermonitors" with 190-mm and 90-mm guns were contemplated in 1917 but never built. Austro-Hungarian monitors and armored patrol boats served in riverine operations against Serbia and Romania, and monitors fired the first shells in anger against Serbian positions at Belgrade, starting the First World War. Two monitors (*Temes* and *Inn*) were sunk by mines, but they were raised and repaired during the war, and by 1917 Austro-Hungarian riverine units operated in the Danube estuary, on the Black Sea, and along Ukrainian rivers.

WAR EXPERIENCE AND EVOLUTION

Wartime Evolution

Surface and Submarine Warfare in the Adriatic

In accordance with the initial war plans, modern Austro-Hungarian naval units were to operate in the Mediterranean together with the Italian fleet and the German Mediterranean Division. In the Adriatic, Italy was to be represented by one old battleship, three armored cruisers, and four destroyer and several torpedo boat flotillas, and Austria-Hungary with three old coastal-defense battleships and five older cruisers, together with several divisions of older torpedo boats. The plan even called for Germany to operate some of its training ships and older cruisers in the Adriatic.

Early on 4 August, *Goeben* and the light cruiser *Breslau* attacked French North African harbors and went to re-coal at Messina. The responding French battle fleet—wrongly informed as to their movements—missed the enemy by forty nautical miles. Although shadowed by British warships, *Goeben* and *Breslau* escaped. The German commander, Rear Admiral Wilhelm Souchon, asked on 5 August for an Austro-Hungarian fleet to come to Messina, but Austria-Hungary was still not at war with Great Britain, and Haus declined. The German ships left Messina on 6 August and set out for the Dardanelles. Meanwhile, two British battle cruisers sailed west to protect French convoys, and only four British armored cruisers were waiting south of Otranto Straits to intercept *Goeben* and *Breslau* (presumed to be sailing to Pola). These, after a short pursuit, gave up in face of a "superior force." In the meantime Haus received instructions to sail south to meet the Germans, supposedly en route to the Adriatic. He left Pola on the morning of 7 August with six battleships of the 1st Squadron, two cruisers, six destroyers, and thirteen torpedo boats. On the evening of 7 August Haus received news that Germans were heading for the Dardanelles, and he returned to Pola. Haus rejected a German proposal to send the Austrian battle fleet to the Dardanelles to operate alongside the German-Turkish fleet against Russia in Black Sea. He considered it impractical because of a slow fleet train and the threat to the Austrian Adriatic coast from expected Italian aggression.

Before May 1915, when the French squadron at Corfu was the main enemy at sea, the Austro-Hungarian fleet remained at Pola, with older vessels in the Bocche ordered to blockade the Montenegrin coast. There on the morning of 16 August the old cruiser *Zenta* and destroyer *Ulan* were surprised by the French battle fleet and British armored cruisers. *Zenta* was sunk with heavy losses, while *Ulan* escaped to the Bocche. The French sustained significant self-inflicted losses when three major guns exploded during the action and two battleships collided afterward. Nonetheless, this action effectively ended the Austrian blockade.

During 1914 the French fleet entered the Adriatic eight more times, escorting single transports with provisions for Montenegro, shelling fortifications protecting the Bocche, or attacking isolated islands. Although it would have been easy to transfer heavy units unnoticed from Pola to the Bocche or to Sebenico, or to attack the French fleet on several occasions, Admiral Haus ignored these opportunities, because of his obsession with Italy. The only sallies made by k.u.k. units occurred on 17 October, when twelve destroyers with six torpedo boats of the 1st Torpedo Flotilla made a sortie from Sebenico, an attempt that was quickly terminated after it was learned the enemy had left the Adriatic. On 3 November the cruiser *Helgoland* led the flotilla to Lissa, returning after French warships departed the area.

Of note is the mission of the semidreadnought *Radetzky*, sailing unopposed from Pola to the Bocche on 21/22 October to neutralize French naval guns that had been mounted on the heights of Lovcen. They had shelled Austrian naval and military installations from 19 October, and the ranges of the guns of older warships in the Bocche had been inadequate to answer. *Radetzky* started a systematical bombardment on 22 October—aided by observation balloons and aircraft—and five days later the French batteries withdrew. *Radetzky* shelled some other targets on the Montenegrin front before returning to Pola on 17 December.

Austro-Hungarian submarines became active in the autumn of 1914, and after several unsuccessful attempts *U 12* (Lieutenant Commander Egon Lerch) torpedoed the French flagship *Jean Bart* on 21 December, compelling her return to Malta for repairs. Another French loss was the submarine *Curie*, which, sent to attack Pola anchorage, became entangled in the harbor boom on 20 December and was sunk by the Austrians. *Curie* was initially towed to Pelagosa by the French armored cruiser *Jules Michelet*. *Michelet* was sighted and the k.u.k. 1st Torpedo Flotilla sailed, but it did not encounter the enemy.

Before Italy entered the war, the French fleet lacked adequate bases. After *Jean Bart* was torpedoed, the French patrol line was moved south of the Otranto Straits. Even there, near the Cape Santa Maria di Leuca, the submarine *U 5* (Lieutenant Commander Georg von Trapp) on 27 April 1915 torpedoed the French armored cruiser *Léon Gambetta*, which sank with heavy loss of life. Afterward the French patrol line retired even farther south.

Italy declared war on Austria-Hungary on 23 May 1915, and at dawn on the 24th the Austro-Hungarian battle fleet, covered by six cruisers, fourteen destroyers, thirty torpedo boats, three submarines, and six seaplanes, attacked Ancona and other Italian Adriatic cities, sinking in the process the small Italian destroyer *Turbine* off Barletta. It was the second and only successful sortie of the battle fleet during the war. The blow to the Italian morale outweighed the material damage inflicted.

Later actions were less spectacular, but Austrian local supremacy on the Adriatic was secured by the repulse of intruding enemy forces and attacks on targets on the enemy coast. On 11 July 1915 Italians landed unopposed on Pelagosa Island. The cruisers *Helgoland* and *Saida,* with six *Tátra*-class destroyers and two torpedo boats, shelled Pelagosa on 28 July, but a counterlanding was aborted when it became clear that the Italian garrison was stronger than anticipated. Italian and French submarines were afterward patrolling off Pelagosa, but on 5 August *U 5* sank there the Italian *Nereide.* In a bombardment conducted on 17 August, Austrian shells destroyed the island's only water cistern; the Italians evacuated one day later.

On 9 June 1915, *U 4* (Lieutenant Commander Rudolf Singule) torpedoed and heavily damaged the British cruiser *Dublin* off the Albanian coast. On 18 July, while an Entente squadron was shelling the railroad line near Ragusa Vecchia, in southern Dalmatia, *U 4* struck again, sinking the Italian armored cruiser *Giuseppe Garibaldi.* Other Italian losses in this period included the submarine *Medusa,* torpedoed on 10 June near Venice by *U 11*; the torpedo boat *5 PN,* sunk on 27 June by *U 10*; and armored cruiser *Amalfi,* torpedoed on 7 July by the German *UB 14.* Newly laid Italian minefields were fatal for Austrian *U 12,* destroyed off Venice on 8 August 1915, and on 13 August *U 3* was lost in the southern Adriatic. Even more serious was the mining of two *Tátra*-class destroyers in December 1915 during a bombardment of Durazzo by the cruiser *Helgoland* and five destroyers; *Lika* and *Triglav* represented one-third of Austria's modern destroyer force. Surviving k.u.k. warships, including the damaged destroyer *Csepel,* returned to base despite enemy pursuit.

An Italian land offensive west of Trieste in May 1915 was stopped on the Isonzo line. Despite a series of bloody battles the front remained stalemated until 24 October 1917, when the Austro-German offensive at Caporetto ruptured the Italian line. The Italians retreated to the River Piave, where the front stabilized. During the trench war that ensued between May 1915 and October 1917, smaller Austro-Hungarian vessels, as noted above, operated on the sea flank as a lagoon flotilla, supplying and supporting the army. The old battleships *Wien* and *Budapest* bombarded Italian positions; when *Wien* was sunk by Italian MAS at Trieste in December 1917, she was replaced by *Árpád.*

German submarines operated in the Mediterranean from Pola and the Bocche, and the Entente tried to block their passage from Adriatic with ships, nets, and the mines of the Otranto Barrage. Submarine losses in the barrage were negligible—in fact, only the Austrian *U 6* and German *UB 53* (and perhaps *UB 44*) were lost in the barrage, with other boats slowed or damaged during passage and the Austrian *U 30* lost nearby to an unknown cause. Fast Austro-Hungarian units were ordered to clear this passage. The greatest attack occurred in the night of 14/15 May 1917, when scout cruisers *Novara, Helgoland,* and *Saida,* under Captain Horthy, attacked British anti-submarine drifters, sinking fourteen; the detached destroyers *Csepel* and *Bálaton* sank one Italian destroyer and a freighter from a convoy of three. This aroused a hornet's nest at Brindisi, and numerous British, Italian, and French warships rushed to intercept the Austrian intruders. They damaged *Novara* during the chase, but all Austro-Hungarian ships escaped to their bases. Skirmishes between Austrian and Entente fast warships constantly occurred along both Adriatic coasts but never led to a decisive battle.

Photo 1.4. Austro-Hungarian cruiser *Helgoland.* The scout cruisers of the *Admiral Spaun* and improved *Spaun* class were the "real capital ships" in the Adriatic. (Courtesy of Eng. René Greger)

After the mutiny in the Bocche in February 1918, Horthy—promoted to the rank of rear admiral—became the navy's new commander in chief, and the fleet was rejuvenated, with several admirals retired and old ships without military value stricken. To improve the morale of the crews Horthy decided to repeat his attack against the Otranto Barrage, but this time taking along four dreadnoughts of the *Tegetthoff* class and three *Erzherzogs* to form seven support groups. On the move from Pola to the south *Tegetthoff* and *Szent István* ran into two Italian MAS, and *Szent István* was torpedoed and sunk. (Ironically, both k.u.k. battleships sunk during the war, *Wien* and *Szent István*, were torpedoed by the same Italian officer, Luigi Rizzo.) After this loss the attack was canceled, practically ending Austro-Hungarian fleet operations in the Adriatic.

Submarine Operations in the Mediterranean

Not counting sorties to the Ionian Sea, Austro-Hungarian submarines operated in the Mediterranean only from autumn 1916, beginning with a cruise of the old *U 4* in the Bay of Taranto. In February 1917, *U 29* started her cruise as the first of the UB II boats, returning prematurely because of mechanical defects. Similar problems plagued *U 30* during her first sortie in March, and in April she disappeared without a trace when under way to the Mediterranean. *U 27*—the most successful of all Habsburg submarines—made her first sortie in April 1917, being followed by other UB II boats, finally by the rebuilt *U 14*. Even the small *U 15* made a sortie into the Bay of Taranto in June 1917, and *U 4* went again to these waters. *U 14* made her last Mediterranean cruise in November 1917, operating afterward in the Adriatic. UB II boats were active in the eastern Mediterranean until 1918. Of interest is the cruise of *U 27*, whose crew discovered that a ton of lubricating oil was missing and that Durazzo, the nearest Austrian-controlled port, was therefore out of reach. The boat went to Beirut, using only the starboard diesel, her electric motors, and even sails. In Beirut there was no oil; *U 27* was finally supplied by the German *U 65*. She completed her cruise and arrived back at the Bocche in September 1918, only a month before the armistice.

Overall, Austro-Hungarian submarines in the Adriatic and Mediterranean sank 196,093 GRT of enemy and neutral merchant ships. The top aces were Lieutenant Commander Zdenko Hudecek and Georg von Trapp, who accounted for 47,788 and 44,595 GRT, respectively. (See table 1.4.)

Summary and Assessment

The Austro-Hungarian navy committed several mistakes before and during the war. The navy did not order enough destroyers and submarines, and the loss of two *Tátra*-class destroyers left it with even fewer of these valuable ships. Six destroyers were canceled in 1914 without logical reason, and

Table 1.4 Results of German and A–H Submarines against Merchant Tonnage in the Mediterranean, 1914–18 (including the Adriatic and Black Seas)

	German Submarines					AH Submarines	
Month & year	Enemy merchantmen sunk	GRT	Neutral merchantmen sunk	GRT	Total GRT	Merchantmen sunk	GRT
11.1914						1	13
03.1915						7	21
05.1915						1	1,065
08.1915						1	1,074
10.1915	17	61,340	1	2,508	63,848		
11.1915	42	146,457	2	6,425	152,882	1	25
12.1915	16	72,463	1	1,278	73,741	5	180
1915 TOTAL	75	280,260	4	10,211	290,471	15	2,365
01.1916	5	27,979			27,979	3	53
02.1916	11	43,144	1	1,266	44,410	1	475
03.1916	4	20,045			20,045		118
04.1916	16	47,779	2	3,407	51,186		
05.1916	32	59,907	5	12,185	72,092	1	2,238
06.1916	42	64,933	1	2,192	67,125	2	11,424
07.1916	30	84,850	3	1,582	86,432		
08.1916	69	113,230	8	16,138	129,368	1	204
09.1916	32	85,623	7	15,807	101,430	1	4,309
10.1916	29	99,555	15	25,597	125,152	32	4,299
11.1916.	27	71,583	9	19,964	91,547		
12.1916	36	110,924	7	21,395	132,319		
1916 TOTAL	333	829,552	58	119,533	949,085	41	23,120

01.1917	20	67,213	4	11,328	78,541		
02.1917		81,216		24,414	105,630		
03.1917		49,480		9,340	58,820		
04.1917		210,324		40,863	251,187	5	23,037
05.1917		156,945		8,889	165,834	4	10,270
06.1917		125,963		16,375	142,338	4	6,877
07.1917		82,660		1,659	84,319	4	16,969
08.1917		63,967		9,436	73,403	9	38,823
09.1917		105,251		5,990	111,241		
10.1917		134,256		9,537	143,793	4	12,663
11.1917		92,681		1,648	94,329	1	4,016
12.1917		134,167		10,123	144,290		
1917 TOTAL	**20**	**1,304,123**	**4**	**149,602**	**1,453,725**	**31**	**112,655**
01.1918					116,146	7	26,020
02.1918					84,118		
03.1918					113,347	4	15,273
04.1918					80,087	1	40
05.1918					112,790	11	9,159
06.1918					58,248		
07.1918					76,629	10	235
08.1918					69,281	1	2,209
09.1918					37,689	15	5,004
10.1918					35,322		
11.1918					10,233		
1918 TOTAL					**793,890**	**49**	**57,940**
WAR TOTAL					**3,487,165**	**137**	**196,093**

Source: E. Sieche, *La Guerra Sottomarina Tedesca nel Mediterraneo 1915–1918.*

the fleet command irresponsibly sold five bigger submarines ordered in Germany on the mistaken assumption that they would not be able to sail to home waters during wartime. The decision to order them abroad in the first place—because of the slightly lower price offered by Germania shipyard at Kiel—was another error, because home-built boats of similar Whitehead or Danubius designs would have been available during 1915.

It was also wrong to refund the financial allocations approved by the 1914 program and to allow the army to send trained shipbuilding personnel to the front. The Austro-Hungarian navy also lacked a mobilization shipbuilding program adapted to its needs for building new destroyers, submarines, minesweepers, tugs, and other vessels. The main reason was, again, savings. Delaying the order for new battleships was no loss for the navy, because these would have been completed too late to be of use. A better option would have been to build three new cruisers and complete the "China cruisers" at Monfalcone before Italy entered the war. Between July 1914 and May 1915 there was enough time to have made them ready for launching, for completion at Pola. During the war only ships already laid down were completed. Important newly built additions included twelve submarines (but four of them of scant military value) and four 850-ton destroyers. At the same time Great Britain and United States, thanks to their broader industrial bases, were building hundreds of bigger and thousands of smaller warships, along with scores of merchantmen. Moreover, the battleship-oriented Austro-Hungarian naval leadership ignored the development of fast motor torpedo boats, starting their trials with this type too late and not completing the designed boats in time for war.

Regarding tactical errors, the cruiser *Zenta* was lost because command failed to use faster vessels or aircraft for reconnaissance in the south. On the following day, it suddenly became possible to send seaplanes to scout the same area. It was also wrong to retain the fleet at Pola during French sorties into the Adriatic, especially on 3 November 1914, when the enemy fleet was sailing without a destroyer screen near Lissa, only 150 nautical miles from Pola. The k.u.k. battle fleet was weaker than the French, but in case of damage all Austrian vessels were near their operational base, the French ships some 750 miles away from Malta. Mistakes committed by the French commander in chief, Vice Admiral Augustin Boué de Lapeyrère—like attacking one old cruiser with every ship at his disposal, and escorting single merchantmen to Montenegro with the whole fleet—were not exploited by Admiral Haus. He was obsessed with the unfaithful Italians, ignoring French movements but in September 1914 sending the whole Torpedo Flotilla to search for an Italian volunteer force incorrectly reported to be landing in Dalmatia.

The French fleet was finally "chased" from the Adriatic, not by k.u.k. battleships but by two small submarines.

The May 1915 bombardment of the Italian coast was successful, being performed without losses on the Austro-Hungarian side. The next failure occurred during the evacuation of the Serbian army from Albania in 1915/16, when Haus neglected to attack the enemy convoys. Only a few cruiser and submarine sorties were envisaged (and these were interrupted prematurely), where an action of the whole fleet would have at least disrupted, if not terminated, the Serbian Dunkirk. An army of 150,000 men was left to escape, to be rearmed at Corfu and play a significant role on the Salonika front later, contributing to the Entente victory. One of the reasons against attacking enemy convoys might have been humanitarian—the Serbians were dragging with them thousands of Austro-Hungarian prisoners through Albania and evacuating the survivors on Allied vessels along with their own troops—but it is not clear whether Admiral Haus was aware of this.

It is inexcusable that during the operations of the Austro-Hungarian scout cruisers in December 1915 and May 1917 there were no heavier units at sea to support them if pursued by a stronger enemy. Armored cruisers sailed from the Bocche only after receiving calls for help. With better strategy it would have been possible to intercept enemy cruisers poised to attack these scouts.

The last and biggest error led to the sinking of *Szent István*. To counter enemy cruisers and destroyers at Brindisi (the Italian main fleet was still at Taranto, too far away to be of concern), four k.u.k. scout cruisers with eight destroyers were more than enough. If stronger vessels had been needed, three *Erzherzog*-class battleships would have been sufficient. Dividing battleships into seven separate support groups was unnecessary and irresponsible, producing more targets for enemy submarines and fast attack craft. If confronted by the enemy battle fleet, these battleships would have been overwhelmed one by one. It would have been better to send the whole Austro-Hungarian battle fleet out as one body, perhaps directly from Pola, to attack Brindisi. An even greater impact would have been achieved by a landing (even a feinted one) on the Italian coast behind the enemy lines somewhere near the estuary of the Po River during the Austrian offensive on the Piave, to distract and disrupt the allies. Another mistake was to send four dreadnoughts south in two separate groups, halving the number of available escorts and doubling the chance of incidental encounter with the enemy. And finally, when *Szent István* developed machinery problems, it would have been better to send her back to Pola than to risk the discovery or delay the whole operation.

It was not necessary to retain so many obsolete warships in service, tying up their crews, and at the same time not permitting leave from fleet units. It would have been better to decommission all vessels of small value, and to "rotate" the crews of active vessels. Lack of coal was another big problem: ships lying idle in harbor became centers of discontent. Other reasons for the mutiny in February 1918 were scarce food rations (an effect of the bad harvest in 1917), lack of replacement uniforms, and war fatigue.

In spite of all this, Austro-Hungarian navy remained effective during the war, retaining control over Austrian coastal waters, preventing enemy landings, chasing superior French forces from the Adriatic, deterring allied battleship squadrons from entering this coastal sea, attacking Italian coastal cities and targets in Montenegro and Albania, supporting Austro-Hungarian army forces and aircraft in their operations, and enabling German and Austrian submarines to operate in the Mediterranean.

The Austrian and the Austro-Hungarian navies went through several phases of evolution, from a Category III, or "third grade," naval power dedicated to coastal defense before 1786 to a Category I ("first grade") sea power in the twentieth century. During the last years of its existence, the Imperial and Royal Navy was a valuable instrument in foreign politics, trade, and economics, making the empire a worthy member of the Central Powers and a respected adversary of the Entente. Austro-Hungarian naval power was not a result only of material resources in the form of ships, submarines, aircraft, naval bases, and industrial foundation but also of the ideas introduced by Tegetthoff, whose spirit guided his successors in building and organizing the navy, making operational control the main issue, and rendering the commander in chief independent in his actions. The Austro-Hungarian navy remained unbeaten until the end, but it dissolved from within, especially after old Emperor Franz Joseph I died in November 1916. The "rejuvenation" of the fleet in 1918 came too late. Horthy was neither Nelson nor Tegetthoff, and his action-at-any-cost principle caused one of the navy's biggest losses during the war. It was followed five months later by the delivery of the fleet to the South Slavs and by the loss of *Viribus Unitis* at Pola from an explosive device installed by Italian frogmen—a symbolic end for this multinational navy.

2

FRANCE

La Marine Nationale

Jean Moulin

BACKSTORY

Pre-1914 History

The creation of the French navy dates back to Cardinal Richelieu, minister of King Louis XIII (1624–42), and its organization to Jean-Baptiste Colbert, minister of Louis XIV (1665–83). From its foundation the French navy alternated between periods of relative splendor when supported by the royal powers and lean periods when the same powers neglected it. In general, however, the crown gave priority to the protection of the northern and eastern borders, the traditional invasion routes into France, not to the navy.

The French navy distinguished itself in the American War of Independence (1778–83), especially in the battle of the Virginia Capes, but was weakened by the revolution that began in 1789, and it was then misused by Napoleon I (1804–15). The defeat at Trafalgar on 21 October 1805 condemned the navy to secondary roles, such as warfare against commerce. The navy, partially restored during the reconstruction period (1815–30), was able to land 35,000 men near Algiers on 14 June 1830, in the prelude to the conquest of Algeria. From that time, the French considered the link between the French mainland and North Africa to be vital.

The imperial navy of Napoleon III (1852–70) was the world's second largest. Its ships were often technologically advanced, in some case even envied by the British. The French and British navies operated together during the 1853–56 Crimean War. The war with Prussia began in August 1870;

France was defeated in the land campaign too swiftly for the navy's blockade of the German coast to be effective. The navy's contributions, such as the pinning down of 100,000 German soldiers to oppose a potential landing and the uninterrupted movement of supplies by sea, remain largely ignored. French sailors stood out, however, during the siege of Paris (18 September 1870–26 January 1871).

The Third Republic replaced the Second Empire. The German annexation of Alsace and part of Lorraine under the Treaty of Frankfurt on 10 May 1871 traumatized France. The nation focused on the "blue Vosges," which marked the new frontier with the German Empire created at Versailles on 18 January 1871, and assigned priority to the army's reconstitution.

In the late nineteenth century, France wanted a war of revenge with Germany and approached Russia with a proposal that it take the Germans from behind. Overseas expansion, blocked several times by the British, was reprised in 1830 but without any real popular support at home, and it was often frustrated by British superiority. The major European powers divided Africa at Berlin in June 1878. This did not prevent crises, however. The Fashoda situation with Great Britain between July and November 1898 had to be resolved by diplomacy because the French were aware that their navy could not oppose the British. The Franco-German Moroccan crises of 1905 and 1911 also ended with diplomatic compromises. Despite these setbacks, France controlled by 1914 a vast colonial empire that included northern and western Africa and Indochina and was the second largest in the world, after only Britain.

By this time, both the French and British—beginning to feel threatened by the development of Germany, including that of its fleet—reconciled and established the Entente Cordiale on 8 April 1904. In 1914, Europe was divided into two blocs: the Triple Entente (France, England, and Russia) and the Triple Alliance (Germany, Austria-Hungary, and Italy, which joined in 1915).

Mission/Function

The French navy's primary mission had long been to oppose Britain's Royal Navy and to prevent any foreign incursions against or "insults" to the French coast (hence the proliferation of torpedo-boat squadrons to cover ports). Coastal defense was the navy's top priority in the 1872 program, which set the fleet's force level and emphasized overseas deployment. As the German navy remained negligible, the main enemy for the French navy was still Great Britain, but there was also a need to account for the Italian threat.

The navy's expansion was required to oppose the British and ensure links with the empire. Normally, the budget voted on annually by the parliamentary assembly provided for the construction of warships according to the navy's demands. But political instability (forty-four navy ministers served between 1871 and August 1914) did not facilitate a coherent policy. Also, technology was changing rapidly between 1870 and 1914, and construction times were excessive due to a disorganized industry. This led to warships that were virtually obsolete by the time they were commissioned.

A new philosophy, that of the Jeune École, or Young School, which disrupted the nation's entire shipbuilding policy, appeared in 1882. Arising from the ideas of Admiral Hyacinthe L. T. Aube (1826–90), this philosophy advocated the construction of many small vessels armed with torpedoes and the near abandonment of large warships, such as battleships, which could be easily sunk by one torpedo. No battleships were ordered between 1882 and 1889. By contrast, 370 torpedo boats were built between 1875 and 1908, including nearly three hundred from 1885. They were distributed among the numerous ports of France and North Africa, ready to repel a British attack and give each port a "mobile defense." The desire to tackle British trade during a *guerre de course* led to the construction of raiding cruisers, many with limited military characteristics, that could operate independently.

In 1890 a new naval statute established a battle-line fleet (twenty-four battleships), a coastal-defense fleet (seventeen coastal battleships, 220 torpedo boats), and an overseas fleet (thirty-four cruisers). Ten battleships were built between 1890 and 1907, forming "the specimen fleet," only three of them identical enough to constitute a homogeneous formation. The navy also constructed coastal-defense battleships, which lacked true nautical qualities, and outmoded armored cruisers. In 1900, however, the submersible torpedo boat *Narval*, designed by the engineer Maxime Laubeuf, was commissioned. *Narval* incorporated many advances, including a periscope and improved surface steam propulsion, and helped pave the way to operational submarines with increased endurance (generally two days).

The 1900 program called for a 1908 fleet of twenty-eight battleships, twenty-four armored cruisers, fifty-two destroyers, 263 torpedo boats, and thirty-eight submarines. The Entente Cordiale eliminated the principal risk of naval war with France's cross-Channel neighbor, but the development of the Italian and Austrian navies increased the danger in the Mediterranean. During 1905, flaws in the Jeune École theory were demonstrated by the battle of Tsushima. The 1900 statute was revised in 1906 to provide for thirty-four battleships, thirty-six armored cruisers, six scout cruisers, 109 destroyers, 131 submarines, and 179 torpedo boats. The emergence of

Dreadnought did not immediately disrupt the building program, since the French laid down in 1907 and 1908 the six 18,000-ton battleships of the *Danton* class. By this time the French, with no battle cruisers or dreadnoughts, had been surpassed by the Germans as a naval power.

The first French dreadnoughts, the four ships of the *Courbet* class, were not laid down until late 1910, becoming operational in 1914. These were followed by three superdreadnoughts of the *Bretagne* type. The navy was stigmatized by several accidents, notably powder detonations that sank two battleships in Toulon, the *Iéna* on 12 March 1907 and *Liberté* on 25 September 1911.

The French naval law promulgated on 30 March 1912 set a 1920 goal for a fleet of twenty-eight battleships, ten scout and ten overseas cruisers, fifty-two destroyers, and ninety-four submarines (twenty-five oceanic and sixty-nine coastal). The twenty cruisers were not specifically defined. The French had commissioned twenty-five armored cruisers between 1895 and 1911 but, despite some studies in 1913, never ordered a battle cruiser. In fact, naval officials attempted to sneak battle cruisers into the authorized program by manipulating the definition of "scout" and "overseas" cruiser, but the onset of war negated such efforts.

The British and French began discussions in 1911 for cooperation in case of war. Three conventions were established in January and February 1913. The British would take responsibility for the Pas de Calais, assisted by French destroyers and submarines operating from Dunkirk, Calais, and Boulogne. The western end of the English Channel would be defended by a French cruiser squadron supplemented by four British cruisers. The North Sea would be the responsibility of the British, who reserved the right to strip the Mediterranean of their warships, leaving the western basin under the care of the French but retaining responsibility for the eastern basin. On 27 January 1913 the two powers also established a cooperation agreement to cover the Far East.

Germany declared war on France on 3 August 1914. The Franco-British Convention of 6 August 1914 provided for a new distribution of naval forces. The general direction of operations was left to the British Admiralty, except for the Channel (set in 1913) and in the Mediterranean, where the direction belonged to France, which was to protect traffic in the Mediterranean and Adriatic and monitor the Gibraltar and Suez choke points. Cooperation with British forces was planned, but each nation retained its autonomy when national interests were at stake.

ORGANIZATION

Command Structure

Administration

In 1914 the minister of marine, who was often an admiral and until 1893 was colonial secretary as well, was the navy's political head and the commander in chief. Housed in the Hôtel de la Marine, on the Place de la Concorde, he was responsible for war preparations. A subsecretary of state supervised finances and administration. On 3 August 1914 Armand Gauthier was as minister replaced by Victor Augagneur. The latter's successors were Admiral Marie-Jean-Lucien Lacaze on 29 October 1915, Charles Chaumet on 10 August 1917, and Georges Leygues between 16 November 1917 and January 1920. However, it was Admiral Augustin Boué de Lapeyrère, minister between 1909 and 1911, who directed much of the navy's reorganization. The central administration was formed by a 18 December 1909 decree and consisted of:

- The Central Military Department, with the General Staff and the Fleet Personnel Bureau
- The central directorates of Naval Construction and Naval Artillery and the Central Bureau of Hydrographic Engineering
- The Central Bureau of Maritime Administration
- The Central Bureau of Health
- The Central Directorate of Navigation and Maritime Justice
- Administration of the Establishment for the Disabled
- Administrative Supervision
- The Central Bureau of Maritime Aviation, established on 10 July 1914.

The central offices were in Paris, and each district had local offices.

The Bureau of Naval Construction, organized by a decree of 11 November 1909 included:

- The Central Directorate of Naval Construction, notably including the Technical Service that designed warships and the arsenals responsible for the maintenance and, in some cases, the construction of the fleet
- The Central Directorate of naval artillery
- The Central Bureau of Hydraulic Engineering and Civil Shipping.

The Chief of the General Staff in Paris was essentially the head of the minister's military cabinet. He ensured the organization of naval forces, their mobilization, and fleet movement, but he did not control operations. This

Photo 2.1. *Danton*-class battleship *Diderot* in Brest dockyard, on the Penfeld River, fitting out in 1911 (Jean Moulin collection)

position was occupied by Vice Admirals Louis Pivet (from 20 May 1914), Charles Aubert (7 December 1914), Marie de Fauques de Jonquières (2 May 1915), and Ferdinand De Bon (10 March 1916 to May 1919). The general staff was organized into four sections:

- Section 1: intelligence, foreign navies
- Section 2: bases and support, mobilization, requisition, transportation, and supply
- Section 3: communications
- Section 4: naval forces, operations.

A fifth section, coastal defense, was added on 21 September 1917, and the fourth section absorbed the third in 1916.

Advisory bodies consisted of mainly the Supreme Council of the Navy, supplemented by technical commissions or committees, or administrative commissions, such the commission for new-warship trials, the committee for naval weapon doctrine, the machinery control committee, and the Board of Health. The Supreme Council, which included the admirals at the top of the hierarchy, determined new ship types and the characteristics desired by the navy. The Naval College, which became in 1922 the Naval Graduate College, annually matriculated fifteen to twenty officers who were destined to become general officers, and it constituted a think tank.

The navy's budgets increased with the threat of war. It was 333 million francs in 1909, 375 million in 1910, 415 million in 1911, 457 million in 1912, 567 million in 1913 (including 222 million for new warships), and more than 600 million francs in 1914 (including 268 million for new construction), in an overall budget of 8.9 billion. Warships under construction at the beginning of the war totaled 257,000 tons.

Command and Fleet Organization

The home fleets (Mediterranean and Atlantic) were each under the orders of a supreme commander, but in reality the main position in the navy was that of the commander of the Toulon battle squadron, in which was concentrated the core of the Mediterranean units. A vice admiral/maritime prefect commanded each maritime district defense and the area's defense. The maritime prefects and their wartime commanders were:

- Cherbourg (1st District), Vice Admirals Le Pord (1912), Pivet (1914), Favereau (1914), Tracou (1916), Jaurès (1917), and Rouyer (1918)
- Brest (2nd District), Vice Admirals Chocheprat (1911), Berryer (1914), Moreau (1915), Pivet (1915), Le Bris (1917), Moreau (1917), and Salaün (1919)
- Lorient (3rd District), Vice Admirals Perrin (1913), de Gueydon (1916), La Porte (1917), Favereau (1917), and Aubry (1918)
- Rochefort-sur-Mer (4th District), Vice Admirals Amelot (1914), Nicol (1916), and Charlier (1917)
- Toulon (5th District), Vice Admirals Chocheprat (1913), De Marolles (1914), Rouyer (1916), and Lacaze (1917)
- Bizerte (Algerian-Tunisian Maritime District), Vice Admirals Dartige du Fournet (from 1913), Nicol (1915), Auvert (1915), Guépratte (1915), and Darrieus (1918).

Local commands were also located overseas.

The war led to some reorganization, the most notable instance being the creation of the Directorate General for Submarine Warfare (MSB) on 18 June 1917. The order of battle, as of 3 August 1914, comprised elements at Toulon, Brest, and Dunkirk.

In Toulon was the Armée navale (Main Fleet), under Vice Admiral Boué de Lapeyrère, comprising:

- Section hors rang (Independent Section) (Vice Admiral Boué de Lapeyrère): *Courbet,* one cruiser (*Jean Bart* after 6 August)

- 1re escadre de ligne (1st Line Squadron) (Vice Admiral Chocheprat): six *Danton*-class battleships
- 2e escadre de ligne (Vice Admiral Le Bris): five *Patrie*-class battleships
- Division de complément (supplemental division) (Rear Admiral Guépratte): four old battleships
- 1re division légère (1st Light Division) (Rear Admiral de Ramey de Sugny): four armored cruisers
- 2e division légère (Rear Admiral Sénès): three armored cruisers
- Division spéciale (special division) (Rear Admiral Darrieus): two old cruisers, seven cruisers, one seaplane carrier, three minelayers, three transports
- Flottille de contre-torpilleurs (destroyer flotilla) (Captain Lejay): 1st, 2nd, 3rd, 4th, 5th, and 6th escadrilles de contre-torpilleurs (destroyer squadrons); thirty-seven large torpedo boats
- Flottille de sous-marins (submarine flotilla) (Captain Moullé): 1st and 2nd escadrilles de sous-marins (submarine squadrons); six torpedo boats, fifteen submarines.

At Brest was the 2e escadre légère (2nd Light Squadron), under Rear Admiral Rouyer:

- 1re division de croiseurs cuirassés (1st Armored Cruiser Division) (Rear Admiral Rouyer): three armored cruisers
- 2e division de croiseurs cuirassés (Captain La Cannelier): three armored cruisers, one training cruiser
- Division des flottilles (Captain Lavenir): three torpedo boats
- 1st, 2nd, and 3rd escadrilles de torpilleurs d'escadre (fleet torpedo-boat squadrons), groupe de réserve des torpilleurs d'escadre (torpedo-boat squadron reserve): twenty-two torpedo boats, two minelayers
- 1st, 2nd, and 3rd escadrilles de sous-marins: seven torpedo boats, twenty-one submarines.

Finally, there was the Dunkerque Mobile Defenses (Commander Saillard): twenty-two torpedo boats, four fleet minesweepers, and four trawlers. In total, there were 690,000 tons of warships in service at the beginning of the war. The naval forces had been reorganized on 31 October 1911, when three battleships squadrons were formed in the fleet. Beginning in August 1914, the domestic forces were divided into the Main Battle Fleet (l'Armée navale) and the 2nd Light Squadron (2e escadre légère).

Photo 2.2. Battleship *Condorcet,* a "semi dreadnought" of the *Danton* class before the war (Jean Moulin collection)

The movement to a war footing was gradual. On 26 July 1914 staff was recalled, the operation of schools was suspended, and supplying completed. On 27 July the training divisions were armed. The arming of auxiliary ships began on the 29th. The navy was reinforced by the division de complément (supplemental division) of Admiral Guépratte, which included the battleships *Suffren, Saint Louis, Bouvet,* and *Gaulois;* the divisions of Morocco and the Levant; and the training division. The oceanic training division, of six armored cruisers (*Marseillaise, Amiral Aube, Jeanne d'Arc, Gloire, Gueydon,* and *Dupetit Thouars*), reinforced the 2nd Light Squadron. The general mobilization order was issued on 1 August.

L'Armée navale was based at Toulon until it was ultimately disbanded in March 1920. The successive commanders, who at the time of mobilization was also the commanders in chief in the Mediterranean, were Admirals Boué de Lapeyrère (beginning on 5 August 1911, on board *Courbet* from 5 January 1914), Dartige du Fournet (19 October 1915, on board *France,* then *Provence* from 23 May 1916), and Gauchet (15 December 1916, on *Provence*). The 3rd Squadron, or Syrian Division, was created on 5 February 1915 with three old battleships and a cruiser.

Italy's entry into the war on 24 May 1915 led to the basing of a French Adriatic Division being at Brindisi to reinforce the Italian navy. It had two destroyer flotillas of six units each and a squadron of six submarines. On 20 September 1915 a mixed antisubmarine flotilla was created with six destroyers and ten trawlers. On 1 July 1918 the fleet consisted of the 1st and 2nd Squadrons, one light division, four torpedo boat flotillas, a flotilla of submarines, the Salonika, Syria, and Aegean Sea divisions, and the Provence, Algeria, and Tunisia patrols.

The 2nd Light Squadron was based in Brest. Commanded by Admirals Rouyer and then Favereau, from 27 October 1914, it was dissolved on 15 November 1915. It was partly replaced by the Eastern Channel and North Sea Fleets. The Atlantic Division of Rear Admiral Grout was created on 28 May 1918 to escort American convoys.

In October 1918 divisions consisting of destroyers and patrol boats operated in the eastern English Channel and North Sea. Naval commands were established in Dunkirk, Calais, Boulogne, Dieppe, and the sea frontiers at Nieuport, Dunkirk, and Calais. (See table 2.1. Some figures are questionable depending on how certain ships are classified, especially third-class cruisers, sloops, and gunboats, whose classification varies according to time and from document to document, even in official papers. Multirole vessels, such as gunboats, minesweepers, and patrol boats, were classified in either category, and figures may be arbitrary, especially for the auxiliaries.)

Many old ships were decommissioned during the war. Thus the number of ships in service on 11 November 1918 does not equal the total of those in service in 3 August 1914 plus newly commissioned ones minus the losses. A portion of the auxiliary cruisers became armed troop transport ships or hospital ships. The Greek warships taken over in 1916 and 1917 are not included.

Communications, Tactical and Strategic

The first tests of radio transmissions (called TSF, for *télégraphie sans fil*) between warships were conducted in 1900 and onboard installations had became widespread by 1904. The devices were bulky and fragile. Communications were made in written form (Morse code), and transmission time was very long, given the time required for encoding and decoding. Ranges were short. The navy adopted the Marine type 1908 wireless and then a post-1916 model of six kilowatts. A network of listening posts was implemented in 1913 for the interception of foreign transmissions. Small, directional devices were available for shipboard use by late 1915.

Merchant ships were progressively fitted with wireless from 1917. The French went from 101 ships with wireless in early March to 359 by the end of the year and 462 in 1918. Seaplanes, especially those engaged in coastal antisubmarine patrols, were being fitted with transmitters by the end of 1916, but deliveries were very slow and the sets were not very reliable.

Table 2.1 French Warship Strengths and Types

Type	In service 3 Aug. 14	Building 3 Aug. 14	Authorized	War losses	Entered service	In service 11 Nov. 18
Dreadnoughts	2	10	4	0	5	7
Battle cruisers	0	0	0	0	0	0
Predreadnoughts	17	0	0	4	0	9
Coastal-defense ships	2	0	0	0	0	2
Armored cruisers	22	0	0	4	0	16
Protected cruisers	9	0	0	1	0	8
Third-class cruisers	5	0	0	0	0	5
Scouts	0	0	1	0	0	0
Aircraft carriers	1	0	0	0	8	1
Destroyers	86	3	0	14	18	89
Torpedo boats	128	0	0	10	0	117
Submarines	50	9	0	14	22	52
Sloops	0	0	0	3	60	57
Minelayers	4	0	0	2	0	2
Minesweepers	7	2	0	7	152	159
Gunboats	8	0	0	2	29	35
Auxiliary cruisers	0	0	0	13	23	5
Patrol boats	0	0	0	46	790	734
Submarine chasers	0	0	0	3	100	97
River gunboats	4	1	0	2	12	10

Aircraft also carried pigeons, which allowed pilots at least to be able to call for help in case of ditching.

In 1914, overseas connections were provided by cables and radio posts, occasionally by the ships themselves. Tahiti was the only colonial post without cable.

Intelligence

Information on foreign navies was provided by naval attachés stationed in major embassies and consuls in foreign ports. From 1915 the French intelligence services intercepted and decoded German radio transmissions. Lack of liaison between the services concerned (the ministries of War, the Navy, Interior, and Foreign Affairs) meant that the best use of decrypts was not always made. For example, the Ministry of War intercepted and decoded a message from the German army attaché in Turkey announcing that Turkey would join the Triple Alliance on 4 August 1914. The Minister of Marine and the fleet commander, however, were not informed, and the fleet commander proceeded to maneuver against the prospect of Italy's entry, as he was unaware of its declaration of neutrality.

By 1917 the French were able to decipher submarine traffic with a twelve-hour delay. The presence of submarines was also disclosed by the obvious sinking of a ship by one of them, as well as by conventional optical means (watchers in coastal stations, seaplanes, or balloons), but exploitation was often limited by the small areas patrolled by warships and the modest performance of the weapons available.

Infrastructure, Logistics, and Commerce

Bases

The navy's main bases were all located in metropolitan France, where industrial support was centered. Toulon, on the Mediterranean, was the main fleet base. Its arsenal, in addition to performing maintenance, constructed small vessels, including submarines. Ten dry docks were in use. La Seyne, which constructed battleships, was across the roadstead from the arsenal. Bizerte was not fully completed in 1914, and the arsenal of Sidi Abdallah, at the base of Lake Bizerte, had only two dry docks. Oran and Algiers in Algeria could supply ships in transit. Torpedo boats were based at Oran.

On the Atlantic coast, Brest was the base of the 2nd Light Squadron, and its arsenal was the navy's largest industrial establishment. It had eight dry docks. Lorient and Rochefort Harbor contained arsenals; each had two dry docks. Brest and Lorient could build large warships, and Rochefort could construct destroyers. Cherbourg, on the southern Channel, could construct submarines and had eight docks. Most docks were old and small in size, and the length and beam of French dreadnoughts were such that these ships could use only a few of them. A program to build larger docks was completed only after the war.

Naval industrial establishments were also located at Indret (propulsion), Ruelle (artillery), and Guérigny (anchors and chains). In Indochina, Saigon's small arsenal had a dock. Facilities at distant stations, with limited supply (coal) and support capabilities, were located at Fort de France, Martinique; Casablanca, Morocco (under construction); Dakar, Senegal (with a dry dock); Diego Suarez, Madagascar (with a dry dock); and Papeete, Tahiti. (See map 2.1.)

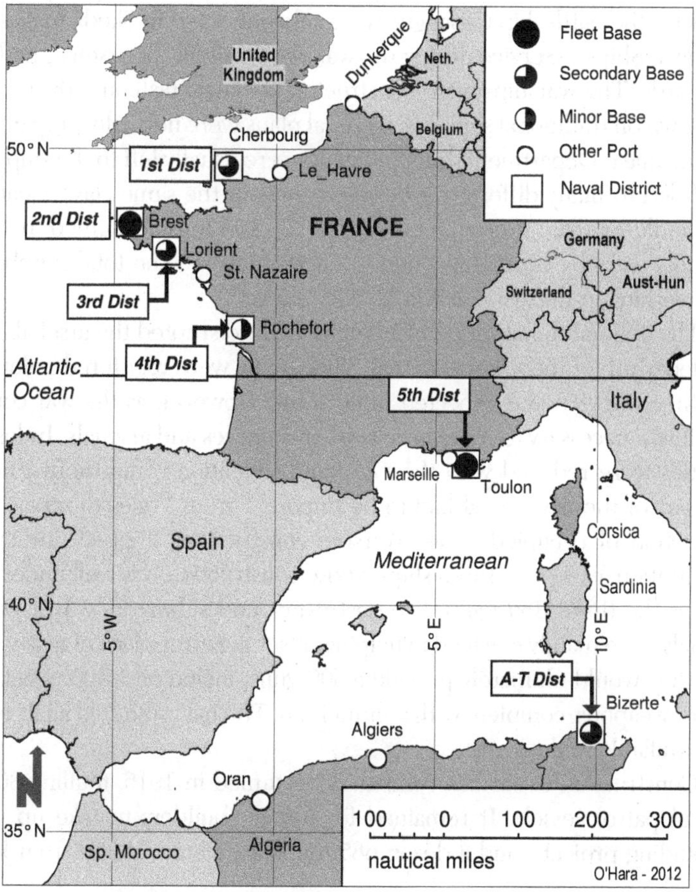

Map 2.1. French Naval Bases

Industry

In the early twentieth century French industry, which relied on the nation's coal and iron resources, was well developed but still behind that of the Germans, British, and Americans. Industrial organization was convoluted, and there were many small businesses involved. French engineers, in the quest for perfection, conceived sophisticated and complex equipment that was often difficult to maintain. Poor communication between the arsenals and competition among private yards limited industry's ability to produce units in series.

Large engineering industries, which the arsenals depended upon to equip ships, were concentrated in the northeast and the Paris regions, far from the ships themselves. Industry could not sustain the fleet's planned expansion, and orders had to be placed abroad. For example, propeller shafts for the battleship *Gascogne* were subcontracted to Skoda in Austria-Hungary. Ships in service during the war were built in the arsenals and private yards. The warships were constructed in classic fashion—riveted and laid down on traditional slipways. General plans were normally prepared by the Technical Department, but the details were usually left to the shipyard, which led to many differences between ships in the same class. Coal was still the fleet's main source of energy; oil (38,195 tons consumed in 1914) was only used by submarines and a few destroyers. The total number of men working in the arsenals was 22,000 to 23,000.

The general mobilization of 1 August 1914 disrupted the arsenals with the departure of mobilized workers, since many were registered sailors. At that time, the war was expected to be short. However, as the war continued, it was necessary to reorganize work in factories and arsenals. Industrial facilities were reduced with the German occupation of northern France, and part of the navy's coal had to be imported from Wales to replace the production of occupied areas. Warship construction stopped during the mobilization, except on those ships whose construction was well under way, such as the three *Bretagne*s, two destroyers, and submarines. In fact, the arsenals were mainly engaged in helping offset the army's lack of heavy artillery; they would ultimately provide 8,500 guns, including 1,500 new large-caliber weapons, complete with ammunition. The navy also sold all its heavy guns available to the army.

Construction of surface combatants resumed in 1916, totaling 80,000 tons of patrol vessels. It remained for foreign builders to take up more demanding projects, and a dozen 685-ton ships were ordered from Japan in 1917. The Americans supplied a hundred submarine chasers, while the British provided some sloops. The French navy, which began the war with 690,000 tons of warships in service, came to 11 November 1918 reduced to 652,000 tons, though with 129,600 tons under construction.

Shipping (Sea Routes and Traffic)

In August 1914 French shipping totaled 2,556,000 tons, including 1,745,000 tons of steamships (about a thousand ships) and 701,530 tons of sailing vessels, including 150 "tall ships" (as known today, the "Cape Horners") and 500 transports. At the end of 1913 there were 29,296 fishing vessels, totaling 271,000 tons, of which 356 were steam powered, 43 were motor, and 27,507 under sail. The construction of a fleet of sailing trawlers was funded and bonuses awarded after 1906 to expedite the construction of domestic warships with steam power. Private companies, often state supported, conducted most of the commercial maritime traffic between the *métropole* and the colonies. Three of these, the Compagnie Générale Transatlantique, the Messageries Maritimes, and Chargeurs Réunies, together owned more than 800,000 tons of shipping.

In addition to the shipping lines to North and South America and the West Indies, most of the traffic from metropolitan France was concentrated in three major shipping routes to North Africa, to West and Equatorial Africa, and through the Suez Canal to Indochina and the Far East.

During the war, requisitioned ships supported the army and naval forces engaged in the eastern Mediterranean. These vessels were fitted out as hospital ships or troop carriers, sometimes switching from one function to another. Initial requisitions included four auxiliary cruisers, over fifty tugs, and two hundred trawlers.

The Maritime Transport Committee was created on 29 February 1916. Shipping was transferred from the Department of the Navy to the Department of Public Works, Transport, and Supply in December 1916, after the creation of a Directorate General for Transportation and Imports on 18 November 1916. A decree of 22 December 1917 brought all French commercial vessels under the orders of the state, and an order of general requisition was finally issued on 15 February 1918.

During the war, the merchant navy lost 3,200 men and 1,128,000 tons of shipping, including 921,000 to enemy action. Losses consisted of 280 steamers (712,000 tons) and 431 sailing vessels.

Personnel

Demographics

On the eve of the war, the navy had 2,850 officers and 62,600 enlisted men. The proportion of officers was 4.4 percent of total personnel. Reservists were called up during mobilization. Crews of the active fleet were brought to wartime levels, and requisitioned ships were manned; some, in fact, were requisitioned complete with crews. Only 30,000 of the 121,500 men initially drafted were enlisted into the navy; the others were retained at their posts or were considered unfit for service for various reasons, such as illiteracy. Draftees were brought into service slowly, to avoid congestion, and mobilization was not completed until 1 March 1915. Surplus personnel were ultimately transferred to the army. At the armistice the navy had 155,000 men in service.

Training

Naval officers were trained at the Naval Academy (École Navale) in Brest after passing a competitive entrance examination. Studies, which were often considered too theoretical, ran two years on *Borda,* an old ship anchored in Brest Harbor, followed by almost ten months on a training ship, which in 1914 was the armored cruiser *Jeanne d'Arc.* These officers might serve within a chain of command or as commanders of smaller warships. Then, after attendance at the Naval War College (l'École supérieure de marine), and toward the ends of their careers, they became the captains of major warships. Other officer graduates of the special schools were distinguished by their specialties, such as engineering, health, supply, naval construction, hydrographics, navigation, and naval artillery. The technicians in maritime engineering were responsible for the construction of warships. They were assisted by officers in that course of study (future engineers).

There were so many officers that progress up the ranks was slow. Lieutenants remained long in their grade, and some were assigned to land positions often held by civilians in other major navies. The proportion of junior officers was higher than in other navies, while the proportion of senior officers was lower. The latter were usually older than their foreign equivalents; a battleship commander was at least fifty-four years of age, ten years older than his British or German counterpart. The rank of lieutenant commander (*capitaine de corvette*), suppressed since 1848, was restored on 1 July 1917.

Officer training was shortened during the war. An applied school (École des chefs de quart) was opened at Lorient for Naval College candidates and students from the merchant marine who had enlisted or been mobilized.

They underwent a course of several months' training in essential practical manners. After the war Lorient returned to being a training school for officers. Many reserve officers, usually from the merchant marine, took positions with the Fleet Auxiliary, including patrol duty, with ships still manned by their premobilization crews.

Petty officers (NCOs), quartermasters, and sailors were groups within the body of the crews of the fleet. There were six main specialties: helmsmen-seamen, gunners, torpedoes, marines, mechanics and stokers, and electricians. This list was supplemented by specialties less "naval" in character, such as steward. Petty officers were usually recruited from the ranks and trained in schools of specialization. Grades ranged from first master to second master.

Sailors were either enlisted (a youth could enter the École des Mousses from age fourteen) or conscripts from the naval draft, a feature dating back to Colbert that mobilized young merchant seamen, fishermen, and arsenal workers for the navy. The time of compulsory military service was three years in 1914. In 1906 half of the navy's needs were covered by the naval draft, the rest by enlisted volunteers—more than 80 percent from the coastal departments. Many enlisted men were from Brittany.

Schools were closed during mobilization, but as the war continued the French needed to reopen the School of Apprentice Mechanics in Lorient, which was done on 2 March 1915. The courses were accelerated, and practice then usually became "on the job."

Culture

A large proportion of officers came from the upper classes of society. Often described as conservative, they had a reputation for resistance to change. Outside of headquarters assignments and service in Paris, they lived in the five major metropolitan ports, somewhat isolated on board ship or together in naval housing. The weight of tradition was strong, an acculturation partly acquired during training at the Naval Academy.

On-board accommodations, lifestyle, food, and education all formed barriers between officers and crew. A comparable barrier also existed, despite often a common origin, between the petty officers and sailors. Symbolic of social organization on board was the organization of the wardrooms (officers) and mess halls (petty officers and crew); on large ships there were no less than six messes: admiral, senior officers, junior officers, petty officers, junior petty officers and medical staff, and crew. Outside of coastal areas, the navy was often ignored and at best poorly understood by the French, the majority of whom were farmers.

THE WAYS OF WAR

Surface Warfare

Doctrine

After many metamorphoses, especially because of the Jeune École, a surface warfare doctrine supported by the Naval Graduate College eventually won the approval of the minister and Parliament. Alfred Thayer Mahan's influence was obvious when the French finally abandoned the doctrine of the *guerre de course* (war against commerce) in favor of a *guerre d'escadre* (squadron warfare) strategy based on the main fleet, although the obsession with coastal defense remained. The goal of the new naval strategy was a decisive clash between battle fleets, clearly along the lines of fleet actions like Trafalgar (ideally with better results, from the French point of view) and Tsushima. The result was a unique main-battle force, l'Armée navale, most of the strength of which was under the command of an *amiralissime,* a commander in chief equivalent to the army's general of the army. The political situation (and the power of the new German navy, with which a direct confrontation was impossible without British support) led, after an agreement with the British, to the concentration of naval forces in the western Mediterranean.

The navy was in disagreement with the army and its policies, which obviously were mainly concerned with the land front in the event of conflict with Germany. The army's plans required that the navy's first duty, upon the outbreak of war, was to cover the passage from North Africa to France of the 19th Corps (38,000 men, 6,800 horses—the divisions of Algiers, Oran, and Constantine—in forty-six ships) and troops from Morocco (11,000 men and 5,000 horses in forty-three ships). The presence of these troops was deemed essential to the Northeastern front for the anticipated great battle with the German army.

Ships/Weapons

The priority given to the battle fleet led to development of the divisions of battleships. In thus passing from one developmental extreme to the other, the French navy came late to the dreadnought race and neglected its light scouting forces.

Battleships

The five 15,000-ton battleships of the *Patrie* class (the sixth, *Liberté,* blew up in 1911) were classic predreadnoughts, with four 305-mm main guns and a secondary battery of eighteen 164-mm (*Patrie, République*) or ten 194-mm (*Démocratie, Vérité, Liberté, Justice*) guns. They were completed between 1906 and 1908.

The six 18,000-ton battleships of the *Danton* class (*Danton, Mirabeau, Diderot, Condorcet, Vergniaud, Voltaire*), described as "semidreadnoughts," were laid down between 1907 and 1908. They carried four 305-mm and twelve 240-mm guns and had turbine propulsion. The dual caliber was upheld by the Supreme Council of the Navy because it could deliver the same amount of a metal per single barrel a minute as the larger caliber, thanks to its higher rate of fire. This would permit a veritable blasting of the enemy's superstructure at the then-current combat ranges of only six thousand meters.

The first French dreadnoughts were the four *Courbets*, which became operational in 1914. They displaced 23,500 tons and carried twelve 305-mm guns. Upon mobilization the dreadnoughts *Courbet* and *Jean Bart* were operational, followed by *Paris* on 9 September, then *France* on 18 October. These ships suffered from teething troubles, particularly jamming of the main gunnery breeches after just a few shots. The class was followed by three *Bretagne*-class superdreadnoughts (*Bretagne, Provence,* and *Lorraine*), a simple adaptation of *Courbet* with ten 340-mm guns. Though laid down in 1912 and their construction well advanced in 1914, they would not be completed until 1916. Five battleships of the *Normandy* class were laid down in 1913, but construction stopped at the beginning of the war. Their twelve 340-mm guns were installed in three quadruple turrets of the same model as before. This same turret would also have fitted out the four units of the *Lyon* class (four turrets) that should have been started in 1915. The other battleships in service were obsolete predreadnoughts, even though the last six, and *Danton,* were in service for three years.

Cruisers

The fleet lacked modern light scout cruisers to guard the flanks of the battleship divisions. A design for an escort (scout) of 4,500 tons was planned for 1915, but the war forced the project's abandonment. Battle cruisers were studied in 1913, but none were ordered before the war.

The twenty-five armored cruisers in service in 1914 had all been built after 1888. The newest was *Waldeck Rousseau,* laid down in 1906 and completed in 1910. All these ships were too big, too poorly armed (194-mm batteries), and too slow (twenty-three knots) to perform the role of scout. The remaining fifteen protected and unprotected cruisers were too old (about fifteen years) and too limited in performance for fleet use. In 1914 the navy did not possess the right type of cruiser for a fleet squadron. Its armored cruisers were outdated but at least had the advantage of an imposing appearance, with their four or six funnels, as well as significant mission performance capability.[1]

Photo 2.3. Armored cruiser *Ernest Renan,* the last class of French armored cruisers (Jean Moulin collection)

Torpedo Boats

In 1914 the navy still had more than a hundred numbered coastal torpedo boats, as a consequence of its past adherence to the doctrine of Jeune École. They served as escorts and patrol boats until the specialized ships that were being hastily put into construction arrived. In some cases propulsion plants were stripped from disarmed torpedo boats to equip *Ardent*-class gunboats built from 1916.

French destroyers comparable to their British counterparts appeared in 1899, with the commissioning of the first three-hundred-ton vessels of the *Durandal* class. In 1914 there were three torpedo gunboats of the *d'Iberville* class, of about nine hundred tons and dating from the 1890s, which were sometimes classified as *contre-torpilleurs* (destroyers). French *contre-torpilleurs* were reclassified as *torpilleurs de haute mer* (oceanic torpedo boats) on 14 March 1913. The term *contre-torpilleur* did not reappear for ships until the *Jaguar* program in 1922 but was still used in the designation of formations.

In 1914 the majority of French destroyers were three-hundred-ton types, of which fifty-five units were constructed between 1900 and 1908. They were obsolete by 1914 and unsuitable as escorts. In August 1914 twenty-nine were in the Atlantic, twenty-one in the Mediterranean, and three in Indochina. Thirteen 450-ton torpedo boats were completed between 1909 and 1912. The construction of eight-hundred-ton torpedo boats started in 1910; sixteen were in service when the war started; two followed shortly thereafter and two more of 850 tons in 1916. A design for a 1,500-ton destroyer was adopted in January 1914 but was not realized until 1922.

On 9 August 1914, the French requisitioned four 990-ton ships under construction for export to Argentina, commissioning them by year's end, but this did not give the navy enough large destroyers to screen the fleet even in good conditions, a problem aggravated by the need to counter the submarine threat. The seizure of twenty Greek destroyers and torpedo boats in December 1916 also gave only partial relief. Given the limits on wartime shipbuilding, the French found the situation so serious that they resorted to ordering a dozen 685-ton ships from Japan in 1917. The rest of the fleet, in addition to submarines, consisted of a collection of old ships, some of them posted overseas (gunboats, transports, auxiliaries).

Weapons

Gunnery had been improved since 1906. A corps of naval artillery engineers succeeded the colonial artillery engineers in 1909. A controlling department for powder was set up after the explosions of *Iéna* and *Liberté*.

In 1914 the gun calibers in use were 305-mm (in six models), 274-mm (the old battleships), 240-mm (*Danton*'s secondary battery), 194-mm (gunnery school, old battleships, and armored cruisers' main batteries), 164.7-mm, 138.6-mm (at the time referred to as "14 centimeters"), and 100-, 75-, 65-, and 47-mm. The best of these was the 240-mm cannon. Guns of 75-, 90-, and-120-mm were supplied by the War Department to equip a portion of the auxiliary fleet.

Sailors and engineers considered that a battle could not be fought at ranges greater than twelve or thirteen thousand meters. The ranges of guns were thus intentionally limited, with low elevation angles for the heavy guns and a plethora of secondary batteries. Range finders and fire control were poor; English Barr & Stroud range finders were purchased at the beginning of the war. The navy did not increase elevations until 1916, after it learned that the 305-mm guns of the Austro-Hungarian fleet could range to 20,000 meters. The superdreadnought *Provence* was commissioned with one of her five 340-mm turrets capable of shooting 21,000 meters instead of 14,500. Torpedoes were originally purchased from Whitehead, Fiume, and were constructed in part at Toulon from 1894. A factory was still incomplete in Saint-Tropez in 1914. Weapons in service were of 356-, 381-, and 450-mm calibers. The first two sizes armed torpedo boats and the first *contre-torpilleurs*. The 450-mm caliber dated from 1892, and five models were in use on the latest destroyers. The 450-mm Model 1906 weighed 648 pounds and had an 86.8-kg warhead. It ranged to 600 meters at 36.5 knots, 1,000 meters at 32.5 knots, 1,500 meters at 27 knots, or 2,000 meters at 24.5 knots.

Submarine Warfare

Offensive

Doctrine

The mission of French submarines was initially to protect harbor approaches, acting defensively toward friendly vessels and offensively against enemies. In 1912 it was planned to have them participate in the *guerre d'escadre*. A division of three submarines, led by a three-hundred-ton torpedo boat, would scout ahead of the fleet and then deploy in front of enemy warships. Submarine squadrons would screen the flanks of the battle fleet, but the low speed of the boats, around twelve knots, made the practice of such tactics very difficult, and they were never applied. During the war, submarines were initially used in a static role to monitor enemy ports in the Adriatic and to form patrol lines in the Channel blockade. This changed when they were assigned an antisubmarine-warfare role and began hunting for enemy submarines.

Boats/Weapons

Overall, French boats were relatively inefficient and fragile. Engineers had created systems that were too complex, difficult to maintain, and ill suited to war service. The systems were too precise for the techniques of the time. The admirals were generally skeptical about the capabilities of the submarine arm, there was no central office or research bureau, private industry was not interested, and there was no coordination. The training of personnel, selected from volunteers, could not make up for the poor design of their craft. Industry could barely make reliable diesel engines, for which the market was so small; therefore, part of the fleet needed to be equipped with a steam engine for surface propulsion, with a diving time (for over ten minutes) incompatible with military necessity.

Operationally, the submarines were divided between offensive units (the more efficient) and defensive (the older submarines), which were placed in ambush positions along the coastal zone. The best submarines were the seventeen steam-driven units of the *Pluviôse* class completed between 1908 and 1911 and the thirteen diesel boats of the *Brumaire* class completed between 1911 and 1912.

The navy had fifty submarines readily operational in August 1914 (the figures vary between thirty-four and sixty-two, depending on how one defines availability). In early August 1914 submarines were deployed as follows:

- The English Channel, with:
  - The 1st Squadron at Cherbourg with eleven boats.
  - The 2nd Squadron at Calais with eleven diesel-powered boats.

- L'Armée navale, with:
  - The 1st Squadron at Toulon with seven stream-powered submarines.
  - The 2nd Squadron at Bizerte with eight diesel submarines.

Nine relatively old boats were assigned to the defense of Cherbourg (four) Toulon (two), and Bizerte (three).

Antisubmarine

In 1914 the concept of antisubmarine warfare was still unclear. The possibilities of submarines had been poorly understood. When on the surface, submarines could be attacked from above or hit by gunfire, but underwater they were virtually undetectable unless revealed by a their own torpedo or periscope.

The first antisubmarine depth charges, which the navy began developing in 1914, were released by a surface vessel, which needed to pass just above the submarine. These first depth charges contained thirty kilograms of gun cotton. Five hundred were constructed, followed in 1915 by depth charges of the Guiraud design, weighing forty-five kilograms with a charge of twenty-five kilograms. A first order was for four thousand, and in 1916 each patrol boat carried six. Depth charges of the naval artillery type with 40-, 45-, and 75-kg of explosives were also ordered in 1916 and 1917. Four thousand CM-type depth charges were delivered in late 1917. They had warheads with thirty-five kilograms of melinite. It was not until 1918 that launching equipment, such as depth charge throwers and mortars, were being shipped in sufficient numbers. By 1916 a towed antisubmarine sweep, the Marseillaise device, was also in service.

Seaplanes engaged in antisubmarine warfare did not have effective weapons. They typically used a twenty-two-kilogram bomb, type D, containing eleven kilograms of melinite. It was dropped from an altitude of one or two hundred meters and exploded at a depth of eight meters. A 47-mm gun fitted to a hundred seaplanes was in service by early 1918.

Submarines were noisy while underwater, and detection was possible by listening for them using a device derived from a stethoscope, but the hunting vessel needed to be stopped. Lieutenant Walser developed a device with acoustic resonators contained in two spherical caps. It could be used at speeds of up to six knots and could give an approximate bearing. It was tried in March 1918 and then mounted on board a hundred warships. Active detection by ultrasound echoes, tested from late 1917 by Professor Langevin, arrived too late for the war. The most common listening device was the Perrin microphone, a simple underwater microphone that required the listening vessel to be at a standstill in order to detect a submarine. This equipped all antisubmarine vessels too small to carry a Walser apparatus.

Mine Warfare

Doctrine

The navy had no real mine-warfare policy. Mines were mostly intended for defensive barriers off ports. Minefields were supplemented by fixed torpedo tubes, including the defense of the Brest Narrows. Despite this, France laid fields within certain anchorages in the English Channel and North Sea, off the Turkish coast, and on the Atlantic side in areas where submarines could operate. France participated in the construction of the Otranto barrier in 1918 with nets and mines. Throughout the war the French navy did not lay more than 4,700 mines.

Ships/Weapons

The Ronarc'h drag method of sweeping—a sweep of two cables in the form of a large V held out by underwater kites—was tested in 1910, then adopted and widely used during the war. The number of sweepers increased with the requisition of new craft, growing from about thirty sweepers upon mobilization to seventy-six in November 1915 and 228 by the end of 1916, then dropping to 110 in July 1918. The number of sweepers rose again to 248 after the armistice to clear mined areas.

Minelaying was carried out by two old torpedo cruisers, *Casabianca* and *Cassini*; by two small specialized ships launched in 1913, *Cerberus* and *Pluton;* and by destroyers equipped with rails. For sweeping, the navy used four minesweepers built in 1913, but most sweepers used during the war were tugs and requisitioned auxiliaries. Torpedo boats, gunboats, and sloops built during the war were also equipped for sweeping.

In 1911 the stock consisted of 2,800 mines, of which only the 1,500 of the model 1906 were not totally obsolete. All mines were contact types. The principal mines were, in addition to the model 1906, Breguet, Sauter-Harle, and the Schneider, for two submarine minelayers completed in 1918.

Amphibious Warfare

Doctrine/Capabilities

Marines represented a specialty within the regular navy, such as engineering or torpedoes, not a separate force as in the U.S. and British navies. Each ship had a team of sailors led by regular officers trained to form a landing company in case intervention ashore was required. Landings were usually accomplished using the ship's boats.

A doctrine for amphibious operations had not yet been codified, and the concept was limited to the notion of a *coup de main* by the companies landed. There were no specialized ships for landing operations; in the event of need, amphibious transports would consist of commandeered ships, especially already-armed auxiliary cruisers.

Coastal Defense

The coastal-defense system was the legacy of the British threat against the French coasts. Controversy between the ministries of the Navy and War (which included the army) led to a shared responsibility for coastal defense, with the navy in charge of Cherbourg, Brest, Toulon, and Bizerte, the Ministry of War of all other coastal zones.

From late August 1914 the Ministry of War began to disarm some of its coastal batteries to recover the guns for use on the land front, due to a lack of heavy artillery. The growing threat of submarines led to a meeting on 12 February 1917 and the decision to strengthen coastal defense with medium-caliber rapid-fire guns, and a decree of 21 September 1917 assigned coastal-defense responsibility to the navy. The mission was entrusted to the Fifth Section (EMG 5) of the navy's General Staff. By the end of 1917, fifty-five defense posts had been installed by the army and armed with the help of the navy, each with two 90-, 95-, or 100-mm guns.

Naval Forces Ashore

From 12 August 1914, as in 1870, surplus sailors available after mobilization were gathered into battalions designed to ensure the safety of Paris. They were finally sent to reinforce the front; two regiments forming the Brigade of Marines were committed from 16 October to 10 November 1914 in Dixmude, Flanders, where they stopped the German advance. The brigade was disbanded 22 November 1915 and replaced by the Bataillon de marche des fusiliers marins, which fought until the armistice.

Spare 37-mm guns armed twenty-six armored-car sections from late September 1914, and eleven sections of light cars were allocated to the army, but the sailors who manned them were recovered by the navy beginning in 1916. The navy was also required to send to the land front gunners to man heavy artillery batteries (305-, 194-, and especially 164-mm), the number of which reached eighteen by 1918, and also, from 1916, to man on the river system a dozen barges armed with a 138- or 100-mm weapons.

Aviation

The navy developed its first aircraft at the end of 1910. The Department of Naval Aviation was created by decree on 20 March 1912, and the Central Bureau of Naval Aviation was organized by a decree of 10 July 1914. A former torpedo cruiser (another legacy of the Jeune École), the *Foudre,* was refurbished in 1911 and used for tests and maneuvers with seaplanes on board. The first flight of an aircraft was made from a forward platform on 8 May 1914, but the war interrupted the development of this technique. At the beginning of the war the navy had seventeen aircraft with fourteen pilots, the seaplane carrier *Foudre,* and a shore base in St. Raphael.

WAR EXPERIENCE AND EVOLUTION

Wartime Evolution

Surface Warfare

Upon the outbreak of war the navy's first priority was providing complete coverage for the transports bringing troops from North Africa to the mainland. The original plan called for the transports to operate separately in order to avoid losing time, with distant cover provided by a special division allocated to the task, while l'Armée navale was ordered to stop the two German ships in the Mediterranean, the battle cruiser *Goeben* and light cruiser *Breslau.* The fleet sailed from Toulon on 3 August 3 at 0400 hours. However, it had only one dreadnought, the *Courbet.* The announcement of the bombardment of Philippeville by *Goeben* and of Bône by *Breslau* early on 4 August disrupted these plans, and the troop transports were then collected into three escorted convoys. Three battleships were detached to search for the Germans before escorting the two dreadnoughts *Jean Bart* and *France* from Brest to Toulon, as the second was still undergoing trials and had no ammunition. *Courbet* was at least 250 miles from the enemy, the French ships were too slow to catch up with the Germans, and no cruisers were fast enough to maintain contact. L'Armée navale covered the transports until 7 August, when the ships left Toulon, this time with *Courbet* and *Jean Bart,* and headed to a rallying point at Malta.

Austria Hungary entered the war against France on 11 August. The battle fleet no longer needed to account for the Italian fleet, as Rome had declared its neutrality, and instead the French sought to bring the Austrian fleet to battle. On 16 August the battle fleet was concentrated when it intercepted just off Antivari the small Austrian cruiser *Zenta* and the destroyer *Ulan*. The latter managed to escape and took refuge in Cattaro, but *Zenta* was shot up by the guns of the French battleships. The incident revealed a certain lack of coordination between the French warships.

The Austrian fleet remained out of reach in the upper Adriatic. Now based in Malta, l'Armée navale, ready for the expected battle, implemented a close naval blockade of the Austro-Hungarian navy by maintaining a cruiser in the Strait of Otranto. While the government asked him to act against ships and Austrian ports, Admiral Lapeyrère had always hoped for a face to face confrontation with the enemy fleet. However, the fine workings of *guerre d'escadre* and squadron warfare was now thrown off by the appearance of the submarine. The torpedoing of *Jean Bart,* damaged on 21 December 1914, and of the armored cruiser *Leon Gambetta,* sunk on 27 April 1915, led the fleet to retreat to Malta, and the blockade was then carried out by light vessels. The entry of Italy into the war on 24 May 1915 placed the navy in the second line behind the Italians.

Malta served as the advanced base, while Toulon remained the base for major maintenance. The navy was quickly reinforced by the dreadnoughts *Paris* and *France* and in 1916 by the three superdreadnoughts of the *Bretagne* class: on 7 May *Provence, Bretagne* on 18 May, and *Lorraine* on 9 August. This force stood ready to strengthen the Italians should the Austrians attempt to sortie. That fleet, however, generally remained at anchor, successively based at Navarino until the end of 1914, at Corfu from January 1916, and Corfu and Argostoli from April 1916. Its outings were limited to forays into the lower Adriatic.

The main fleet lost some of its forces to peripheral operations. The most important was that of the Dardanelles. The British monitored the outlet of the straits from which the *Goeben* could appear at any time. Two battleships, *Suffren* and *Vérité,* were detached to Tenedos and put under British orders on 27 September 1914. On 29 October Turkey attacked Russia in the Black Sea. On 3 November *Suffren* and *Vérité,* along with the British battle cruisers *Indefatigable* and *Indomitable,* conducted the first bombardment of the Turkish forts at the entrance of the straits. War was declared on 5 November. A second operation was conducted on 19 February 1915. The allied fleet assembled a battle cruiser and eighteen battleships, including five French ships of the division commanded by Rear Admiral Guépratte (*Suffren, Bouvet, Gaulois, Charlemagne,* and *Saint Louis*). A new bombardment was conducted on 25 February.

A purely naval attempt to force the Dardanelles began on 18 March 1915 but failed, with the loss of the French battleship *Bouvet* and the British *Ocean* and *Irresistible.* Battleships *Suffren* and *Gaulois* were badly damaged, and the latter was only just saved. *Bouvet* struck a mine, capsized, and sank in less than a minute. This failure affected the navy, which would thereafter refuse nearly all efforts against coastal defenses until the Second World War. On 25 April the allies landed at the entrance of the Dardanelles, a French brigade being put ashore at Kum-Kaleh, on the Asian side. In the face of Turkish resistance, the allies were finally reembarked on 9 January 1916. The Dardanelles French squadron was renamed the Fourth Squadron on 1 January 1916 and was disbanded in March 1916 with its ships joining the Naval Division of the East in June 1916.

The navy was involved in the defense of the Suez Canal during the Turkish attack on the night of 2 February 1915. The bombardments by the coastal battleship *Requin* and the cruiser *D'Entrecasteaux* were decisive. Operating out of Port Said, French ships blockaded the Turkish coast in the eastern Mediterranean. The French occupied Ruad Island on 1 September 1915 and Castelorizo on 28 December. On 12 September 1915 French vessels embarked three thousand Armenian refugees being hounded by the Turks near the northern tip of Ras Al Mina. Two armored cruisers participated in Red Sea patrols in 1915.

In the Far East, the armored cruiser *Dupleix* was involved in hunting Admiral Spee's East Asian squadron. The torpedo boat *Mousquet* was sunk by *Emden* at Penang on 28 October 1914. The armored cruiser *Montcalm* acted as an escort in the Indian Ocean. French ships also engaged in the initial operations against Cameroon in September 1914.

In the Mediterranean, the navy supported the Serbian army. Naval 14-cm guns participated in the defense of Belgrade in November 1914. French warships evacuated the Serbian army to Corfu in January 1916 and

Photo 2.4. *Torpilleur 319* (Jean Moulin collection)

in April and May 1916 transferred it to Salonika, which the allies had occupied on 5 October 1915.

War with Bulgaria and, especially, a complicated relationship with Greece led to the creation of the 1st Franco-British Special Squadron between 25 November and 22 December 1915. Later, in late August 1916, a second squadron was activated. On 1 December the landing of 2,900 men at Athens led to gunfire and fifty-four French deaths. Fire from the battleship *Mirabeau* stopped the Greeks. Eventually, after some complications, and like it or not, Athens joined the allies on 21 June 1917. Meanwhile, the navy seized many Greek ships, including seventeen destroyers.

Armored and auxiliary cruisers of the 2nd Light Squadron maintained a blockade line at the western entrance of the English Channel until April 1915 before being replaced by light warships and auxiliaries. Pas de Calais was guarded by destroyers and submarines until December 1914.

A naval command under Vice Admiral Ronarc'h was established on 1 May 1916 to support the Dover Patrol. This command had a dozen destroyers, a squadron of submarines, and a naval aviation center. Part of its mission was to block the Straits of Dover to German submarines operating from Flanders. There were a few skirmishes with German forces off Flanders, and the torpedo boat *Bouclier* sank the German torpedo boat *A 7* on 21 March 1918.

The French armored cruisers operating from Brest were relatively underutilized and in early 1916 formed two new divisions, one in Dakar and the other in the Caribbean, to address the threat of German surface raiders. In fact, from 1915 the threat of submarines was what guided the deployment of these warships.

Although the fleet was supported by four dreadnoughts in late 1914 and three superdreadnoughts by 1916, no new cruisers were constructed. Four large destroyers of 990 tons being built for Argentina were requisitioned on 9 August 1914 and commissioned in October and November 1914, and twelve 685-ton destroyers were constructed in Japan in 1917. Two eight-hundred-ton torpedo boats (*Enseigne Roux* and *Mécanicien Principal Lestin*) were completed in 1916. Twenty-four submarines were completed, including three boats being built for export, along with one more captured from Germany (*UB 26* became *Roland Morillot*).

The most spectacular development was in the patrol and escort fleet, which in November 1918 totaled 111 torpedo boats and destroyers, 63 sloops, 153 patrol boats and submarine chasers, and 734 armed trawlers. The navy lost four battleships (*Bouvet* mined on 18 March, 1915, *Gaulois* torpedoed 27 October 1916, *Suffren* torpedoed 26 November 1916,

Danton torpedoed 19 March 1917); five cruisers (*Léon Gambetta* torpedoed 27 April 1915, *Amiral Charner* torpedoed 8 February 1916, *Kléber* mined on 27 June 1917, *Châteaurenault* torpedoed 14 December 1917, and *Dupetit Thouars* torpedoed 7 August 1918); twenty-three destroyers, thirteen submarines, three sloops, eight-six patrol boats, requisitioned trawlers and submarines chasers, and eight auxiliary cruisers.

Submarines

The submarine division based at Calais was initially to oppose any attempt by the German fleet to force the Pas de Calais. Two mine barrages were located at Pas de Calais and between Le Havre and Portsmouth. After the appearance of enemy submarines in the English Channel, French submarines were kept in port to avoid confusion and were posted to Dunkirk in 1916 to defend the coast of Flanders and then in 1917 to Brest. Submarines were also towed underwater by sailing vessels as U-boat traps but, sadly, to no avail.

The submarines of l'Armée navale followed it to Malta and then later to the Greek anchorages. They operated in the Adriatic; however, to do so their range needed to be increased, so they were first towed to the Strait of Otranto by a cruiser. The French lost *Curie* in the Adriatic on 25 December 1914 while attempting to force Pola, *Fresnel* on 5 December 1915, *Monge* on 28 December 1915, *Foucault* on 15 September 1916 to aircraft bombs, *Bernoulli* mined on 15 February 1918, and *Circe* to a torpedo on 20 September 1918.

Six submarines were sent to the Dardanelles in October 1914. Only the *Turquoise* succeeded in operating (for ten days) in the Sea of Marmara; she ran aground and was captured by the Turks on 30 October 1915. The others did not manage to pass through the straits, and three were lost: *Saphir* 15 January 1915, *Joule* 2 May 1915, and *Mariotte* on 26 July 1915.

Six submarines were based at Brindisi in 1915, and a squadron was established in Morocco in 1917. Another squadron was created in Bizerte on 17 June 1917, with five submarines. In 1917 and 1918 submarines were deployed operating from the Atlantic coastal ports to confront their German counterparts and to cover American convoys, in cooperation with maritime aviation. The ability of French submarines to receive messages while submerged allowed greater control over their operations. Submarines were also based in Brest, Gibraltar, and Bizerte to monitor the Sicilian Channel. The results of their operations were small. Four submarines were lost outside the Adriatic Sea and the Dardanelles: the *Ariane* torpedoed off Bizerte on 19 June 1917, *Diane* disappeared in the Atlantic 11 February 1918, and *Prairial* and *Floreal* in collisions on 29 April and 2 August 1918.

French submarines had limited success. They sank four and damaged three Austrian warships. The torpedo boat *Bisson* sank the Austrian submarine *U 3* on 13 July 1915, and the submarine *Circe* sank the German *UC 24* on 24 May 1917. Statistics kept between 2 August 1914 and 1 January 1918 established that the percentage of nonavailability was 31 percent for steam submarines and 42 percent for the diesel boats. The average proportion of time spent on war cruises was only 9 percent. French submarines conducted nearly four thousand patrols, but these were all short-range. The navy had sixty-four submarines by the armistice, but twenty-two had reduced crews. French submarines were excluded from the battle line, contrary to prewar intentions.

The fight against German and Austro-Hungarian submarines became increasingly important. Weapons and detection equipment, however, were developed relatively slowly. Antisubmarine defense was initially restricted to the direct escort of valuable ships only. Then, in June 1915, two patrol flotillas were established on the ocean and in the Mediterranean.

In late 1915 the allies established a system of patrol routes, first in the Mediterranean, which was divided into eighteen zones—four British, four French, and ten Italian—and then in the English Channel. The navy began arming the merchant fleet in 1915, typically with 90-mm guns provided by the Ministry of War. Ships armed with guns also had special gun crews and were called AMBC ships (*armement militaire des bâtiments de commerce,* military-armed merchant vessels). By 16 December 1916, 418 ships were thus armed, a number that rose to 591 steamships and 137 sailing vessels by 31 December 1917, and finally to 1,140 by the end of 1918.

The French navy requisitioned 280 patrol vessels, and the fleet was expanded through purchases and orders, especially abroad. The French purchased trawlers from Belgium, Brazil, Greece, Iceland, Italy, Japan, the Netherlands, Norway, Sweden, Spain, and the United States. Thirty-seven antisubmarine vessels were commissioned from French shipyards, and a hundred were constructed in the United States, but only eight of the latter were in service by the armistice.

Patrolled routes were widespread in the Mediterranean in 1916 but proved to be a failure. In March 1917 the number of patrol squadrons was increased from nineteen to twenty-five, including twelve in the Mediterranean. The real solution was the escorted convoy, which was finally implemented in early 1917 for slow cargo ships bringing coal from Wales to France, in May 1917 in the Mediterranean, and finally along the Atlantic coast in June 1917.

By October 1917 nine patrol divisions were in place in the North Sea, eastern Channel, western Channel, Brittany, Gascony, Algeria, Tunisia, eastern Mediterranean, and off Provence. These divisions came under the orders of the maritime prefects on 30 December 1917.

Aviation

The development of aviation and maritime airships was linked to submarine warfare. Several maritime aviation development programs were approved in January 1916. Aviation detachments were located from mid-1916 on all coasts, organized into Centers of Maritime Aviation (centre d'aviation maritime, or CAM) with eight to twelve aircraft, and combat stations (poste de combat, or PC) with a maximum of six units. At the end of 1916, ten centers were located from Dunkirk to Salonika. Development accelerated in 1918, and by the armistice the navy operated thirty-seven CAMs and twenty-four PCs, of which three centers were transferred to the Americans. The Maritime Air Station (L'Aérostation maritime, or balloon division) began arming airships from December 1915. Ten centers were equipped in metropolitan France, three in North Africa, and one on Corfu.

At the armistice the naval air section had 1,264 aircraft (650 were active), 37 airships, and 200 balloons, with 580 pilots and 550 observers. Naval air mobilized 11,000 men, with 4,300 for airships. The naval air section conducted 155 air attacks, 124 by aircraft and 31 by airships.

French seaplanes played a decisive role, thanks to their reconnaissance of Turkish forces advancing toward the Suez Canal. The main fleet too used seaplanes, mostly for reconnaissance. They operated in the Mediterranean in March 1916 from the converted freighter *Campinas,* which could operate in areas not covered by maritime aviation centers.

The Dunkirk CAM, shared with the British, operated against the Germans based in Belgium, had seaplanes for surveillance and patrol, and also operated against land-based fighters. Overseas, CAMs were located on the coast of North Africa and in early 1918 at Dakar. A center was set up in Venice by the end of May 1915. A CAM was also based at Corfu and Mytikas, Greece, in August 1917. The navy deployed a number of seaplane carriers, including *Foudre* in August 1914, *Campinas* from 1916 to 1919, *Nord, Pas de Calais,* and *Rouen* in 1916, and *Dorade* and *Normandie* in 1917.

Navy seaplanes participated in the neutralization of two German submarines, *UC 38* on 14 December 1917, sunk by *Lansquenet,* and on 18 May 1918 *U 39,* obliged to seek internment in Cartagena, Spain. Maritime aviation and airships played a decisive role in antisubmarine warfare, forcing submarines to remain submerged (hence costing them their ability to observe and, especially, their mobility) and driving them away from the coast.

Summary and Assessment

By the time of the armistice of 11 November 1918, France had mobilized about 8.4 million people and suffered 1.4 million dead or missing. The navy was exhausted. It had lost 19,495 men: 11,388 dead, 607 wounded, and 7,500 prisoners.

Apart from building antisubmarine forces in the shipyards, equipment had not been renewed and was worn out by the demands of war service. Ships and men also often served far from the industrial support of metropolitan France. Prepared for a classic war fleet, sailors who completed training for work in submarines and battleships often found themselves allocated to sloops and patrol vessels. For the French sailors the war effectively continued until late 1920, due to operations against the Bolsheviks in Russia, especially within the Black Sea. The delayed demobilization led to on-board mutinies, which were quickly controlled.

In early 1922, after the return of requisitioned ships, the disposal of the oldest and most worn-out units, and the incorporation of former enemy warships (including five light cruisers), the fleet's total tonnage in service stood at 485,000 tons, with 25,400 tons under construction and 81,600 projected. The reconstruction of the fleet began with the 1922 program.

Liaison was not always good between the different levels of responsibility. On 3 August 1914 Paris did not advise Admiral Lapeyrère that Italy had declared neutrality, which he needed to know in order to operate appropriately. The capabilities of submarines were underestimated, but fortunately the time taken by the Germans to decide on unrestricted submarine warfare in the Atlantic worked to the advantage of the allies.

The cooperation with the British, good comrades in battle, was more labored at higher levels. Responsibility in the Mediterranean, in theory left to France, was actually shared between the French, British, and Italians, each wishing to benefit from reinforcements provided by others but not wishing to lose any of their own authority within their areas or when they considered that their interests were at stake. The Mediterranean was finally divided into areas assigned to the respective navies of the three countries at a conference at Malta on 2 March 1916. The convoy system, in a case of forgetting history, was implemented much later.

If French sailors proved their courage and their capabilities, they were frequently disappointed by their often fragile, unreliable, and difficult-to-maintain equipment. It has been written that the French sailors had more problems with their equipment than they did with the enemy.

For the French overall, World War I was symbolized by trench warfare. The battles of the Marne, Verdun, and the Chemin des Dames marked every family. The evasion of the Austro-Hungarian fleet and then the entry of Italy into the war did not allow the navy its great battle in the image of Jutland. Submarine warfare, the major threat until 1917, remained virtually unknown outside of the coastal populations, as did the ultimately successful effort to oppose it.

The navy benefited from the war's lessons, and its reconstruction starting in 1922 was difficult but successful. Unfortunately, this new navy would be virtually eliminated in difficult and unpredictable conditions during the Second World War.

3

GERMANY

Kaiserliche Marine

Peter Schenk with Axel Niestlé and Dieter Thomaier

BACKSTORY

Pre-1914 History

The Kaiserliche Marine developed enormously in the forty-three years from its very humble beginnings at the foundation of the German Empire in 1871 as the amalgamated Prussian and North German Federation navies to the beginning of World War I. In the centuries before 1871 the German Empire never created a navy, letting the coastal cities and kingdoms guard their own maritime interests. After the empire's collapse in the Napoleonic wars and its acquisition of the Baltic territory of Pomerania from Sweden, Prussia established a small navy. In 1848 the German revolutionary National Assembly formed a fledgling navy to serve in the war against Denmark. The outnumbered fleet fought a small battle at Helgoland but could not break the Danish blockade. In the Prusso-Danish War of 1864 the Prussian fleet, together with an Austro-Hungarian squadron, met the Danish blockade fleet off Helgoland but once again failed to drive the Danes from their station.

In the following years the Prussian fleet, under the command of Prince Adalbert, trained officers and crews while new ships slowly entered service. A North Sea base was established in Wilhelmshaven and another in the Baltic at Kiel. In 1867 the North German Federation was founded under Prussian supremacy, and a new national ensign, which flew until 1918, was hoisted on the ships. Anticipating conflict with Denmark, the navy ordered small gunboats of questionable value. But soon France was seen as a potential enemy, so three armored frigates were ordered in France and Britain, as well as four more in Germany, to support the construction of iron ships—an industry just beginning in Germany. When war with France broke out in 1870 only three armored frigates were in service, and once again the German navy found itself unable to prevent a superior enemy fleet from blockading its coasts.

In 1871, at the end of the war, the German Empire was formed when the four South German states joined the North German Federation. Whereas the armies remained separate, acting together only in war, the navy came under the emperor's direct control. Its growth accelerated when Emperor Wilhelm II was crowned in 1888. Two months later the parliament readily granted his request to fund a division of four modern *Brandenburg*-class battleships. Soon the emperor noticed a young captain, Alfred Tirpitz, who had distinguished himself in the development of torpedoes and torpedo boats. Although at this time the Jeune École school of naval theory envisioned torpedo boats as coastal craft, Tirpitz called for high-seas torpedo boats to operate together with the battleships. In 1892, at the age of just forty-two, he was appointed chief of staff of the Naval High Command and in 1897 State Secretary of the Reichs Marine Amt (Naval Administration), becoming the de facto naval minister.

Wilhelm II favored a fleet of cruisers, but he could not impose this idea on Tirpitz, who redirected Germany's naval policy to an offensive orientation. In fact, Tirpitz considered a fleet of seventeen battleships and six torpedo boat flotillas necessary in order to cope with the French and Russian navies simultaneously. The parliament balked at these plans and only reluctantly approved funds for two additional battleships of the *Kaiser* class to join the three already authorized. In 1898, however, parliament accepted a bill asking for nineteen battleships in two squadrons plus two reserve ships; twelve of this total number, including old, coastal, armored ships, were already in service. Three battleships were laid down in 1899 and three more in 1900. Tirpitz felt this rate of construction was desirable, but as it could not be sustained under the existing naval law, which dictated construction through 1903, Tirpitz convinced the emperor to build at a rate that would lead to forty-five battleships by 1920. Tirpitz's aim was a battle fleet strong enough to deter Britain from entering war with Germany. He assumed a decisive battle in the southern part of the North Sea and from 1907 on had the ships constructed to the prerequisites of such a battle: smaller-caliber guns, slower speed, but superior protection.

In the second naval bill of 1900 Tirpitz asked for four squadrons of battleships of eight units each, with two flagships and four reserve vessels—that is, thirty-eight battleships. The old, coastal, armored ships were to be quickly replaced. The "*Dreadnought* leap" resulted in additional supplementary bills in 1906, 1908, and 1912, which were pushed through parliament and would have eventually led to a German fleet of sixty-one battleships. However, against Tirpitz' expectations, Great Britain reacted violently, and by 1910 it became clear even to Tirpitz that a naval arms race with Britain could not be won. Fiasco was imminent. It was too late, however, to stop what had become a runaway train.

At the beginning of the twentieth century, many in the Imperial German Navy considered submarines useless for a powerful navy that could sustain the Germany's world position. In fact, at this time no existing submarine anywhere offered features that inspired confidence in the type's capabilities in a future conflict. Insufficient sea-keeping qualities, speed, and endurance prevented submarines from deepwater operations with battle fleets. Instead, they were seen as defensive weapons for protecting harbors or sealing limited areas against enemy raids; they were often regarded in the same category as mines and barriers.

Thus, Germany was the last major naval power to employ submarines. The private German shipbuilding companies Howaldtswerke AG and the Krupp-owned Germaniawerft AG had constructed military submersibles since 1898. Only in 1904 was Germaniawerft AG awarded a contract to build the German navy's first submarine. The boat was based on a design for the Russian navy, and changes repeatedly delayed its completion. In accordance with common German practice for small naval units, the vessel received no name but a designator—the letter *U,* for *Unterseeboot,* or *U-Boot,* and a number, starting with *1.* On 14 December 1906, *U 1* was commissioned at Kiel. Several improved designs followed with increased displacement and endurance and enhanced technical reliability, but the early boats still suffered from insufficient battery capacity, and their low-power, petroleum-driven main engines produced telltale smoke clouds during surface travel. In 1913, following the development of powerful and reliable diesel engines, the first series of diesel-powered U-boats (*U 19–U 22*) entered service. Prewar maneuvers had shown them capable of patrols lasting a week under all weather conditions.

Mission/Function

In an 1892 study the Naval High Command planned to prevent an enemy blockade of the German coast, as experienced so often in the past, and to act offensively in the event of war with France and Russia. The French Atlantic Squadron was to be destroyed first, before it could unite with the

Mediterranean Squadron, even at the risk of the devastation of Danzig by the Russian fleet. Hostilities with Britain were not officially taken into account until later. When they were, the planners assumed the British would implement a close blockade and envisioned meeting the British fleet between Thames Estuary and Helgoland in a decisive battle.

When Tirpitz became secretary of state of the empire's navy department (Reichsmarineamt, or RMA) in 1897, the imperial navy possessed a disparate assortment of vessels. The most powerful units were the four battleships of the *Sachsen* class (7,368 tons) and the four *Brandenburg*-class units (10,000 tons). Some coastal armorclads of the *Siegfried* class (3,500 tons), built in accordance with the expired defensive doctrine, were also in service.

Photo 3.1. *U 27* loading torpedoes. (Peter Schenk collection)

Under construction or authorized were three battleships of the *Kaiser Friedrich III* class (11,100 tons). For these vessels the design criterion of the strongest main artillery possible—a feature of the *Brandenburg* class—was abandoned. Instead, on the basis of contemporary experience, these ships were armed with quick-firing guns, in order to deluge the enemy with shells. The so-called heavy artillery at this time consisted of four 24-cm guns (*Schnellfeuergeschütz*-Sk)—the largest caliber capable of sustaining a high rate of fire. In fact, the eighteen 15-cm Sk guns were the real main weapons of this ship class. The belt armor consisted of 300 mm of the newly developed Krupp Cemented (KC) armor. Speed reached nearly eighteen knots. In the first fleet law, two more of these ships were authorized. The next, five-unit *Wittelsbach* class (11,700 tons) was a follow-on design. Its armament was identical; the main modification was rearranged armor plating. A 75-mm armored-deck slope was positioned behind 225-mm belt armor, and speed was increased slightly.

Emperor Wilhelm II had great interest in the navy, and he was especially fond of cruisers. Thus he strongly influenced the conception of the *Hertha*-class cruisers (5,660 tons). The armament consisted of two 21-cm and eight 15-cm Sk guns. The speed (19.5 knots) and protection (armored deck only) of these vessels were insufficient, however, and this type was not continued after Tirpitz entered office. Contemporaneous to the *Kaiser Friedrich III* class was the first German armored cruiser, *Fürst Bismarck* (10,690 tons). She was a cruiser version of the aforementioned battleships armed with four 24-cm and a dozen 15-cm Sk guns. Her speed was only nineteen knots, but the belt armor was up to 200 mm thick amidships.

The armored-cruiser equivalent to the *Wittelsbach* class was *Prinz Heinrich* (8,890 tons). She was a little smaller than her predecessor but, at twenty knots, slightly faster. Armament had been reduced to a pair of 24-cm and ten 15-cm Sk weapons. Protection consisted of a 100-mm thick layer of belt armor and a 50-mm armored-deck slope. The material was KC steel for the belt armor and nickel steel for the armored decks.

From 1897 the need for a type suited to fleet and colonial use resulted in the light cruisers of the *Gazelle* class (2,660 tons). Capable of up to twenty-two knots, these cruisers were armed with ten 10.5-cm Sk guns. There was only local shielding and an armored deck for protection. Many of the older cruisers served in colonial stations and were then assigned auxiliary tasks.

Torpedo boats played a role in Germans doctrine second only to battleships. Tirpitz himself strongly affected the progress of this type from 1878, as a leader of the technical development of torpedoes, and then from 1886 to 1889 as chief inspector of the torpedo department. Very different boats were investigated, with the goal of vessels as small and fast as possible. Since the speed, range, and directional control of the early torpedoes were inadequate, the boats had to close very near to their targets and so required conditions of low visibility to operate successfully. In this first phase, boats of the Elbinger shipyard, in Schichau, proved very useful. A larger unit was also designed as a division leader.

When Tirpitz became secretary of state, a typical torpedo boat was *S 82*, with a displacement of 142 tons and a speed of twenty-five knots. She was armed with three 45-cm torpedo tubes and a 5-cm Sk gun on a torpedo-boat gun carriage (a combination known as Tk). A corresponding leader was the division torpedo boat *D 9*, with a displacement of 350 tons, a speed of 23.5 knots, three 45-cm torpedo tubes, and three 5-cm Tk guns.

As weapons improved, consideration regarding the ideal size for torpedo boats was ongoing. Positive experience with the division torpedo boats encouraged an enlargement of the type, which would also improve their seaworthiness. The result was the high-seas torpedo boat with a displacement between 310 and 580 tons and a speed of twenty-seven knots. Armament consisted of three deck-mounted 45-cm tubes and three 5-cm Tk guns. The division torpedo-boat type was suspended.

According to Tirpitz' strategic conviction, the decisive instrument of sea power was the battle fleet. The so-called standard ships of the line formed the basis for Tirpitz' planned fleet expansion. As a first step he consciously accepted that the size and characteristics of these ships were below international norms. The battleships of the planning years 1900–1903 were the five *Braunschweigs* (13,200 tons) and five *Deutschlands* (13,200 tons). Their armament was moderately enhanced to four 28-cm and fourteen 17-cm Sk guns. The armor strengths remained the same for the first ships and changed only insignificantly in the last ones. The maximum speed reached eighteen knots.

The contemporaneous two-unit, armored-cruiser classes of the *Prinz Adalbert* (9,050 tons) and *Roon* (9,530 tons) types carried four 21-cm and ten 15-cm quick-firing guns. Their armor resembled that of their predecessors, but the *Roons* were one knot faster. Significant improvements were not achieved until the two ships of the 1903/04 *Scharnhorst* class (11,600 tons). That class's armament consisted of eight 21-cm and six 15-cm quick-firing guns. The deck armor improved somewhat, and the belt armor thickened to 150-mm. The maximum speed was 23.5 knots. Apart from colonial duties, German armored cruisers could undertake reconnaissance in force and support the battle fleet.

Systematic firing tests conducted in 1904 at Meppen demonstrated that the 100-mm belt armor of the armored cruisers was insufficient, while comprehensively investigating the interaction with the deck slope behind the belt armor. Such firing experiments on actual-sized ship modules played an important role in the design of new units. As soon as the end of 1904, several influences were generating discussion about increasing battleship sizes. These influences included an increased accuracy and rate of fire of heavy gunnery, the growing threat presented by torpedoes and mines, and initial lessons from the Russo-Japanese War.

At first such considerations were retarded by German reluctance to appear as a driver in the expansion of ship sizes. Furthermore, an increase in battleship size would require costly expansion of locks and widening of the Kiel Canal. Rumors of larger British battleships and then the construction of the *Dreadnought* provoked this policy's reversal. The result was the first German all-big-gun battleships, the *Nassau* class (18,900 ton). They were armed with twelve 28-cm and twelve 15-cm naval guns. The hexagonal arrangement of the six 28-cm twin turrets was thought to offer advantages during a melee. The maximum speed was twenty knots. The ships had a new and effective underwater protection system and a maximum belt armor of 300 mm.

An unusual feature of the design organization was that parallel to the titular head of the construction office was a young official, Hans Bürkner, designated by Tirpitz to be responsible for capital-ship construction. Many of his design measures led to the remarkable survivability of German capital ships. He conceived of a large float (called *Ponton I*) for underwater explosion tests. This allowed for actual-sized ship sections to be stressed with explosion charges and torpedo-bulkhead prototypes to be tested under near-real conditions. The cruiser design corresponding to the *Nassau* class was *Blücher* (15,840 tons), the Germans' ultimate expression of the classical armored cruiser: twelve 21-cm guns in the same main-battery arrangement as *Nassau,* a secondary battery of eight 15-cm guns, protection featuring torpedo bulkheads, and twenty-five knots. Despite the considerable progress from her forerunners, *Blücher* remained an armored cruiser, not a battle cruiser (both types were labeled "large cruisers" in the imperial navy).

The German answer to *Invincible* was the battle cruiser *Von der Tann* (19,400 tons), with eight 28-cm and ten 15-cm guns. Speed was twenty-seven knots. With torpedo bulkheads and strong armor (belt armor maximum 250 mm) she was very well protected. Along with these radical changes in capital-ship design, systematic development was occurring in light cruisers and torpedo boats.

ORGANIZATION

Command Structure

Administration

From 1899 on, the kaiser was the Kaiserliche Marine's supreme commander. The offices reporting to the kaiser included the commanders of the Naval Cabinet, of the Naval Staff, of the High Seas Fleet Command, of the Cruiser Squadron, of the North and Baltic Sea naval stations, of ships on foreign station, and finally, the State Secretary of the Naval Administration, Grand Admiral von Tirpitz. Tirpitz headed the naval administration, which had personnel, technical, and educational departments. Thus, the navy did not have a centralized professional leadership. This led to contradictory strategic proposals. All orders had to be given by the kaiser, in contrast to the army. Von Tirpitz' request for general command over the navy was rejected. He was finally removed from his post in March 1916. Only in September 1918 did Admiral Reinhard Scheer, newly appointed head of the Admiralty Staff, succeed in establishing an operational branch (Seekriegsleitung) at the Grand Headquarters at Spa, thus taking de facto the high command from the emperor.

The budget of the navy for the 1912/13 fiscal year amounted 462 million marks, compared to 899 million marks for the British navy in the same period. The next year's budget was 476 million marks, compared to 1,051 million marks for the Royal Navy.

As for command and fleet organization, territorial commands administered the North Sea coast (Marinestation Nordsee) and the Baltic coast (Marinestation Ostsee). There were also six overseas stations. The cruiser squadron was stationed at Qingdao, Germany's only foreign base with docking facilities. In the Mediterranean the battle cruiser *Goeben* and the light cruiser *Breslau,* and in the Caribbean the light cruiser *Karlsruhe,* were deployed without a German base. The cruiser *Königsberg* was stationed in East Africa and smaller units in West Africa and the South Pacific. The navy's inspector-general was Grand Admiral Prince Heinrich von Preussen.

Fleet Organization and Order of Battle

At the beginning of the war the High Seas Fleet was in Wilhelmshaven, under the command of Admiral Friedrich von Ingenohl, on board his flagship *Friedrich der Große.* There were three squadrons; the first, under the command of Vice Admiral Wilhelm von Lans, comprised the eight battleships of the *Nassau* and *Ostfriesland* classes. The second squadron, (II Squadron) under Scheer, who had become a vice admiral in 1916, was made up of the five predreadnoughts of the *Deutschland* class and the predreadnoughts *Hessen* and *Lothringen.* The third squadron, under Rear Admiral Felix Funke, comprised the four battleships of the *Kaiser class.* Later, in 1914, the four new battleships of *König* class and in July 1916 *Bayern* were included in this squadron. In 1917 *Baden* became the flagship, and then a fourth squadron was formed with the five battleships of *Kaiser* class, splitting the third squadron. The second squadron left the High Seas Fleet after Jutland. A fourth and fifth squadron that existed in 1914 consisted of old predreadnoughts, soon relegated to secondary service.

The first reconnaissance group, under Rear Admiral Franz Ritter von Hipper, comprised the battle cruisers *Seydlitz, Moltke,* and *Von der Tann* and six small cruisers. Later, in 1914, *Blücher* and *Derfflinger* were added, with *Lützow* coming in during 1916 and *Hindenburg* in 1917. The second, third, and fourth reconnaissance groups had five light cruisers each. There were eight torpedo-boat flotillas with eleven or twelve boats each, with additions made during the war. (See table 3.1.)

Table 3.1 Strength of Kaiserliche Marine

Predreadnought-era ships Type	Aug. 1914	Losses, 1914–18	
Battleships	22	1	
Armored cruisers	9	6	
Protected cruisers	5	0	
Light cruisers	18	7	
Torpedo boats	48	10	
Dreadnought-era ships Type	Aug. 1914	Losses, 1914–18	Nov. 1918
Battleships	14	0	19
Battle cruisers	4	1	5 (1 to Turkey)
Light cruisers	16	12	18
Destroyers	0	1	13
Torpedo boats	84	57	134
Submarines	27	178	195
Minelayers	7	4	14

Communications

Tactical communications were conducted with flag signals during the day and by signal lights at night. To ensure receipt, by the time of the battle of Jutland, signals were repeated by wireless.

Wireless telegraphy had become an indigenous and reliable communication system by 1900, and in 1912 a monopoly quarrel between the British Marconi and the German Telefunken systems had been settled. In 1905 the navy built a wireless station with a range of two thousand nautical miles at Norddeich, in cooperation with the post ministry. In 1908 Telefunken introduced an innovative long-wave transmitter that could be carried by all Kaiserliche Marine ships. From 1911 a long-range transmitter at Nauen, near Berlin, with a range of five thousand nautical miles, was able to reach German colonies. Airships and bigger planes were equipped with small wireless sets. In the summer of 1914, however, the building of a worldwide wireless net had not been finished. There were big stations at Kamina in Togo, at Windhuk (in modern Namibia), at Qingdao, and on Yap in the Carolina Islands, and a number of smaller ones. But the stations in Tabora in Deutsch-Ostafrika and on Sumatra were not yet finished, so parts of the Indian and Pacific Oceans remained out of range.

Intelligence

The Nachrichtenbureau (N) in the Imperial Naval Administration collected intelligence from other navies. At the beginning of the war no naval deciphering service existed. In March 1915 a radio station of the Royal Bavarian army's Funkerkommando 6 at Roubaix observing enemy wireless traffic succeeded in breaking the British patrol-boat code and in July 1915 the British fleet code. From 1917 the British and French naval signal books were broken. Also, from spring 1915 the positions of allied merchant vessels could be determined by taking the bearings of wireless transmissions. Later in the war the Royal Navy introduced more sophisticated codes that were harder to decipher. These code-breaking successes were accidentally achieved by the ex–University of Würzburg mathematics professor Ludwig Föppl, then twenty-six years old, who had been sent to the wireless station by chance. In February 1916 the navy created the Beobachtugs- und Entzifferungsdienst (B.u.E. Dienst) at Neumünster, under Lieutenant Commander Martin Braune, for observation and deciphering of enemy radio messages. Braune had been sent to Föppl to learn from him. The information gathered from this activity was often stunning; it ranged from the deployments of Q-ships to minefields and losses in them, as well as to exact numbers of merchant ships around Britain.

The practice of wireless communications was still very young in 1914, and the German Naval Staff was unaware of the security problems connected with it. Some simple precautions were thought to be sufficient. A secret signals book was used, and tables were changed from time to time. Germany used three code books, one (*Handelsverkehrsbuch*) for the merchant vessels and smaller warships, one (*Verkehrsbuch*) for the diplomatic service and interservice communication, and the navy's signals book (*Signalbuch der Kaiserlichen Marine*), issued only to larger units on important missions.

All radio messages from ships were to be sent with the lowest possible signal strength, in the belief that enemy land stations would not then be able to intercept them. The normal procedure was for the main radio station, usually on the flagship, to ask every single recipient of a message for an acknowledgment. The practice generated excessive traffic, with many repetitions, from which enemy observers could conclude a great deal.

When the German light cruiser *Magdeburg* ran aground in the Baltic in August 1914, the Russians captured the ship's signals book, a copy of which they handed over to the British. A new set of codes was ordered instantly, but it took two month to distribute. From 1915 codes were replaced at first monthly, later daily. But the request of the commander of the Baltic Forces for a new signals book was rejected by the Admiral Staff in May 1915. Only in December 1915 was the signals book improved. Two new signals books, for fleet and general signals, were finally introduced in 1917. As a result of all this, on the eve of the battle of Jutland the British were fully informed about German intentions from German radio signals, and the Grand Fleet went to sea in time to intercept the German High Seas Fleet.

Positive results and a more cautious attitude toward radio signals could be observed in October 1917 during a mission of the cruisers *Bremse* and *Brummer* against a convoy east of Lerwick. The cruisers kept wireless silence and remained undetected. *Brummer* had a radio observation squad on board that could jam the alarm message of the British destroyers escorting the merchant vessels. The cruisers sank eight merchant vessels and one destroyer. British messages giving the positions of intercepting forces were deciphered and courses were adjusted so that the cruisers' return was unmolested. Another dash of the High Seas Fleet against the Bergen-Shetland convoys in April 1918 was also undetected because of German radio silence until a machinery malfunction on *Moltke* forced her to broadcast. By that time it was too late for the Grand Fleet to intercept.

Infrastructure, Logistics, and Commerce

Germany entered the war unprepared, in the firm belief that it would be over by autumn. It soon became clear that this would not be the case. The complete blockade of overseas supplies was quickly felt. Industrial managers pointed out that the supplies of saltpeter imported from Chile for production of explosives would last only half a year. As a result, a department for war raw materials (Kriegsrohstoffabteilung) was established, with military and civilian deputies, and the chemical industry was brought together in a syndicate to mass-produce artificial saltpeter from nitrogen gas.

Also, food production began to suffer from a shortage of labor as farmers and their sons were conscripted and workhorses requisitioned. Germany had to import 10 percent of its food before the war. At the end of 1914 a central grain organization was set up, followed in 1916 by a war food administration, which, however, proved inefficient. By the end of 1916 a crisis existed in terms of transportation and coal, caused by the lack of railroad workers. The winter of 1917 became notorious for people having only turnips left to eat. The need for labor in industry was partly alleviated by the employment of five million women.

As most German warships used coal, a fuel that Germany had in abundance, there was no scarcity in this sphere. The need for oil was much smaller than it would be in the Second World War, but nevertheless it was critical, as of the 1.3 million tons consumed in 1913 only 90,000 tons were produced domestically. At first oil could still be imported from Galicia, then a part of the Austro-Hungarian Empire. But the region was soon occupied by the Russians, until regained in spring 1915 (luckily the Russian army did not bother to destroy the oil wells when it retreated). Romania also stopped its oil exports, under allied pressure, and a crisis in supplies occurred in 1916. Romania entered the war that year and was occupied in spring 1917 by German and Austro-Hungarian forces. The British destroyed the oil wells before the allied retreat, but German workers quickly repaired them, and by the end of the year production had been restored to half its previous level. Overall, Germany could provide about 80 percent of its prewar annual oil consumption, which compared unfavorably with allied countries, which doubled their supplies during the war.

Manganese ore, an important raw material for steel production, was imported from Turkey. Only after Serbia was overwhelmed in October 1915 could it be shipped by rail from Constantinople to the Danube and from there to Germany. When the railway in Serbia was reopened at the end of 1915 the traffic became faster, and from three to five thousand tons per month could be sent to Germany.

Bases

The two chief military ports with docking and supply facilities were Wilhelmshaven and Kiel. On the North Sea coast there were also harbor commanders for Geestemünde (today Bremerhaven), Cuxhaven, and Helgoland. In 1895 the Kiel Canal was opened, connecting the North and Baltic Seas without the detour around Jutland. The locks were widened for the new battleships in 1914, just before the war. The only German overseas base for the cruiser squadron was at Qingdao, which possessed a floating dry dock. Because of the need to supply the overseas cruisers in the event of war, the German navy prepared a number of stations, called *Etappen,* in Qingdao and in neutral countries, commanded by naval officers who cooperated with businessmen in chartering German and neutral coal ships to rendezvous with raiders. These stations were officially part of the embassies and were connected by wireless with ships and naval commands. There were such stations in China, Japan, Manila, Batavia, San Francisco, Peru, Valparaiso, La Plata, Rio de Janeiro, the West Indies, New York, West Africa, East Africa, and the Mediterranean. With the destruction of most raiders by the end of 1914 and the declaration of war against Germany by many countries, the stations lost their importance. During the war, more bases were set up in occupied countries—for example, Zeebrugge and Ostend in Flanders,

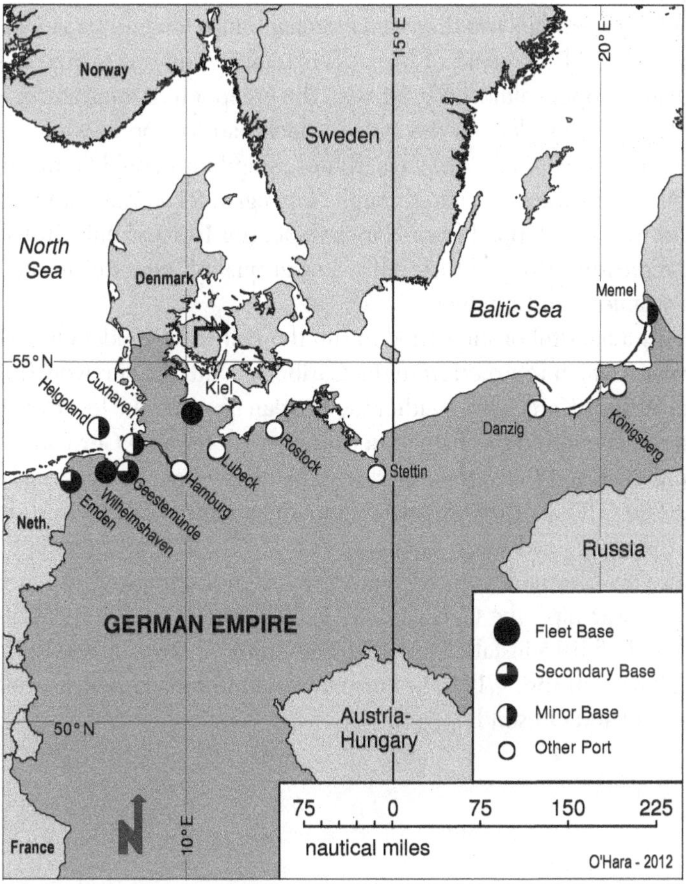

Map 3.1. German Naval Bases

and Memel, Libau, and Riga in the Baltic. At Zeebrugge, submarine pens were built. In the Black Sea, small bases were built at Varna and Costanza. (See map 3.1.)

Industry

The navy had its own shipyards at Wilhelmshaven and Kiel. There were larger, civilian yards at Emden, Geestemunde, Hamburg, Lübeck, Rostock, Stettin, Danzig, and Elbing. In 1900 there were a total of thirty-nine yards, with 154 slipways and twenty-seven docks. Krupp at Essen produced armor and guns, and armor was also made at Dillingen. Before the war Germany ranked second only to the United States in coal and steel production. The country had very good rail and canal networks.

Shipping

In 1914 Germany had two thousand merchant ships totaling 5,134,720 GRT, amounting to 11.3 percent of the world's total. When war started German merchant shipping almost ceased, with the exception of the iron-ore traffic from Lulea in Sweden via the Baltic, which had to stop in winter due to ice. Some 7 percent of Germany's iron-ore shipments could be maintained from Narvik by the safe route through Norwegian territorial waters. A large amount was also shipped from Narvik to neutral Holland until British diplomatic pressure stopped this traffic. Lower-quality "minette" iron ore was also available from Lorraine.

Only a handful of ships tried to run the British blockade. One was the *Rio Negro,* which returned from the Caribbean with the survivors from the sunken cruiser *Karlsruhe.* Neither the Russian navy nor the few British submarines that entered the Baltic Sea caused much harm to Germany's Baltic traffic. British and Russian submarines sank fourteen merchant vessels totaling 28,000 GRT in 1915, Russian submarines sank another three ships in 1916; there were no losses to submarines in 1917–18. Apart from diplomatic pressure on Denmark and Sweden to close the Baltic's western entrances to enemy warships, the German navy laid minefields, ordered patrols, and at the end of 1915 installed a net barrage from Wustrow to Gedser. More nets followed in spring 1916 in Langeland and Fehmarn Belt, as well as in Baagösund and Öresund.

Personnel

Demographics

In 1914 the Kaiserliche Marine had 3,878 officers and 65,091 ratings, plus 3,582 clerks. A further 13,200 ratings could be activated from reserve status at the beginning of the war, but as this exceeded the need at that time they were mostly used in the Marinekorps Flandern, on the western front.

Training

The navy conscripted for military service all men over seventeen years of age who had at least three months' experience on ships or river craft. Volunteers from the technical professions were also inducted for a period of three years and then placed into the reserve for a further four years. Boys could enter the navy from age sixteen and after graduation to sailors could become noncommissioned officers.

Every April the navy accepted two hundred officer candidates (in 1914 the number was raised to three hundred). They were given one month of infantry training, then were sent on board a sail training vessel that spent several weeks cruising the Baltic before departing overseas, to return the following spring. The cadets had to pass an examination to become midshipmen. They were then educated for another year at the naval academy, which from 1910 was situated in an impressive brick building in Flensburg-Mürwik. After another examination they received an additional two years' training on board ship.

Engineer officer candidates had to first apprentice for thirty months in facilities building ship's machinery. Then, after infantry drill, they spent half a year on board ship and another six months in education on land. An examination followed, after which the candidates had another two years of shipboard training.

Culture

In the nineteenth century, before forced to change the system, the Prussian army had only officers of noble birth. The navy, as a younger branch of the armed forces, did not have this limitation, and in 1914 only 9 percent of naval officers were nobles. There was much discussion over whether candidates passing their college final examinations should have a shortened training period, as was the case in the army. Those in favor considered a broader education to be advantageous, while opponents—who won the argument—feared a lower esprit de corps and a less malleable group of young men. The lower status of the engineer officers was another source of friction, which was not solved until after the war.

Generally the naval officer corps was very loyal to the kaiser, to whom they owed much. There was little or no tolerance for free discussion, and differing opinions tended to be suppressed.

THE WAYS OF WAR

Surface Warfare

Doctrine

The strategic aim of the Kaiserliche Marine was to win a major battle against the British Grand Fleet in the southern North Sea, under conditions favorable to the German side. It was assumed that the Royal Navy would mount a close blockade of the German ports and that it could be worn down by mine warfare, torpedo boats, and submarines prior to this decisive battle. After substantial losses had been inflicted on the Grand Fleet, it was hoped, German overseas traffic could resume. Opponents of this approach, such as Vice Admiral Karl Galster, favored a "cruiser war" concept but had no answer to the problem of the disruption of German overseas traffic and thus were silenced by Tirpitz. Shipbuilding policy, gun development, and tactical training all advanced the strategic aim of a decisive fleet engagement.

The greater gun caliber and range of the British dreadnoughts was acknowledged, but in the primarily misty conditions prevalent in the North Sea the performance of German guns at shorter range was initially deemed superior. (The battle of Dogger Bank occurred on one of the rare days of good visibility.) A battle was to be fought in line ahead, with torpedo boats making attacks from the lee side. Tirpitz considered a close-in melee between the battle fleets as a means to tackle the superior enemy fleet. Therefore, the German battleships had medium guns for close-range action and, in the early classes, a hexagonal turret layout to allow engaging on both sides. Tirpitz also hoped that with their good protection even heavily damaged ships would be able to make it back to their nearby home ports.

Ships

Battleships

Of the predreadnoughts, the ten ships of the *Braunschweig* and *Deutschland* classes were still in service with II Squadron at the start of the war. The following units formed the core of the battle fleet, including the *Nassau* class, already described.

The four ships of the *Helgoland* class (22,800 tons) were the first armed with 30.5-cm cannon, of which they had twelve, plus fourteen 15-cm guns. The hexagonal arrangement was retained for the six twin 30.5-cm turrets. Speed was twenty-one knots, protection was similar to the preceding class.

The following *Kaiser* class (24,700 tons) had five ships. Armament consisted of ten 30.5-cm and fourteen 15-cm guns. The turret positions had now been changed—one turret on the forecastle, two turrets "en echelon" amidships, and two turrets aft in a superfiring arrangement. Armor was considerably strengthened—for example, 350-mm in the main belt and 40-mm on the torpedo bulkheads. Speed increased to twenty-two knots. For the first time, a diesel engine was planned for one of these ships, *Prinzregent Luitpold*, as propulsion for the central shaft. However, it took until 1917 to perfect a satisfactory diesel engine, and by that time it could no longer be installed.

One ship of the four in the next, *König*, class (25,800 tons) was commissioned before the outbreak of the war. The remaining three were completed by November 1914. Armament remained the same, but now all five turrets were arranged on the centerline, two forward and two superimposed aft. Armor was similar, with the torpedo bulkheads strengthened to 50 mm.

Only two of the four ships of the *Bayern* class (28,500 tons) were completed during the war, joining the fleet in 1916 and 1917. For the first time a main armament of 38-cm caliber was chosen. There were eight of these guns, in four twin turrets, and sixteen 15-cm cannon. Armor corresponded roughly to that of the *König* class, with a top speed of twenty-two knots. Further battleship designs did not get beyond the planning stage.

Armored Cruisers and Battle Cruisers

Some of the older armored cruisers had been reactivated and were still in service for reconnaissance purposes at the start of the war. Three of these were lost to mines or torpedoes very early in the conflict. *Scharnhorst* and *Gneisenau* were posted to the East Asian station at the beginning of the war; after a victory at Coronel they were sunk in the battle of the Falkland Islands on 8 December 1914. The most modern armored cruiser, *Blücher*, served with the battle cruisers in 1st Scouting Squadron until her loss at the battle of Dogger Bank in January 1915.

With the previously mentioned *Von der Tann* the German navy also undertook the construction of battle cruisers. Not privy to Sir John Fisher's thinking, the Germans took their own path to the type, enhancing the armored cruiser's firepower with battleship-caliber guns, with increases also in protection and speed. This progression did not accord with the ideas of Tirpitz, who did not envision armored cruisers serving in the battle line. In fact, it was a step in the direction of the fast battleship.

The next two ships, of the *Moltke* class (23,000 tons), were armed with ten 28-cm and twelve 15-cm guns. The additional turret was arranged in superfiring position aft. Armor and torpedo bulkheads were strengthened and speed increased to 25.5 knots. Soon after the war started the second ship, *Goeben*, was passed on to Turkey, where she was renamed *Yavuz Sultan Selim*. (She remained in Turkish service after the war and following World War II carried NATO pennant number B70 until decommissioned in 1954.)

The following *Seydlitz* (24,700 tons) was an enlarged and better protected *Moltke*. The immediately visible difference was an additional weather deck in the forecastle area. Armor (belt armor 300-mm) and torpedo bulkheads (up to 50 mm) were strengthened, with practically the same armament and a slightly higher speed (26.5 knots).

The transition to 30.5-cm caliber was accomplished with the three ships of the *Derfflinger* class (26,600 tons). All three were commissioned after the war broke out. Armament consisted of eight 30.5-cm and twelve to fourteen 15-cm guns. The four turrets were arranged in a purely centerline arrangement. Armor roughly approximated that of the previous class. The torpedo bulkheads were now generally 45 mm thick. Trial speed at one mile was approximately twenty-six knots. This was achieved in shallow water, due to wartime circumstances, and corresponded to twenty-eight knots in deep water. For propulsion all German battle cruisers had four-shaft systems with turbines, unlike the battleships, which always had three-shaft systems. (Up until the *Helgoland* class battleships all had reciprocating machinery, the following classes all having turbines.)

At the end of the war four ships of the *Mackensen* class (31,000 tons, eight 35-cm guns) and one ship of the *Ersatz Yorck* class (33,500 tons, eight 38-cm guns) were in various stages of construction. Another two *Ersatz Yorck*s were planned.

Light Cruisers

The construction of light cruisers of a unified type for fleet and colonial use started with the previously mentioned *Gazelle* class, whose design was consistently further developed. This, of course, inevitably led to compromises. Thus these cruisers were neither as fast nor as agile as Britain's fleet cruisers. (See table 3.2.)

Regarding armament, the navy stuck with the 10.5-cm gun for a long time. A direct order from Tirpitz in 1913 caused the switch to the 15-cm gun. Some of the older cruisers were reequipped during the war. From the *Magdeburg* class onward, light belt armor and an improved bow form were incorporated. The older cruisers had a cork dam, of doubtful value, on their sides. The two cruisers *Pillau* and *Elbing* were under construction for the

Photo 3.2. Battle cruiser *Derfflinger* (Peter Schenk collection)

Russian navy at the start of the war and were completed after being requisitioned. They proved welcome reinforcements. *Brummer* and *Bremse* were built as minelaying cruisers; in addition to minelaying duties they proved highly suitable for fleet service. They were the fastest cruisers in the fleet. Outline studies for a pure fleet cruiser were carried out during the war, but none got past the drawing-board stage. Eight *Cölns* remained unfinished at the end of the war.

Torpedo Boats

The high-seas torpedo boats, as previously mentioned, started with *S 90*. These boats were preferably funded and built in divisions of six units. Because of their small size the torpedo boats did not get names but rather letter-number designators. For the majority of the boats the letter indicated the shipyard of construction:

B	Blohm & Voss, Hamburg
G	Germaniawerft, Kiel
H	Howaldtswerke, Kiel
S	F. Schichau, Elbing
V	Vulcan-Werke AG, Stettin.

Exceptions to this rule were the following designations: *A* for small torpedo boats for coastal use, and *D* for division torpedo boats. The numbering of the torpedo boats with shipyard codes was done consecutively—that is, as each boat was laid down, regardless of the letter assigned. The *A* and *D* boats were numbered separately.

The size of the boats continued to increase moderately with each new series. These vessels grew from the 310-ton *S 90* to the 660-ton *G 197*.

Table 3.2 German Light Cruiser Classes

Class	Number	First ship commissioned	Displacement (tons)	Speed (knots)	Armament
Gazelle	10	June 1901	2,660	21	10 x 10.5-cm
Bremen	7	May 1904	3,250	22	10 x 10.5-cm
Königsberg	4	April 1907	3,400	24	10 x 10.5-cm
Dresden	2	Nov. 1908	3,600	24	10 x 10.5-cm
Kolberg	4	June 1910	4,360	26	12 x 10.5-cm
Magdeburg	4	Aug. 1912	4,560	27.5	12 x 10.5-cm
Karlsruhe	2	Jan. 1914	4,880	28	12 x 10.5-cm
Graudenz	2	Aug. 1914	4,900	27.5	12 x 10.5-cm
Pillau	2	Dec. 1914	4,400	27.5	8 x 15-cm
Wiesbaden	2	Aug. 1915	5,150	27.5	8 x 15-cm
Brummer	2	April 1916	4,300	29	4 x 15-cm
Königsberg (2)	4	Aug. 1916	5,300	27.5	8 x 15-cm
Cöln (2)	10	Jan. 1918	5,600	27.5	8 x 15-cm

Note: The *Lubeck* of the *Bremen* class was the first German cruiser with turbine propulsion. Different propeller sizes and arrangements were tested with this ship. From the next two classes, only one ship each had turbines, again as a trial. Not until the *Kolberg* class were all cruisers equipped with turbine systems.

Speed increased from around twenty-seven to approximately thirty-two knots. Armament was originally three deck-mounted 45-cm torpedo tubes and three 5-cm cannon but was later increased to four 50-cm torpedo tubes and two 8.8-cm guns. The *S 125* and *G 137* were the first German torpedo boats with turbine propulsion. Starting with *V 161,* this became standard for all boats.

In 1911 the shipyard numbering scheme was restarted, with *V 1* through *S 24* (boats of 569 tons). The older boats kept their previous numbers but were switched to the designation *T* instead of their previous shipyard letter codes as new vessels with the same number sequence were commissioned. Armament and speed of these boats roughly corresponded to those of the preceding series.

The next torpedo boat series, encompassing boats *V 25* through *G 95,* displaced 812 tons. Speed increased to thirty-six knots. Armament consisted of six 50-cm torpedo tubes and three 8.8-cm cannon (later up to three 10.5-cm Tk or Utof—the latter a quick-firing gun on an antiaircraft mount for submarine or torpedo-boat use). Two of these boats were already in service at the start of the war.

Altogether, the navy had in 1914 132 high-seas torpedo boats, or "large torpedo boats," as they were called at that time. Two boats were at Qingdao on the East Asian station. The ten *D,* or division, torpedo boats and approximately seventy small torpedo boats still in service were mainly used for other purposes. Some were employed as training boats and others refitted as minesweepers, coast-defense boats, or tenders.

The series beginning with *G 96* and *V 125* and running through *H 169* (displacement 990 tons) was intended to include forty-six boats; however, only twenty entered service. From another planned design for a series of fifty-four boats, a few were laid down, but none were completed. A special type of small torpedo boat had been designed for use off the coast of Flanders; the boats *A 1* through *A 113* were planned, in three series. However, from the last series twenty-one were never completed. Many of these boats also served as minesweepers. The series from *B 97* to *V 100* and from *B 109* to *B 112* resulted from a yard design for Russian destroyers. These ships had a displacement of 1,350 tons and a speed of up to thirty-seven knots. Their armament consisted of six 50-cm torpedo tubes and four 8.8-cm Tk (later four 10.5-cm Tk). Four destroyers under construction for Argentina were confiscated and became *G 101* to *G 104* (displacement 1,116 tons). They were capable of reaching thirty-three knots, with armament corresponding to that of the previously mentioned destroyers. However, from a series of large destroyers, only *S 113* and *V 116* entered service. These ships displaced

2,060 tons and were fast, making up to thirty-seven knots. Armament consisted of four 60-cm torpedo tubes and four 15-cm Utof guns.

Weapons: Gunnery

Since Krupp delivered the first guns to the Prussian army in 1860, this company had become the most important supplier of artillery in Germany. Therefore the navy's guns were also from that firm. The fundamental structure of the gun barrels consisted of an inner tube, with shrunk-on tubes and hoops, and an outer casing. The process of shrinking-on tubes in a heated condition produced a bias stress on the inside. Such a barrel could better withstand the strong internal pressure of firing. The breech was a sliding-wedge breechblock. For large guns the breechblock's orientation was horizontal. Large guns also used a two-part propellant charge; the forward charge was in a silk bag, the main charge in a brass casing. The warheads of armor-piercing shells were hardened, with mild steel caps. This improved penetration when hitting at an angle. (See table 3.3.)

With the increase in battle distances and firing ranges, effective fire control became imperative. An important step toward achieving this was the introduction of stereoscopic range finders. These were first offered by Carl Zeiss in 1905, and from 1908 they were generally installed on German warships. On capital ships the turrets were equipped with the six-meter base model on 28-cm turrets and an 8.2-meter base on 38-cm turrets. Further important elements of the fire-control system were telescopic sights, the *Abfeuergerät*, and analog fire computers. The *Abfeuergerät* worked with gyros and indicated the right moment to fire in relation to the ship's roll. An analog fire-control computer tracked and accounted for distances and changes in the relative locations of the fighting ships. Synchros coupled the elements of this system with each other.

Centralized fire control with range measurement from the foretop was not available until after the battle of Jutland. The lack of this capability had an adverse effect if turret commanders could not take the target's bearing due to poor visibility. After Jutland the Germans worked to further develop their fire-control system.

Submarine Warfare

Offensive

Doctrine

Before World War I, German U-boats were designed and their crews trained exclusively to attack enemy warships. German operational tactics

Table 3.3 German Guns

Bore (in./mm)	Cal.	Model	Shell (lbs.)	MV (f/s)	Range (yds.) / elevation (deg.)	F/C (sec.)	Ship or classes
15.0/380	45	SK C/13	1,653	2,625	22,146 / 16	26	*Bayern* *Ersatz Yorck*
12.0/305	50	SK C/08	893	2,805	17,717 / 13.5 22,310 / 16	20	*König* *Kaiser* *Helgoland* *Derfflinger*
11.1/283	50	SK C/08	666	2,887	19,794 / 13.5 23,731 / 22.5	20	*Seydlitz* *Moltke*
11.1/283	45	SK C/06	666	2,805	20,669 / 20	20	*Nassau* *Von der Tann*
11.1/283	40	SK C/01	529	2,690	20,888 / 31	40	*Deutschland* *Braunschweig*
6.7/170	40	SK C/01	141	2,789	15,843 / 22	12	*Deutschland* *Braunschweig*
5.9/150	45	SK C/06	101	2,920	17,273 / 22	9	capital ships light cruisers
4.1/105	45	SK C/06	35	2,756	13,342 / 30	8	light cruisers torpedo boats
3.5/88	45	SK C/13	21	2,920	11,695 / 25	6	capital ships torpedo boats
2.0/50	40		4	2,743		5	torpedo boats

called for submarines to establish watch positions and scouting lines for harbor and coastal defense or to find the enemy in the open North Sea. When the enemy was located in a favorable position for an attack, boats were to engage submerged, firing torpedoes at a target angle of ninety degrees (that is, from abeam of a target) in order to bring all forward and aft tubes to bear. However, the relatively slow speeds of the U-boats compared with modern ships of the line, as well as their small radius of observation, made valid attack opportunities rare. Radio communication was still in its infancy, making controlled operations almost impossible. Consequently, expectations regarding U-boat operations were rather low within the higher circles of the German navy. The focus was entirely fixed on a decisive engagement between the opposing battle fleets.

Boats/Weapons

Germany started the war with twenty-seven submarines in commission and a further fourteen under repair or in various stages of construction. The recently commissioned diesel submarines *U 23* through *U 28* were still working up, while the oldest boats (*U 1, U 3,* and *U 4*) were already relegated to training duties in the Baltic. With new fleet-type U-boats taking seventeen to twenty-four months to build, a rapid increase in numbers was unlikely. Therefore, in autumn 1914 a total of thirty-two quickly constructed but small boats of the UB I torpedo and UC I minelaying types, displacing only 150 tons, were ordered for use in the eastern part of the English Channel from the newly captured bases on the Belgian coast. To differentiate the new designs from the larger, fleet-type submarines, these new U-boats were somewhat confusingly designated in different series, with letters *UB* or *UC* and numbers starting from one, as in *UB 1* and *UC 1.*

In a similar manner, ten Type UE I medium-sized fleet minelayers were ordered for distant operations. Production of the larger but ultimately more capable mobilization (Ms-Type) fleet torpedo submarines continued on a small but steady scale.

As a continuation of the first small-boats program, a new building program was begun in 1915 for 260-ton UB II torpedo-carrying U-boats, in combination with 420-ton minelaying subs of the UC II type. After the U-boat war had been scaled down in September 1915 following repeated American protests, mining operations were seen as more useful employment for the submarines. However, the still limited size and endurance of the new boats restricted their operational use to the North Sea, the English Channel, and areas within reach of German bases in the Mediterranean. With unconditional antishipping operations by German U-boats again halted in summer 1916, the German Admiralty came to favor the construction of large U-cruiser types to allow for operations according to prize regulations in the open Atlantic and other far-distant areas.

In parallel with the U-cruiser program the building of new medium-sized UB III torpedo-armed boats was begun to supplement the larger fleet U-boats, especially in the Mediterranean. Also, the few remaining UE I minelayers were followed by the much larger Type UE II boats. In the final phase of the war, U-boat construction was concentrated on a few main types. Wartime experience led to the design of the new 350-ton UF-Type boats, which were intended for quick production at small yards not hitherto involved in building U-boats, and the Type UC III, as an improvement to the previous UC II design. The latter two types, however, came too late to see operational service during the war. Tables 3.4 and 3.5 show the slow and often erratic course of the German U-boat building program during the war years.

In 1891 the 450-mm-diameter torpedo model C 45/91, with a speed of thirty-two knots, and the 350-mm, twenty-nine-knot C 35/91 were introduced as the German navy's first modern torpedoes. They were still useful twenty-five years later, when employed by German submarines during the First World War. After several steps the German navy in 1907 adopted the G/7 torpedo for battleships, with a diameter of 500 mm, a length of seven meters, and a range of 9,300 meters at twenty-seven knots, or four thousand meters at thirty-five knots. The six-meter-long G/6 was intended for smaller ships and submarines. It had a range of 8,400 meters at twenty-seven knots and 3,500 meters at thirty-five knots. By 1914 the 500-mm, pressure-driven

Photo 3.3. Light cruiser *Ariadne* (Peter Schenk collection)

Table 3.4 U-Boat Building Contracts and Overall Deliveries, 1906–18

Period	Building contracts	Commissioned prewar	Commissioned 1914	Commissioned 1915	Commissioned 1916	Commissioned 1917	Commissioned 1918	Not commissioned
Prewar	45	28	10	6	-	-	-	1
Foreign prewar	6	-	1	5	-	-	-	-
1914	49	-	-	33	16	-	-	-
1915	102*	-	-	8	74	19*	-	-
1916	123**	-	-	-	18	66**	18	21
1917	266	-	-	-	-	2	69	195
1918	221	-	-	-	-	-	-	221
Total	812	28	11	52	108	87	87	438

* Includes the privately contracted civilian transport U-boats *Deutschland* and *Bremen,* with the former taken over in 1917 as *U 155,* while *Bremen* was lost in 1916 in its civilian role.

** Includes six privately contracted civilian transport U-boats taken over before completion in 1917 by the German navy as U-cruisers *U 151–U 154,* and *U 156–U 157.*

Table 3.5 German U-Boat Types Contracted and Delivered, 1906–18

U-Boat types	Contracts	Prewar	Commissioned 1914	Commissioned 1915	Commissioned 1916	Commissioned 1917	Commissioned 1918	Not commissioned
Prewar & foreign designs	51	28	11	11	-	-	-	1
MS-type	99	-	-	1	25	25	9	39
Large MS-type	60	-	-	-	-	-	2	58
U-cruiser	41	-	-	-	-	-	4	37
UB I type	15	-	-	15	-	-	-	-
UB II type	30	-	-	5	25	-	-	-
UB III type	202	-	-	-	-	42	47	113
UF type	92	-	-	-	-	-	-	92
UC I type	17	-	-	17	-	-	-	-
UC II type	64	-	-	-	51	13	-	-
UC III type	113	-	-	-	-	-	16	97
UE I type	10	-	-	3	7	-	-	-
UE II type	10	-	-	-	-	-	9	1
Deutschland class	8	-	-	-	-	7	-	-
Total	812	28	11	52	108	87	87	438

G/6, carrying a contact-fused 160-kg explosive warhead and fitted with a plus-or-minus-ninety-degrees target-angle director, had become the standard torpedo on board boats from *U 19* onward. Further developments shortly before the end of the war included the H/8 for the *Baden*-class battleships, with a caliber of 600 mm and a range of 12,000 meters at thirty knots; the electrically driven E/7; and a magnetic detonator. For the torpedo planes the C 45/91 was used. Production of torpedoes took place at BMAG, the navy-owned Torpedowerkstatt Kiel, and also at the Whitehead factory, which had been moved from Fiume to St. Pölten in Austria.

Antisubmarine

With the main focus of German naval activity on battle-fleet and torpedo-boat operations, antisubmarine warfare consisted mainly of the heavy mining of coastal waterways in the North and Baltic Seas. This worked well for much of the war, as the threat from mines prevented allied submarines from operating close to German-held coastlines. Even the threat presented by the transfer of a British submarine flotilla to the Baltic in late summer 1915—to operate against the iron-ore traffic from Sweden to Germany—was quickly brought under control, following some initial losses. In addition to mines, great use was made of nets and barriers to close vital passages and harbors to submarines. Sometimes the nets were armed with small explosive charges. During the large-scale German amphibious operations against the Estonian island of Ösel, the landing area in Tagga Bay was completely sealed off with a twelve-kilometer-long net barrier to protect the supporting battle-fleet units against submarine attacks.

Early in the war, detection of submerged submarines was almost impossible. From 1915 onward primitive listening gear provided limited means of detection. Antisubmarine weapons included towed nets and paravanes carrying explosive charges that detonated on contact. Depth charges came into use from 1916 but were ineffective due to the rare opportunities for attack. In the absence of purpose-built ships, advanced antisubmarine location gear or weapons, or specially trained personnel, antisubmarine operations were normally conducted by converted fishing vessels, minesweepers, and old torpedo boats—these being used as escorts for fleet units and merchant ships in areas of known enemy submarine activity. Given this background, it is not surprising that during the entire war only two allied submarines fell victim to German surface warships, both sunk by gunfire. German U-boats became the most successful submarine killers but usually encountered or attacked their allied counterparts as targets of opportunity while on their own patrols.

Mine Warfare

Doctrine

In the event of war the German navy planned to establish defensive mine barrages off its North Sea bases and in the entrances to the Baltic, as well as to stage offensive minelaying operations along the British east coast. The defensive mine barrages were laid in the war's first days. In August 1914 a first—and very risky—offensive minelaying operation was carried out in the Thames estuary by the twenty-knot auxiliary minelayer *Königen Luise*. The ship was sunk by the cruiser *Amphion* and an accompanying destroyer flotilla, but later *Amphion* herself sank on one of *Königen Luise*'s mines, which would also eventually claim four minesweepers and eight merchant vessels. Subsequently, minelayers *Nautilus* and *Albatros* conducted successful missions off the British east coast. However, a dangerous operation in the Downs by four torpedo boats led to their destruction. The armed merchant cruiser (AMC) *Berlin* had better luck in October 1914, managing to slip through the British patrols and lay two hundred mines off the west coast of Scotland near Lough Swilly, where part of the Grand Fleet was exercising. The modern battleship *Audacious* was lost on one of her mines.

The AMC *Meteor* laid mines off the port of Arkhangelsk that accounted for twelve merchant vessels and a minesweeper. On her second sortie, *Meteor* mined the Moray Firth on the east coast of Scotland. During this mission she was discovered by the British AMC *Ramsey*, which *Meteor* was able to sink, but on her return four British cruisers hunted down the German ship off Jutland. Light cruisers laid minefields during the raids of battle cruisers against the British east coast. However, by mid-1915 only submarines were able to mine the waters around the British Isles.

Despite the Russian defeat in East Prussia in 1914, the advance in the East was slow. The Russian navy remained mostly on the defensive, behind mine barrages protected by coastal batteries. German cruisers made sorties to mine and thereby block the port of Libau, where British submarines were based. After the armored cruiser *Friedrich Carl* hit two mines and sank during one such mission, these operations were stopped. In August 1915 two battleships and two cruisers entered the Bay of Riga and shelled Pernau. The Russians too laid offensive mine barrages off Memel, later off East Prussia and east of Bornholm, and even one barrage north of Rugia in the winter of 1914/15. These mines accounted for several ships lost or damaged. In 1916 there was one smaller Russian mining operation near Libau, which Germany had occupied in May 1915, and none thereafter.

Ships/Weapons

In 1914 Germany had only two purpose-built minelayers, the *Nautilus* and *Albatros,* each capable of twenty knots. In 1916 fast minelayers *Brummer* and *Bremse* (twenty-eight knots) were commissioned, and these ships performed well. A variety of fast passenger vessels and ferries served as auxiliary minelayers.

At the beginning of the war the German navy had forty-five converted torpedo boats organized into three minesweeping divisions. Soon specialized minesweepers were ordered: the coal-fired M-boats, of about five hundred tons and sixteen knots, plus F-boats, motor minesweepers of twenty tons and ten knots, for coastal waters. In 1918 these were joined by the FM-boats, two hundred tons and fourteen knots. In all, 145 M-boats were commissioned, of which twenty-seven were lost to mines and three to other causes. In addition, fifty-seven F-boats and six FM-boats were built. Numerous fishing craft also acted as auxiliary minesweepers.

In 1877 Germany bought its first mines, of the anchored C/77 type, which had a 40-kg charge with potassium ignition. The subsequent C/05 and C/06 had 80-kg charges. New-standard mines were introduced in 1912 with the EMA (150-kg charge) and EMB (225 kg). U-boat minelayers carried one of two basic moored-mine types (UC 120 or UC 200), in each case with hundred-meter mooring cables. Measuring eighty centimeters in diameter, they differed in length according to the size of the charge, as indicated by the name (120 kg for the UC 120, 200 kg for the UC 200). These mines were dropped either from flooded vertical mine chutes penetrating the pressure hull (UC-type minelayers) or from horizontal mine-ejection tubes at the stern, loaded from a dry mine storage compartment inside the pressure hull (UE-type minelayers). During the war, wet-stored mines showed a tendency to explode prematurely, which caused several U-boat losses. In the course of the conflict special 50-cm torpedo mines were developed to be ejected from the torpedo tubes of normal U-boats (the P-Mine, length about three meters, and TEKA-Mine, length about two meters, each carrying a 100-kg warhead).

The German navy laid 45,000 mines during the war. The dreadnought *Audacious,* three predreadnoughts, four cruisers, one monitor, thirty destroyers, nine torpedo boats, and a large number of minor craft were lost on these mines. Mines also caused an estimated 10 percent of allied merchant shipping losses.

Amphibious Warfare

Doctrine/Capabilities

The Kaiserliche Marine did not consider the problem of transporting troops and their equipment other than port garrisons. Three *Seebataillone*—battalions of naval infantry—were formed but not trained for beach assault. There was, however, cooperation with the army engineer corps, whose commander, General Colmar von der Goltz, ordered developmental work on the landing of troops on open beaches, holding a first exercise in 1900. At the beginning of the war one engineer battalion was trained for such operations, equipped with inflatable rubber boats and unpropelled landing craft to transport horses, guns, and small vehicles. These craft could be towed from the transports by motorboats and pulled on cable lines through the surf.

Photo 3.4. Battleship *Westfalen* during landing operations on the Aland Islands off Finland on 18 March 1918 (Peter Schenk collection)

One company was used to help cross the Danube at various places in October 1915, November 1916, and January 1917. A bigger operation was carried out in October 1917, the landing of a reinforced division on the Russian Baltic island of Ösel. After the first assault, under a curtain of covering fire from no less than eleven battleships, twenty transport steamers were unloaded by landing boats and barges, unmolested by enemy submarines due to a protective net barrage that had been laid the same day.

Coastal Defense

Helgoland was heavily fortified, with four 305-mm twin turrets and four single 210-mm guns. There was also Battery Friedrich August on Wangerooge with six 305-mm guns, Battery Grosser Kurfürst at Pillau with four 280-mm guns, and medium batteries at Borkum, Norderney, Sylt, and Schillig, near Wilhelmshaven. To protect the submarine ports of Ostend and Zeebrugge against shelling by British monitors, the coastal artillery emplaced five batteries, with guns up to 280-mm caliber, by March 1915. In autumn 1915 Battery Tirpitz was put into service, with four 280-mm guns and a range of thirty kilometers. In spring 1916 Battery Kaiser Wilhelm II became operational, with four 305-mm guns ranging to thirty-seven kilometers, which prevented further shelling of the bases. In all, twelve heavy and eleven medium batteries were mounted in Flanders.

Another means to counter the British monitors involved wire-controlled unmanned explosive motorboats (*Fernlenkboote*). Two were sunk by artillery in 1916 while trying to attack monitors *M 23* and *Erebus,* but one destroyed part of the mole at Nieuport.

Aviation

The value of this new weapon was recognized when World War I was still in its infancy. The German naval air arm began the war with one airship at Hamburg, six seaplanes at Helgoland, two airships in the Baltic, and four seaplanes at Kiel. The airships of the Marineluftschiffs-Abteilung, founded in 1912, soon proved their value in long-range reconnaissance over the North Sea and Baltic. In good weather three airships could cover the German Bight. The seventy-eight naval airships carried out 1,148 reconnaissance sorties during the war. Airships could also spot minefields and mark them with buoys. They were also used with army airships for bombing raids. The 197 tons of bombs dropped mainly on London from 1915 to 1917 in two hundred night raids had a great psychological effect, until these operations had to be stopped due to mounting losses.

Nordholz, near Cuxhaven, was the main airship base and headquarters, with ten hangars. Other bases were at Hage, Ahlhorn, and Tondern on the North Sea coast, and at Seddin (near Stolp), Seerappen (near Königsberg) and Weinroden (near Libau) in the Baltic. Airships were also deployed to the Black and Adriatic Seas. In September 1917, *LZ 104* attempted an epic journey from Bulgaria to East Africa loaded with supplies for the isolated troops there. But near Khartoum the airship had to turn back when a message arrived that German forces had had to withdraw from the stipulated landing place. The zeppelin returned to its base after a round trip of six thousand kilometers.

Naval aircraft were concentrated in the I Marineflieger-Abteilung (MFA) at Kiel-Holtenau and II MFA at Wilhelmshaven. In September 1915 these detachments were renamed Seeflieger-Abteilungen (SFA). Like the Marineluftschiffs-Abteilung, they reported to the *Befehlshaber der Marine-Luftfahr-Abteilungen* (BdL), Rear Admiral Otto Phillip. In December 1916 the naval airships got their own commander, known as the *Führer der Marineluftschiffe* (FdL), a title held by Commander Peter Strasser until his death in August 1918. The BdL was renamed as *Befehlshaber der Marine-Fliegerabteilungen* (BdFlieg) and then in July 1917 *Marine Flugchef.*

Naval planes were deployed at thirty-two sea bases and seventeen airfields on the Baltic and North Sea coasts, in Belgium, on the Black Sea, and in the Mediterranean. A total of 1,478 sea and land planes were taken into service, of which 673 were frontline seaplanes and 191 frontline land-based aircraft. Personnel numbered in 1918 some 16,122 men, of whom 2,116 were pilots and aircrew.

The planes of the era were lightly armed and could only carry small bombs. Thus their main role was reconnaissance. In spite of this, German naval aircraft shot down 270 enemy planes and two airships, and they sank one Russian destroyer, three submarines, four motor torpedo boats, four merchant vessels, and twelve minor craft.

Much effort was devoted to the development of torpedo planes, seen as the only means to destroy larger ships from the air. A special command for this branch of the air arm was formed at Flensburg under Commander Konrad Goltz. A first, unsuccessful, attack was flown against Russian warships in the Gulf of Finland on 12 September 1916. The first "kill" was the British cargo ship *Genua* in the English Channel on 1 May 1917. Another steamer, *Storm of Guernsey,* was sunk on 9 July 1917 in the same area. In all, during eleven missions twenty-eight torpedoes were launched and six hits achieved. In the summer of 1917 these torpedo planes successfully mined Russian Baltic ports using mines developed for submarines.

At the beginning of the war the Marineflieger-Abteilung ordered seaplanes for fighter and reconnaissance purposes. For the fighter role the Hansa-Brandenburg KDW seaplane was introduced in 1916, and sixty were built. Forty of the Rumpler 6B1 seaplane fighters were also taken into service starting in 1916. In the same role, 114 of the Albatros W 4 type were built from 1917 on. In addition, land-based fighters were found necessary to protect bases from enemy air attacks, and the Pfalz D III was ordered. The torpedo squadron used the Freidrichshafener Flugzeugbau FF 41 and the

Gotha WD 7; both were two-engined float biplanes and were also used in the reconnaissance and bomber roles.

The fifty-nine German naval airships were mostly built according to the zeppelin design, with aluminum ribs, but there were also two Parseval (blimps) and nine Schutte-Lanz types with timber ribs. Hydrogen-gas volume varied between 56,000 and 69,000 cubic meters and payload between forty and fifty tons. Five or six Maybach engines gave airships a speed of 100 to 130 km per hour. The airships proved very efficient at long-range reconnaissance, as they could stay in the air for many hours. From 1916 trials were undertaken for launching from airships radio- or wire-controlled torpedoes attached to gliders, but this came to nothing.

Shipboard aviation started early, with the conversion of two cargo vessels into seaplane tenders. *Answald* and *Santa Elena* were commissioned for the High Seas Fleet in mid-1915 as *Flugzeugschiff I* and *II*. A third, *Oswald*, was converted in 1918, and a fourth, *Glyndwr*, had been used as a training vessel since 1914. The aircraft used on board were Friedrichshaftener Flugzeugbau types, mainly the FF 33. One cruiser, *Friedrich Carl*, received two planes in September 1914 but was mined and sunk in the Baltic soon after. The light cruiser *Stuttgart* was rebuilt with a hangar for two planes in 1918. The armed merchant cruiser *Wolf*, battle cruiser *Derfflinger*, light cruiser *Medusa*, and several mine-destruction vessels made good use of embarked aircraft. An innovative project to convert the unfinished liner *Ausonia* into an aircraft carrier, with a hangar deck for wheeled fighters and another below for two-engined torpedo planes, could not be started before the war ended.

WAR EXPERIENCE AND EVOLUTION

Wartime Evolution

Surface Warfare

The war had come much earlier than Tirpitz had wished, and in summer of 1914 the German fleet in the North Sea was inferior to the Royal Navy by a factor of one-third. In the first phase of the war the navy hoped for an early defeat of the allied forces in northern France. Having in mind a short war, the High Seas Fleet, under Admiral Friedrich von Ingenohl, remained in port awaiting the actions of the British Grand Fleet. During this time German cruisers were active in the Pacific and South Atlantic, drawing away three Grand Fleet battle cruisers to deal with the threat they presented. This effect had been expected by the Germans but was not exploited. Another strategic option would have been to attack the supply and transport of the

British Expeditionary Force in the English Channel, but this was deemed too risky.

On 28 August, the British raided the cruisers supporting the patrols off Helgoland, after British submarines had observed a daily routine of torpedo boats being escorted to their night patrols by cruisers. The British appeared with five battle cruisers and eight cruisers, plus destroyers, sinking the German cruisers *Mainz, Cöln,* and *Ariadne,* as well as a torpedo boat. German battle cruisers sent to intervene arrived too late. This type of hit-and-run battle would thereafter be repeated often. German battle cruisers shelled Yarmouth on 3 November 1914 and struck Hartlepool, Whitby, and Scarborough on 15 December 1914. On 24 January 1915, the next German raid—four battle cruisers under Admiral Franz Ritter von Hipper against the fishing fleet at Dogger Bank—was intercepted by a squadron of five British battle cruisers under Admiral Sir David Beatty. A running fight developed, with the British chasing the Germans, in the first battle between examples of this new class of capital ship. *Seydlitz* was hit, burning out her two aft turrets, and *Blücher* took a hit that affected her machinery, so that the ship fell behind and was sunk. On the British side, *Lion* was heavily damaged. The commander of the High Seas Fleet, having remained in port with the battleships, was now replaced. Admiral Hugo von Pohl became the new commander, with an admonition to be more cautious.

Pohl died in February 1916, and Admiral Reinhard Scheer, an energetic leader, gained command. The raids on the British east coast were resumed on 25 April 1916, with the shelling of Lowestoft and Yarmouth. Scheer expected his next sortie to generate a major battle, and when he sailed from Wilhelmshaven bound for the Skagerrak on the morning of 31 May 1916 he brought with him the six predreadnoughts of II Squadron. Deciphered signals had informed the British of this sortie, and they also went to sea in full force, with a superiority of about a third.

The battle-cruiser squadrons, sailing in advance of their respective fleets, clashed first. A running fight developed, with the Germans under Rear Admiral Hipper retreating toward Scheer's battle fleet. *Indefatigable* and *Queen Mary* were both hit and fatally exploded. The four fast battleships of the *Queen Elizabeth* class that followed prevented further losses. Meanwhile, Scheer, with his sixteen battleships and six predreadnoughts, came up to assist Hipper and engaged the *Queen Elizabeth*s. The three battle cruisers of the British third squadron approached the German battle cruisers, and another British battle cruiser, *Invincible,* suffered a vital hit and exploded. On the German side, *Lützow* had to be abandoned. Finally the commander of the Grand Fleet, Admiral Sir John Jellicoe, with twenty-four battleships, arrived on the scene and tried to destroy the leading German ships by crossing the T of Scheer's formation and concentrating fire on the head of the latter's line. Scheer reacted with a surprising maneuver, the simultaneous turning of each ship on the spot, which allowed the Germans to avoid the danger and break contact. After another turn to east the battle fleets met once again, and the German battle cruisers at the head suffered badly. German torpedo-boat attacks forced the British line to turn away, and both fleets separated in the night to steam south. Jellicoe hoped to resume the battle in the morning but did not succeed in reestablishing contact; the High Seas Fleet reached port.

The battle had not forced a decision. The blockade had not been lifted, and it was felt in Germany all the more. Tactically the battle of Jutland demonstrated how difficult it was to command the great fleets at the given gun ranges, in conditions of poor visibility, and with faulty communications.

Submarines

In the early months of the war, German U-boats were mainly employed on single patrols or scouting lines, in the North Sea, or against troop transports in the eastern English Channel. In October 1914, *U 20* rounded Britain for the first time. Wartime conditions demonstrated that longer patrols, lasting by July 1915 up to twenty-five days, had no negative effect on crews or material.

Actual results during the first six months of the war nevertheless confirmed pessimistic prewar expectations regarding the efficiency of submarines in operations against enemy fleets. Although the destruction of three old British armored cruisers in the North Sea on 7 September 1914 by *U 9* made its commander, Otto Weddigen, a national hero and boosted German morale, the sinking of a total of ten outdated warships in exchange for the loss of seven submarines during that period had no real impact on British superiority at sea. However, the appearance of German U-boats all around Britain did markedly affect the disposition and operations of the British Grand Fleet, due to the fear of substantial losses in possible encounters. As a result, the strategic impact of German U-boats in the early phase of the war greatly exceeded their tactical success.

In November 1914 the British government declared a total naval blockade against Germany and its allies. Spurred by this flagrant violation of international law and the dawning apprehension—after the transition to trench warfare—that the conflict would not be over in a matter of months, the German Admiralty gradually came to adopt the idea of a counterblockade in retaliation. Under the military and political situation existing at the beginning of 1915, German U-boats offered the only option available to enforce such a blockade in the waters around France and Britain. On 4 February 1915 Germany declared the waters around Britain a war zone, effective from 18 February, where all enemy merchant shipping was subject to attack. In accordance with the British precedents, prewar legal restrictions on this kind of warfare were thereafter successively dropped, especially after the British Admiralty lifted the nonbelligerent status of British and allied merchant ships by arming them and instructing their masters to attack U-boats whenever possible.

Exceeding the German Admiralty's expectations, the few U-boats available in early 1915 were rather successful in their new role. By the end of April 1915 seventy-one merchant ships, comprising 155,000 gross tons, were sunk. Quickly appreciating this new threat to their war effort, the British government started a widespread public propaganda campaign against German U-boats and their crews, caricaturing them as perfidious and bloodthirsty pirates. At the same time, diplomatic steps were taken to bring the neutral countries in Europe and overseas, especially the United States, in line with the war interests of the Entente. Due to the strong cultural and economic links of its political and industrial elites with Britain and its empire, the U.S. government soon sided with the British, while openly insisting on the rights of neutral states, including free trade even within the declared blockade zone. This was evidently only in favor of allied war aims, since no American ship ever tried to sail for German ports during the war. German diplomatic countersteps failed to influence the American position.

Following the sinking of the British passenger liner *Lusitania,* carrying many U.S. citizens as well as war material, inside the German blockade zone by *U 20* on 7 May 1915—resulting in heavy loss of life, including 110 Americans—the U.S. government protested strongly against German submarine-warfare policy. Since the political opinions held by the kaiser and his government still dominated military views at this time, in the following months the German Admiralty was forced to scale back its successful U-boat campaign in order to avoid further tension with the U.S. government. On 19 August 1915 the *Arabic* incident, involving the loss of eight U.S. citizens, triggered further diplomatic protests from the Americans. Eventually, on 18 September 1915, the German Admiralty stopped all attacks against trading vessels west of Britain and in the English Channel, reverting to prize regulations in the North Sea. Except in the Mediterranean theater, the military use of U-boats in the months thereafter was mainly confined to mining operations and attacks against naval vessels.

Repeated attempts thereafter by the Admiralty to restart an unconditional tonnage war were thwarted by the compliant attitude of the German government toward American protests and demands for free neutral trade inside the war zone. This self-destructive German position culminated in the almost total abandonment of antishipping operations around Britain on 4 May 1916, in response to American protests following the torpedoing of the Belgian cross-Channel ferry *Sussex* on 24 March 1916. In the following months the German fleet U-boats were used, with only marginal success, in scouting operations against the British Grand Fleet or were diverted to other theaters, especially the Mediterranean Sea. This restrictive German policy undoubtedly saved the Entente several hundred thousand tons of shipping during 1916.

At the end of 1916 German political and military leaders realized that their chances for victory against the Entente were dwindling. With the High Seas Fleet effectively blocked in the North Sea, the resumption of unconditional U-boat warfare was seen as a final option for victory, or at least renewed peace negotiations. When the campaign of unrestricted submarine war began on 1 February 1917, the German U-boat arm was confronted with the task of defeating the British almost single-handedly.

German hopes were supported by a 22 December 1916 Admiralty memorandum predicting victory over Britain in five months if sinkings of merchant vessels could be raised to 600,000 tons monthly. This statement was never questioned or scientifically verified, and the actual results of unconditional U-boat warfare soon proved the opposite, although the tonnage sunk exceeded the amount demanded by the German Admiralty.

On 1 February 1917 just 105 U-boats of various types were available for frontline use. With a number of boats detached to sideshows like the Baltic or Black Sea, in fact only ninety-two boats were available for antishipping operations—including many Type UC II purpose-built minelayers, in addition to a number of small Type UB I and UC I boats unfit for high-seas operations. This figure did not meet the number demanded in an April 1915 memorandum by the U-Boat Inspectorate Bureau, which calculated that 154 large boats were required for a successful tonnage warfare campaign. In a later memorandum from the Admiralty staff to the kaiser as many as 350 boats were deemed necessary to achieve victory. The reason an insufficient number of U-boats was available for operations lay with the hesitant attitude of the RMA toward the intensification of U-boat construction at the expense of other shipbuilding programs, especially capital ships, and the ongoing misconception among some Admiralty planners that the war would soon be won.

The widespread introduction of a convoy system in the eastern Atlantic, the Mediterranean, and along the coasts of Britain in summer 1917 made it harder for individual U-boats to find targets in the vast areas of sea. Existing technical standards on board U-boats and limited ranges in radio reception made coordinated actions against convoys almost impossible. After the convoy system had been fully implemented, monthly sinking figures dropped considerably. The tonnage-war strategy slowly faded into an antisupply campaign, merely trying to interfere with the steadily increasing flow of American supplies for the depleted European allies. Nevertheless, the German U-boats remained a threat to the allied war effort until the end of the war.

From the technical point of view, German submarines were second to none in shipbuilding and board weapons technology. The rounding of Great Britain was seen as an outstanding example of the performance of German U-boats early in the war. Four years later the large U-cruisers had extended the operational radius to the waters along the North American east coast and well into the South Atlantic off West Africa, with individual operations lasting up to 135 days.

Tactically the U-boats were still equal to allied antisubmarine-warfare technology. The lack of effective location devices meant that allied antisubmarine forces in the air and at sea could not prevent successful daylight submerged attacks or night-time surface attack, once a U-boat had located a target and was able to close within torpedo-firing distance. The use of aircraft over the open sea and the development of ultrasonic detection devices (Asdic) were only in their infancy and had no significant effect before the end of the war. Allied mines along the inward- and outward-bound routes in the North Sea and Dover Strait presented the biggest hazard for German U-boat operations. This hazard capitalized on Germany's geostrategic disadvantage due to its lack of bases with direct access to the Atlantic. Mining became the most frequent cause of U-boat losses in the final phase of the war—forty-four in 1917/18, which represents 33 percent of the total losses over that period. Table 3.6 gives the nominal strength of the German U-boats for each month during World War I. Between 1 August 1914 and the armistice on 11 November 1918, German U-boats sank a hundred warships and almost 6,400 merchant ships of 12 million gross tons, equaling about one-third of the prewar British merchant fleet. In the same period 178 U-boats were lost to enemy action during frontline service.

The war in the Baltic was less dramatic. Germany stationed there only a coastal-defense division, with seven cruisers, some torpedo boats, submarines, and minor vessels. The Russian navy had not recovered from the Tsushima disaster and did not pose a real threat, although four Russian battleships were completed during the war. Germany tried to maintain an offensive posture to disguise its own weakness in the Baltic and on certain occasions also brought battleships into the area.

Table 3.6 Nominal and Operational Strength of German U-Boats during World War I

Date	Commissioned	Loss to enemy action	Other frontline losses	Total frontline losses	Decommissioned	Losses home waters	Available at start of month
Aug. 14	3	2		2			27
Sep. 14	3	-		-			28
Oct. 14	1	-		-			31
Nov. 14	2	1		1			32
Dec. 14	2	2		2			33
Jan. 15	2	2		2			33
Feb. 15	4	-		-			33
Mar. 15	8	3		3			37
Apr. 15	6	1		1			42
May 15	8	1		1			47
Jun. 15	6	2	1	3	1		54
Jul. 15	5	3		3	1		56
Aug. 15	2	2		2			57
Sep. 15	2	3		3			57
Oct. 15	2	1		1			56
Nov. 15	2	1	1	2			57
Dec. 15	6	-		-			57
Jan. 16	3	-		-			63
Feb. 16	5	-		-			66
Mar. 16	9	2		2			71
Apr. 16	9	3		3			78
May 16	9	2		2	1		84
Jun. 16	8	1		1			90
Jul. 16	9	3		3			97
Aug. 16	10	2		2			103

Sep. 16	10	-		-			111
Oct. 16	10	1		1			121
Nov. 16	13	5		5			130
Dec. 16	14	3		3			138
Jan. 17	6	2		2			149
Feb. 17	4	5	1	6			153
Mar. 17	4	3	1	4		1	151
Apr. 17	5	1		1			150
May 17	5	7	1	8			154
Jun. 17	8	2	1	3			151
Jul. 17	12	6	1	7	2		156
Aug. 17	13	5		5			159
Sep. 17	8	11	1	12			167
Oct. 17	13	5	1	6			163
Nov. 17	5	8		8			170
Dec. 17	6	8		8		1	167
Jan. 18	3	10		10			164
Feb. 18	6	2		2			157
Mar. 18	8	5	1	6		1	161
Apr. 18	9	8		8			162
May 18	11	13	2	15		1	163
Jun. 18	12	3		3			158
Jul. 18	10	6		6			167
Aug. 18	8	7		7			171
Sep. 18	12	9		9		1	172
Oct. 18	12	6	14	20			174
Nov. 18	2	-	1	1			168
Total	355	178	27	205	5	5	

The cruiser *Magdeburg* was lost by grounding in August 1914. Russian cruisers made dashes and successfully laid mines in German waters. The German navy retaliated with minefields in the Gulf of Finland and along the Russian coast. A landing operation on the islands of Ösel, Dagö, and Moon in 1917 succeeded with support from battleships. After the October Revolution, the Russian ships retreated to Kronstadt. In March 1918 strong German naval forces supported by three battleships landed a division in Finland to help nationalist "White" forces in their struggle against Finnish and Russian "Reds."

The Mediterranean division, with the battle cruiser *Goeben* and cruiser *Breslau,* was offered to Turkey after two Turkish battleships ordered in Britain had been confiscated for use in the Grand Fleet. The division's commander, Rear Admiral Wilhelm Souchon, left the Austro-Hungarian base of Pola in July and, following the declaration of war against France on 3 August, shelled Bône and Phillipeville in Algeria during the early hours of 4 August. The British battle cruisers *Indefatigable* and *Indomitable* pursued but had to wait until war had actually been declared by the British government at 2300 that night, and the German division was able to break contact. Souchon's force coaled in Messina and departed to the south, while the British battle cruisers waited in the north. *Goeben* and *Breslau* reached Constantinople unscathed. They then went under the Turkish flag and, renamed *Yavuz Sultan Selim* and *Midilli* but retaining their German crews, conducted raids in the Black Sea.

A cruiser squadron under Vice Admiral Maximilian Graf von Spee, with two armored cruisers and three light cruisers, sailed from the Caroline Islands to Chile, where it sank the British cruisers *Good Hope* and *Monmouth* on 1 November 1914. After refueling in Valparaiso the squadron rounded Cape Horn to attack Port Stanley in the Falkland Islands. The battle cruisers *Invincible* and *Inflexible,* which were hunting the German squadron, had just arrived there. Instead of attacking the unprepared ships, Spee turned away and was chased down a few hours later, on 8 December 1914. Only *Dresden* made her escape, hiding in a bay in the Magellan Strait, until finally caught at the island of Mas y Terra on 14 March 1915.

Emden carried out a marvelous raiding cruise in the Indian Ocean, with attacks on Madras and Penang, before being sunk 9 November 1914 off Cocos island. *Königsberg* hid in the Rufiji Delta in East Africa and made a successful sortie to Zanzibar, where she sank the British cruiser *Pegasus* on 20 September 1914. She was discovered and sunk by British monitors on 11 July 1915. Another very successful raider was the cruiser *Karlsruhe,* which arrived on the Caribbean station just before the start of the war. After arming a German passenger liner for service as an armed merchant cruiser, *Karlsruhe* sank sixteen cargo ships until she was destroyed by an internal explosion on 4 November 1914.

Summary and Assessment

The High Seas Fleet's war planning was based on the expectation that the Grand Fleet, following Royal Navy precedent set over previous centuries, would impose a tight blockade on the North Sea ports. However, even immediately before the war doubts about this possibility had arisen, and in May 1914 von Tirpitz asked the commander of the High Seas Fleet, Admiral Friedrich von Ingenohl, "What are you going to do if the British don't appear in the German Bight at all?" Neither man had an answer. The concept of reducing the Grand Fleet's superiority in small actions near the German harbors did not work, because the blockade actually undertaken by the British was a distant one. The option of attacking the transport of the British Expeditionary Forces in the Channel was rejected as risky and because it required precise timing. The option of attacking the Grand Fleet while its battle cruisers were away in the South Atlantic chasing the German cruiser squadron was ruled out, because in summer 1914 the hope was still for a short war and the fleet was to be saved for later. Neither several German fleet sorties nor the battle of Jutland altered the basic strategic situation in the North Sea.

The German U-boat arm in World War I progressed from a belittled service at the start of the conflict to a highly sophisticated fighting force at the beginning of its final campaign of unrestricted warfare in February 1917, which was intended to defeat the Entente powers, against all odds, by itself. This steadily increasing demand on the performance of German submarines and their crews was not matched by the wartime policy of the German Admiralty until 1917. Prior to that, the Admiralty failed to provide the building programs to supply the basic number of operational boats required. This is particularly surprising in light of repeated attempts by the German Admiralty in the prior years to begin unconditional U-boat warfare.

Until 1917 the awarding of U-boat construction contracts had been guided by existing capacities at submarine building yards or main-engine construction companies, instead of by ambitious operational plans or strategic necessities. Repeatedly changing military requirements and operational policies during 1914–16 resulted in several special-purpose U-boat designs (such as coastal types, U-boat minelayers, and long-range U-cruisers). This reduced the production of torpedo-carrying U-boats, which eventually proved to be the most efficient ship killers after the start of unrestricted U-boat warfare.

Examination of the U-boat building contracts before and during World War I from the viewpoint of subsequent availability of boats for operations leads to the conclusion that Germany fought its U-boat campaign in 1917–18 almost exclusively with types and boats that had been designed and contracted before 1916—that is, before the reorganization of the building program and the final decision for unconditional U-boat warfare. Subsequent designs and building contracts either had no significant operational effect or were not completed before the armistice. This refers especially to the labor-consuming and material-intensive U-cruiser types contracted from 1916 onward for operations in distant theaters.

The German U-boat campaign's chance for success during World War I was essentially lost in the years 1915–16 owing to political and organizational failures. Only reluctantly did the Imperial German Navy turn away from its prewar battleship doctrine, under the pressure of the strategic and operational conditions created by the British Grand Fleet, which denied the Germans the decisive battle they had planned for. Full commitment to the U-boat tonnage-warfare strategy came too late, and when political approval for unrestricted U-boat warfare did materialize, it confronted this new branch of the service with an unsolvable problem. Likewise, the German army high command came to support the idea of unrestricted U-boat warfare only at the end of 1916, when its own strategy on the European battlefields no longer offered prospects of success, at least in 1917. By then, preparation for a buildup of sufficient forces, in terms of the boats and logistics, to ensure a successful U-boat campaign, was no longer feasible. Surprisingly, the possibilities for success of an all-out U-boat campaign in 1917 or earlier have not yet been examined in detail. However, the example of the German economy under the pressure of the allied blockade has given striking evidence that, in the age of total warfare, large industrial economies cannot be seriously affected by economic warfare within a short period severely enough to effect political destabilization.

4

GREAT BRITAIN

The Royal Navy

John Roberts

BACKSTORY

Pre-1914 History

At the opening of the twentieth century, Great Britain was the world's leading naval power, and the Royal Navy enjoyed a considerable reputation both at home and abroad. The greater part of this reputation was founded in its long history and its success in Britain's wars with France a century before. In the intervening years, however, the Royal Navy had not been involved in any major fleet actions, and technology had moved forward at a considerable pace. This situation had generated two substantial problems. First, the fleet, while an efficient peacetime organization that was more than capable of dealing with police duties and minor conflicts, lacked the extensive experience of war that had made Nelson's fleet such a formidable adversary. Second, the nature of fleets had changed so radically that while history still provided a guide to the essential nature of naval strategy, naval tactics had to be adjusted to accommodate the improved mobility and weapons of modern warships.

The period from the introduction of Britain's first oceangoing ironclad, the *Warrior* of 1860, until the end of the 1880s saw a rapid evolution in warship design that produced a considerable variety of types that in turn made the development of a homogenous fleet impracticable. In the space of thirty years wood construction gave way to iron and then steel, sail power to steam machinery, and muzzle-loading guns to breechloaders. Warships increased in size and speed, along with their powers of offense and defense, and a steady stream of innovation saw the introduction of improved armor, torpedoes, torpedo boats, quick-firing guns, machine guns, and electric and hydraulic power supplies. Warship design stabilized during the decade from 1894 to 1904, and a considerable expansion of the construction programs to meet the two-power standard (a navy equal to the next two largest—France and Russia) gave the Royal Navy a fleet that greatly outnumbered any of its potential rivals. This period was not, however, without its innovations, which included the introduction of the torpedo-boat destroyer in 1893, face-hardened all-steel armor (which led to the reintroduction of the armored cruiser), gyrostabilized torpedoes (which increased effective range and provided a large part of the initial impetus for the development of long-range gunnery), and the initial stages of the installation of wireless communication.

The new century brought new problems for the continuance of Britain's naval supremacy. The expansion of the navies of the United States, Japan, and Germany threatened to undermine the two-power standard at a time when the cost of maintaining the fleet was placing a heavy burden on the national economy. The two first-named countries did not pose any immediate threat to peace, but the planned expansion of the German fleet was clearly intended to challenge Britain's assumed command of the seas and, in a more general sense, upset the balance of power in Europe. Initially circumstance served to favor the British, the danger of conflict with a combination of naval powers being considerably reduced by the Entente Cordiale with France in 1904 and the reduction of Russian naval power during the Russo-Japanese War of 1904–1905. These, together with the signing of the Anglo-Japanese alliance in 1902, allowed for a considerable reduction in ships on foreign stations, principally in the Mediterranean and Far East, and for a concentration of the fleet in home waters. This concentration served as both an economic measure and as a counter to the threat from Germany, the former rapidly giving way in importance to the latter.

At the same time the navy was subjected to major reforms under the direction of Admiral Sir John Fisher (First Sea Lord, 1904–10). These were intended to both improve the efficiency of the Royal Navy and to reduce costs; they included improvements in the training of officers, the nucleus-crew system, and the wholesale scrapping of obsolete warships. There was also a major change in warship development, with the introduction of the all-big-gun battleship and armored cruiser (*Dreadnought* and the *Indomitable* class, respectively). What has become known as the Dreadnought Revolution was again built around economy, especially as the construction program could be reduced while other naval powers considered their replies. The possibility of Germany reconsidering its intentions may well have crossed some British minds, but in the event that nation rose to the challenge, precipitating a naval race between Berlin and London. Ultimately the challenge failed, Britain abandoning attempts at economy and answering every increase in German construction with larger programs of its own. In the process the two-power standard was abandoned in favor of a 1.6:1 ratio between the British and German dreadnought fleets.

On the outbreak of war in 1914 the Royal Navy's Grand Fleet consisted almost entirely of ships completed within the previous ten years, the bulk (dreadnoughts and their associated ships) within the last seven years. It was in many ways an untried weapon. The most recent fleet actions had been fought in the Russo-Japanese war between predreadnoughts, and although these had provided some lessons, mainly in regard to the dangers of mines and torpedoes and to the possibilities of long-range gunnery, much new technology had been introduced in the meantime that had major implications for the employment and tactics of the fleet. Critical among these were the introduction of submarines and aircraft, long-range gunnery, and long-range "heater" torpedoes. It remained to be seen how well peacetime plans and exercises would translate into war conditions.

Mission

The primary roles of the Royal Navy were defensive—the protection of seaborne trade and the prevention of invasion of Britain or the colonies and dominions of its worldwide empire. Traditionally, these roles had been met by the strategy of commanding sea communications with superior force and blockading the enemy fleet in harbor—either to prevent the latter's passage to sea or to be in a position to intercept it when it did so.

In 1914 the import/export trade was critical to the British economy. The country was not self-sufficient; it imported well over 50 percent of its foodstuffs, while industry was dependent on large amounts of imported raw materials, particularly iron ore and oil. The importance of trade was reflected in the size of the empire's merchant marine, whose gross tonnage represented 45 percent of the world's shipping. On the outbreak of war the eastern entrance to the Channel was quickly closed and Britain's premier fleet—the Grand Fleet—was already in position guarding the northern exits to the Atlantic. This greatly limited the ability of Germany to send out raiding cruisers or armed merchantmen to attack British shipping, the majority of the disruption caused in this way came from enemy ships that were already abroad when war broke out. Even then, the vast size of the British merchant fleet meant that the losses were economically insignificant. The only real impact resulted from the disruption of regular trade and a disproportionate number of warships required to patrol the trade routes.

As for defense against invasion, the only area of vulnerability was the east coast of England, and although this danger exercised the minds of the naval and military authorities, it was more imagined than real. The coast *was* vulnerable, due to the concentration of Britain's main fleet in the north, but any attempt at invasion, even given a successful landing, would have certainly failed. In the event the only attacks made were a few "tip-and-run" naval bombardments of towns on the east coast.

The Royal Navy's primary offensive roles were to support the army and to deny the seas to enemy trade. The former was mainly a case of defending troop transport and supply shipping to and off foreign shores, and general support, including bombardment operations in coastal areas. In the case of trade it proved fairly easy to eliminate the passage of the German merchant marine, but it remained possible for goods to reach Germany in neutral ships and via neutral countries. Although few ships could evade the blockade, its overall effectiveness was compromised by the difficulty of determining whether goods bound for neutral countries would ultimately end up in Germany, as well as by problems in defining "contraband" goods. This problem was exacerbated by a reluctance to antagonize the neutral countries concerned—primarily the United States, the Netherlands, Denmark, and Sweden.

ORGANIZATION

Command Structure

Administration

The Royal Navy was directed centrally from the Admiralty in London. The Admiralty controlled shore establishments and fleet commands covering everything from general policy to supply and training. Compared with the past, its ability to direct the movements of ships and fleets had improved considerably with the advent of wireless communication and wireless intelligence—interception and decoding of enemy signals and direction finding (D/F). This greatly enhanced centralized information gathering, which, combined with the ability to communicate rapidly on a worldwide basis, made the Admiralty the logical center of strategic control. This control should have been limited to ordering ships to sea, with outline instructions as to the objects of their movements and information on possible enemy intentions, leaving subsequent events to the discretion of the commander on the spot. However, this was not always the case, and early in the war the

Admiralty's interference at the local level led to some dangerous decisions; in particular, it was a contributory factor in the loss of a large part of the South America Squadron to the German East Asiatic Squadron off Coronel in November 1914. Moreover, the supply of intelligence to ships at sea was often handled badly, particularly during the battle of Jutland in 1916.

Control of the navy (including the Royal Marines) was the responsibility of the Board of Admiralty, which in August 1914 consisted of:

- The First Lord, political head of the board and a member of the cabinet, providing the link between the government and the navy
- The First Sea Lord, senior naval member of the board and naval advisor to the government
- The Second Sea Lord, responsible for personnel
- The Third Sea Lord and Controller, responsible for material, with superintendence of the departments of the Director of Naval Construction (DNC), Director of Naval Ordnance (DNO), Engineer in Chief (EinC), Director of Naval Equipment (DNE) and Director of Air Department (DAD)
- The Fourth Sea Lord, responsible for stores and their transport.

In addition to the above there were three other political posts: the Civil Lord, to oversee civil establishment staff, naval works, buildings, dockyards, and marine schools, charitable funds, and Greenwich Hospital; the Additional Civil Lord, for naval contracts and dockyard business; and the Parliamentary and Financial Secretary, to control financial matters. Finally, there was the Permanent Secretary—a civil servant of considerable power, responsible for Admiralty correspondence and head of the Admiralty Secretariat. Reporting to the board members were various Admiralty departments, both naval and civilian, most with their own directors.

A Fifth Sea Lord was added in January 1917 to serve as Chief of Naval Air Services. A reorganization in May 1917 produced increased representation for the Naval Staff (see below), and removed the term "Controller" from the Third Sea Lord's title making it a separate political appointment, with the primary function of overseeing the shipbuilding industry. The new post was terminated in June 1918, at which time the Third Sea Lord regained his full title. A Deputy First Sea Lord was added to the board in September 1917 and in January 1918 a Second, Third, and Fourth Civil Lord; all these posts were terminated shortly after the war ended.

In 1912 the Admiralty set up the Admiralty War Staff, an advisory organization to prepare war plans and gather intelligence. It was composed of three divisions—the existing departments of Intelligence and Mobilization

Photo 4.1. Admiral Sir John Fisher (First Sea Lord 1904–10, 1914–16) was the leading figure in the technological and organizational advances of the Royal Navy during his years in office. He also was responsible for several of its shortcomings. (John Roberts collection)

and a new Operations Division—and was headed by a chief of staff, under the supervision of the First Sea Lord. A Trade Division was added on the outbreak of war to deal with the blockade of Germany and the defense of British shipping, and in December 1916 an Anti-Submarine Division and a Signals Section were also added.

Expansion of the staff progressed steadily through the war; its increasing importance and size were formalized in May 1917 with a change of name to "Naval Staff" and the placing of the First Sea Lord at its head as CNS (Chief of Naval Staff), which had the effect of moving it beyond its previous advisory status. The original staff chiefs became the DCNS (deputy chief) and ACNS (assistant chief), both of whom had seats on the board. Several more divisions were added between this time and the end of the war. In their final wartime configuration the departments of Intelligence and Training and Staff Duties reported direct to the First Sea Lord, the foreign section of the Operations Division direct to the Deputy First Sea Lord. The remaining divisions were split between those covering home waters under the DCNS (Plans, Operations [Home], Air and Signals) and trade protection under the ACNS (Trade, Antisubmarine, Mercantile Movements, and Minesweeping).

Organization: Fleet Organization and Order of Battle

The organization of the British Fleet underwent several changes during the years preceding the outbreak of war that were primarily intended to concentrate its main force in home waters and minimize running costs. In 1912 a major reorganization established a Home Fleet on three levels of readiness. The 1st Fleet consisted of the most modern ships of the navy, all of which were fully manned; it included all three dreadnought battle squadrons (1st, 2nd, and 4th BS) and one predreadnought battle squadron (3rd BS—relocated to Rosyth in 1914 and to Sheerness in 1916, when it ceased to be part of the Grand Fleet), together with most of the modern cruisers and destroyers. The 1st Fleet was redesignated as the Grand Fleet on the outbreak of war and shifted its base to Scapa Flow, with the exception of two destroyer flotillas and their attendant light cruisers, which were based at Harwich. Although part of the Grand Fleet, the Harwich Force generally operated as an independent command.

The 2nd Fleet was composed of two predreadnought battle squadrons (5th and 6th) and two cruiser squadrons, whose ships had nucleus crews (60 percent of complement) but could be brought to full complement rapidly. The battleships and one of the cruiser squadrons formed the Channel Fleet, based at Portland, while the second cruiser squadron was temporarily transferred to the Grand Fleet as a substitute for the 4th Cruiser Squadron, which had been detached to the West Indies before the outbreak of war.

The 3rd Fleet, in effect the Reserve Fleet, contained the Royal Navy's older ships. On the outbreak of war preference was given to manning its five cruiser squadrons for patrol and trade-protection duties in home waters and the Atlantic. Its battleships (7th and 8th BS) were mainly employed in subsidiary roles, usually as guard ships at various ports, although a few operated for a short period with the Channel Fleet during the passage of the British Expeditionary Force (BEF) to France and several were later transferred to the Mediterranean. (See tables 4.1 and 4.2.)

Table 4.1 Strength of British Royal and Dominion Navies

Predreadnought-era ships			
Type	Aug. 1914	Losses, 1914–18	
Battleships	41	10	
Armored cruisers	34	13	
Protected cruisers	44	6	
Scout cruisers	8	1	
Destroyers	110	17	
Torpedo boats	73	2	
Sloops	16	0	
Dreadnought-era ships			
Type	Aug. 1914	Losses, 1914–18	Nov. 1918
Battleships	21	2	33
Battle cruisers	9	3	11
Light cruisers	24	5	57
Destroyers and leaders	106	48	329
Torpedo boats	36	6	30
Submarines	76	54	159
Aircraft carriers	1	3	12
Monitors	-	6	34
Escorts	-	10	224
Minesweepers	14	19	138
Minelayers	7	4	14

Notes: The above covers only ships built for naval service and does not include merchant conversions with the exceptions of aircraft carriers and minelayers. The minelayers and minesweepers listed for 1914 are respectively old cruisers and old torpedo gunboats converted to their new roles within the dreadnought era. The minelayers listed for 1918 do not included fleet cruisers, destroyers, or submarines adapted for minelaying.

In addition to the above, the waters around the coasts of the United Kingdom were provided with flotilla craft defense, in the form of Patrol Flotillas and Local Defence Flotillas (LDFs). The former, under the Admiral of Patrols, consisted of middle-aged destroyers and torpedo boats, with their attached light cruisers, based in the Humber, Forth, and the Tyne, as well as at Dover. The Dover Patrol soon became a separate command,

Table 4.2 Royal Navy Order of Battle, 10 September 1914

Home commands
Grand Fleet (Jellicoe): 22 BB, 12 OBB, 6 BC, 10 AC, 10 CL, 40 DD, 1 DL, 9 MS
Harwich Force (Tyrwhitt): 3 CL, 40 DD, 1 DL
Channel Fleet (Burney): 16 OBB, 3 CL
Northern Patrol (De Chair): 9 C, 2 AMC
7th Cruiser Squadron (Campbell): 4 AC
Patrol Flotillas (Ballard): 8 CL, 67 DD, 23 TB
Local Defense Flotillas: 34 DD, 58 TB, 15 SS
Submarine Flotillas (Keyes): 2 DD, 46 SS
Sheerness: 7 minelayers
Atlantic
North American and West Indies Station, 4th CS (Phipps Hornby): 1 OBB, 4 AC, 1C, 1 AMC
Cape Verde—Canaries Station, 5th CS (Stoddart): 1 OBB, 1 AC, 1 C, 3 AMC
West Coast of Africa Station: 1 AC, 1 C, 1 sloop
Finisterre Station, 9th CS (de Robeck): 1 OBB, 5 C
Irish Station, 11th CS (Tottenham): 1 AC, 5 C
West Channel Patrol, 12th CS (Wemyss): 4 C
SE Coast of America Station (Cradock): 1 OBB, 3 AC, 2 CL, 3 AMC
Cape Station (King-Hall): 1 AC, 3 C, 2 AMC
Foreign stations
Mediterranean Fleet (Carden): 2 BC, 4 AC, 4 CL, 16 DD, 6 TB, 3 SS, 1 AMC (plus 11 TB, 3 SS at Gibraltar)
China Station (Jerram): 1 OBB, 2 AC, 1 CL, 8 DD, 4 TB, 3 S, 4 AMC, 2 DS, 13 GB, 1 ML
East Indies Station (Peirse): 1 OBB, 1 CL, 1 C, 2 DS
Australian Fleet (Patey): 1 BC, 2 CL, 1 C, 3 DD, 2 SS, 1 GB
New Zealand Station: 3 C, 1 DS
Pacific Station: 1 CL, 1 C

in recognition of its strategic importance in protecting the supply route to France and maintaining the blockade of the Dover Straits.

The LDFs, intended for the close support of naval bases, employed the oldest of the destroyers, torpedo boats, and submarines. The largest of these forces defended Portsmouth, Devonport, and the Nore, but smaller groups were provided for Pembroke, Queenstown in Ireland, and the Clyde. There was also an LDF at Gibraltar. As the war progressed both the patrol flotillas and LDFs were expanded to include other ports and bases, eventually providing the core of the escort-force organization for the defense of trade and the war against the U-boat.

The entire Home Fleet was under a single commander in chief, but after the outbreak of war the new C in C, Admiral Sir John Jellicoe, was effectively limited to controlling the main forces operating in northern waters and the North Sea—the Grand Fleet, the Harwich Force, and the Northern Patrol—the majority of the 2nd and 3rd Fleets being dispersed to duties too distant for effective control from Scapa Flow.

The battleships of the fleet were nominally grouped into battle squadrons of eight ships grouped in two divisions, with a vice admiral in overall command and a rear admiral for the second division. The Grand Fleet battle cruisers were initially formed into a single battle cruiser squadron (1st BCS) under Rear Admiral David Beatty, who was given the acting rank of vice admiral (he was promoted permanently to vice admiral in August 1915). On the outbreak of war 1st BCS consisted of four ships, but by early 1915 Beatty's command had increased to three squadrons of three ships each (1st, 2nd, and 3rd BCS—each commanded by a rear admiral), plus Beatty's flagship, *Lion,* which, like *Iron Duke,* was an independent command. In February 1915 this force, now based at Rosyth, was redesignated by the Admiralty as the Battlecruiser Fleet, although it remained an integral part of the Grand Fleet. Its separate existence at Rosyth increased its sense of nominal independence. On becoming First Sea Lord at the end of 1916, Jellicoe, as one of his first acts, changed its title to the Battlecruiser Force.

The cruisers too were organized into squadrons, usually of four ships under a rear admiral, or, for most of the light cruiser squadrons, a commodore. There were originally three LCSs, and, light cruisers being faster than the older cruisers, all the squadrons were transferred to Rosyth with the battle cruisers. Additional LCSs were formed and allocated to the battle fleet as new construction allowed.

The destroyer flotillas of the Grand Fleet nominally consisted of twenty ships each, with a light cruiser or a flotilla leader for the flotilla commander. The latter was normally a captain (D), but the Harwich Force was under Commodore (T) Reginald Tyrwhitt, whose rank reflected his original role as senior commander of all 1st Fleet flotillas. (The "[D]" indicated command of destroyers, "[T]" command of fleet torpedo craft.) Initially there were two flotillas with the battle fleet, but these steadily increased in number as new construction became available.

The prewar cutbacks on foreign stations in favor of home waters had substantially reduced the number of ships operating abroad. This even applied to the Mediterranean Fleet, regarded as the most prestigious of Britain's foreign commands and second in importance only to the Home Fleet. Its area of command included the Suez Canal and the Red Sea. In 1905 it included eight battleships based at Malta and could if required call on a similar number from the Atlantic Fleet, based at Gibraltar. By August 1914 the Atlantic Fleet no longer existed, and the Mediterranean Fleet had been reduced to three battle cruisers (2nd BCS), two cruiser squadrons, and a destroyer flotilla. All these ships were fairly modern and would have been valuable additions to the Grand Fleet, but Britain was unwilling to entirely abandon the Mediterranean to French control, despite the Entente Cordiale. Early in 1915 the fleet was reinforced, mainly with predreadnoughts, for operations against Turkey in the eastern Mediterranean and later to support the Italian navy against Austria in the Adriatic.

The remaining foreign stations had, after a few months of excitement pursuing German warships and raiders and dealing with German colonies, a relatively quiet war. In August 1914 these were as follows:

- The China Station, based at Hong Kong
- The Australia Station, under the control of the newly formed Royal Australian Navy (RAN), with its principal base at Sydney
- The New Zealand Station, based at Auckland
- The East Indies Station, with bases at Aden, Bombay, Colombo, and Singapore
- The Cape Station, at Simonstown, South Africa
- The North America and West Indies Station, with its main bases at Halifax and Bermuda.

With the exception of the Mediterranean, the strength of the above stations varied little during the war apart from their few battleships, which all transferred to the eastern Mediterranean in 1915. Most of the stations were commanded by a rear admiral, but that of China had a vice admiral, as he could in theory become C in C of an Eastern Fleet, combining the forces of the China, East Indies, Australia, and New Zealand Stations.

Other stations, which normally had little more than token presences, were the South East Coast of America (the western Atlantic from Brazil southward), the South America Station (the Pacific coast of South America south of Ecuador), and the Pacific Station (the area north of the New Zealand and South America Stations). Shortly after the outbreak of war the single light cruiser on the South East Coast of America Station was joined by the predreadnought *Canopus*, three armored cruisers, and a second light cruiser. This force was to guard the valuable trade routes in the area in case the German East Asiatic Squadron took its most likely (and actual) route home across the Pacific and around Cape Horn. For similar reasons a new West Africa Station was created that extended from the Gold Coast to Angola and covered the coasts of the German colonies of Cameroon and Togoland (German West Africa).

Apart from the main force of the Royal Navy, the Dominions of Australia and Canada had opted to create their own naval forces, an arrangement formalized in 1911 with the creation of the Royal Australian Navy and Royal Canadian Navy (RCN). Both were intended for home defense but were expected to come under the control of the Royal Navy in wartime. The Australian force was the larger, and its flagship (the battle cruiser *Australia*) transferred to the Grand Fleet in 1915, followed in 1917 by two of Australia's modern light cruisers. Australia's four destroyers joined the Mediterranean Fleet in 1917. Its service was otherwise in the Far East, Pacific, and the North America and West Indies stations. The Canadian force was limited to two old cruisers and a few small craft and was not developed to any appreciable extent until the 1920s.

Communications

Communication at sea was provided by wireless (W/T), flag signals, and signal lamps. W/T was well established prewar and continued to develop as the war progressed. However, the primary means of intership communication during the day remained flags, because they were quick (wireless signals were relatively slow, due to shipboard paperwork and the need to code and decode messages) and because the general practice was to maintain wireless silence at sea. The latter was not, of course, necessary once contact with the enemy had been made, and much use was made of W/T during the battle of Jutland, an episode that revealed several weaknesses of method—primarily inadequate and ambiguous reporting of the enemy. Signal lamps were employed to repeat signals, especially when poor visibility or distance made it unlikely that a flag signal could be read. They were also employed at night, and Jutland revealed another weakness in that when a German ship made note of a British recognition signal it relayed this to other enemy ships, information that considerably aided them in their encounters with British ships during the night. In the later years of the war several innovations were introduced to assist intership communication for concentration of fire—that is, two or more ships firing on a single target. These included range indicators operated from control positions, bearing scales painted on turrets, and dedicated fire-control W/T sets.

Worldwide communications, which were not always fully reliable in the early years of the war, were greatly improved with the provision of higher-power transmitters and more numerous W/T stations. However, signals between shore stations and ships in home waters were normally transmitted on relatively low power to reduce the chance of enemy interception.

Intelligence

The Naval Intelligence Division (NID) became part of the Admiralty War Staff in 1912. Its main functions were intelligence gathering; assessment of foreign navies and of their plans and intentions; and, in the case of potential enemies, developing strategies to counter those intentions. Information was obtained by various means, primarily from naval attachés, consuls, and port visits by British warships, but also from the study of the naval legislation and programs of foreign governments, the effect of naval pressure groups (such as the German Navy League), and the events reported and opinions expressed in newspaper and magazine articles. There was also some covert work, involving agents noting such things as activity in dockyards and the strengths of port and coast defenses. The Admiralty also obtained secret documents, including plans of the battle cruiser *Seydlitz,* reports of German fleet gunnery practice in the Baltic during 1912–13, and the 1914 tactical orders for the High Seas Fleet. The latter was used by Jellicoe when formulating the intended tactical deployment of the Grand Fleet.

The primary intelligence source for the British throughout the war was the wireless communications of German ships, submarines, and shore bases—specifically through the interception and decryption of wireless messages and the location of enemy vessels at sea by wireless D/F. In August 1914 the Admiralty had only one station, Stockton on the northeast coast of England, dedicated to interception of German wireless messages. This was quickly expanded by the employment of W/T stations belonging to the Post Office, the Marconi Company, and a few amateur wireless enthusiasts. The provision of D/F came later, with a network of direction-finding stations covering the North Sea established during 1915–16; this network was followed by a similar arrangement in Ireland to cover the area west of the British Isles, a network that proved invaluable both in tracking enemy surface ships and U-boats.

In August 1914 the navy organized a decryption center to deal with incoming coded messages. This was Room 40OB (Room 40 Old Building), largely manned by civilians. Recruiting was initially from the teaching staffs at Osborne and Dartmouth Colleges, later from the universities and individuals possessed of the required skills—especially mathematicians and German speakers. However good this setup was, it would not have been of the inestimable value that it was to be but for the fact that the Admiralty had by the end of 1914 obtained copies of all three of the German navy's primary code books. The first was recovered from the German merchantman *Hobart* at Melbourne by the RAN, the second by the Russians from the German cruiser *Magdeberg* (which ran ashore on the coast of Estonia), and the third from a steel box jettisoned by the sinking German destroyer *S 119* in October and trawled up from the seabed by a British trawler in November. The British were thus served well by fortune, if less so by failures to use the intelligence gained to its best effect during the first years of war.

The constant decoding and monitoring of German wireless traffic eventually gave the staff of 40OB considerable insight into enemy intentions, but it was not until after Jutland that this pool of acquired knowledge was effectively employed or, for that matter, acknowledged. Information was filtered out through the Operations Division, whose personnel, being naval rather than civilian, considered themselves the best people to analyze the information received and, if necessary, to determine whether it was necessary to pass it on to the commanders in the field. This situation was not helped by the fact that the information forwarded was often limited in both its distribution and content. This came to a head at the time of Jutland, when the serious deficiency of the information sent to Jellicoe and Beatty was a contributory factor in Jellicoe's erroneous assumption of the German fleet's course during the night.

A change in methods after Jutland created a system of greater integration and cooperation between the departments concerned. The staff of 40OB was allowed greater freedom to analyze information and issue reports. Detailed and more frequent communications regarding enemy movements and possible intentions were sent to senior commanders afloat, which allowed them to better utilize the information available. The improvement was timely, as the dissemination of wireless intelligence during the critical campaign against the U-boats in the last two years of war was to be a vital component in the campaign's favorable outcome.

Infrastructure

Bases

Prewar, all the Royal Navy's primary bases in home waters were located in southern England—at Devonport, Portsmouth, and Chatham. All these were Royal Dockyards, with substantial construction, docking, repair, base, and supply facilities, together with several of the experimental and training facilities. The establishment of the main fleet base at Scapa Flow initially required ships to sail down the west coast for repair and their annual refit. This created problems with maintaining fleet strength, lengthened the time a ship was absent from the fleet for such reasons, and required careful management to ensure that the number of ships undergoing such work simultaneously was kept to a minimum. The first step in reducing these detachments was the establishment of a repair base, with a floating dock, at Invergordon in the Cromarty Firth; it was operational before the end of 1914. The base was provided with a second floating dock in 1916. Use was

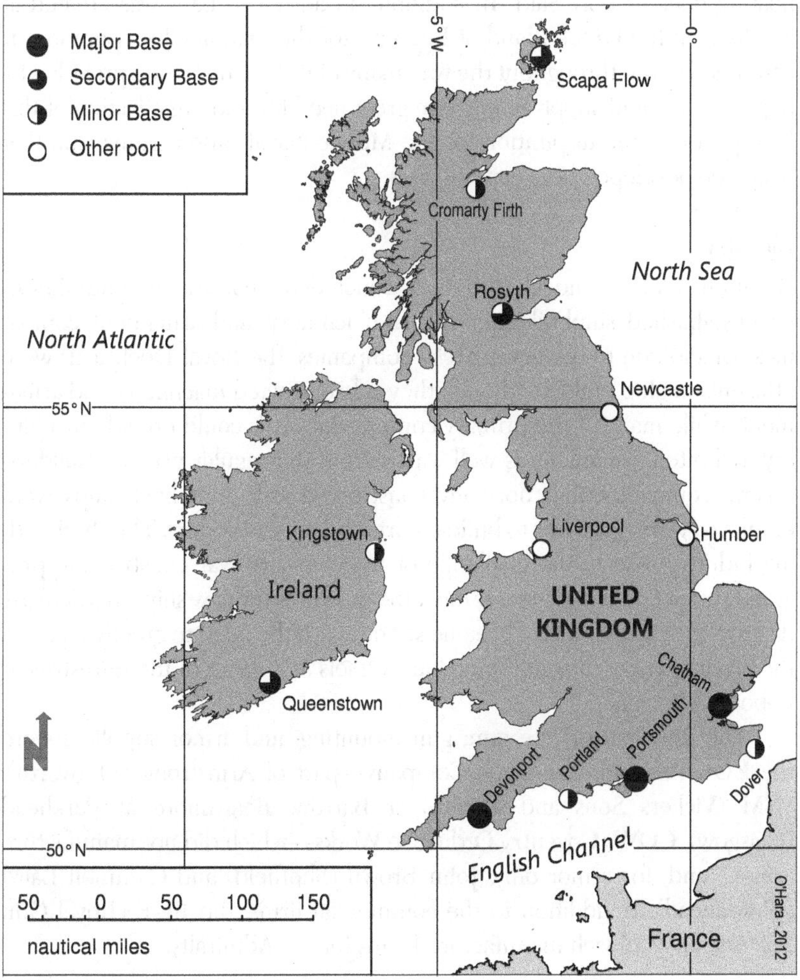

Map 4.1. British Naval Bases

also made of commercial docks, especially those on the Tyne. The need for a northern repair facility had been realized as early as 1903, when it was proposed to build a new dockyard at Rosyth, but construction did not begin until 1909. Owing to various delays and difficulties, this did not become usable until early 1916 and was not fully complete until November 1917. (See map 4.1.)

In the Mediterranean the base and dockyard facilities were located at Malta and Gibraltar. These were inconveniently distant for the convenience of ships operating in the Aegean against the Turks, so Alexandria in Egypt was used as a naval base during the war; it also provided a single floating dock, which could take cruisers and smaller vessels. There was also a small floating dock at Port Said. In addition, an advanced base was created at Mudros, on the Greek island of Lemnos, for the Dardanelles operation. It continued in use throughout the war, many of its facilities being provided by depot, repair, and supply ships. The great need for and organization of this base provided the inspiration for the Mobile Naval Base organization that would be developed between the wars.

Industry

Britain had a large industrial base that included a considerable number of well-established shipbuilding, marine machinery, and armament companies. In addition to the commercial companies, the Royal Dockyards were efficient warship builders, though they subcontracted machinery and armament, while many of the primary commercial yards could provide machinery and often armament as well. Apart from the regular warship builders, several companies that normally constructed only merchant ships were employed during the war to build escorts and minesweepers. The shipbuilding industry rose to the challenge of the extensive war construction programs, but it could not entirely meet the demands for new ships, particularly destroyers, a situation that became serious with the need to greatly increase the numbers of escorts and merchant vessels as a result of the unrestricted U-boat campaign.

The principal private gun, gun mounting, and armor suppliers were the EOC (Elswick Ordnance Company—part of Armstrong Whitworth), VSM (Vickers Sons and Maxim) at Barrow, Beardmore at Parkhead (Glasgow), COW (Coventry Ordnance Works—which did not manufacture armor), and, for armor only, John Brown (Sheffield) and Cammell Laird (Birkenhead). In addition to the commercial firms, the RGF (Royal Gun Factory) at Woolwich manufactured guns for the Admiralty.

The EOC, VSM, and Cammell Laird also supplied projectiles, although the two leading producers were the Sheffield firms of Hadfield and Firth. As there were few major naval engagements, there was a relatively low demand for new supplies of armor-piercing shell until the post-Jutland production of improved versions began in 1917. It was, however, necessary to increase the reserve of high-explosive (HE) shell, and to meet this demand several companies expanded their existing plants.

Torpedoes were manufactured by the Whitehead Factory in Weymouth and the newly constructed RNTF (Royal Navy Torpedo Factory) in Greenock. Shortly after the outbreak of war the Whitehead Factory was taken under Admiralty administration. In 1915 the Admiralty, with some assistance from Vickers and Armstrong, constructed a new factory, at Caton Moor, near Lancaster, to increase torpedo production. As Caton Engineering it manufactured torpedoes from late 1916 until closure in 1919.

The manufacture of explosives, both HE and propellants, was split between trade and the government factory at Waltham Abbey. In 1915 the Admiralty decided to build its own factory for the production of gun propellant. The resulting RNCF (Royal Navy Cordite Factory) at Holten Heath, in Devon, started production in January 1916. In full production the RNCF was making about four hundred tons of cordite a month, compared with the approximately 1,800 tons from commercial companies. The war raised serious concerns about quality control of trade-manufactured cordite following losses of ships to magazine explosion both in action and in harbor—the latter indicating the likelihood of spontaneous ignition. It should be noted, however, that these losses, especially those in action, could be laid at the door of other contributory factors or a combination thereof. Problems were also encountered with the HE known as Lyddite employed in the majority of APC shells, as its sensitivity caused premature detonation on impact with armor. This problem was overcome in the new heavy APC shell supplied to the fleet in 1918 by the use of a new mixture known as Shellite, which was to remain in use until after World War II.

Shipping and Trade Protection

The Royal Navy had few supply problems and had little use for replenishment at sea, due to its worldwide store and refueling depots, combined with the fact that most of its wartime operations did not involve extended periods at sea. Coal was almost entirely carried in chartered colliers, but the oilers that supplied the ships of the fleet were Admiralty-owned vessels of the Royal Fleet Auxiliary (RFA). The navy also employed a considerable number of supply vessels, the majority taken up from trade during the war, although not all were under direct control of the Admiralty. In general the only causes of concern were the losses in merchant ships, in particular ocean tankers, created by the unrestricted U-boat campaign.

Despite the fact that escorted convoys of merchantmen had been successfully employed in the days of sail, the general attitude in 1914 was that this was not practical for a modern war, the main argument being that convoying would cause serious and damaging restrictions to the flow of trade due to the large numbers of ships involved. Instead, the trade routes were to be patrolled by cruisers that could both be directed and keep in touch with each other with wireless communications. This policy was justifiable in relation to surface raiders, given their limited effect. Greater problems were caused by German warships that found themselves in foreign waters on the outbreak of war than by any specific raider sent out from home, and most of those already at sea were intercepted and destroyed during the war's first few months.

It was realized prewar that Britain's trade was vulnerable to submarine attack, but it was considered that international law, which required the safe removal of crew and passengers, would prevent this from becoming a serious problem. Some foresaw, however, that Germany would find it difficult to resist the considerable gains to be had by ignoring the rules. This expectation was fulfilled in February 1915, when Germany declared the waters around the British Isles a war zone in which all ships, including neutrals but excepting passenger vessels, were liable to be sunk without warning. The subsequent U-boat war was to some extent intermittent, as Germany adjusted its campaign in the face of neutral protests, but the general trend was toward ever-increasing losses in the flow of trade in both home waters and in the Mediterranean.

Up to mid-1916, shipping losses, while serious, could be absorbed, but increases in the number of operational U-boats and in the aggressiveness of their campaign saw the loss of over 1.5 million tons of shipping during the five months from September 1916 to January 1917. In February 1917 Germany introduced a completely unrestricted war on trade, and losses immediately increased to well over a half million tons per month—an unacceptable rate in both imports and ships. The answer was the introduction of convoys, which had been in partial use for trade with Scandinavia from the end of 1916 and for the cross-Channel coal trade (at French request) from February 1916. The Admiralty, nevertheless, resisted the implementation of wholesale convoying until April 1917, when a conference, instigated by Beatty, recommended a full convoy system for the North Sea trade with Scandinavia.

The recommendation was accepted, and its success so weakened the Admiralty's position that it was finally agreed to introduce ocean convoys on a trial basis. Two experimental ocean convoys that sailed in May, one from America and one from Gibraltar, lost no ships. Four that sailed from America in June were equally successful. After this the convoy system expanded rapidly to include both outward- and homeward-bound ships. During July 1917–November 1918, 610 homeward and 537 outward Atlantic convoys lost only 167 merchantmen from a total of 16,994—less than 1 percent. Overall shipping losses began to fall significantly toward the end of 1917, and the majority that did occur were vessels not in convoy. The methods finally developed for organizing and operating the convoy system were highly successful and provided the pattern for that adopted on the outbreak of the Second World War.

Personnel

Demographics

In mid-August 1914 the personnel of the Royal Navy and Royal Marines numbered just over 200,000, compared with 146,000 a month before. This included 174,000 in the Royal Navy, of which just over 11,000 were officers, and 25,000 Royal Marines. Thirty percent, a little under 50,000 men, were from the naval reserves—the Royal Fleet Reserve, Royal Navy Reserve (RNR), Royal Navy Volunteer Reserve (RNVR), and the Marine Reserve.

Photo 4.2. A youthful gun crew standing by its charge, the forward 6-inch gun of the light cruiser *Phaeton*. At the men's feet is a 6-inch capped shell. (John Roberts collection)

The Fleet Reserve was made up of ex–service personnel, the RNR mainly from merchant navy officers and seamen; RNVR personnel came from all walks of life, although many had sea experience. A special section of the RNR, designated the trawler section, or RNR(T), was created prewar for men from the British fishing fleet, whose skilled seamanship and knowledge of the waters around the British Isles was recognized as an invaluable asset. Their main employment was to man the trawlers requisitioned for naval service, but they also saw service in other auxiliary and patrol craft.

The marines were divided between the Royal Marine Artillery (RMA) and the Royal Marine Light Infantry (RMLI). The marines afloat were mostly in the fleet's larger ships and served to man some of the ships' guns. They also provided buglers and bands, wardroom servants, and security forces (performing sentry/guard duty, not police duties, which were the province of the petty officers of the Regulating Branch).

A Women's Royal Navy Service was begun in November 1917 to provide shore-based domestic services and release men to other duties. It was disbanded in 1919.

By the end of the war the personnel numbers had doubled to 407,000. War losses amounted to 2,074 officers and 20,337 men killed in action, plus 400 officers and 11,443 men lost from other causes. The Royal Navy Division, which spent the war fighting ashore, seeing action at Gallipoli and on the western front, lost a further 8,590 men. (See table 4.3.)

Table 4.3 Royal Navy and Royal Marine Personnel, 1914–18

	15 August 1914		15 November 1918	
	Officers	Men	Officers	Men
Royal Navy	9,600	117,200	13,700	198,500
Fleet Reserve, RNR, RNVR	1,600	45,200	16,000	110,000
Royal Marines (afloat)	300	12,900	500	17,100
Royal Marine Reserve	20	2,400	50	3,900
Royal Marines (ashore)	Inc. in men	9300	1,100	28,000
Coastguard	Inc. in men	1,900	Inc. in men	4,300

Note: 74,400 of those in service in November 1918 were HO (hostilities only). Numbers are rounded to nearest hundred.

Training

Peacetime officer training began with two years at Royal Navy (RN) College Osborne, on the Isle of Wight, followed by two years at RN College Dartmouth, in Devonshire—the latter including sea experience on board training cruisers. Cadets who opted for careers in engineering transferred to RN College Keyham, near Devonport. The colleges were modeled on the fee-paying English public-school system, with cadets starting at thirteen and a half years of age. From the colleges the cadets joined the fleet as midshipmen and after three to four years were promoted to acting sublieutenants and thereafter, on satisfactory completion of examinations, sublieutenants. This was followed by advanced courses at the RN College, in Greenwich, and at various specialist training establishments before promotion to lieutenant. After a year at this rank an officer could elect to specialize in gunnery, torpedoes, navigation, or signals, which involved intensive training courses and more examinations but provided the best routes to promotion. Those who did not choose to specialize remained "general service" officers.

Enlisted men followed similar paths but naturally with shorter and much less academically demanding training periods. Boys joined at the age of fifteen and underwent about one year's training in seamanship prior to being selected for gunnery, wireless, or signals training. The main boys' training establishments were at Harwich (HMS *Ganges*) and Devonport (HMS *Impregnable*). On leaving the training establishment boys were sent to sea as first-class boys, boy signalers, or telegraphist boys, to continue their training and education until promotion to ordinary seamen, ordinary signaler, or ordinary telegraphist on reaching age eighteen. The training period for the engineering branch was much longer, at around four years, and took place in specialist schools. Boy artificers went either to HMS *Fisgard,* at Portsmouth, or HMS *Indus,* at Devonport, while training for mechanicians was provided at Chatham, in HMS *Tenedos.*

The war brought a substantial reduction in training periods in order to fulfill the manning requirements of the fleet. Compensation was obtained by increased training within the fleet—especially the Grand Fleet, where certain officers were appointed as acting schoolmasters. In December 1915 Admiral Jellicoe requested and obtained the appointment of an experienced schoolmaster to each of the battle and battle cruiser squadrons—an arrangement expanded during 1916 to include every ship of light-cruiser size and larger.

THE WAYS OF WAR

Surface Warfare

Doctrine

The primary British strategy was the containment of the High Seas Fleet within the confines of the North Sea, where, it was hoped, it would be brought to battle by the Grand Fleet. It was established well before 1914 that close blockade of the enemy coast would not be feasible in the face of submarines and mine warfare, and the alternative "distant blockade" was adopted. For this purpose the Grand Fleet was stationed at Scapa Flow, where it guarded the northern exits to the Atlantic and supported the Northern Patrol in the interception of merchantmen bound for enemy ports. It was hoped that the strangling of German seaborne trade would force the German fleet to seek battle, but this proved optimistic, given the limitations involved in controlling neutral shipping.

With the fleet based so far north there were concerns about enemy invasion of, or raids on, the east coast, concerns that generated demands for a greater presence in more southerly bases. In general these demands were resisted, but the bombardment of Scarborough and Hartlepool by German battle cruisers on 16 December 1914 resulted in the Admiralty ordering the battle cruisers to be based at Rosyth. The intended tactics for a fleet action involved employing what was regarded as the Grand Fleet's overwhelming firepower and superior fire control at long range and then closing to decisive range as the enemy's strength was reduced. This confidence in gunnery superiority was shattered at Jutland in 1916, which revealed many problems with British methods and equipment and, in several important respects, the superiority of German ones.

Ships

Prewar ships can be divided between vessels of the predreadnought and dreadnought eras, reflecting broadly the effects on design initiated by Admiral John Fisher. The older vessels date approximately from the decade 1894–1904. The dreadnought-era ships can be broadly differentiated from the earlier vessels by their steam-turbine propulsion, higher speeds, and, in the case of battleships, uniform armaments.

Battleships

The earlier predreadnought battleships (twenty-eight ships completed during 1895–1904) mounted four 12-inch, twelve 6-inch, and sixteen 12-pounder guns and displaced 12,000–15,000 tons. In the eight ships of the

Photo 4.3. The battleship *Dreadnought* anchored in the Solent at the head of a line of predreadnoughts during the Fleet Review of August 1907 (John Roberts collection)

King Edward VII class (17,500 tons) completed during 1905–1906 an intermediate battery of four 9.2-inch was added; in the final two ships, known as the *Lord Nelson* class (16,500 tons), the entire secondary battery consisted of guns of this caliber. Maximum speeds varied from 17.5 knots in the earliest ships to nineteen knots in the last. There were also two ex-Chilean ships (*Swiftsure* and *Triumph,* 11,800 tons, four 10-inch, fourteen 7.5-inch, twenty knots), purchased in 1903 while under construction.

The dreadnought battleship classes readily divide into three groups differentiated by the caliber of their main-armament guns. The first ten mounted ten 12-inch guns in twin turrets, three on the centerline and two in wing positions. The only other offensive gun armament was an anti–torpedo boat battery of 4-inch guns (12-pounder in *Dreadnought*). All had a design speed of twenty-one knots (the dates in the list below are those of the ship's completion).

1	*Dreadnought* (1907)	17,900 tons
3	*Bellerophon* class (1909)	18,600 tons
3	*St. Vincent* class (1910)	19,250 tons
1	*Neptune* (1911)	19,900 tons
2	*Colossus* (1911)	20,000 tons.

The next twelve dreadnoughts were armed with ten 13.5-inch guns in centerline twin turrets. In the last four of this group the anti–torpedo boat battery was increased to 6-inch caliber. All had a design speed of twenty-one knots.

4 *Orion* class (1912) 22,500 tons
4 *King George V* (1912–13) 23,000 tons
4 *Iron Duke* class (1914) 26,400 tons.

Each of the final two classes consisted of five ships, each ship armed with eight 15-inch guns mounted in twin turrets, two forward and two aft. All were prewar designs, but none completed until after the outbreak of war. The first was the *Queen Elizabeth*–class fast battleships of 27,500 tons (completed 1915–16), which adopted oil-fired boilers and had sufficient power for a design speed of twenty-five knots. Due to additions during construction they completed well above their design weight, and in practice they could not make much over twenty-four knots. They were followed by the 25,750-ton ships of the *Royal Sovereign* class, completed during 1916–17, whose design reverted to coal/oil-fired boilers and a speed of 21.5 knots. However, during construction they were modified for oil fuel only, which increased speed to twenty-three knots. Three battleships under construction for foreign navies in British yards were requisitioned shortly after the outbreak of war. Two, intended for Turkey, were completed in 1914 as *Agincourt* (fourteen 12-inch guns) and *Erin* (ten 13.5-inch guns); one, intended for Chile, was completed in 1915 as *Canada* (ten 14-inch guns).

Cruisers

Armored cruisers replaced the earlier first-class protected cruisers at the end of the 1890s—both groups representing the largest ships of the cruiser class. In the later armored cruisers, turret-mounted guns of increased caliber gradually superseded the casemate 6-inch guns of the earlier ships. This culminated in the three all-big-gun armored cruisers of the *Indomitable* class (17,250 tons, eight 12-inch guns, twenty-five knots), initiated at the same time as *Dreadnought* but not completed until 1908. These were the first of Fisher's battle cruisers—a classification that became official only in 1911. Although Fisher, who had a strong belief in speed and gun power at the expense of protection, favored the type, he appears to have had little support in perpetuating it until Germany began to build similar ships. This stimulus produced the *Indefatigable* (18,750 tons), completed in 1911, effectively a repeat of the *Invincible* and an inadequate reply to German construction, which tended toward the fast battleship rather than the armored cruiser. This was possibly excusable for *Indefatigable*, given the initial lack of knowledge of the German design at the time, but less so for her two sisters—*Australia* (for the RAN) and *New Zealand*, whose construction began later. The next four ships—*Lion*, *Princess Royal*, *Queen Mary*, and *Tiger*, completed during 1912–14—were armed with eight 13.5-inch guns, the last-named also adopting the 6-inch-gun secondary battery. They were better protected and faster at twenty-eight knots but still showed weaknesses in their armor arrangements.

Further battle-cruiser construction halted with the introduction of the *Queen Elizabeth* class but began again with the return of Fisher as First Sea Lord in 1914. His war construction program included *Renown* and *Repulse* (26,500 tons, six 15-inch, 31.5 knots—little more than larger, faster versions of *Invincible* with 15-inch guns) and the bizarre *Courageous* and *Glorious* (18,600 tons, four 15-inch, thirty-one knots) and *Furious* (19,500 tons, two 18-inch, 31.5 knots). These last three were originally designated "large light cruisers." Their function is far from clear, although Fisher insisted they were built for proposed operations in the Baltic. Postwar, they were all converted to aircraft carriers—*Furious* being partially modified for this role before completion in 1917.

Fisher advocated a fleet that consisted almost exclusively of large, preferably fast, armored ships and flotilla vessels, and during his original period as First Sea Lord (1904–10) he showed little interest in the development of second- and third-class cruisers. No such ships were laid down from early 1904 until 1909, apart from two scout cruisers intended to support destroyer flotillas. However, demands from the fleet for cruisers of greater speed than the aging second-class cruisers initiated the construction of the seventeen second-class cruisers of the Town classes. In 1913 all these ships, including the scouts and the older second- and third-class cruisers, were redesignated as "light cruisers," while first-class protected cruisers became simply "cruisers."

Although the "Towns" proved to be excellent fleet cruisers, it was the scouts that formed the basis of future cruiser development. This began with the *Arethusa* class, whose eight ships were improved versions of the three *Active*-class scout cruisers of the 1910–11 program with oil-fired boilers, increased speed and high-tensile steel side protection built into the hull structure. They were followed by the early C classes, constructed during 1913–16 as repeats of *Arethusa* but with both 6-inch guns mounted aft. The first eight (the *Caroline* class) were designed with three funnels, like the *Arethusa* class, but two (*Calliope* and *Champion*) were experimentally fitted with geared turbines and had two funnels rather than three (a feature repeated in all later C- and D-class ships). In the later years of the war the *Arethusa*- and early C-class ships (except *Centaur* and *Concord*) were rearmed, initially receiving a third 6-inch gun in place of two 4-inch during 1916–17 and, in the C group only, a fourth 6-inch in place of the remaining 4-inch (low-angle) guns in 1918. All these ships also had their torpedo armament doubled to four twin tubes as a result of experience at Jutland.

The first of the later C classes (*Caledon* class) were modified versions of *Centaur* but, following successful trials in *Calliope,* were fitted with four-shaft geared-turbine machinery. The last two groups, the *Ceres* and *Carlisle* classes, adopted an improved gun layout, having the second 6-inch gun mounted in B position (superfiring over A, the forwardmost position) rather than abaft the bridge. These were followed by the D, or *Danae,* class, in which displacement was increased to accommodate a sixth 6-inch gun and a larger torpedo armament. The last ships of the series, the 7,300-ton, thirty-three-knot E class, were not laid down until late 1918 (two completed 1926, one canceled).

The majority of the above mentioned war-construction cruisers were primarily intended for fleet operations in the North Sea. There was, however, a perceived need for some fast, modern ships to operate on ocean trade routes against raiding cruisers. Design work on these ships began in 1915, and the resulting four ships of the *Hawkins* class (9,750 tons, seven 7.5-inch guns, thirty knots) were constructed during 1916–25. Only one (*Cavendish*) completed during the war, and she was modified during construction to serve as an aircraft carrier. (See table 4.4.)

Destroyers

The navy's older destroyers were twenty-seven-knot (A, B, and C classes) and thirty-knot (D class) vessels of 280–400 tons, with turtle-back forecastles, constructed during 1893–1903. Being constructed by a variety of builders to a basic Admiralty specification, they varied considerably in detail, especially machinery and funnel arrangements, but all were armed with one 12-pounder and four 3-pounder guns and mounted two single torpedo tubes. These were followed by the larger E class, which introduced the raised forecastle that became standard in all subsequent British destroyers. These were slower but more seaworthy vessels, capable of maintaining speed with the fleet in any reasonable weather conditions. Progress at this point deviated briefly with the arrival of Fisher as First Sea Lord, who, following his standard penchant for high speed, initiated the design of the F-class destroyers and the destroyer leader *Swift,* both employing oil-fired boilers—neither design proving particularly successful. At the same time, Fisher initiated the design of thirty-six small (240-ton), twenty-six-knot coastal destroyers of appearance similar to the old turtle-back destroyers and armed with two 12-pounders and three 18-inch torpedo tubes; these vessels were subsequently reclassified as torpedo boats.

Prewar construction returned to more moderate vessels with the coal-fired G class, which provided the basis for the following oil-fired

Table 4.4 Particulars of British Light Cruisers, 1905–18

Class	Completed	Displacement (tons)	Armament (guns/torpedo tubes)	Max speed (knots)
Scouts				
Adventure (8)*	1905	2,670–2,940	10 x 12pdr/2 x 18-in.	25.5
Boadicea (2)	1908–09	3,300	6 x 4-in./2 x 18-in.	25
Blonde (2)	1909–10	3,350	10 x 4-in./2 x 21-in.	24.5
Active (3)	1911–13	3,440	10 x 4-in./2 x 18-in.	25
Town classes				
Bristol (5)	1910	4,800	2 x 6-in., 10 x 4-in./2 x 18-in.	25
Weymouth (4)	1911–12	5,250	8 x 6-in./2 x 21-in.	25
Chatham (5)**	1912–13	5,400	8 x 6-in./2 x 21-in.	25.5
Birmingham (3)†	1914	5,440	9 x 6-in./2 x 21-in.	25.5
Birkenhead (2)***	1915–16	5,200	10 x 5.5-in./2 x 21-in.	26.5
Light cruisers				
Arethusa (8)	1914–15	3,750	2 x 6-in., 6 x 4-in./4 x 21-in.	29
Early C (14)****	1914–16	4,220–4,320	2 x 6-in., 8 x 4-in./4 x 21-in.	29
Later C (14)*****	1917–19	4,120–4,290	5 x 6-in./8 x 21-in.	29
D (8)††	1918–22	4,970	6 x 6-in./12 x 21-in.	29

Notes: Numbers in parenthesis refer to number of ships in class.
The Town classes and *Centaur* and *Concord* of the early C class were fitted with broadside submerged torpedo tubes; all other light cruisers were fitted with above-water tubes.

* Actually four subclasses of two vessels each. All had their 12-pounder guns replaced by nine 4-inch during 1911–12.

** Including two RAN ships. A third RAN ship *(Brisbane)* was built in Australia and completed in 1916.

*** Building in UK for Chili and taken over by Admiralty on outbreak of war.

**** Consisted of four subclasses. The last two ships, *Centaur* and *Concord,* were fitted with a uniform main armament of five 6-inch guns to improve their capability in engaging both cruisers and destroyers.

***** Consisted of three subclasses.

† A fourth unit *(Adelaide)* was built in Australia but did not complete until 1922.

†† Four further ships were canceled at the end of the war.

H-to-M-class designs. The need for command vessels for the increased numbers of destroyers and a demand for vessels of higher speed than the scout cruisers resulted in the construction of the seven *Lightfoot*-class destroyer leaders—essentially enlarged destroyers with additional accommodation for the flotilla commander and his staff. Six repeats of this design (the *Parker* class) followed during the war, while a further four vessels of this type (*Botha* class) under construction in British yards for Chile were requisitioned upon the outbreak of war.

The Emergency War Programs included the construction of ninety-seven repeats of the M class, fifty-five of the R class, and sixty-nine S class. All were of generally similar design, except that the R and S classes were fitted with geared turbines and were faster. In 1916 work began on the design of a new leader similar to, but smaller than, the *Lightfoot,* which resulted in the five V leaders. They differed from the earlier ships in having geared turbines and superimposed gun arrangements forward as well as aft. False concerns that the German navy was introducing larger destroyers resulted in this design being repeated in twenty-five V-class destroyers. The V-class was again repeated in the W class, which differed only in having two triple torpedo tubes instead of twins (postwar, the V class were also fitted with triple tubes). The V and W classes proved to be one of the best destroyer designs of the time and served as a pattern for future British vessels of the type. The last of the wartime destroyers, of the Modified W class, were enlarged Ws with four 4.7-inch guns, but none of these were completed before the end of the war. (See table 4.5.)

Other Naval Types

The navy developed specialized coast-bombardment vessels, designated as monitors, whose main employment was in the eastern Mediterranean and off the coast of Belgium. Fourteen large and nineteen small monitors were completed in 1915. Purpose-built patrol vessels consisted of the P-boats and the Kil class. The forty-four P-boats (six hundred tons, one 4-inch gun, two 14-inch torpedo tubes, twenty knots) built during 1915–18 were designed as patrol and antisubmarine vessels for coastal waters. Their low silhouettes and fair speed gave them a passable chance of ramming a submarine on the surface, for which they had a strengthened stem (used successfully against four U-boats). A further twenty, the PC boats (690 tons, one 4-inch, two 12-pounder guns), were modified to resemble merchantmen and completed as Q-ships in 1917–19. The Kil class "double-ended" patrol gunboats were ordered in large numbers, but only a few became operational. The Admiralty took into service a very large number of merchant vessels to serve

Table 4.5 Particulars of British Destroyers and Leaders, 1903–18

Class	Completed	Displacement (tons)	Armament (guns/torpedo tubes)	Max speed (knots)
Destroyers				
E (River)	1903–09	540–560	5 x 12pdr/2 x 18-in.	25.5
F (Tribal)	1907–09	865–1,090*	5 x 12pdr/2 x 18-in.	33
G (*Beagle*)	1909–10	915–975	1 x 4-in., 3 x 12pdr/2 x 21-in.	27
H (*Acorn*)	1910–11	720–770	2 x 4-in., 2 x 12pdr/2 x 21-in.	27
I (*Acheron*)**	1911–12	780–800	2 x 4-in., 2 x 12pdr/2 x 21-in.	27
K (*Acasta*)	1912–13	935	3 x 4-in./2 x 21-in.	29
L (*Laforey*)	1913–15	968–1,010	3 x 4-in./4 x 21-in.	29
M	1915–17	1,000–1,100	3 x 4-in./4 x 21-in.	34
R	1916–17	1,040	3 x 4-in./4 x 21-in.	36
S	1918–19	1,090	3 x 4-in./4 x 21-in.	36
V	1917–18	1,280	4 x 4-in./4 x 21-in.	34
W	1917–18	1,280	4 x 4-in./6 x 21-in.	34
Leaders*				
Swift	1907	2,200	4 x 4-in./ 2 x 18-in.	35
Lightfoot	1915–16	1,600	4 x 4-in./ 4 x 21-in.	34
Botha	1914–15	1,700	6 x 4-in./ 4 x 21-in.	31
Parker	1916–17	1,670	4 x 4-in./ 4 x 21-in.	34
Shakespeare	1917–19	1,750	5 x 4.7-in./ 6 x 21-in.	36
Scott	1918–19	1,750	5 x 4.7-in./ 6 x 21-in.	36

* The later ships of this class were larger and were fitted with two 4-inch guns in place of two of the 12-pounders.

** Six units of this design were completed for the RAN during 1910–15. They differed from the RN ships in having one 4-inch and three 12-pounder guns and three 18-inch torpedo tubes.

*** V Leaders are included with the V-class destroyers.

as auxiliary war vessels. The largest of these were sixty-seven AMCs, most of which were acquired in 1914–15, to supplement the older cruisers in trade protection and patrol work. The smaller vessels included yachts and paddle steamers, but by far the largest number came from the British fishing fleets—trawlers, drifters, and whalers, which among other duties served as patrol, escort, and antisubmarine vessels and as minesweepers. The number of trawlers that could be taken into service was limited by the detrimental effect on commercial fishing capacity caused by these requisitions, worsened by war losses and the paucity of new construction (by the end of 1916 over 70 percent of British trawlers were in naval service). To make up the shortage and provide vessels for the postwar fishing fleet, the Admiralty began its own program of construction—completing 540 "Admiralty trawlers" by the end of the war. In order to preserve it, the remaining trawler fleet was taken over by the government in 1917, thereafter nominally operating under the white ensign but continuing its commercial activity.

Coastal Types

On the outbreak of war a large number of privately owned motorboats were taken into service as inshore patrol vessels. These having proved their value, the Admiralty ordered 550 motor launches from Elco in the United States; all had been delivered by the end of 1916. They were capable of nineteen knots, and their standard armament was one light gun and depth charges. They were employed for patrols, antisubmarine duties, and inshore minesweeping. Further development of coastal craft began in 1916, with the completion of thirteen coastal motorboats (CMBs). These stepped-hull, hydroplaning boats were forty-foot, twenty-five-knot vessels, armed with a single 18-inch torpedo (launched over the stern from a trough) and machine guns. A further twenty-two completed in 1918 were fitted with more powerful engines, for a speed of thirty-six knots. A larger, fifty-five-foot class followed capable of thirty-six to forty-one knots (depending on engine fitted), with depth charges added to their armament. Six completed in 1917 and fifty in 1918; some carried two torpedoes, while others were fitted for minelaying.

Weapon Systems

Surface Gunnery

The majority of guns were of wire-wound construction, a technique originally developed to save weight but in time showing less advantage as metallurgical developments improved the quality of steel. Guns were either BL (breechloading, employing bag charges) or QF (quick-firing, with cartridge cases). All guns above 6-inch and the majority of those of 4-inch to 6-inch caliber were BL, with screw breechblocks. The older, medium-caliber QF guns of the 1890s also had screw breechblocks, but light guns were fitted with sliding breechblocks, as were the modern 4-inch and smaller QF guns. Apart from the heavy guns, most mountings were single, but a triple 4-inch was introduced in the *Renown* and *Courageous* classes.

Until 1910 capital ships were consistently fitted with 12-inch guns firing 850-pound projectiles. Improved performance was obtained by increased length, from 35 calibers in the Mk VIII of the *Majestic*-class predreadnoughts to the 50-caliber Mk XI high-velocity gun of the *St. Vincent* class. The latter proved a disappointment, and to increase hitting power the alternative of increasing caliber and reducing velocity was adopted in the 13.5-inch gun, firing a 1,250-pound projectile (increased in later versions to 1,400 pounds). The success of this weapon, which had a low wear rate and good accuracy, set the pattern for the following 15-inch gun (1,920-pound projectile), which proved to be one of the best-performing heavy guns of the period. Unfortunately, the armor-piercing shell for all heavy-caliber guns was insufficiently developed and lacked strength, which, combined with an oversensitive filler and inadequate fuse, reduced its effectiveness in oblique impact with armor. This problem revealed itself at Jutland, and subsequent investigation resulted in the development of a very effective armor piercing shell; this was in supply by 1918, and over 15,000 new shells had been supplied to the Grand Fleet by the end of the war.

Antiaircraft Gunnery

The development of antiaircraft (AA) guns began prewar, with the introduction of 3-inch QF and 2-pounder pom-poms—the latter mostly fitted in destroyers and smaller craft. To increase numbers, old 3-pounder and 6-pounder QF guns were converted to high-angle fire and widely distributed through the fleet, later supplemented by a purpose-built 3-pounder. By the end of the war most of the larger ships of the fleet had one or two 3-inch or 4-inch AA guns.

Torpedoes

Substantial advances in torpedo design occurred during 1909–10, with the introduction of the long-range heater torpedo, the angled gyro for submerged tubes (which allowed torpedoes to change direction after launch), and an increase of size from eighteen to twenty-one inches. In 1914 the latest torpedoes were provided with two speed settings—three thousand yards at forty knots or six thousand yards at twenty-eight knots for the 18-inch, and for the 21-inch, 4,500 yards at forty-five knots or ten thousand yards at twenty-eight knots for the 21-inch (although these figures varied slightly depending on the weapon's mark and subtype). In 1915 Jellicoe requested that 21-inch torpedoes be provided with an extreme-range setting; this need was met in 1916 with the introduction of torpedoes with their low-speed setting altered to 14,000–15,000 yards at twenty-three or twenty-five knots and, in battleships and battle cruisers only, 17,000–18,000 yards at eighteen to twenty-one knots for conditions of high visibility. The former was later redefined as a "medium speed," while the latter retained the ER (extreme range) designation. British warships fired 778 torpedoes during the war, of which 575 were fired by submarines—517 at naval and 58 at merchant vessels, obtaining 106 hits (76 sinkings). Destroyers sank ten ships for 134 torpedoes fired (thirty-two hits), cruisers two for thirty-six fired (seven hits), and CMBs one for twenty-three fired (six hits).

Submarine Warfare

Offensive

Doctrine

During the latter part of the nineteenth century the Admiralty discouraged the development of submarines, convinced that in time such craft could seriously threaten its own surface fleet. Once it was realized that this policy could no longer be sustained, it ordered five U.S.-designed Holland boats from Vickers, which completed during 1902–1903. By the outbreak of war seventy-six submarines were in service—a larger number than possessed by any other naval power. Fifty-nine of these craft (which included two constructed for the RCN) were coastal types of the A, B, and C classes, and sixteen (including two constructed for the RAN) more modern, longer-range patrol (or "oversea") submarines of the D and E classes. A further 137 submarines were completed during the war. Fifty-four were lost—thirty-five to enemy action or unknown causes, eleven to accidents, friendly fire, or stranding, and the remainder deliberately destroyed (seven at Helsingfors in April 1918 to avoid capture and one blown up during the attack on Zeebrugge in April 1918).

In August 1914 the majority of the coastal boats were stationed on the east and south coasts of Britain to provide harbor defense and coastal patrols. Three of the B class were stationed at Gibraltar and three at Malta—all later transferred to Venice to operate with the Italian navy. The patrol submarines were stationed at Harwich for offensive operations into the southern North Sea and patrols into the Helgoland Bight, operations that were continued throughout the war. Home waters were to remain the main area of operation, but the navy's submarines also saw service in the Dardanelles and Sea of Marmora, against Turkey; in the Adriatic, cooperating with the Italian navy; and in the Baltic. Unlike the German U-boats, their primary targets were normally warships, mainly because there were very few opportunities to attack trade.

The main successes achieved by submarines against naval targets were sinkings of U-boats—fifteen in home waters, one west of Cape St. Vincent in the Atlantic, and one in the Adriatic. British submarines also accounted for three German cruisers and two old Turkish predreadnoughts. Although less successful in this respect than the German U-boats, they did manage to damage a number of dreadnoughts, something that the U-boats failed to do in their operations against the Grand Fleet—although it should be noted that the British had more opportunity, given that U-boats were primarily concentrated against trade.

Boats/Weapons

The early coastal submarines of the A to C classes were larger versions of the U.S. Holland boats to an improved design by Vickers. Surface propulsion was provided by petrol engines, and like all subsequent coastal types, they were of single-hull construction with internal ballast tanks and mounted all their torpedo tubes in the bow (except the F class, which also had a stern tube). The first of the patrol type were saddle-tank designs, the Ds introducing a stern tube and diesel engines (first tried experimentally in *A13*) and the Es beam tubes (one firing to port and one to starboard), while the modified E9 class added a second bow tube. Six of the Es completed during 1916–17 were fitted for minelaying, the beam tubes being omitted and vertical tubes for twenty mines fitted in the saddle tanks.

Vickers' contractual arrangement with the Admiralty gave it a virtual monopoly of submarine construction for several years, and it built the majority of the prewar boats of the A to E classes, apart from a few constructed under license by Chatham Dockyard. This monopoly ended in 1913, but before this date the Admiralty had invested in the construction of double-hull boats of foreign design that did not infringe the Vickers agreement. The primary purpose was to increase the number of builders with experience in submarine construction, given that the existing arrangement severely limited capacity, together with a desire to investigate the qualities of the double-hull type. The coastal boats built to foreign design were the Italian (Laurenti) S class and the French (Laubeuf) W class; all six were transferred to the Italian navy in 1915.

Requirements for double-hull coastal and patrol submarines were laid down by the Submarine Committee in 1912. From these Vickers designed the V class and *Nautilus,* while the Admiralty produced the F class. The *Nautilus,* begun in 1913, had a substantial torpedo armament of two bow, four broadside, and two stern tubes, but Vickers found it impossible to accommodate the twenty-knot surface speed desired by the committee. *Nautilus* did not complete until 1917, due to delays in producing her high-power diesel engines, and was not employed operationally. The *Swordfish,* based on a Laurenti design and representing a second attempt to achieve high speed, employed steam turbines; she proved a failure and was converted into a surface patrol vessel in 1917.

War construction of patrol submarines was split between saddle-tank (E and L) and double-hull (G and J) boats, while the H class and the R class reverted to single-hull design. The Ls were essentially enlarged Es with a higher speed, greater endurance, and no stern tube; the later vessels of the class had 21-inch bow tubes (five of the Ls were fitted as minelayers, sixteen mines replacing the beam tubes). The Gs, originally part of a program aimed at increasing the number of patrol submarines, were double-hull variations of the E but each with a 21-inch stern tube. The J class boats were the largest and fastest of the conventional submarines, the increased power being provided by three sets of diesels driving three shafts in place of the more conventional two. The torpedo tubes were arranged as in the E class, except for the omission of the stern tube.

The original H-class boats were of U.S. design. Ordered from Bethlehem Steel late in 1914, the first ten were to be built in Canada with U.S.-supplied material, while the second ten were to go to the Fore River Yard in Massachusetts for delivery postwar. Only four of the Fore River boats were delivered (in 1918), of which two were transferred to the RCN. Utilizing the same design the Admiralty ordered in 1917 from British yards an enlarged version (H21 class) that substituted 21-inch torpedo tubes for the 18-inch but was otherwise generally similar.

The remaining war construction could best be described as specials—the steam-powered K-class submarines (intended to work in conjunction with the Grand Fleet), the R-class antisubmarine boats (hunter/killers, in modern terminology), and the submarine monitor *M1.* The last-named was fitted with a single 12-inch gun that could be fired on the surface or, for a single round, with the boat at periscope depth. The general idea was that the gun could be employed either as a supplement to the torpedo in attacks against surface vessels or for shore bombardment, but the opportunity to use it never arose. (See table 4.6.)

Antisubmarine Doctrine

At the opening of the war, antisubmarine tactics were largely passive. Jellicoe kept his fleet at sea for most of the time while the defenses of Scapa Flow

Table 4.6 Particulars of British Submarines, 1903–18

Armament (Surface)	Date completed	Displacement surf/sub (tons)	Speed (kts) surf/sub	Endurance nm @ knots	Torpedo
Coastal type					
A5–13	1905*	190/205.5	11.5/7	325/11	2 x 18-in.
B	1905–6	287/316	13/7	740/12	2 x 18-in.
C	1906–10	290/320	13/7.5	910/13	2 x 18-in.
S	1914–15	265/324	13/8.5	1600/8.5	2 x 18-in.
V	1915–16	390/455	14/8.5	2800/9	2 x 18-in.
W	1915–16	330/500	13/8.5	2500/9	2 x 18-in.
F	1915–17	360/440	14.5/8.75	3000/9.5	3 x 18-in.
H1 – 20	1915	364/464	13/11	1600/10	4 x 18-in.
H21 – 52	1918–19	438/504	13/10	1600/10	4 x 21-in.
Patrol type					
D1	1909	483/595	14/9.8	1750/11.2	3 x 18-in.
D2–8	1911–12	495/620	14.5/10	2000/11.5	3 x 18-in.
E1–8	1913–14	655/796	15/9.5	3000/10	4 x 18-in.
E9–56	1914–17	667/807	15/9.5	3000/10	5 x 18-in.
Swordfish	1916	932/1105	18/10	3000/8.5	2 x 21-in., 4 x 18-in.
Nautilus	1917	1441/2026	17/10	5300/11	8 x 18-in.
G	1915–17	703/837	15.5/9	3160/10	1 x 21-in., 4 x 18-in.
J	1916–17	1204/1820	19.5/10	5000/12.5	6 x 18-in.
L1–8	1917–18	891/1074	17/10.5	3800/10	6 x 18-in.
L9–33	1918–26	914/1089	17/10.5	3800/10	2 x 21-in., 4 x 18-in.
Fleet type					
K	1916–18	1980/2566	24/9	12500/10	8 x 18-in.**
Monitor type					
M1***	1918	1594/1946	16/10	3840/10	4 x 18-in.
Hunter/killer type					
R	1918–19	410/503	9.5/15	2000/8	6 x 18-in.

Note: A number of vessels in the above sequence of numbers for the H21 and L9 classes were canceled postwar. Gun armaments varied considerably; several (including all the coastal types) carried none, but the standard in patrol submarines was a single 12-pounder or 3-inch. Some of the Js and all the Ls were fitted with 4-inch guns, and the Ks one 3-inch and one 4-inch.

*A13 did not complete until 1908. The earlier A1–4, which differed slightly from the later boats were taken out of service before 1914.

** Increased to 10 x 18-inch during construction by the addition of a twin mounting in the superstructure.

*** Two sister boats were completed postwar and a third canceled.

were sufficiently improved to prevent the entry of U-boats into his base. At sea the fleet relied on speed and zigzagging (as also became standard practice for convoys) to reduce the chances of a submarine's obtaining a good attack position. These methods, together with maintaining a lookout for torpedo tracks and periscopes, continued throughout the war. Destroyers were positioned to screen the battle fleet, but without a means of attacking a submerged U-boat (apart from ramming, which required a high degree of luck), they served only to spoil a submarine's chance of attack.

More direct means of dealing with U-boats began with the laying of minefields off their bases in the southern North Sea and along their expected routes, especially in the areas off the Flanders coast and the Helgoland Bight. In addition, the Dover Straits were heavily patrolled by auxiliary warships and closed off with a mined net barrage between the Goodwin Sands and a position west of Dunkirk, as well as, from late 1917, a deep minefield between Folkestone and Cap Gris Nez. These barriers claimed several U-boats, but nonetheless, submarines regularly passed through them to attack shipping in the Channel and beyond. The U-boats had a relatively safer but longer route to the Irish Sea and western approaches, that of passing around Scotland, but the distance involved reduced their period on station. An attempt to close the northern route began in March 1918 with an extensive Anglo-American mining project known as the Northern Barrage. This involved laying a minefield from Orkney to Norway; the center section, by U.S. minelayers, gave coverage from the surface to a depth of two hundred feet, while the eastern and western ends were British-laid deep minefields (allowing the passage of surface ships) that were to be continuously patrolled in order to force submarines to pass through them submerged. By the end of October 1918, 56,033 American and 15,093 British mines had been laid, but the barrage claimed few U-boats (most estimates give six as possible). In addition to the Northern Barrage, the Helgoland Bight minefields were substantially extended during 1917–18 (the total number of British mines laid in this area during 1914–18 was 42,899, most in the last two years of war). Channels were constantly being cleared through these fields by German minesweepers and were just as regularly closed off by further minelaying, so U-boats often took the safer route through the Kattegat, which again reduced their time on patrol. In fact, the disruption to U-boat operations caused by North Sea minefields was of greater value than the direct losses they caused.

Other antisubmarine measures included:

- Submarine patrols: British submarines sank during 1916–18 nineteen U-boats, of which seventeen were torpedoed and two

Table 4.7 British Warship Losses to Submarines, 1914–18

Type	Home waters/Atlantic	Mediterranean
Predreadnoughts	2	3
Cruisers	8	0
Flotilla leader	1	0
Destroyers	4	3
Torpedo boats	2	0
Submarines	3	1
Torpedo gunboat	1	0
Sloops	7	4
Monitors	1	0
Seaplane carrier	1	0
Minelayers	1	0
Armed merchant cruisers	11	0
Armed boarding vessels	5	4

Note: Auxiliary and coastal craft are not included. The higher loss rates for AMCs, ABVs, and sloops relates to their employment in trade protection. The cruiser losses include three (*Aboukir, Cressy,* and *Hogue*) sunk on the same day in September 1914 due to a combination of being inexcusably placed in harm's way and badly handled when attacked.

lost in minefields. Two of the torpedoed U-boats were lost to old submarines towed by decoy trawlers—U-boats being in the habit of sinking trawlers with gunfire.

- Aircraft patrols: Airplanes and airships searched for submarines from coastal air bases. Mostly this served for intelligence on enemy movements, but forcing a submarine to dive also had value. Although the aircraft carried bombs, only one U-boat was sunk by this means. In addition, convoys were provided with a wider area of observation from escorting airships and kite balloons flown from destroyers.
- Q-ships: Converted merchant vessels (and some naval escorts designed to look like merchantmen) were employed as decoys to tempt U-boats to the surface, where they could be engaged by a hidden armament. They sank eleven U-boats during 1915–17.
- Dazzle painting: Employed on both merchant ships and warships during 1917–18, this technique was intended to increase the difficulty of estimating a ship's course and speed. These were critical factors for submarines, which tended to keep periscope observation to a

minimum to avoid detection. A related development on this theme was the construction of some escort vessels as "double-ended" ships with central, symmetrical superstructures and the same hull profiles at stem and stern (often with false bow waves painted aft).

- Arming of merchant ships: As this would have made ships legitimate targets for sinking without warning, it was not begun until February 1915. Progress was initially slow, due to the limited availability of weapons, but by the end of 1916 over 1,300 merchantmen had been fitted with guns, by the end of the war over four thousand.
- Patrol concentrations: These involved swamping a large area with antisubmarine craft at times when intelligence had indicated the likely passage of U-boats through that area. This was intended to force the enemy to submerge and, ideally, exhaust his batteries so that he could be attacked on returning to the surface. (See table 4.7.)

Antisubmarine Weapons

Overall, mines produced the greatest losses to U-boats during 1914–18, accounting for about forty-eight (excluding a further ten lost to German mines), but for a given period the most effective offensive antisubmarine weapon proved to be the depth charge. In 1918, with supply and tactics well established, they accounted for twenty-two U-boats, compared with eighteen sunk by mines. They were supplied to light cruisers, destroyers, escort vessels, and coastal craft; they were initially simply dropped over the stern from racks, but by mid-1917 depth-charge throwers had been introduced. There were also towed explosive devices: the explosive paravane, which was difficult to operate, unpopular, and achieved little; and the explosive sweep, which was employed mainly by auxiliary patrol vessels and accounted for only three submarines.

Experiments with hydrophones, developed from prewar sound-signaling apparatus, to detect the engine and propeller noises of submarines produced a system that was employed as both a static defense and on board ships. In the former case, the hydrophones were laid in arrays on the seabed in coastal areas, with a shore-based listening post. In addition to warning and tracking functions, these stations were often used in conjunction with controlled minefields. Apart from those around the coasts of Britain, listening stations were established in Italy and at Malta. The shipboard use of hydrophones was at first hampered by the need for the vessel in which they were fitted to be stopped, due to the excessive noise created when moving. This problem was solved by the adoption of towed units, and this in turn led to their use by airships and seaplanes, from which the hydrophone was lowered into the sea (although seaplanes had to alight on the surface). A much-improved ultrasonic detector was developed during the war but was not brought to completion until shortly after the war ended—this was Asdic, which was to become the standard submarine-detection device of the future.

Mine Warfare

Doctrine

Mine development was neglected prewar, and the standard Elia mine in use in 1914 had a firing mechanism that often malfunctioned. To improve matters the Admiralty purchased Carbonit mines from Russia, eventually producing a reliable home-manufactured type by copying the essential features of the German horned mine. Early problems with both quality and numbers limited most minelaying to defense fields, but from early 1917 there was greater emphasis on offensive minelaying, this activity being reflected in the number of vessels adapted for the purpose during this period. Britain also developed the first magnetic mine—the M sinker, which was employed primarily on the U-boat routes off the coast of Belgium. The central section of the Northern Barrage employed U.S. antenna mines.

Mine and Patrol Vessels

At the instigation of Admiral Fisher, the early war-construction programs included many minesweeping and small patrol vessels. War-construction minesweepers belonged to the Flower, Racehorse, Ascot, and Hunt classes. Over seventy of the Flower class were ordered in 1915, a further twelve in January 1916, and twenty-eight in January 1917. They proved adaptable for escort service, and the last two groups were built for this purpose—the 1917 ships being constructed to resemble merchantmen, in order to blend with their charges or to serve as Q-ships. The Racehorse class minesweepers were "double-ended" ships, while the thirty-two of the Ascot class were paddle steamers ordered during 1915–17. The Hunt class consisted of over a hundred vessels, but only fifty-two were completed before the end of the war.

Minelayers

The RN had no purpose-built minelayers, all such vessels being either modified warships or merchant vessels. Seven old second-class cruisers were converted prewar, but no other warships were adapted for this purpose until 1917, except for destroyer leader *Abdiel*, completed in 1916 for service with the Grand Fleet (two of her sisters were similarly modified in 1918). During 1917–18 the old first-class cruisers *Ariadne* and *Amphitrite*, the predreadnought *London,* the battle cruiser *Courageous* (temporarily), eleven light cruisers, and fourteen destroyers were adapted for minelaying. Ten merchant vessels were converted to minelayers, most during 1915, together with sixteen trawlers during 1915–18.

Amphibious Warfare

The navy was involved in only two amphibious operations of any note. The first was support to the landings in Gallipoli, which began in April 1915 following an abortive attempt to force a passage to Constantinople through the Dardanelles with ships alone. British and French warships provided a bombardment force and guarded the beachheads. The campaign proved a costly failure, with 205,000 British and 47,000 French casualties and the loss of three predreadnought battleships. In contrast, all Allied personnel were evacuated in December 1915 without a single casualty.

Troops were landed on the Gallipoli Peninsula from a variety of craft, including a converted collier (*River Clyde*) that was run ashore to allow troops to disembark rapidly from specially fitted ramps. Specially constructed landing craft arrived later in the campaign—160-ton X lighters, driven by oil engines, and small Y "dumb," or non-self-propelled, lighters (a few were powered by small outboard engines). The construction of X lighters continued through 1916, the type providing general service in the transport of troops and stores, especially in Mesopotamia. The navy also built three 2,500-ton pontoons intended to land troops, guns, and tanks as part of an invasion of Belgium in combination with a land advance by the army planned for mid-1917. The latter (the third battle of Ypres) failed, and the whole operation was canceled.

The second amphibious operation of note was the attack on Zeebrugge on 23 April 1918. This was a night raid in which the Royal Marines were to suppress the outer harbor defenses while three old cruisers were sunk across the mouth of the canal that linked the U-boat base at Brugge with the North Sea. The assault was well executed and resulted in the awarding of eight Victoria Crosses, but the blockships were not sunk to best effect, and U-boats were able to get past them only a few days after the attack. In addition, secondary attacks on Ostende failed completely.

Aviation

The Admiralty began to show a serious interest in aviation in 1909. In April 1912, following the recommendation of the Aerial Sub-Committee of the Committee of Imperial Defence, the Royal Flying Corp (RFC) was formed, with both military and naval wings that shared resources but were effectively under separate control. Shortly after this an Air Department was added to the Admiralty's organization. The separation of the two air services was recognized in July 1914, when the naval wing officially became the RNAS (Royal Naval Air Service). It survived until 1 April 1918, when it was combined with the RFC to become a completely separate third service—the Royal Air Force (RAF).

Photo 4.4. View, looking aft, of the midships ("Q") 13.5-inch turret of the battle cruiser *Lion* in 1918. The aircraft on the flying off ramp is a 2F1 Sopwith Camel. (John Roberts collection)

In August 1914 the RNAS had ninety-three land and seaplanes and six airships, while its personnel consisted of 138 officers and 589 men. By the end of March 1918 this force had increased to 2,949 airplanes (of which about a third were seaplanes), 5,378 officers, and 49,688 men. The majority of the air personnel transferred to the RAF, but the Admiralty retained control of its airships until the end of 1919. In November 1918 the RAF aircraft on naval flying duties numbered a little over 1,700; the naval airship service included 103 airships, 580 officers, and 6,534 men.

Shortly after the outbreak of war two RNAS squadrons transferred to France to support the Naval Brigade. This presence was retained throughout the war and was substantially increased in late 1916 to provide additional support to the RFC in covering military operations on the western front. In the early months of the war these squadrons pioneered strategic bombing, conducting the first air raids on Germany (against the zeppelin sheds at Düsseldorf and Friedrichshafen) and the first night bombing raid (against Ostende), while one of their aircraft was the first to destroy a zeppelin (Z9, at Düsseldorf). The RNAS also had the task of home defense against air attack until early 1916, when the RFC assumed this responsibility.

In the maritime war the major part of the air resources of the RNAS was employed from coastal stations in home waters. Land planes, seaplanes, flying boats, and airships continually patrolled in search of enemy warships, U-boats, minefields, and zeppelins. Air patrols did not produce much in direct action against enemy assets, but they proved extremely valuable in exerting a deterrent effect, reporting enemy vessels, gathering intelligence on enemy movements, and in the later years of the war providing air escorts for convoys. Naval aircraft also served in coastal operations off Belgium; in the assaults on the Dardanelles and Gallipoli; in the Aegean, Adriatic, and Red Seas; in Palestine; and East and Central Africa. Their activities included spotting for naval bombardments, bombing, and carrying out reconnaissance and aerial photography of enemy positions.

The idea of employing aircraft with the fleet was conceived early but developed slowly due to the difficulties of operating from the open sea. Early aircraft were comparatively light structures, and initially the only suitable aircraft were seaplanes, whose floats reduced their performance compared with land planes. Even the main advantage that they possessed—that they could be launched and recovered from the sea—was limited by the need for the ships carrying them to stop (making them vulnerable to attack and compromising their operation in conjunction with a fleet) and by the requirement of moderate sea conditions. In 1917 the development of shipboard aircraft moved toward employing wheeled aircraft launched from ramps and flight decks.

The principal roles initially envisaged for fleet aviation were reconnaissance and sea-launched attacks on coastal positions. On Christmas Day 1914, three seaplane carriers launched an air attack against the airship sheds at Cuxhaven. The attack failed in both its primary object and a secondary one—the hope that the attack would draw out the German fleet—but nevertheless demonstrated the potential of naval airpower. Further sea-launched raids on enemy airship bases were attempted in 1916, but it was not until a raid on the Tondern airship sheds by aircraft from HMS *Furious* in July 1918 that such an operation succeeded: both airship sheds were set alight, and the zeppelins *L54* and *L60* were destroyed.

Given their small size, the bombs of the era were unlikely to achieve a great deal in attacks on armored ships. The weapon that had the most potential in this respect was the air-launched torpedo, first tried in July 1914, when a 14-inch torpedo was dropped from a Short Folder seaplane. In August 1915 a Short 184 seaplane was the first aircraft to torpedo a ship from the air—a grounded Turkish supply vessel. Two more Turkish vessels were torpedoed by aircraft a few days later; one did not sink, though it became a total loss, while the second, a tug, was torpedoed when the aircraft was afloat rather than in the air. These isolated events served to demonstrate both the potential and the shortcomings of employing aerial torpedoes—not least the fact that the aircraft involved could barely take off with the weight of a torpedo. Toward the end of 1916, work began on the world's first torpedo bomber, the prototype of which appeared in June 1917. This became the Sopwith Cuckoo, a land plane suitable for operation from an aircraft carrier. The first operational squadron was allocated to the carrier *Argus* in October 1918 and began working up for a planned torpedo attack on the ships of the High Seas Fleet in harbor. It was intended to make this attack in 1919, but the end of the war intervened.

The initial impetus for fitting takeoff platforms to fighting ships was to provide improved reconnaissance capability and a means of dealing with zeppelins. Land planes were essential in this latter role, not simply because of their superior performance in comparison to seaplanes (especially a higher rate of climb) but because they required a shorter takeoff run. The problem of recovery was solved by the adoption of air bags that could be inflated by compressed air shortly before landing, but that of having to stop to recover aircraft remained (if necessary, the aircraft could be picked up by a destroyer or abandoned). The first takeoff platform in a fighting ship was fitted over the forecastle of the cruiser *Yarmouth* in June 1917. (Four cruisers of the Harwich force were fitted with flying-off ramps in 1915, but these achieved little and were soon removed.) Shortly after, her aircraft succeeded in shooting down zeppelin *L23*, and, with the encouragement of this singular—and as it turned out, only—success, a further twenty-one light cruisers were fitted with platforms by the end of 1918.

The next step was the fitting of flying-off platforms to capital ships, beginning with the battle cruiser *Repulse*, which successfully launched aircraft from ramps fitted to the roofs of her B and Y (the latter the aftmost) turrets in October 1917. By the end of the war a further ten battle cruisers and twenty-five battleships had been fitted with two turret ramps each. The provisional outfit in each ship was one fighter and one reconnaissance aircraft. At the end of 1918, 103 aircraft were allocated to the fighting ships of the Grand Fleet. In March 1918 serious work began on developing aircraft spotting for the battle fleet, but this had not been advanced to a fully workable system before the war ended—not least because of the difficulties of communication. Aerial spotting for guns had in fact started earlier, from kite balloons, which, being tethered to ships, did not suffer the same communication problem. They were first used from kite-balloon ships during the Dardanelles and Gallipoli campaigns in April–July 1915, spotting for ships bombarding Turkish positions. During 1917–18 kite balloons were installed in sixteen battleships, four battle cruisers, five light cruisers, and twelve destroyers of the Grand Fleet. Although their primary role was spotting, they were also intended for observation of enemy movement in a fleet action and could provide general observation for a cruising fleet. However, the latter role was limited by the fact that being visible from some distance, they might give advanced warning of the fleet's approach.

Another mode of operating aircraft with the fleet employed a high-speed (hard-chine), fifty-eight-foot lighter that could be towed by a destroyer. These were originally introduced in 1917 to extend the range of flying boats by towing them out into the North Sea. In 1918 a number of these craft were fitted with flying-off ramps for fighters and, under tow by a destroyer, accompanied various raiding operations. They achieved one success—a Sopwith Camel flown from a lighter on 10 August 1918 shot down zeppelin *L53* during a sweep by the Harwich Force toward Helgoland.

In the development of aircraft and seaplane carriers, experiments in operating aircraft from ships began in 1912, with seaplanes being launched from temporary takeoff ramps built over the forecastles of a few predreadnoughts. In the following year the old cruiser *Hermes* was converted into the navy's first seaplane carrier. Fitted with a flying-off ramp over her forecastle and canvas hangars fore and aft, she was sunk by *U 27* shortly after the outbreak of war. The shortfall was made up by converting fast passenger ferries into seaplane carriers—three in 1914, two in 1915, one in 1916, and two in 1917. All these vessels had a similar configuration—a hangar aft for seaplanes and a flying-off ramp forward for wheeled aircraft (except for the first three, which had a second hangar forward and no ramp). There were also two ex-German merchant ships operated as seaplane carriers in the eastern Mediterranean during 1915–17.

The development of more capable aviation vessels began with the 7,450-ton *Ark Royal*, a cargo vessel purchased in May 1914 while under construction and completed as a seaplane carrier/aircraft depot ship in December. The next project involved the conversion of the 20,000-ton ex–Cunard liner *Campania* into a seaplane carrier for operation with the Grand Fleet. She was purchased by the Admiralty in November 1914 and entered service in April 1915 with a 165-foot flying-off platform forward and two hangars for ten to twelve aircraft. In 1916 the flying-off platform was extended aft to 245 feet by splitting the forward funnel into two uptakes. The thirty-one-knot hybrid battle cruiser *Furious* was completed in July 1917, with a 228-foot takeoff deck forward, to meet the need for a high-speed aircraft carrier to operate with the Grand Fleet. During 1917–18 she was further modified to accommodate a 284-foot landing deck between her funnel and the stern. A similar but smaller-scale arrangement was adopted for the conversion of the cruiser *Cavendish,* completed as the *Vindictive* in September 1918 with a 106-foot flying-off platform forward and a 193-foot landing platform aft.

Experience with *Furious* pointed to the need for carriers with clear, full-length flight decks. The first of these was *Argus,* converted during 1917–18 from an incomplete Italian liner. She had a 550-foot flight deck and no bridge structure, apart from a small, retractable pilothouse. Her 350-by-68-foot hangar was served by two aircraft lifts and could accommodate twenty aircraft. She did not complete until September 1918 and was too late to take an active part in the war. Two more carriers were begun during the war but did not enter service until the 1920s. Both showed the configuration generally adopted for the majority of later carriers, with full-length flight decks and starboard "island" superstructures. The first was the 21,000-ton *Eagle,* converted from an incomplete battleship originally building for Chile, and the second the 10,850-ton *Hermes*—the first aircraft carrier to be designed as such from the outset.

WAR EXPERIENCE AND EVOLUTION

Wartime Evolution

At the commencement of war the population of Britain saw little reason to doubt the navy's supremacy at sea or its ability to continue its glorious traditions. However, the confidently expected new Trafalgar failed to materialize, and a series of failures and inconclusive engagements eroded the high regard generally held for the service's commanders, ships, and equipment. In part this resulted from a limited understanding of the nature of the naval war and the fact that the navy was undergoing a learning process in the conduct of modern warfare. There were nevertheless less excusable examples of poor judgment and arrogance that slowed this process—most seriously in the late introduction of ocean convoys due to the inadequate methods adopted to evaluate their likely success, combined with general resistance to policy change.

In the first few months of war the navy lost one dreadnought (*Audacious*), nine cruisers (two at the battle of Coronel), and in the Mediterranean failed to prevent the battle cruiser *Goeben* and the cruiser *Breslau* from escaping to Constantinople—one of the factors that encouraged Turkey to enter the war. On the plus side, the navy raided the Helgoland Bight in August, sinking several German ships without loss, and avenged Coronel at the battle of the Falklands in December. However, these were little more than minor actions, and they revealed further problems: the Helgoland Raid succeeded only in spite of poor Admiralty planning, while the Falkland Island battle involved an excessive expenditure of ammunition. The following year was little better: at the battle of Dogger Bank the German battle cruisers escaped from Beatty, with the loss of one armored cruiser, while the Dardanelles operation and the following Gallipoli campaign proved costly failures. Finally, in mid-1916, the one major fleet engagement of the war, the battle of Jutland, produced more losses in ships and men to the British than to the German fleet, no victory for either side, and no change in the strategic situation.

The main fleets did not meet again, and it is not difficult to see that a feeling developed, not least within the fleet itself, that the Grand Fleet was contributing little to the war compared with the sacrifices being made by the army on the western front. While this had some validity in terms of "sacrifice," it was far from correct in terms of strategy.

The Grand Fleet, in its distant northern bases, was there to contain the High Seas Fleet and support the blockade, and in the overall strategic sense it was completely successful in achieving these objects. It was essentially achieved by stalemate—the High Seas Fleet did not wish to engage the full strength of the Grand Fleet and failed in its attempts to draw its enemy into U-boat traps or intercept detached squadrons in the hope of redressing the balance and making a fleet engagement more equitable. At the same time the Grand Fleet, despite several attempts to do so, failed to develop any strategy that would lure the High Seas Fleet to sea. The Admiralty was subjected to much criticism, especially from its own younger officers, for its lack of initiative, but these criticisms seldom suggested any practical means of overcoming the stalemate, and it is difficult to see, with one notable exception, what could have been done to draw out the German fleet. The one exception was the blockade, whose strangulation of German trade should in theory have brought out the fleet in an attempt to break it. Unfortunately, the blockade did not become fully effective until after the United States entered the war, and by the time it was causing severe problems to Germany the High Seas Fleet's ability to fight had been greatly reduced by internal dissension. In this respect the Grand Fleet had something of an advantage over its elusive enemy, in that the morale of its men remained high through the end of the war.

The greatest challenge the navy faced was not, however, the High Seas Fleet but the unrestricted U-boat campaign, which could easily have brought about a British collapse. Its response to that challenge was also its greatest success and represented a true victory in keeping with its traditions—albeit without the great battle-fleet action expected by the public and so desired by the men of the Grand Fleet.

Summary and Assessment

One of the major problems of the North Sea strategy was that the High Seas Fleet could choose its moment to emerge and would almost certainly do so when at maximum strength. The Grand Fleet, on the other hand, had to be constantly ready to meet any challenge and viewed reductions in fleet strength with great concern. This was a particularly difficult problem in the early months of war but eased progressively as new ships joined and earlier problems diminished—principally the detachment of battle cruisers on trade-protection duties, the need to send ships to southern dockyards, and problems with ship's condensers. The early battles of the war were limited in the lessons they provided, and these in some cases were not quite as valuable as they appeared at the time—principally the perceived need to conserve ammunition in the opening stages of action (as a result of the Falkland battle) and the desire for rapid fire (from the battle of Dogger Bank). It was Jutland that provided the most important lessons in regard to fleet action and warship design. This battle saw the loss of three battle cruisers and an armored cruiser to magazine explosions, which were the main causes of the higher number of British ships and men lost during the battle. These explosions—and the fact that other ships had come close to suffering the same fate—led to a tightening of ammunition-handling procedures and improvements in the isolation of magazines and ammunition supply. The losses suffered at Jutland also brought into question the level of armor protection provided for British capital ships, especially battle cruisers.

The arrival of a U.S. squadron of battleships at Scapa Flow in 1917 to join the Grand Fleet as the 6th Battle Squadron gave it absolute battleship preponderance, but there remained considerable concern about the relative strength in battle cruisers and destroyers to the end of the war. The battle cruisers were not only considered insufficient in number but substantially inferior to their German opposite numbers. In the case of destroyers it was simply a perceived lack of numbers, especially as there was no guarantee that those attached to the Grand Fleet would be available in the case of a fleet action, given that several were likely to be absent escorting convoys or covering raids or minelaying operations. Other ships of the Grand Fleet were also likely to be dispersed as close or distant cover, and these were open to attack by superior enemy raiding forces.

These considerations, together with the need to provide capital ships with new shells, magazine isolation, and improved protection to magazines and turret roofs, resulted in a change in policy. This change was initiated by Beatty at an Admiralty Conference in January 1918 at which it was concluded that action with the High Seas Fleet was something best avoided until fleet strength improved and the technical changes had been effected. This change simply resulted in the abandonment of enticement schemes; it did not mean that the Grand Fleet would not engage the High Seas Fleet if it put to sea. The enemy fleet did in fact sortie once more, in April 1918, to cover a raid on the Scandinavian convoy route by its battle cruisers. Fortunately, there were no convoys at sea at the time, and, less fortunately, the German fleet retired before the Grand Fleet could reach an interception position.

While the battle squadrons spent the last two years of war patrolling, exercising, and occasionally providing distant cover for light-force operations, the smaller ships of the fleet were very active. Regular raids took place into the area to the north of Helgoland and into the Skagerrak against enemy patrol vessels, minesweepers, and aircraft, together with numerous assignments covering and escorting convoys and minelaying operations. In general, the commanders of the navy's light forces fought with distinction and showed greater ability to adapt to modern war than the more senior officers of the battle squadrons. In part this was due to greater opportunity, but they were also younger and less imbued with the deference to seniority and rigid adherence to accepted methods that had marked the Victorian age. This showed particularly in the balance of British-German destroyer engagements in the North Sea and English Channel, where the losses on each side were relatively equal despite the generally held view that German flotilla craft were superior in speed, armament, training, and doctrine.

Beyond the North Sea, the navy maintained its hold on the sea communications with Great Britain's worldwide empire with relatively little difficulty, primarily because the German navy, with the exception of its U-boats, had little opportunity to cause serious problems. It was also a relatively simple matter to contain the Ottoman fleet (most importantly the *Goeben*) in the Dardanelles and to support the Italian navy in containing the Austro-Hungarians in the Adriatic.

At the outbreak of war the Royal Navy had the advantage of a large, modern fleet that represented a substantial investment of the nation's wealth. There was, however, considerable scope for improvement in correcting areas of neglect, while other problem areas were revealed by war experience, particularly in relation to ammunition, fire control, and signaling. Solutions to the many difficulties that arose were found in the construction of new types of ships and the introduction of a considerable amount of new equipment and improved munitions. Great progress was made in the development of naval airpower, antisubmarine weapons, fire control, bombardment, and minesweeping equipment (both for sweepers and self-defense). Much of this, especially airpower and submarine detection, was only just reaching maturity in 1918 and had only a limited chance to show its full potential. More importantly, the navy learned and adapted, albeit somewhat slowly at first, and emerged from the war with a well-developed understanding of the methods and ships required for modern warfare. In its junior ranks were men of experience who would serve it well in the next war.

5

ITALY

Regia Marina

Enrico Cernuschi and Vincent P. O'Hara

BACKSTORY

Pre-1914 History

The Regia Marina was established upon the foundation of the united Italian kingdom in 1861. Like any armed service, it developed programs and plans to meet the threats its government considered most likely at the time. Unfortunately for Italy, the theme of the late nineteenth and early twentieth centuries was one of too many potential foes.

Up through 1866 the Regia Marina hurriedly commissioned thirteen ironclads into a force centered on the Sardinian navy, which had hitherto only operated wooden frigates. Its main purpose was to confront the similarly developing Austrian navy and seize Venice as soon as possible. This mission stressed the officer and noncommissioned-officer (NCO) corps, which consisted of a stew of personnel from five navies and was in any case numerically unequal to such a task. The lack of integration was demonstrated by the results of the 1866 battle of Lissa, in which the Austrian fleet defeated its Italian counterpart in the largest naval action fought in the hundred years between Trafalgar and Tsushima.

After the 1866 conflict, the navy struggled with the questions that attend a significant defeat amid a deep budgetary crisis. Meanwhile, Austria remained a bitter opponent, because of the territorial losses it had sustained in the subsequent peace, which included Venice. At the same time a dangerous new threat loomed in the form of the British Mediterranean Fleet, which Rome considered a probable opponent within the framework of a larger confrontation between Paris and London—regarded as a real possibility in Europe during the many war scares of those years. However, when the Franco-Prussian War erupted in 1870, the Italian government ignored French requests for help, and the Regia Marina confined itself to the easy task of supporting the Italian army's advance along the coast as it swiftly absorbed the remnants of the French-protected Papal States into the kingdom.

In 1873 Vienna finally accepted the existence of the unified Italian kingdom and, as a gesture of goodwill, demilitarized the island of Lissa. Meanwhile, the 1866 annexation of Venice vastly improved Italy's naval situation in the Adriatic. In 1871 the increasingly efficient Italian navy began a generic modernization, driven by the need to face threats on 360 degrees, and played an important role in maintaining the Mediterranean balance of power in an atmosphere of growing tension, as the major European states practiced an increasingly dangerous form of nineteenth-century brinkmanship.

In 1877 rumors of a preemptive British strike against Leghorn and Naples as part of a policy to forestall a brewing Russo-Turkish war, as well as Russian attempts to secure control of the Dardanelles, induced the Italian government to abandon its recent policy of rapprochement with Austria-Hungary and Russia. There was another war scare in 1879, when Vienna, after its rupture with Russia, embarked upon a policy of revenge against Italy. Berlin stopped that threat, but it was immediately followed by the more significant crisis of 1881–82, when the French suddenly occupied Tunis and the British asserted control over Egypt. These landgrabs motivated Italy to sign an alliance with Germany and Austria-Hungary in 1882. There finally being an answer to the fundamental question, "Who is the enemy?" Italian navy programs, from 1882 until the early twentieth century, at last had a strategic focus: war against France.

Mission/Function

In a war against France, the Italian intention was to defend the Alps and send a dozen divisions by rail to Germany to contribute to operations in Alsace-Lorraine. The navy would threaten French troop convoys from North Africa. If these reinforcements could be stopped or even delayed—given the planned swiftness of the German invasion of France—the Regia Marina would have accomplished its task. In this type of war Alfred Thayer Mahan's concept of a decisive naval battle made no sense. Given the German navy's modest size at the time, the Regia Marina would be smaller than the Marine Nationale in the Mediterranean Sea, unless, in a best-case scenario, a large fraction of the French fleet was diverted to fight the British in the English Channel.

To wage a traffic war against Paris, the Regia Marina's planners calculated that they required quality battleships and cruisers, individually stronger and faster than the enemy's more numerous units. The innovative talents of the Italian navy engineering corps, already demonstrated in the 1870s by the modern battleships of the *Duilio* class and the proto–battle cruisers *Italia* and *Lepanto,* created an integrated, high-speed force that began entering service in 1885. This combination was continued, following the same formula, by the battleships of the *Re Umberto, Emanuele Filiberto, Regina Margherita,* and *Vittorio Emanuele* classes supplemented by the armored cruisers of the *Marco Polo, Carlo Alberto, Garibaldi, Pisa,* and *San Giorgio* classes, which could also operate with the battle line. Its units individually faster and more powerful than their more numerous French counterparts, this relatively cheap force allowed Italy to face its military commitments on a third of its Latin neighbor's budget, adopting a deterrent strategy fifteen years before the German admiral von Tirpitz' well known *Risiko* policy toward Britain.

In addition to this core of heavy units the Regia Marina commissioned between 1885 and 1917 seventeen protected cruisers and some sloops and gunboats for colonial service, as well as, from 1881 to 1913, 133 torpedo boats supplemented by fifteen torpedo cruisers for the defense of the kingdom's long coastline. The average strength of this coastal force, divided between the Tyrrhenian, Ionian, and Adriatic Seas, was roughly seventy torpedo boats, led by a dozen torpedo cruisers. A coastal submarine force supplemented the torpedo boats after 1905.

In 1914 the Italian merchant navy, the world's third largest in tonnage in 1877, was still rebounding from a slow and economically difficult modernization process following the advent of metal hulls and the adoption of steam machinery during the 1890s. Excluding ships smaller than a hundred tons, the Italian merchant fleet totaled 1,282,115 gross registered tons (GRT) consisting of steamers (933,156 GRT) and sailing vessels (348,959 GRT). This fleet could handle half of the country's peacetime traffic and was supplemented by swarms of small, wooden sailing vessels conducting an intense coastal trade (about 190,000 daily sailings any year during that decade).

For economical and doctrinal reasons the navy did not order battle cruisers, as the Regia Marina was oriented toward the fast battleship principle, which materialized in the 1913 design of the superdreadnought *Caracciolo.* The four *Caracciolo*s were to sail by the end of the decade, supported by three lightly protected five-thousand-ton 6-inch cruisers ordered in 1914.

Although the main purpose of the Italian battle force was to threaten French traffic in the western Mediterranean, in 1906 the naval staff began to consider the possibility of conflict against the improving Austro-Hungarian fleet. Nonetheless, war against France remained the dominant concern, especially after Paris' and London's harsh reaction to Italy's 1912 conquest of Libya. For this reason Regia Marina staff decided to improve operational effectiveness with Germany and Austria-Hungary by implementing procedures for an integrated Triple Alliance fleet in the Mediterranean. In February 1913, after a German request, Italy even ordered three large, special-type destroyers of the *Poerio* class, whose task would be to escort German battle cruisers assigned to perform independent, high-speed missions in the western Mediterranean.

These initiatives demonstrated that in the years between 1909 and 1914 there existed an excellent partnership between Italy and Germany at sea. Berlin was increasingly concerned by the growing tension with Britain and decided to inject some technology into the veins of its Mediterranean allies. The Regia Marina responded to this opportunity enthusiastically. The first and most important benefit was in gunnery. *Dante* had the maximum elevation of her four triple 12-inch batteries increased from twenty to twenty-seven degrees, which expanded potential engagement range from the Tsushima-era limit of seven to eight thousand meters to 24,000 meters.

Nonetheless, when war came in the summer of 1914, Italy was the continent's only major power to resist the siren call to battle. The reasons for this decision were complex. For the purposes of this chapter it is enough to note that they had much to do with the fact that Austria-Hungary had instigated a war of aggression, with the House of Savoy's personal attitudes toward its Teutonic partners, and with the government's perceived interests, which did not correspond to the interests of its allies in this situation. Not surprisingly, Germany and Austria-Hungary were bitterly disappointed by Italy's failure to march with them into battle.

Rome soon discovered, however, that it was not easy for a great power to remain neutral in the frenzy of a continent gone crazy. Both alliances tried to lure Italy into joining their sides, through fair means and foul. For example, the Franco-British coalition practiced polite blackmail in the form of a naval blockade. However, by the spring of 1915 the allied situation had so deteriorated that Italy secured extravagant promises from London, Paris, and, finally, St. Petersburg in payment for a declaration of war against Vienna. These promises, if realized, would secure for Rome an appreciably improved position in the global panorama. On 24 May 1915, the kingdom declared war against Austria-Hungary (but not Germany), seeking the defeat of Vienna but the preservation of Europe's general balance of power as the best guarantee for the nation's autonomy. Thus, Rome found itself confronting a nation it had been allied to for thirty-three years alongside the erstwhile enemy it had constructed a fleet to fight. This situation complicated relations with its allies—especially after Rome brusquely rejected calls to send its battleships through mine-infested waters and submarine ambushes to seek impossible battles with the Austro-Hungarian fleet while the French fleet waited events at Corfu and the British kept their squadron of elderly predreadnoughts at Taranto. It also made the Italian naval staff sensitive to the importance of a powerful fleet in the postwar world.

ORGANIZATION

Command Structure

Administration

The naval ministry administered the navy, set construction programs, and appointed the fleet commander. The position of chief of staff was instituted in 1889, and for almost twenty years a division of responsibilities existed in which staff members concentrated on technical matters while the fleet commander (*Comandante in Capo dell'Armata*) controlled planning and operations.

Command and Fleet Organization

On April 1913 Admiral Paolo Thaon di Revel became chief of staff. A successful cruiser division commander during the Turkish war, he possessed a revolutionary vision of his role and assumed some of the prerogatives of the naval minister, including construction policy, as well as some of the planning functions of the fleet commander, by centralizing planning in Rome.

In August 1914 Admiral Luigi Amedeo di Savoia, Duke of Abruzzi, the king's cousin and third in the line of succession, was appointed fleet commander. The duke favored an active role for the battle fleet in a war against Austria Hungary, in contrast to Thaon di Revel's concept of an opportunistic and calculated-risk guerrilla campaign, which envisioned a fleet action only if enemy battleships sortied to challenge the Strait of Otranto. These contrasting philosophies introduced an element of tension into the Regia Marina's higher echelons. Seeking roles for his fleet, the duke ordered bombardments of the enemy coast and a landing on Pelagosa Island. These activities had scant military value and led to the torpedoing of the armored cruisers *Amalfi* and *Garibaldi* and the British light cruiser *Dublin* by Austrian submarines. These losses worsened the relationship between Thaon di Revel and the duke. On 30 September 1915 Admiral Camillo Corsi, the duke's chief of staff and a skilled politician, became navy minister. He cleverly played his old commander against Thaon di Revel, and on 11 October 1915 the latter resigned his post to become commander in chief at Venice. This allowed Corsi to add to his ministerial role the functions of chief of staff of the navy.

The duke continued to exercise the battle fleet in preparation for the long-awaited decisive general action; however, the mining of the predreadnought *Regina Margherita* on 11 December 1916 off Valona, Albania, with the loss of 684 men, eroded his position. The duke finally resigned on 4 February 1917 for reasons of health, but in fact the real reason for his departure was the reappointment of Thaon di Revel as chief of the naval staff and commander of the Mobilized Naval Force—with full rights to dictate the actions of the admirals. Admiral Corsi held his ministry desk until 16 June 1917, when he too resigned. With the fall of his rivals, Thaon di Revel became the navy's paramount leader. Thereafter a series of admirals held the fleet command, always on a temporary basis, while, for the balance of the war, Thaon di Revel answered to no one but the king.

Photo 5.1. Admiral Thaon di Revel and Captain Costanzo Ciano inspect a pair of Grillo attack craft in the spring of 1918. (Enrico Cernuschi collection)

On 24 May 1915 the fleet was organized into commands, and the individual ships were grouped into squadrons. The Duke of Abruzzi commanded the battle fleet, based at Taranto. Under his command he had four dreadnought and four predreadnought battleships, five armored cruisers (four new and one old), four destroyers, and nine torpedo boats. At Brindisi, Vice Admiral Ernesto Presbitero commanded a squadron consisting of two predreadnoughts and four old armored cruisers. Also present there were three of the modern scouts, five protected cruisers, one torpedo cruiser, three armed merchant cruisers, ten destroyers, twenty torpedo boats, and eight submarines. At Venice, under Rear Admiral Giovanni Patris, the navy had based three predreadnoughts, two old armored cruisers, an old protected cruiser, eleven destroyers, twenty-nine torpedo boats, and thirteen submarines. Another submarine was located at Ancona. (See table 5.1.)

Table 5.1 Regia Marina Order of Battle

Type	Service 24 May 1915	Building 24 May 1915	Authorized 24 May 1915	War losses	Entered service	In service 11 Nov. 1918
Dreadnoughts	5	4	1	1	1	5
Battle cruisers	0	0	0	0	0	0
Predreadnoughts	8	0	0	2	0	6
Coastal-defense ships	5	0	0	0	0	4
Armored cruisers	10	0	0	2	0	5
Protected cruisers/ML	9	2	0	1	0	8
Torpedo cruisers/ML	6	0	0	1	0	5
Scouts	3	0	0	0	0	3
Flotilla leaders	0	9	1	0	9	9
Destroyers	34	7	0	8	18	44
Torpedo boats	68	2	0	6	35	97
Submarines	21	3	34	8	51	50
Sloops	2	0	0	0	0	2
Minelayers	1	0	0	0	0	1
Minesweepers	22	0	0	7	112	127
Gunboats	3	1	0	2	10	11
Auxiliary cruisers	15	0	0	6	2	11
Patrol boats	10	0	0	6	60	64
Submarines chasers	0	0	0	4	99	95
MAS boats	0	2	0	12	181	169

Another factor that affected Italian fleet organization and command structure was an agreement between Rome, London, and Paris signed just prior to Italy's entry into the war, under which Italy reserved for itself command of all allied naval forces operating within the Adriatic. Italy's naval leadership was sensitive to the way alliances could easily shift and the fact that its current allies might be its enemies once the conflict concluded. It also envisioned a sortie of the Austro-Hungarian fleet from Pola, and it did not want to be in a position in which the Regia Marina bore all the risk and cost of meeting such a sortie. Thus, France committed itself to provide twelve large and modern destroyers to Adriatic operations under Italian command, while the British would provide a pair of modern light cruisers and a division of four battleships. Collectively, these forces, along with Italy's Adriatic squadrons, would form the First Allied Fleet and be under Italian command. A Second Allied Fleet, formed by the French battleships and other warships at Corfu and any British and Italian units in the area outside the Adriatic, would operate under French command.

Communications: Tactical and Strategic

Tactical communications were carried out with signal flags supplemented by signal lights. In the area of strategic communications, following experiments conducted by Guglielmo Marconi, the Regia Marina started in 1897 its first land-based wireless system, completing it in 1907. That same year the navy introduced radios on board warships down to the size of destroyers. The development of the technology led from 1914 to an increase in shipboard and land radio stations from 250 to 1,048 by 1918. The navy added an additional 1,410 telegraphic and telephonic stations. In October 1916 it established the Istituto Elettrotecnico e Radiotelegrafico della Regia Marina (MARINELETTRO) at Leghorn. This would become the first Italian electronics center, and in 1917 it produced the first Italian triodes.

In 1917 an Italian direction-finding network began operation, giving the navy's centralized antisubmarine command, the Ispettorato della Difesa del traffico, valuable help in pinpointing the location of enemy submarines and allowing convoys to be directed away from danger zones.

Torpedo and MAS boats had no wireless facilities, as these this equipment was still too cumbersome for such small vessels. Submarines did have them but strictly observed the rule of radio silence. They could receive, of course, but had to surface to transmit and were authorized to broadcast only critical messages, such as the sighting of the always-awaited sortie of the enemy battle fleet from Pola or raids by the Austrian squadron based at Cattaro.

Jamming was also studied, but the frequencies of about 750 kilocycles per second used during those years made this type of electronic warfare ineffective. Another inhibiting factor was that the electric power on warships during this period was about one-fifth of that available in 1940.

Intelligence

In 1908 the Italian navy began to regularly use wireless codes and ciphers. Security, however, was primitive. Italy began to practice signals intelligence (SIGINT) in 1913 by monitoring the volume and characteristics of Austro-Hungarian and French radio traffic. In November 1914 the 2° Reparto established contacts with British intelligence in North Africa during the fight against the Senussi revolt. This partnership proved effective and was developed during the following years to the extent of laying a telegraphic cable between Cyrenaica and Alexandria for rapid and secure communications. On 10 May 1915 the future western allies signed an agreement to exchange information related to the Mediterranean. The system was activated on 24 May 1915 and worked reasonably well during the war.

After Italy entered the war, the Austro-Hungarian navy could read some of the Regia Marina's wireless traffic. Fortunately, the intercepted messages were mainly administrative and of little tactical value. The Italian army initiated efforts against Austro-Hungarian traffic, cracking the enemy's main army code in the summer of 1916. The Regia Marina followed the next year, as a consequence of its recovery from the wreck of the Austro-Hungarian destroyer *Lika* (mined on 29 December 1915 off Durazzo) of the full set of Habsburg naval codes and handbooks. Vienna had changed its codes after the loss, of course, but general knowledge of the system, once integrated with information accumulated over the previous three years, greatly helped Italian and allied code-breaking efforts. Even more important was the April 1916 recovery of German and Austrian codes by Italian divers from inside the wreck of *UC 12*, which sank off Taranto after the explosion of one of her own mines. Austrian-Hungarian codes were not immediately changed, so this coup appreciably increased Italian knowledge of the enemy's wireless habits. The benefits were significant and were demonstrated by opportune changes of convoy routes that explain why the German U-boats newly arrived in the Mediterranean initially enjoyed little success. Regia Marina intelligence also relied heavily on informers, including some junior k.u.k. naval officers, as sources of information.

In the late spring of 1917 the Austro-Hungarian navy totally changed its wireless codes and systems, causing a blackout in Italian and French SIGINT activities. In August of that year the British sent assistance, including a few of their best code breakers, who taught Regia Marina personnel some of the Royal Navy methods used against the Germans. The British appreciation was, however, that the situation in the Adriatic Sea was quite different from that in northern waters. First, the Habsburg navy used its wireless stations sparingly; no more than thirty daily messages were intercepted, compared to a German naval volume that averaged five times more. In addition, the Austro-Hungarians were very careful and followed strict wireless discipline. Nonetheless, British intervention led to some partial successes from autumn 1917 until January 1918, despite code changes subsequent to the desertion to Italy of the crew of the torpedo boat *Tb 11* on 5 October 1917. At the beginning of 1918, however, extensive changes in the Austro-Hungarian naval codes led to another SIGINT blackout.

The most spectacular aspect of the shadow war fought in the Adriatic Sea and beyond was the thrust and parry of sabotage and countersabotage between the Austrians and Italians. The Austrians had dedicated considerable effort to planting agents in Italy. By a clever use of Italian army deserters and using parallel webs activated throughout the peninsula, the naval section of the Evidenzbureau (Austria's directorate of military intelligence) conducted a series of sabotage actions against Italian facilities. Austro-Hungarian intelligence claimed credit for sabotaging the predreadnought *Benedetto Brin* at Brindisi on 27 November 1915 and the dreadnought *Leonardo da Vinci* at Taranto on 2 August 1916. While the Austro-Hungarian claim against *Leonardo da Vinci* has long been disproven, recent research has established that *Brin*'s loss was also caused by an accidental magazine explosion.

Habsburg's claims sparked a strong reaction as Italy inserted double agents into their adversary's network and identified its hub as being the Habsburg consulate in Zurich. Italian agents broke into the consulate on carnival night of February 1917 and forced the safe. According to the Italian minister Ferdinando Martini's diary they discovered the names of more than forty Austro-Hungarian agents, including three members of the Italian parliament. This coup completely unraveled Vienna's spy networks in Italy and allied countries. In fact, in some respects it proved too successful as it jeopardized painstaking Italian efforts to establish Austro-Hungarian trust in Rome's network of double agents. Thus, hoping to regain some of this lost trust, the Italians blamed Habsburg saboteurs when the training cruiser *Etruria* was sunk on 13 August 1918 in the accidental explosion of an ammunition barge alongside, allowing these agents to perform useful services.

Infrastructure, Logistics, and Commerce

During the First World War the Regia Marina easily met its requirements for munitions, food, and uniforms, despite the army's huge demands. The navy's greatest logistic concern during the conflict was coal. Its consumption averaged 60,000 tons a month in 1915 and increased over the next two years to 72,000 tons (allied vessels bunkering in Italian depots included). Navy stocks were 423,000 tons on 31 July 1914, and the Anglo-French blockade prevented much of an increase once war began—by May 1915 reserves totaled only 494,000 tons. Stockpiles stood at 870,000 tons by December 1915, but this was the highest total achieved. From the autumn of 1916 British exports declined, and the navy's reserves dropped to 740,000 tons by December 1916. At that point new cuts in shipments imposed the use of low-caloric Sardinian lignite for navy consumption on land, reserving the best-quality Bristol coal for ships. By autumn 1917, however, the Regia Marina had to surrender 250,000 tons of coal to industry, and in 1918 another 72,000 tons followed. In the meantime, monthly consumption dropped to 35,000 tons, remaining at this level until the end of the war.

The Regia Marina's perceived coal shortages affected operations. As the dreadnoughts had to maintain full readiness and could not jeopardize their training, the navy staff reduced the availability of the four *Vittorio Emanuele*–class battleships at Brindisi, transferring them to Taranto in April 1918. On September 1918 the fuel crisis was considered finally over, as the imports of American coal reversed the decline in the reserve experienced since late 1916.

The Regia Marina's oil situation during the war was better, given the small percentage of oil-fired vessels. In May 1915 there were 129,630 tons available, all imported from Texas in Italian tankers. Imports throughout the war totaled 719,627 tons.

Bases

Italy's network of military harbors during the First World War was inferior to what the 1940–45 situation was to be. On the Adriatic Sea, Venice was the only base that could adequately support the battle force. Its defenses were appreciable and were improved during the war. As long as the city remained in Italian hands the Regia Marina's light forces could bottle up the main Austro-Hungarian fleet at Pola. If the enemy had seized Venice they would have gained the strategic initiative in the upper Adriatic. (See map 5.1.)

Porto Corsini was a channel harbor subject to strong tidal influences and could accommodate only torpedo and MAS boats. Ancona was open to the Adriatic's strong, sudden winds and could shield only coastal forces; its railway links were inadequate and its local industrial base tiny. Bari was a commercial port open to the wind and without naval infrastructure. To find a suitable harbor it was necessary to sail to the excellent and large anchorage of Brindisi. The work to transform Brindisi into a base for light cruisers, flotilla leaders, destroyers, and submarines began in 1908 and was almost complete by the end of the war. Brindisi hosted floating docks of 4,700 and 2,300

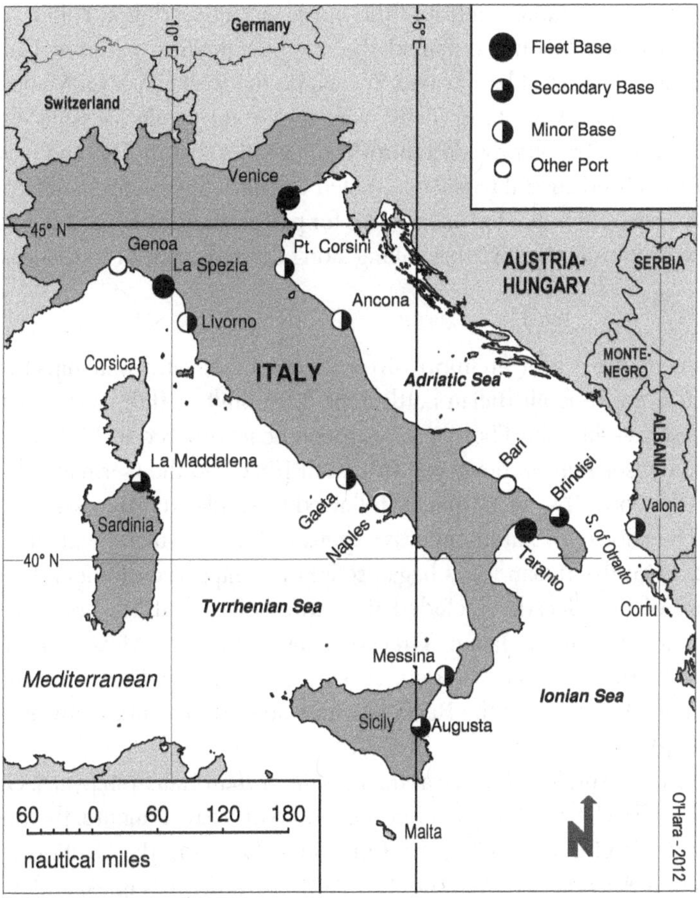

Map 5.1. Italian Naval Bases

tons and some workshops and depots that could perform maintenance, but not major repairs. The lack of yards and industrial facilities and the region's modest rail capacity prevented Brindisi from being a major base.

The other pillar of the Otranto channel was Valona. It had a huge anchorage open to winds, rife with dangerous sandbanks, and with no facilities beyond the moles. The Regia Marina concentrated there its few mobile base resources, including depot ships, the floatplane tender *Europa*, tugs, water carriers, oilers, transports, barges, pontoons, floating cranes, and small floating docks of 145 to 250 tons. The minor Albanian harbors of Porto Palermo and Santi Quaranta served as temporary anchorages.

Taranto was the Regia Marina's major base. Should the enemy battle fleet at Pola sortie, Taranto's strategic value depended on the fleet's ability to exercise continuous control of the upper Adriatic, while the light forces at Brindisi and Valona contained the enemy squadron based at Cattaro. The other main naval base was at Spezia, on the west coast. La Maddalena in Sardinia and Augusta in Sicily were important, while Messina, Gaeta, Leghorn, and Tripoli provided third-level facilities. From 1916 the requirement to defend coastal traffic compelled the navy to organize a network of minor bases and protected anchorages for patrol boats, MAS, and seaplanes, as well as for merchant vessels sailing along the Italian and Libyan coasts.

Industry

Italian engineers have an impressive resumé of innovative warships to their credit. After 1865 all Italian battleships were built in Italy, and new types of warships—like the Thornycroft torpedo boats ordered in 1876, the protected cruiser *Bausan* bought in Britain in 1882, and the German Schichau destroyers of 1899—were quickly followed by similar Italian vessels.

The choice for autonomy was expensive but paid high dividends from 1892, when the Italian yards began selling warships to customers that over a span of two decades included the navies of Argentine, Brazil, China, Denmark, Germany, Japan, Greece, Haiti, Morocco, Mexico, Portugal, Romania, Russia, Spain, Sweden, Turkey, and Uruguay. These exports paid for about 40 percent of the Regia Marina's new construction between 1896 and 1914.

In 1914 Ansaldo Genoa was the most important Italian shipyard. Others included FIAT San Giorgio of Spezia, Odero of Sestri Ponente, the Società Esercizio Bacini of Riva Trigoso, Orlando at Leghorn, the Cantieri Navali Riuniti at Ancona and Palermo, the Pattison yards in Naples, and Tosi at Taranto. The Regia Marina's arsenals at Venice, Spezia, Taranto, and the Regio Cantiere di Castellamare di Stabia also constructed warships. Five of these yards—Castellamare, the Spezia Arsenal, Ansaldo Genoa, Odero Genoa, and Orlando at Leghorn—were capable of constructing battleships. The Italian shipbuilding capability was sufficient to offset losses of warships and undertake necessary refits and repairs, working on a total of 7,411 ships, (708 allied), in 166,588 working days (15,933 for allied vessels).

Shipping

In 1916 the Regia Marina began to escort important freighters along its coasts. With the acquisition of additional auxiliary patrol boats (usually fishery vessels bought abroad), the navy progressively extended coastal convoys and in January 1917 introduced convoys to Sardinia and later to the eastern

Mediterranean and Gibraltar. These efforts and others, like centralized control of domestic tonnage, guaranteed the critical traffic with Gibraltar from January 1918. The numbers for that last year of war were 197,692 GRT of Italian shipping sunk in the Mediterranean Sea and 68,356 in the Atlantic. The coastal trade suffered fewer losses, and during the year the tonnage situation of Italian imports was finally secured with the help in 1918 of 126,000 GRT of American merchant vessels.

Italian imports totaled, in millions of tons:

1915	16.2
1916	15.3
1917	10.7 (and 0.5 from France by rail)
1918	10.6 (and 3.1 from France by rail).

Losses at sea, negligible in 1915, totaled 104,000 tons of supplies in 1916, 241,000 in 1917, and 77,000 in 1918—that is, 1.1 percent of the materials sent by ship during those years. These numbers confirm the hard fact that if little arrived from the autumn of 1916, it was because little was shipped.

The parallel story of littoral shipping defense followed the same lines. Coastal traffic was a pillar of Italian interior communications, engaging 614,000 GRT, excluding vessels under one hundred tons. Between 1915 and 1918, submarines and mines sank 47,151 GRT of wooden sailing ships under five hundred tons. By year, these losses break down as follows:

1915	1,020
1916	13,329
1917	22,658
1918	10,144.

During the period, new construction of about 70,000 GRT of wooden sailing ships more than replaced these losses. The vessels sunk and the cargo lost were of minor strategic relevance, in spite of the psychological effect, compared to the decisive role that coastal traffic played in sustaining Italy's economy. In 1917 the expansion of the coastal convoy system correspondingly led to the increase of coastal forces stationed along the Tyrrhenian and the Ionian Seas and associated defenses, such as shore batteries, protected anchorages, air patrols, and minefields. By November 1918 convoys had become the rule rather than the exception, due to the large number of small escorts under the orders of the *Dipartimenti* (regional commands)—twenty old destroyers, forty-five torpedo boats, 182 MAS, and 206 auxiliary patrol vessels, compared to less than fifty escorts available in early 1916. Eighteen small auxiliary cruisers—joined from early 1917 by a collection of old torpedo cruisers, old destroyers, and torpedo boats—escorted high-seas traffic. The Italian navy introduced 624 hydrophones (including twelve coastal stations created in 1918) during the war's last two years.

An impressive effort created a network of *Punti rifugio* (protected anchorages) where merchant vessels menaced by enemy submarines could seek refuge. The materials used for this system included 9,370,061 square meters of steel nets, 3,500 anchors, 345 kilometers of chain, 6,500 kilometers of steel wire, 2,200 buoys, 6,000 floating cylinders and 400 beacons. By 1918 minefields and shore batteries protected these refuges, as well as Spezia, La Maddalena, and Taranto, for a total of 481 mines and 334 batteries armed with 702 guns manned by navy and army personnel. They engaged German submarines 167 times, usually saving the merchant vessels under attack.

Personnel

Demographics

In 1914 the Regia Marina had 2,139 officers and 45,707 enlisted men. The naval command had already judged the number of its officers inadequate for war during the 1911–12 conflict against the Ottomans, but the selective training and promotion system in place since 1880 did not permit rapid expansion. The five-year curriculum at the Regia Accademia Navale produced 140 to 250 cadets annually. Through calling up the personnel in the naval reserve, many of whom came from the merchant fleet, and other emergency measures, the Regia Marina ended the war with six thousand officers. This number was still short of requirements, given the many land billets, and it imposed on the men at sea heavy service and frequent changes of ships. The number of enlisted men increased from 76,620 in 1916 to 130,213 by 1918.

The number of NCOs was adequate, although some technical billets experienced shortages. In 1914 the enlisted force included one-third volunteers, with the balance being three-year draftees. The availability of large numbers of merchant sailors and fishermen recruited in the maritime provinces allowed the Regia Marina to acquire men of high physical standards. According to an excellent study by Francesco Zampieri of the Italian navy's prewar social history, 43.2 percent of enlisted personnel were merchant sailors who had entered that career as boys and had thus learned much of what was needed to serve; 31.8 percent were fishermen; 9.7 percent riverine professionals; 9.8 percent were workers in yards or factories that supplied the navy; 2.9 percent were shipwrights or carpenters; and 1.7 percent were engine personnel (usually stokers), with the balance other categories.

Training: Culture

About two-thirds of the navy's officers hailed from the northern provinces, while the proportion of enlisted personnel was roughly the inverse. Aware that a poorly amalgamated officer and NCO corps had contributed to the disaster at Lissa, the Italian navy concentrated its training on producing professionals bound to the navy first and last. Naval officers served long-term and were graduates of the Regia Accademia Navale di Livorno, which was established in 1881.

In spite of traditional wisdom that considered the Regia Marina more devoted to the monarchy than was the army, the service's greatest loyalty was actually to the united state and to Italy's enduring naval traditions, principally embodied by the maritime states of Genoa and Venice. Between 1891 and 1905 only 11 percent of the officer corps harkened from the nobility, and this number declined in the ensuing decades. This was quite a change from the old Sardinian navy. No social barriers existed from the early 1870s that precluded qualified individuals from obtaining the positions of admiral, minister of the navy, or chief of staff. This access encouraged innovation and discipline. During the world war the concern traditionally shown by officers for their men's welfare, the service's relatively limited size (compared to the 5.2 million men in the Regio Esercito, or army), and the professional nature of the sailors (who as civilians mostly belonged to the maritime world) allowed the Regia Marina to always maintain discipline without the crises that affected some other navies.

THE WAYS OF WAR

Surface Warfare

Doctrine

The fire-by-salvo doctrine adopted by the Regia Marina in 1902 mirrored contemporary Royal Navy practice, but by 1914 advances in fire-control technology in Great Britain, the United States, and Germany had surpassed Italian procedure, which was based on the output of fire directors supplemented by manual tables and instruments like slide rules to perform the necessary calculations. Not until 1919 did Italy introduce an electromechanical fire-control table calculator, the Salvagnini model. That same year saw the first installation, on the new destroyer *Falco,* of follow-the-pointer dials and a director and bearing transmitter of the Girardelli type with electrical data transmission and training motors, which itself was inspired by a French experimental Le Prieur system studied in 1915.

In 1915 the plan for a fleet action called for the dreadnoughts, the modern predreadnoughts, and the four most modern armored cruisers to sail to contact with the enemy in separate divisions. A scout division consisting of *Quarto* and the two *Bixio*s would give warning of the enemy fleet and allow the battle fleet's divisions to unite into one battle line and adopt the proper dispositions. Given the fire-control limitations, battle ranges would not exceed 10,000 meters.

Since 1905 night-fighting doctrine had been based on searchlights and regarded the torpedo as the primary weapon. The navy's designers preferred single tube mountings, as rapidly developing engagements at short ranges were considered most likely, affording only brief chances to aim and launch. The navy considered night gunnery on destroyers and torpedo boats of minor importance. The lack of flashless charges (for either guns or torpedo tubes, until 1924) and of illuminating shells confirmed the low priority the Italian navy assigned to night combat and helped explain the inconclusive results of the many night actions fought in the Adriatic Sea between 1915 and 1918.

Ships/Weapons

The Italian navy responded to the naval revolution caused in 1906 by the all-big-gun *Dreadnought* with the 1909 *Dante* class. It introduced scout cruisers in 1909, with the *Quarto.* By 1916, six 12-inch battleships—1913's *Dante,* 1914's *Da Vinci* and *Cesare,* 1915's *Cavour* and *Duilio,* and 1916's *Doria*—formed the core of the Italian battle fleet. To support the fleet the Regia Marina could deploy three modern scouts (*Quarto, Bixio,* and *Marsala*) and a new generation of 740-ton destroyers (the *Indomito* class) to replace the 350-ton destroyers commissioned between 1900 and 1910.

The evolution of warship design in the Mediterranean was by 1910 less advanced than in the North Sea, where the world's two main navies had been competing for almost twenty years. Paris, Rome, and Vienna—not to mention Madrid, Athens, and Constantinople—had not reached by 1914/15 the state of the art achieved by their northern counterparts in weaponry and fire control. This gap was only partially filled during the war and can be considered equalized only from the early 1930s. In the context of the regional role to which it was thus limited, Italian warship design, as tested during World War I, proved effective. More numerous and powerful than their k.u.k. counterparts and with better turns of speed, the Italian dreadnoughts kept that adversary at bay, in a small-scale version of the Anglo-German confrontation in the North Sea. The same words can be used for the three modern light cruisers. Like the four similar Austro-Hungarian scouts, they were a vital complement to the battle line, with the task of supplying the admiral information about the enemy formation. They were a poor man's answer to the proud battle cruisers in the North Sea but one proportional to the size of the opposing fleets in the Adriatic.

The Italian navy was, however, able to develop during the war its own *esploratori leggeri,* nine flotilla leaders without equivalent in the Habsburg navy, which could only appreciate those well-armed and speedy warships and dream of ordering something similar from its own impoverished yards. The French were likewise impressed by these useful ships and rushed to construct their own *contre-torpilleurs* after the war.

Regarding Italian destroyers, it was always Admiral Thaon di Revel's policy to order repeats of well-tested designs. His preference for quantity above all else proved sound. This principle saw the repetition of the useful PN-type torpedo boats. However, the Regia Marina also proved capable of innovation, as demonstrated by that most famous component of its "mosquito fleet," the MAS motor torpedo boat. Although the navy commissioned swarms of them (244 boats), giving useful, if far from ideal, support to coastal antisubmarine defenses, experience soon proved that only the best commanders and crews (never more than two dozen) could achieve results in the Adriatic Sea in the offensive role. Nevertheless, accurate planning, seamanship, and the correct application of the principle of expendability allowed the Regia Marina to reap an excellent harvest, inducing the enemy to assign to those little wooden boats fantastic characteristics, from speed to armor, and to try, with no result, to square the circle by projecting and building a poorly designed twenty-six-ton *Panzerboote* as a reply. Special attack craft were another Italian innovation that went on to earn an illustrious record in war.

The ragtag escort fleet of armed merchant cruisers, old torpedo boats, converted fishery vessels, and motor boats gathered by the Regia Marina was improvised, but it worked to control the German submarine menace, with the help of a progressively improved air branch and central command.

On the other side of the coin, submarines had few opportunities to achieve more than incidental results. Only increased numbers and experience gained in sweat and blood could help in such a task, and once again the policy was to order the greatest number of boats the yards could deliver. The mass production of the proven F class, actually an updated *Medusa,* was a correct course at the time. The Regia Marina, however, had deeply studied, before and during World War 1, the development, tactics, and doctrine of the submarine, and after 1918 it was the first to project and order new boats based on untested formulas. The transition from boats that were able to dive only to forty meters to boats that could reach three hundred meters by 1922 was an extraordinary adventure in naval architecture, one that confirmed the great (maybe excessively great) hopes the governments and the naval staff lavished on the submarine branch despite its modest role between 1915 and 1918.

Photo 5.2. The cruiser *Pisa* at Constantinople in 1919 (Enrico Cernuschi collection)

Guns

In 1871 Italy lacked the ability to independently develop modern artillery, for budgetary and technological reasons. Only in 1884 did the navy begin constructing weapons, under license from Armstrong Elswick. Relationships with other foreign companies followed. Finally, in 1916, Ansaldo began to slowly develop its own projects. Guns based on British experience proved serviceable, but their mountings suffered problems. Fuses were all Krupp types. Range finders were tested from 1894 and adopted at last in 1907. The models chosen were the classic Barr and Stroud coincidence models of 0.8-, 1.37-, 2.74-, and 4.57-meter (fifteen-foot) bases imported from Britain, until 1918, when the Italian enterprises Galilei of Florence and San Giorgio of Genoa were able to commence production. The German navy proposed in 1909 its brand-new Zeiss stereoscopic range finders, but the staff considered these too complicated. (See table 5.2.)

Torpedoes

Although Italy first produced torpedoes in 1887, the navy's attention was focused on gunnery, and it paid modest attention to torpedoes throughout the war. The torpedo branch was assigned relatively few personnel and did not attract the highest-quality people. This was one reason why torpedoes

Table 5.2 Italian Guns

Bore	Cal.	Model	Shell (kg)	MV (m/s)	Range (yds.) / elevation (deg.)	F/C (rds./min.)	Ship or class
15.0/381	40	Vickers 1914	884	700	n/a	1.2	*Caracciolo*
12.0/305	46	Armstrong and Vickers 1909	452	840	18,000 / 20 22,310 / 16	2	*Dante, Cesare, Doria*
12.0/305	40	Armstrong 1904	385	770	14,000 / 25	1	*Regina Elena*
10.0/254	45	Armstrong	227	870	25,000 / 25	2.6	*Pisa, San Giorgio*
7.48/190	45	Armstrong	90.9	864	22,000 / 25		*Pisa, San Giorgio*
6.0/152	50	Vickers	50	870	n/a	3.5	
6.0/152	45	Schneider 1911	47	830	n/a	3.3	*Doria*
4.7/120	50	Armstrong Vickers 1909	22.75	840	n/a	6	*Dante, Cavour, Quarto, Bixio*
4.7/120	45	Armstrong 1913	22	750	15,400 / 32	7	
4.0/102	45	Schneider-Canet 1917	16	840	14,600 / 30	7	
4.0/102	35	Armstrong 1914	15	755	11,700 / 45	7	*Pilo, Sirtori*
3.0/76	50	Vickers 1908	7	815	n/a	15	*Dante, Cavour*
3.0/76	45	Schneider- Canet 1911	6.5	760	n/a	15	*Doria*
3.0/76	40	Armstrong 1912	5.9	680	10,000 / 42	15	*Regina Elena*

accomplished relatively little during the war. In May 1915 the Regia Marina had 1,924 torpedoes, including old 356-mm models and new 450-mm ones imported from Austria-Hungary. To accommodate war demand, the British enterprise Whitehead created a new plant at Naples in 1915, and production began the next year. A total of 624 weapons were accepted before the war's end. These torpedoes proved to be sound. The Regia Marina expended 448 torpedoes during the war. The weapons used ranged from the 356-mm model B57 of 1885, which had a 57-kg warhead and a range of six hundred meters at twenty-four knots and a thousand meters at twenty-one knots; to the 450-mm A90 of 1898, with a 90-kg warhead and a range of three thousand meters at thirty-one knots; to the 450-mm A115 of 1914, with its 115-kg warhead and a range of a thousand meters at forty-one knots and three thousand meters at thirty-one knots.

Photo 5.3. Torpedo tube on the torpedo boat *34 PN* (Enrico Cernuschi collection)

Submarine Warfare

Offensive

Doctrine

The Italian navy initially considered the submarine a defensive weapon. The first attempts to enlarge small "Adriatic" boat projects into deepwater cruisers resulted in the disappointing *Pietro Micca* class, ordered in 1914 and commissioned from 1918. This experience confirmed that Italy's designs and doctrine lagged far behind German standards. The navy also pursued an ambitious effort to design a single-engine submarine with the ability to operate underwater at relatively high speeds without the need to surface to recharge batteries. This seemed an attractive shortcut to sea power that was far cheaper than constructing battleships, but the effort proved vastly premature, despite considerable resources expended. Italy also constructed midget boats beginning in 1915, but they achieved almost no results. This mess of ideas confirmed, however, the submarine branch's initiative spirit and enthusiasm, and in April 1916 it received a new central command, the Ispettorato sommergibili e aviazione, dedicated to the appointment of personnel, training, maintenance, new construction, and planning. This initiative confirmed the influence of Admrial Thaon di Revel's ideas about the decisive "third dimension" role of submarines and naval air forces in a modern navy.

When the war begun, Italian attack boats were tasked with harassing the enemy in the Adriatic Sea. Operations against merchant vessels initially followed the Hague Convention prize rules. This political choice precluded any success, as Austro-Hungarian traffic sailed behind the Dalmatian island barrier and was further protected by minefields, shore batteries, and sighting stations. Moreover, Italian torpedoes had defective pistols, as was discovered when a torpedo fired by the submarine *Velella* against the Austro-Hungarian destroyer *Uskoke* on 15 August 1915 failed to explode. This problem plagued the Italian navy throughout the war despite many tests and modifications. Fifteen torpedoes launched by submarines and MAS boats hit their targets but did not detonate, thus sparing one battleship, two destroyers, three submarines, two torpedo boats, and five other vessels.

The Italian submarine force's main task was to supplement the minefields and torpedo boats penning the enemy battle fleet in port. Scouting the enemy coast and harbors was another role, and it greatly assisted the navy's actions against Austro-Hungarian bases. Another task was hunting enemy submarines based at Cattaro. Any opportunity to target warships was, of course, welcome. After January 1916 the government authorized unrestricted warfare against Austro-Hungarian traffic, and this prompted the Habsburg navy to escort convoys from Fiume to Durazzo. With no more than one or two Italian boats on offensive patrol along more than four hundred miles of coasts with some thousands of islands, submarines were only a nuisance force. During the war's last two years, numbers increased as new and more efficient F-class boats replaced the worn-out submarines commissioned before the war and doubled the force available, allowing a daily presence in the Adriatic of three to four Italian and one allied boat. Minelaying missions commenced with an operation in May 1918 by a pair of Italian submarines in company with the British *E46*.

Given such a state of affairs, the results submarines obtained in the Adriatic Sea were modest: four steamers and a submarine were sunk by Italian submarines, and two destroyers, one torpedo boat, and an auxiliary escort vessel were damaged. French submarines sank three steamers and a submarine and damaged one destroyer, one torpedo boat, and one hospital ship. The British sunk an enemy submarine (and an Italian one). The price paid for these successes was high: seven Italian, five French, and two British boats were lost.

In any case, there was no possibility that a successful tonnage war could be fought against the Austro-Hungarians, who had plenty of freighters laying idle along the Adriatic coast. Throughout the war Vienna lost or had damaged approximately 20 percent of its available tonnage of small steamers—the agent of loss being almost equally submarines and mines.

Boats/Weapons

Italy entered the war with a submarine fleet comprising small coastal units. The five boats of the *Glauco* class of 1905–1909 and the eight units of the *Medusa* class of 1911–13 were supplemented by seven miscellaneous boats from one- or two-unit classes launched between 1908 and 1914. These twenty boats ranged in size from the 157-ton *Glauco* class to 345 tons in the two-unit *Pullino* class of 1913. All had two bow 17.7-inch torpedo tubes and carried two spare torpedoes. Their maximum ranges hovered at around a thousand nautical miles, and speeds were as great as fourteen knots on the surface and nine submerged.

Antisubmarine

The first antisubmarine weapons adopted in 1915 were towed torpedoes. On 21 February 1918 the Italian torpedo boat *Airone* achieved one of the few successes with this kind of system, sinking the Austro-Hungarian *U 23* off Valona.

In 1916 the Regia Marina began using British-made depth charges with 50-kg charges. These weapons were manufactured in Italy the following year. War production totaled 5,656 depth charges, while consumption was just 603. Only a few depth charges were carried by escort ships, but the real problem was the lack of sensors. Experimental hydrophones did not materialize on Italian ships until 1917. The lack of effective sensors during the Great War (and for almost twenty years thereafter) reduced the interest that the naval staff took in antisubmarine warfare. Lack of money did not help, of course, but the common appreciation was that according to the experiences of 1917–18, the antisubmarine needs of a war in the Mediterranean could be met by implementing convoys escorted by auxiliary warships and floatplanes, allowing destroyers and specialized torpedo boats to protect the sorties of the bigger warships.

Mine Warfare

Doctrine

In 1913 when Admiral Paolo Thaon di Revel became chief of staff, Italian mine inventories increased dramatically from two hundred to more than three thousand modern weapons in May 1915. The upper Adriatic was shallow and easily mined. Thaon di Revel envisioned large minefields that would alter geography and deny the Austrian battle fleet access to the high seas and thus reduce the naval conflict to a guerrilla and fleet-in-being confrontation.

Weapons

At the beginning of the conflict Italian mines were all of the Bollo type. Local auxiliary vessels and the old torpedo cruisers *Goito, Minerva, Partenope,* and *Tripoli* conducted defensive minelaying operations, while destroyers and torpedo boats and, after 1917, MAS boats conducted offensive operations. The first Italian minelaying submarines followed in 1918; these were the former enemy boat *UC 12* (sunk by its own weapons off Taranto on March 1916, raised, and reconstructed under the new name *X 1*) and a pair of similar boats, *X 2* and *X 3*.

During the war new fields were laid continuously, and old fields needed maintenance, because strong Adriatic gales often broke mooring cables and hundreds of mines became floaters—often still armed due to unreliable security devices. During the war the navy yards and the private enterprises of Pignone in Florence and San Giorgio of Spezia produced 11,735 new Bollo mines of the moored contact type and some dozens of the new S.G. 125/1916 for submarines—a direct derivative of German weapons found off Taranto. An additional 2,279 mines were imported from France. They were the small Breguet type, with 62 kg charges, used by the MAS, and three Sautter-Harlé models (75/1911, 70/1916, and 100/1916), all of the usual contact type and which could be moored in water up to 125 meters deep. These characteristics permitted the effective mining of the upper Adriatic but not the deep waters off Cattaro, a fact that allowed enemy submarines to operate from that base. Between 1915 and 1918 the Regia Marina laid 12,293 mines. The Otranto Barrage required 1,800 Bollo mines; the remainder were mostly laid in the upper Adriatic and along the lower Adriatic coasts, as well as in defensive minefields and some small barrages off major west-coast harbors.

German minelayer submarines proved a major menace to Italian shipping. They placed a total of 565 weapons along the Italian coasts outside the Adriatic (76 in 1916, 287 in 1917, and 202 in 1918). These mines, which in the final 1918 version reached the depth of 220 meters, caused the loss of most of the sixteen Italian steamers mined between 1915 and 1918 (one in 1915, four in 1916, nine in 1917, and two in 1918). To face this challenge Italian minesweeping forces—in 1915, a mere dozen motorized fishing vessels with Oropesa mechanical devices—increased in the western Mediterranean to more than eighty auxiliary minesweepers, joined later by the first RD-class military vessels. A quarter of the force was always at sea, screened from the beginning by patrol boats, gunboats, torpedo boats, and old destroyers of the escort force. They recovered or destroyed 309 German mines, all of the moored contact type, outside the Adriatic between 1916 and 1918.

Italy's extensive mining effort was an important factor in limiting the enemy battle fleet's access to the upper Adriatic. (The old Italian battleships in Venice suffered, of course, a similar limitation, needing significant sweeping and escort forces whenever they sortied.) The total losses suffered by both sides to mines were nearly equal: at least ten Austro-Hungarian steamers sunk and seven damaged, along with two destroyers, one torpedo boat, and two submarines sunk. In additional to the aforementioned steamers, the Regia Marina lost the battleship *Regina Margherita*, one destroyer, one torpedo boat, and two submarines. That predreadnought's loss (caused by a German submarine minefield but attributed during the war to Italian mines hit due to a navigational error and bad weather in Valona Bay on 11 December 1916) was in fact a brilliant success, but at the time the rule that mine warfare is tactically self-canceling in the long run seemed confirmed once again.

Amphibious Warfare

<u>Doctrine/Capabilities</u>

In 1892 Regia Marina doctrine dictated that amphibian operations would be conducted by landing companies from cruisers and battleships, using the warships' steam-driven boats and barges. After this coup de main had secured a beachhead, army troops, heavy weapons, and horses and carts would follow, using pontoons (*zatteroni da sbarco*) ferried on the decks of transports and towed to shore by the steamboats. Such a scheme required an extended period of good weather and a lack of opposition.

In 1907 the Regia Marina and the Regio Esercito began to train together. The original program was to prepare for landings in Albania and Dalmatia in response to an Austro-Hungarian invasion of Albania, but from

1909 the stricter partnership with Germany and the need to get Berlin's support for the future occupation of Libya induced the alliance staff to project an Italo-Austrian invasion of Malta. The plan was completed in 1911 and thereafter constantly updated. The Italian army was confident, especially as the island garrison was less than a brigade, but the navy had many doubts. The landing at Tripoli on 5 October 1911, which was occupied by fewer than 1,600 sailors of the battle fleet's *compagnie da sbarco,* confirmed that Italian interservice efficiency was far from ideal, as it took six days for army troops to replace this weak force. In 1912, confirming the alliance's optimistic assessment of the Mediterranean strategic situation—given the planned arrival of a German squadron, French inferiority to the combined Regia Marina and k.u.k. battle fleets, and the British Mediterranean Fleet's reduction to a pair of battle cruisers—the Italian army also planned a landing in Provence, a scheme it updated until the summer of 1914.

During the world war, in September 1914, Italian sailors occupied Saseno (Sazan) Island off Valona, then Valona itself in October. On 9 July 1915 a naval force landed on Pelagosa Island. The assault was a modest affair, but the fact that the small force of sailors was able to repulse a much larger Austro-Hungarian counterlanding operation on 28 July gave this enterprise a certain notoriety. Further landings were conceived in 1916 against the Curzolari Islands and Sabbioncello Peninsula, but the Italian army withheld the troops needed for these enterprises. The same happened in 1917 for a projected landing in Istria.

Beyond penny-packet raids by sailors and *Arditi* (Regio Esercito shock troops) landed by MAS boats along the River Piave, the upper Adriatic coasts, and Lake Garda, a new cycle of Regia Marina landing operations finally began in October 1918. The harbors of Durazzo, San Giovanni di Medua, Alessio, Scutari, Dulcigno, and Pelagosa Island were occupied from the sea on 14 and 30 October and on 1, 2, and 3 November respectively, following the Austro-Hungarian retreat and before the arrival of Italian army troops.

Coastal Defense

Italian ports, particularly along the Adriatic coast, were well defended by an array of coastal batteries. By May 1917 Venice's defenses consisted of the modern Batteria Amalfi at Punta Sabbioni, a twin 15-inch turret (originally made for the *Caracciolo* battleships), six 12-inch guns (two recovered from the sunken battleship *Benedetto Brin*), six old 12.64-inch guns, twenty four old 280-mm howitzers, six 9.45-inch guns, twenty-nine 6-inch, and twenty-six 4.7-inch, as well as twenty 4-inch antiaircraft guns and sixty-seven 3-inch antiaircraft guns. The base's decisive importance justified such firepower.

Porto Corsini, like the mouths of the River Po and the small fishery harbor of Comacchio, had 6- and 4.7-inch batteries, together with 3-inch antiaircraft guns. Ancona's coastal batteries consisted of two 10-inch guns on the dominating Monte Conero, a single 8-inch gun, and nine 280-mm howitzers. Bari was initially protected by 6- and 4.7-inch guns. Brindisi was reinforced by two 15-inch twin turrets and a single mounting of the same caliber, supplemented by a 12-inch gun. Before those three batteries were completed the harbor was defended by four 10-inch guns and eight 280-mm howitzers. Valona, after its seizure in 1914, had a dozen 6- and 4.7-inch guns emplaced on the small island of Saseno, which dominated the bay. The predreadnoughts *Dandolo, Italia, Re Umberto,* and *Sardegna* also served as floating batteries in various southern ports, depending upon need. Six- and 4.7-inch batteries also protected the small Albanian harbors of Porto Palermo and Santi Quaranta.

Aviation: Naval Aviation

The Regia Marina's first step along the road of naval aviation came in June 1905 with the private development of a functional airship, *Italia*. In October 1907, after years of experiments with a tethered naval-kite float, the navy adapted a telephonically linked balloon towed by the 2,800-ton protected cruiser *Elba* for mine detection. Next Italy commissioned its first military airship, *N.1,* in September 1908. The navy validated the potential of shipborne air in 1911 using a *draken* kite balloon tethered to the brig *Cavalmarino;* the balloon spotted for warships during the bombardments of Tripoli. In 1913–14 the dreadnought *Dante,* the predreadnoughts *Vittorio Emanuele* and *Roma,* and the armored cruisers *San Giorgio* and *San Marco* deployed Curtiss float biplanes. These aircraft were disembarked in June 1914 in favor of using *Elba* as a fleet floatplane carrier. By May 1915 the Regia Marina had thirty floatplanes and two airships. The efficiency rate was modest, the Italian aviation industry was in its infancy, and Austro-Hungarian air superiority was a fact.

In May 1915 the Regia Marina added another seaplane tender, *Europa,* formerly the freighter *Quarto.* Four months later *Elba,* which could carry only two Curtiss flying boats, was transferred to other duties, while *Europa* went to Brindisi. Her ten flying boats performed useful reconnaissance services, but the ship was too slow to serve with the battle fleet as a real seaplane carrier. Transferred to Valona in January 1916, the *Europa* remained there until the end of the war as a seaplane and submarine depot ship, with a complement of Macchi L1 (and later Macchi L.2), FBA, and M.5 fighters.

Reconnaissance and ASW patrol duties were conducted by the Macchi L.1, L.2, and L.3 flying-boat types, which could carry two hundred kilograms of bombs. In 1918 some SIAI S.8 floatplanes and Macchi M.8 and M.9 flying boats, all with greater range, joined the antisubmarine patrols.

The fighter role, both pursuer and escort, was performed from 1916 by the Macchi L.1 and the small Macchi M.3 flying boat. They were replaced after July 1917 by the similar but more powerful Macchi M.5, an excellent aircraft that could down even the most modern Austro-Hungarian fighters.

WAR EXPERIENCE AND EVOLUTION

Geography and the nature of the opposition dictated the course of Italy's naval war. The Regia Marina faced the k.u.k. navy across the long and narrow Adriatic Sea. In the Adriatic, Italy's major naval concerns were to contain the enemy's battle fleet, harass his coastal traffic, protect the Italian army's seaward flank, and guard the national coastline, coastal traffic, and communications with Albania. After the appearance of German submarines in the Mediterranean the Regia Marina was also forced to develop a large antisubmarine force and a doctrine for its employment. Efforts to block enemy submarines from transiting the narrow Straits of Otranto, first with drifters and trawlers and later with a fixed mine barrage, was another major project, although most of the resources involved were British or French.

The Adriatic Sea consists of upper and lower zones, each with unique characteristics. In the upper Adriatic were located the major Italian base, at Venice and, just sixty miles east-northeast, the major Austrian harbor of Trieste, and also, ninety miles southeast of Venice, the main base of the Habsburg fleet, Pola. Despite the proximity of these strongholds and the presence in Venice of some old battleships and armored cruisers used for shore bombardments and coastal defense, supplemented sometimes by a single modern flotilla leader, the naval war in the upper Adriatic was fought mainly by destroyers, torpedo boats, MAS, shore batteries, and floatplanes. The strategic and psychological impact of shore bombardments and air attacks against towns and shipping was always modest. On both sides of the Adriatic few warships and merchant vessels were sunk or damaged by aerial bombs in actions against enemy bases. The threat of submarines and mines was omnipresent and further impeded the deployment of large warships, especially after an Austro-Hungarian submarine torpedoed and sank the large cruiser *Amalfi* on 7 July 1915, when the ship ventured out of Venice in support of Italian destroyers.

Both the Italians and the Austro-Hungarians used barges to supply the flanks of their armies. The amount of material transported by Italian ships in this region rose from 61,900 tons in 1915 to 524,956 in 1916, to 769,500 in 1917, and finally 1,381,900 tons in the war's last year. By 1918 the corresponding Habsburg traffic averaged five thousand tons a month.

The perceived need to undertake aggressive, even decisive, action, inherent in every naval professional's blood, induced the Regia Marina staff to develop a harbor-attack doctrine using, from 1918, dedicated special craft like the climbing boats of the Grillo type and the torpedo-rigged *S 1* and *S 2 Mignatta.* This doctrine also envisioned the introduction of frogmen into enemy bases using specially modified midget submarines. The Regia Marina undertook seventeen base-forcing actions between 1915 and 1918, sinking two freighters, the coastal battleship *Wien,* and the dreadnought *Viribus Unitis.*

In the lower Adriatic the Dalmatian island barrier and its minefields and gun emplacements shielded Austro-Hungarian operations and coastal traffic. This advantage gave the initiative to the k.u.k.'s fast scouts and destroyer divisions, based at Cattaro and supported by the brief sorties of older, bigger cruisers. Assisted by intelligence and air reconnaissance, the Austrians practiced hit-and-run warfare, attacking both the sea-lanes between Italy and Albania and the Adriatic coastal route (the Italian railway system lacked the capacity to handle all the traffic required along the coast) and also, as a secondary and mainly propagandistic target, towns along the Adriatic shore. The tactical situation favored the Austrians, as the three to four Italian and British light cruisers available at any given time could not be tied down as escorts, nor could they constantly patrol the routes of approach. Given this situation the allied scouts could only hope to catch the enemy if they could sortie before the k.u.k. warships could retire to the protection of their coastal-defense system. The more powerful but much slower Italian predreadnoughts and armored cruisers based at Brindisi and Valona had no chance of intervening in such fast-moving actions.

Despite these handicaps and some brilliant Austro-Hungarian raids, the Regia Marina and its allies were successful in the strategic protection of traffic. Between 1915 and 1918 thirteen transports were lost from 1,076 sailings. Transports carried 630,000 men to Albania and Greece, at the cost of 2,057 personnel, while 568,393 ton of materials were delivered, along with 485 guns and 159,813 horses and mules.

Other targets of k.u.k. raids were British trawlers and the other units of the allied splinter fleet maintaining the barriers across the Straits of Otranto. Losses were about 4 percent of the total patrol force active in that strait.

These results confirmed the guerrilla nature of the Adriatic naval campaign. Maybe the Austro-Hungarian navy's greatest strategic accomplishment was the fact that six modern *Tatra*-class destroyers (supported by some older and smaller destroyers) were able to tie down in the lower Adriatic between 1915 and 1918 no less than thirty modern enemy destroyers. The absence of these allied destroyers from the German submarine–infested Mediterranean sea routes was finally balanced, from April 1917, by the coming of a dozen of modern Imperial Japanese Navy destroyers, followed later in 1918 by some U.S. Navy and Brazilian warships.

Wartime Evolution

Surface Warfare

The nature of the Italian navy's activities in its various zones of operation was captured by the popular wartime nicknames of the forces assigned to these zones. The Italian battle fleet at Taranto, the only base other than Spezia that could support the most modern and powerful battleships, was known as *la Marina del piacere* (the pleasure navy), a sharp contrast to the upper Adriatic squadron's nickname *la Marina dell'onore* (the navy of honor). The lower Adriatic force carried the name of *la Marina del dovere* (the navy of duty), while the squadron stationed along the malaria-ridden Albanian coast was known as *la Marina del dolore* (the navy of sorrow).

Photo 5.4. The Italian battle fleet sailing from Taranto 1 December 1916 (Enrico Cernuschi collection)

Reflecting its popular name, the activity of the main surface battle force was dominated by training, although the destroyer flotillas attached to the battle fleet frequently rotated to the Adriatic stations. This is not to say that a long and bitterly contested surface war was not being fought. Including MAS actions, the allies fought thirty-nine surface engagements in the Adriatic against Austro-Hungarian warships: twenty-nine involved Italian ships only, one only French, one only British; there were five with a mix of British and Italian vessels; and three with Italian, British, and French participants.

Excluding submarine actions and harbor attacks, allied warships sank one Austo-Hungarian battleship, one protected cruiser, and two destroyers in surface actions. They damaged five cruisers, fifteen destroyers, and seven torpedo boats. In turn, the allies lost three destroyers and had two cruisers, seven destroyers, two torpedo boats, and two MAS boats damaged in these actions.

The nature of the naval actions fought in the Adriatic Sea can be illustrated by relating a typical incident. On the night of 29/30 September 1917 an Italian squadron consisting of eight destroyers departed Venice at 2145 to support an aerial bombardment of Pola by ten Caproni aircraft and also in response to intelligence indicating that the Austrians had an operation in the works. In fact, a flotilla of four k.u.k. destroyers and four torpedo boats were off the coast supporting an aerial attack against Ferrara's airport by five naval flying boats. The Austrian attack destroyed the airship *M.8,* and as the flotilla turned for home at full speed it crossed paths with the Italian destroyers off the Po River delta. The Italians, steaming at twenty-two knots, engaged from three thousand meters just before midnight; in the exchange of fire the Austrians hit the Italian flagship *Sparviero* five times, wounding three men. The next destroyer in line, *Orsini,* was also hit. In return, *Ardito,* followed by *Acerbi* and *Stocco,* crossed the tail of the enemy flotilla and, shooting from one to two thousand meters, lightly damaged *Huszár* and roughed up *Velebit,* the last ship in the Austrian line. As *Velebit* caught fire and lost steering control *Acerbi* launched two torpedoes, but these missed. Both sides had ceased fire by 0030. *Streiter* took *Velebit* under tow, and the Austrian warships retreated toward the Parenzo minefields. They had another brush with the Italians, led by *Sparviero,* inside the minefields at 0045; the k.u.k. torpedo boat *98 M* suffered one casualty. After this both squadrons returned to port without further incident.

In this context, it is relevant that on the sole occasion when the main Austro-Hungarian battle fleet sortied after its war-opening coastal bombardments, the battleship *Szent István* fell victim to a lowly MAS boat. This costly outcome showed that the belligerents had it right, leaving the surface war to the flotilla and coastal craft.

Antisubmarine Warfare

At the start of war the Italian navy mobilized forty-seven fishing boats, tugs, and small steamers to serve as auxiliary coastal escorts and patrol boats, joining five armed yachts and three gunboats already active in that role. In July the Regia Marina staff began to arm freighters, and by the war's end 948 had received guns manned by navy personnel. The navy also provided wireless radio systems and operators to commercial vessels that lacked such facilities.

In 1915, as the Italian fishing industry could not offer more vessels suitable for escort duties, the navy bought forty-six-odd units from around Europe. In 1916 it purchased forty-seven sturdy and standardized motorized fishing vessels in Japan, and in 1917 these began to operate in the Mediterranean under the names *G 1–G 47.* In 1917 and 1918 the navy integrated MAS boats and motor launches into this coastal force, and it, along with the naval air service's flying boats, proved capable of adequately covering the Italian coasts.

The Regia Marina coastal escort forces command was the aforementioned Ispettorato della Difesa del traffico, which, after its activation in February 1917, absorbed the antisubmarine duties of the various regional departments. The problem of defending Italian and allied high-seas traffic in the Mediterranean was, however, of a completely different scale and nature. As the Austro-Hungarian submarine fleet never had boats bigger than 350 tons, its operational zone extended at best to the Ionian Sea and did not threaten allied Mediterranean sea-lanes. The minor traffic along the western Adriatic proceeded with almost no problem during the war, employing small and expendable wooden sailing vessels (*bragozzi*) that crept slowly but safely along a chain of guarded ports and anchorages under the protection of small escorts and shore batteries.

The appearance in the Mediterranean of the much more capable German submarines in the summer of 1915 immediately caused problems out of proportion to the relatively small number of boats deployed. Those difficulties fatally increased as the number of German submarines rose, the more so because their operations were largely unrestricted by any of the diplomatic limitations imposed in the Atlantic between 1915 and 1916.

In 1915, Italian merchant fleet losses were 62,122 GRT in the Mediterranean and 6,159 GRT elsewhere. New construction totaled 133,000 GRT of Italian ships larger than a hundred tons between 1915 and 1918, to which may be added 250,000 GRT of Austro-Hungarian and

German tonnage seized in Italian harbors. In 1916 the number of German boats based in the Adriatic Sea rose to two dozen, and the effect of that increase was pronounced from the second half of that year. By 31 December 1916, 356,836 GRT of Italian shipping had been sunk, of which 288,738 were lost in the Mediterranean.

In October 1916 the battle fleet commander, the Duke of Abruzzi, advocated the adoption of convoys in the Mediterranean to offset the growing submarine menace. This suggestion was not followed, but on 15 January 1917, during a naval council in London, the Italian representative, Captain Alfredo Baistrocchi, again proposed Mediterranean convoys, stating the Regia Marina was ready to begin at once under its newly created traffic-defense command, using dozens of high-seas escorts, consisting initially of old torpedo cruisers and small auxiliary cruisers, along the vital Gibraltar-Genoa route. The British rejected the Italian proposal, and, with some doubts, so did the French. During 1917 German U-boats ravaged allied traffic. Italian losses that year totaled 436,675 GRT, of which 220,431 were lost in the Mediterranean Sea.

The lack of effective sensors—the first hydrophones could be used only when the ship was motionless—handicapped the escorts, and losses suffered by the German and Austrian submarines were insignificant. Only ten German and eight Austro-Hungarian boats were lost in the Mediterranean between 1915 and 1918; eleven German boats were scuttled on 28 October 1918, during the collapse of the Habsburg Empire. The Regia Marina had seven confirmed kills and two probables.

The allies finally implemented the first, small convoys in the eastern Mediterranean on 25 May 1917. In October 1917 through convoys across the inner sea were introduced, and the decisive Gibraltar-Genoa (GOG) convoys began running in January 1918. The Italian central high-seas escort command was responsible for the protection of Italian freighters bound for Italy. The most important Italian traffic came from the Atlantic Ocean—49 million tons of imports between 1915 and 1918, compared to two million tons from Suez (mostly cereals from Australia) in 1917 and 1918.

From September 1915 the allies attempted to impede the passage of submarines from the Adriatic between Brindisi and Albania by establishing a permanent patrol of mostly British drifters that trailed steel nets to trap submarines or alert surface forces to their presence. While largely unsuccessful, especially considering the resources it consumed, this barrage provided a convenient target for Austro-Hungarian naval forces, which raided it two dozen times over the course of the war. Notable raids on the nights of 31 May, 9 July, and 22 December 1916 produced small results. A larger on the night of 14 May 1917 by three k.u.k. light cruisers sank fourteen drifters and provoked a large reaction by Italian, French, and British warships. During the pursuit all of the Austrian cruisers were damaged, one severely, but all made it back to port under the cover of heavy units that sortied from Cattaro.

In a five-month-long Franco-Italian project undertaken in the spring and summer of 1918, a fixed boom was created in the Otranto channel between Brindisi and Corfu. It was a complex of two hundred steel nets sixty-six kilometers long, fifty meters high, and hanging ten meters under the sea surface, attached to 429 buoys and armed with 1,200 de Quillacq mines. Most of the materials were manufactured in France, after Britain, which opposed the program from the first, declined to supply the necessary steel wire. The results of this barrage were modest: it caused the lost of only one submarine, *UB 53* on 3 August 1918.

Aviation

The Italian naval air service experienced tremendous development during the war. On 1 November 1918 it had in service 552 flying boats and floatplanes, eighty-six wheeled aircraft, four airships, and eighteen blimps. During the war 1,472 flying boats and floatplanes were delivered, along with 158 land aircraft, eleven airships, and thirty-six blimps. Personnel rose from 403 in 1915 to 3,325 men manning the squadrons and the naval stations. Combat losses were 114 aircraft and six airships; 893 aircraft, four airships, and twenty-four blimps were lost in accidents or paid off as worn out. (See table 5.3.)

Table 5.3 The Regia Marina's Ispettorato per l'Avizione Air Service War Activity

	1915	1916	1917	1918
Bombardment	12/13	42/96	179/684	229/1382
Reconnaissance	240/278	795/1454	2068/4579	5772/12900
ASW beyond the Adriatic Sea	-/-	-/-	2337/2337	8048/8048
Fighter	9/14	21/50	103/261	2987/4173

Note: The first number indicates total missions, the second aircraft participating

The two Italian air services dropped about six hundred tons of ordnance against naval targets. The Regia Marina used for this task the Macchi L.1 (a copy of an Austrian Lohner L seized on 28 May 1915), the Macchi L.2, and the Macchi L.3 and FBA flying boats—which could carry only two hundred kilograms of bombs. Admiral Thaon di Revel supported the development of a wheeled torpedo-bomber squadron. Experiments were conducted in 1917 with a pair of borrowed army Caproni Ca.3 biplanes, and one of them made an unsuccessful night attack in Cattaro Bay on 3 October 1917.

Summary and Assessment

The main responsibility of the Regia Marina was to control the Adriatic Sea. This control had three facets: to protect allied traffic, prevent the Austro-Hungarian fleet from challenging Italy's position, and interdict enemy traffic. Secondary responsibilities included support of the army's maritime flank and protection of traffic outside the Adriatic from enemy submarines.

In the Adriatic, the Regia Marina successfully fulfilled its responsibilities by pioneering a form of naval warfare suited to its particular situation and the geography dictating that situation. This warfare—which flew in the fact of the traditional naval wisdom that a decisive battle was the proper object of every fleet—was based on the principles of Admiral Paolo Thaon di Revel. This officer forged a doctrine and a way of making war that incorporated new technology into his clear-sighted vision of what Italy needed to do to win its naval war at the lowest possible cost. He relied on mines, submarines, aircraft, motor torpedo boats, and special-attack weapons to achieve Italy's logical goals and did not feel compelled to use dreadnoughts just because they existed. His policies and practices created conflicts within Italy's own command structure until Thaon di Revel achieved complete control of the navy in 1917, and they also caused misunderstandings with Italy's partners, who resented the way Thaon di Revel placed Italy's interests above those of the alliance. The results vindicated Thaon di Revel's doctrines and formed the foundation of Italian naval policy in the second round of the Great European Civil War that would be fought between 1939 and 1945.

6

RUSSIA

Rossiiskii imperatorskii flot

Stephen McLaughlin

BACKSTORY

Pre-1914 History

On the eve of the First World War the Russian Imperial Navy was certainly among the world's most ridiculed armed forces. Its performance in the Russo-Japanese War—particularly the humiliating defeat at Tsushima—and the widely publicized revolt on board the Black Sea Fleet battleship *Kniaz Potëmkin Tavricheskii* had led both its allies and its potential enemies to assume that the Russian navy would be a negligible factor in a maritime war. Yet despite occasional blunders, its performance in two and a half years of war was on the whole competent and effective. How had this change come about in the nine years between Tsushima and Sarajevo?

From its founding by Peter the Great in 1696 until the Crimean War (1853–56) the Russian navy had performed creditably, if not always brilliantly, and had been an essential factor in Russia's expansion in both the Baltic and Black Sea regions. By the mid-nineteenth century Russia's structural weaknesses—underdeveloped industry, a backward social system, and a cumbersome government—were undermining the navy's ability to defend the empire, but in the Russo-Turkish War of 1877–78 the Black Sea Fleet had still managed to gain ascendancy over a nominally stronger enemy thanks to improvisation and boldness.

But between 1878 and 1904 a series of events sapped those qualities out of the navy. Starting in the 1880s the officer corps was subjected to a rigid promotion scheme, the *tsenz*, that focused the attention of officers on obtaining the right billets for promotion rather than on professional competence. The effects of this system were exacerbated by the navy's dramatic expansion between 1895 and 1904, during which time the number of enlisted men rose from 26,000 to 64,400 without a corresponding increase in the number of officers. The rapid expansion of the navy under Emperor Nicholas II (r. 1894–1917) was the result of his belief that Russia's future lay in Asia and the Pacific; by 1904 most of the navy's battleships and cruisers were based in Port Arthur and Vladivostok, where facilities were lacking and logistical support was dependent upon the single-track Trans-Siberian Railway.

All of these factors played roles in the disastrous war with Japan. When revolutionary disturbances wracked the nation in 1905–1907, these same factors contributed to numerous naval mutinies, of which the *Potëmkin*'s was only the most protracted and embarrassing. The government was eventually able to muster enough loyal troops to crush the rebellions, but the situation remained tense in both society and the armed forces.

In the wake of war and revolution the navy began to address the worst of its problems. Incompetent officers were weeded out, promotions were freed from the restrictions of the *tsenz,* conditions on the lower deck were improved, and the creaky administrative machinery of the Naval Ministry was subjected to a number of changes. The most important of these was the founding in April 1906 of the Naval General Staff (NGS), which was intended to prevent the sort of mismatch between national policy, building programs, and base facilities that had hampered the conduct of the war with Japan.

At sea, a rigorous training program was inaugurated in the Baltic Fleet under Admiral N. O. Essen, a hero of the Russo-Japanese War; improvements in the Black Sea Fleet came more slowly, but there were advances nonetheless. The biggest problem confronting the seagoing forces was the lack of modern ships; war and revolution had undermined the empire's economy, and recovery began only around 1910, so for several years the navy had to watch anxiously as other powers laid down dreadnought after dreadnought. The first Russian all-big-gun battleships, the Baltic Fleet's four *Sevastopol*-class ships, were started only in 1909, and even then work was slow due to a lack of funds.

Reform efforts really began to pick up speed with the appointment of Admiral Ivan Konstantinovich Grigorovich to the post of naval minister in April 1911. Grigorovich was a man of great talent and energy, with clear ideas on what needed to be done to reinvigorate the navy. He was also willing to deal honestly with the new legislature, the State Duma, and soon turned its negative attitude toward the navy into a positive one. As a result, the Duma voted money for a series of warship programs: in 1911, after almost two years of uncertainty, the construction of the *Sevastopol*-class battleships was finally put on a firm financial basis; a program for the Black Sea (three dreadnoughts of the *Imperatritsa Mariia* class) was approved; in 1912 funding was granted for four huge *Izmail* battle cruisers for the Baltic; and in early 1914 a fourth Black Sea dreadnought (*Imperator Nikolai I*) was approved. These programs also included light cruisers, powerful destroyers, and submarines.

By August 1914 the Russian Imperial Navy was in the midst of a renaissance. Although most of its ships were obsolete, the shipyards were humming with new construction. The quality of its officers corps was still uneven, but the service possessed many competent—and a few brilliant—men. The technical training of crews was generally at a high level, equipment was up to date, and procedures were carefully thought out. Only two things stood in the way of Russia's aspiration to become a great sea power: the uncertain loyalty of the navy's enlisted men and—the most important factor of all—time.

Mission/Function

Geography compelled the Russian navy to maintain several separate forces—the Baltic and Black Sea Fleets and the Siberian, Caspian, and Amur River Flotillas. The two fleets were by far the largest and most important formations, but both were isolated in enclosed seas. Moreover, the only access to the Black Sea, the Turkish Straits—the Dardanelles and the Bosporus—were closed in peacetime by international treaty to all warships except those of Turkey; thus the Baltic and Black Sea fleets could never operate together. Although naval officers trained together and were transferred from one sea to the other, the two fleets faced completely different conditions and developed independent traditions and a certain degree of rivalry.

In terms of Russian naval war planning, there were two basic assumptions: first, that the war on land would be the dominant factor in determining victory or defeat; second, that a future war would be short. These assumptions were especially important in the Baltic, where the navy's main task was to prevent the Germans from launching maritime attacks on St. Petersburg (renamed Petrograd in September 1914). The navy was also charged with preventing German landings that could outflank the army's land defenses. The Russian territory of Finland was seen as especially vulnerable, since a German landing there might trigger a revolt among a population unhappy with Russian rule.

The Baltic Fleet's 1912 war plan, which was put into effect in August 1914, had been developed by the NGS in cooperation with the Baltic

Fleet staff. Its central feature was a dense minefield, dubbed the "Central Position," barring entrance to the Gulf of Finland. A cruiser patrol line to its west would warn of the approaching enemy. When that warning came, destroyer flotillas based on the flanks of the central position would come out to launch massed torpedo attacks; their primary targets would be troop transports (if the enemy planned a landing) and capital ships. Once these attacks had been carried out, the destroyers and cruisers would fall back to the east of the central position, where all forces would concentrate for the defense of that position. At best, this system would prevent an incursion by the far stronger German fleet into the Gulf of Finland; at worst, it would hold off the enemy for at least fourteen days, which would give the army time to mobilize to defend against a German amphibious assault.

In the Black Sea, developing a war plan proved more difficult—the NGS was in favor of an aggressive campaign to blockade the Bosporus, while the fleet staff was more cautious and tended to focus on defending Russia's coasts. The upshot was that when the Turco-German fleet attacked on 29 October 1914 the fleet went to war without a plan, which led to some confusion in the initial operations.

In the Pacific, Russia had come to terms with Japan, whose naval power she could no longer hope to match. A 1907 treaty sorted out spheres of influence in Manchuria, trade, fishing rights, and the other desiderata left over from the war. Russia's naval force in the Far East, the Siberian Flotilla, could therefore be limited to a pair of cruisers and a few obsolete destroyers and submarines. Many of these vessels would be recalled to European waters after the war began. The Caspian and Amur River Flotillas were minor forces, intended primarily for police and border-protection functions. As for the north, it was completely ignored in naval plans—a corollary to the short-war assumption, which did not envision the massive imports of arms and material that a long war would require.

ORGANIZATION

Command Structure

Administration

The Naval Ministry was housed in the Admiralty (Admiralteistvo) in St. Petersburg. The naval minister was always a serving admiral; he, like all other ministers, was appointed by, and responsible solely to, the emperor. By far the most outstanding of the naval ministers in this era was I. K. Grigorovich, who held the post from April 1911 to February 1917. During his period in office the naval administration was streamlined, with overlapping departmental functions eliminated by regulations that clearly spelled out the authority of the various branches. Grigorovich also managed to repair the navy's frayed relations with the State Duma while simultaneously retaining the emperor's trust—not an easy tightrope to walk. As a result of his efforts the naval budget increased dramatically in the last few years before the war, as shown in table 6.1.

Table 6.1 Russian Army and Navy Expenditures, 1905–14 (in rubles)

Year	Total defense budget	Army	As % of total	Navy	As % of total
1905	1,633,568,000	1,516,874,000	92.86%	116,694,000	7.14%
1906	1,033,019,000	921,378,000	89.19%	111,641,000	10.81%
1907	679,136,000	591,425,000	87.08%	87,711,000	12.92%
1908	673,778,000	580,294,000	86.13%	93,484,000	13.87%
1909	647,898,000	555,674,000	85.77%	92,224,000	14.23%
1910	650,493,000	537,757,000	82.67%	112,736,000	17.33%
1911	671,325,000	550,356,000	81.98%	120,969,000	18.02%
1912	814,840,000	638,757,000	78.39%	176,083,000	21.61%
1913	961,565,000	716,718,000	74.54%	244,847,000	25.46%
1914	2,459,557,000	2,245,453,000	91.30%	214,104,000	8.70%

Notes: The exchange rate at the time was $1.00 = 1.94 rubles, or £1 = 9.46 rubles.
The navy's expenditures for 1910 included 16,851,000 rubles for paying down the ministry's outstanding debts.

Source: L. G. Beskrovnyi, *Armiia i flot Rossii v nachale XX v.: Ocherki voenno-ekonomicheskogo potentsiala* (Moscow: Nauka, 1986), 226, 227, 229.

Although the minister had broad powers over the naval administration in peacetime, a number of key appointments in the navy were made directly by the emperor and so were outside the minister's control. This opened the door to court politics and intrigue. Among the officers appointed by the emperor were the fleet commanders and some of the major department heads. One of these imperial appointees was the head of the Naval General Staff, which was charged with defining Russia's naval requirements in the various theaters, determining strategies to meet those needs, and formulating the programs to make those strategies work, in terms of both shipbuilding policy and shore facilities. Initially the NGS was small—fifteen officers—and it received little support from the naval ministers. This placed it in a weak position within the ministry's bureaucracy, but under Grigorovich it gained considerable power.

During the war some administrative changes were introduced. The most important came in 1915 with the creation of two assistant ministers, one for combatant affairs and the other for technical and financial matters. The first assistant, who was in charge of the ministry in Grigorovich's absence, was Vice Admiral A. I. Rusin, who was simultaneously the chief of the Naval General Staff; the technical/financial assistant minister was Vice Admiral P. P. Muravev.

After the February Revolution of 1917 the administration of the navy was subjected to numerous changes, and lines of responsibility became blurred. In the event, none of these changes had much influence on the conduct of the war, since after the February Revolution the power of the central authorities was increasingly tenuous.

Organization

Command Organization

The emperor was the commander in chief of the armed forces, although in 1914 he appointed his soldierly uncle, the Grand Duke Nikolai Nikolaevich, as supreme commander. The high command—*Stavka,* in Russian—was established at Baranovichi in Poland. Following the army's great defeats in the summer of 1915, Stavka was relocated eastward to Mogilev, and Nicholas II assumed the title of supreme commander. The actual running of the war was entrusted to the emperor's chief of staff, General M. V. Alekseev.

Once war began, the Naval Ministry became a purely administrative organ—as Naval Minister Grigorovich often remarked, "The fleet requires—we fulfill."[1] Belying its name, the Naval General Staff did not assume direct command functions over the major fleets, a task for which it was neither intended nor equipped. Instead, the Black Sea Operations Section of the NGS, headed by Rear Admiral D. V. Neniukov, was transferred to Stavka, to which the Black Sea Fleet was directly subordinated. The Baltic Fleet, on the other hand, was subordinated to the VI Army, charged with the defense of St. Petersburg, and the Baltic Operations Section of the NGS was incorporated into VI Army headquarters.

The naval administrations at Stavka and VI Army headquarters were small organizations that could do little more than pass reports upward and directives downward, while the higher authorities were generally too preoccupied with the land fronts to interfere with the operations of the fleets. This somewhat vague framework gave the fleet commanders a considerable, perhaps excessive, degree of independence. For example, Stavka's naval administration was constantly frustrated by the Black Sea Fleet's failure to respond to its directives. On the other hand, the Baltic Fleet bridled under the cautious policies of VI Army command, although it obeyed them nonetheless.

Admiral Grigorovich considered these arrangements unsatisfactory, and after the emperor assumed command at Stavka he began pressing for a reorganization. The eventual result of this pressure was the establishment in January 1916 of an Imperial Naval Field Staff within Stavka; the chief of the Naval General Staff, Vice Admiral A. I. Rusin, became chief of the Naval Staff. In practice, however, these changes had little effect on the conduct of the war.

Fleet Organization and Order of Battle

The Russian navy's major combatant formations were the Baltic and Black Sea Fleets, commanded in August 1914 by Admirals N. O. Essen and A. A. Ebergard, respectively. Upon the outbreak of war, the fleet commanders automatically assumed authority over the ports and other naval facilities in their theaters.

Photo 6.1. The Black Sea Fleet's dreadnought *Imperatritsa Ekaterina Velikaia* fitting out at Nikolaev in the summer of 1915. The bowsprit-like structure on her bow was part of the fore-trawl, a paravane-like mine-protection device; in service it proved fragile and was soon removed. *Ekaterina Velikaia* exchanged fire with *Goeben* on 8 January 1916. Having fled Sevastopol in April 1918 to avoid falling into German hands, she was sunk at Novorossiisk by torpedoes from the destroyer *Kerch* on 18 June 1918. (Courtesy Sergei Vinogradov)

For battleships and cruisers, the fundamental unit was the brigade (*brigada*) of four ships, while for destroyers it was the flotilla (*divizion*) of nine ships; two flotillas formed a brigade, two brigades a division (*diviziia*). For submarines the basic unit was the section (*otdelenie*), consisting of two large or three small boats; two to four sections would make a flotilla, and two flotillas would make up a brigade. A detachment (*otriad*) was a separate formation of ships; these might be temporary, as for a special purpose, or more permanent, such as the Artillery Training and Torpedo Training detachments.

Although the division-brigade-flotilla structure remained in place throughout the war, in 1915 new tactical formations were introduced. The fleets were divided into a number of "maneuvering groups." In the Baltic, each of these consisted of two battleships, a cruiser, and a number of destroyers; if the Germans attempted to penetrate the defensive mine barrier at the entrance to the Gulf of Finland, the groups would maneuver independently in protecting the minefields. In the Black Sea, the maneuvering groups consisted either of a single dreadnought or several predreadnoughts, the idea being that each group should by itself be more powerful than the Turco-German battle cruiser *Goeben*, so that each could operate independently without fear of being overwhelmed by the faster German ship.

Communications

Tactical

Like other navies, the Russian navy used flag signals and signal lamps for maneuvering at sea; maneuvers could also be conducted by low-power radio. Before the war a great deal of attention was devoted to circumventing enemy jamming by coordinated frequency changes; this was considered especially important given the defensive system of the Baltic war plans, in which scouting forces would have to alert the fleet to the enemy's approach by radio in time to effect a concentration.

As for codes and ciphers, until 1916 Russian communications used, in the words of one officer, "naïve" ciphers; he went on to say that "the entire difference between the Germans and ourselves was the fact that we transmitted little, while they were garrulous."[2] New ciphers, employing superencryption, were finally issued in the summer of 1916. As for codes, there were different ones for large ships, light forces, submarines, and auxiliary vessels. Thus if a submarine was lost, only that code had to be replaced. Messages were not to be repeated in different codes; instead, large surface ships had copies of all the other codes, so that they could both send and receive messages from the smaller units operating with them without having the same messages broadcast in different codes, which would have provided any German code breakers with a point of entry into the codes.

Strategic

Most strategic communication was conducted via cables running over Russian territory or under waters controlled by Russia. This provided a secure means of communication between Stavka, the Naval Ministry in St. Petersburg, the Baltic Fleet base in Helsingfors (modern Helsinki), and the Black Sea Fleet command in Sevastopol, as well as the various outlying forces. The Hughes Teletype system was much used; although somewhat slow, it provided for secure strategic communications throughout the war. For communicating with ships at sea, the main fleet bases at Helsingfors and Sevastopol were equipped with powerful (thirty-five-kilowatt) radio stations.

Intelligence

The Third Branch of the Naval General Staff was responsible for intelligence; naval attachés, who reported directly to it, were encouraged to develop espionage networks. They obtained some successes. In the Baltic a number of agents were infiltrated into German territory and observation posts were set up in the eastern Danish islands to report on the movements of German warships in the vicinity of Kiel. Matters proved to be more difficult in Turkey; although the Russian navy established espionage rings in Constantinople, they were often short-lived, and the timely transmission of information remained problematic.

But the Russian navy's main source of intelligence was the decryption of German naval radio messages, thanks to the codebook and other materials captured after the cruiser *Magdeburg* ran aground in Russian territory on 26 August 1914. The Russians initially did not establish a centralized codebreaking office to exploit the material; instead, decryption was carried out by both the Intelligence Section of the Baltic Fleet's staff and the Service of Observation and Communications (Sluzhba nabliudeniia i sviazi, or SNIS), under Captain 1st Rank A. I. Nepenin. Eventually, however, the SNIS took over most of the decryption work, which was carried out by a specially assembled staff at the Shpitgamn radio station, in Estonia. SNIS prepared daily summaries of the situation, based on radio decrypts and radio direction finding (by 1915 the SNIS was operating a network of D/F stations). The fleet staff, in turn, prepared weekly summaries based on the SNIS materials, as well as agent reports and other sources. During the war it was standard practice for ships going out on missions—including the British submarines operating in the Baltic—to get briefings on the current situation at SNIS headquarters in Revel (modern Tallinn, Estonia).

Little information is available regarding code breaking in the Black Sea; however, as the Naval General Staff reported to the British Room 40, "We know all ciphers in Black Sea except for the 3-letter-groups W/T [wireless] messages."[3] Overall, however, the published literature suggests that the Black Sea Fleet's radio intelligence was not as well organized as that of the Baltic Fleet.

Infrastructure, Logistics, and Commerce

Bases

Kronshtadt, located about fifteen nautical miles west of St. Petersburg on Kotlin Island, had long served as the Baltic Fleet's main base. The fleet's major schools and depots were located there, as were ship-repair facilities. Its greatest disadvantage was that it was usually icebound from around the end of December until April, so any ships based there were immobilized for about four months. In 1912 the NGS decided that Revel would make a better base, since icebreakers could keep it open year-round, and a vast program of harbor expansion and improvement was undertaken. This work was far from complete in August 1914, and therefore Revel was used only by destroyers and submarines, while the big ships were based at Helsingfors, which was generally frozen from late January to mid-April. During the war, forward bases were established in the Åland Islands and in the Gulf of Riga.

In the Black Sea the main base was Sevastopol, a deep inlet on the western coast of the Crimean Peninsula. During the war Batumi was used as a support base for units operating in the Caucasus and along the northern coast of Anatolia, but facilities there were minimal.

In the Russian north the few facilities available originally belonged to the Ministry of Trade and Industry but were transferred to the navy after the outbreak of war. The main bases were the ancient port of Arkhangelsk on the White Sea and the ice-free port of Romanov-na-Murmane (now Murmansk), which was developed during the war. (See map 6.1.)

Industry

Russia's state shipyards were known for their slow pace of construction and their corruption. These faults became all too obvious after the Russo-Japanese War, when it was revealed that naval shipbuilding was in essence a gigantic Ponzi scheme, under which the cost overruns of incomplete ships were being paid for by credits allocated to new ships. Thus in the wake of the war, when new shipbuilding funds dried up, all work, even on ships

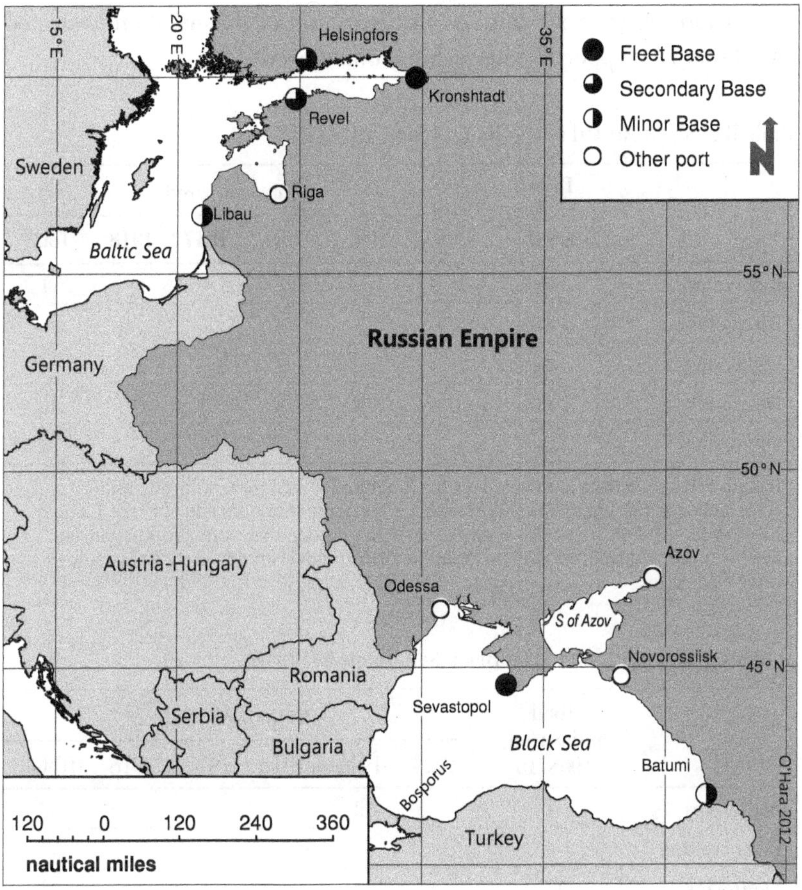

Map 6.1. Russian Naval Bases

well advanced, slowed to a crawl due to lack of money. This situation persisted until 1911, when the Duma granted 16.85 million rubles to pay off the Naval Ministry's debts. Once he was appointed naval minister, Admiral Grigorovich was able to replace ineffective managers and reorganize several of the institutions involved in shipbuilding. As a result, the state facilities were soon operating at a much increased tempo.

Grigorovich also sought to encourage private industries, recognizing that thanks to a massive influx of foreign investment eager to win profits from Russia's naval reconstruction, these firms had enormous capital to work with. Foreign concerns either partnered with existing Russian firms or founded completely new shipyards. In addition to financial backing, the foreign firms provided sorely needed technical expertise; although Russia had a cadre of excellent naval constructors and engineers, there were too few of them to support the navy's burgeoning needs.

Table 6.2 Ships Added to the Baltic Fleet, 1914–18

	Total authorized, 1908–15	Ships delivered					
		1914	1915	1916	1917	1918	Total
Battleships	4	4	-	-	-	-	4
Battle cruisers	4	-	-	-	-	-	-
Light cruisers	4	-	-	-	-	-	-
Destroyers	36	-	2	9	5	-	16
Submarines	35*	-	3	13	5	-	21

* Includes six submarines authorized for the Siberian Flotilla; these were still under construction in the Baltic when war broke out and were therefore added to the Baltic Fleet. Also included are twelve boats of the 1915 program that were never begun and five boats ordered from the United States in 1915 and delivered in sections by railway from Vladivostok.

Table 6.3 Ships Added to the Black Sea Fleet, 1914–18

	Total authorized, 1908–15	Ships delivered					
		1914	1915	1916	1917	1918	Total
Battleships	4	-	2	-	1	-	3
Light cruisers	4	-	-	-	-	-	-
Destroyers	17	4	5	-	4	-	13
Submarines	32*	-	5	1	4	1	11

* Includes 8 boats of the 1915 program that were never started, as well as six Holland boats ordered from the United States in 1916–17 and delivered in sections by railway from Vladivostok.

Nevertheless, the industrial underpinnings of Russia's shipbuilding industry remained weak, and enormous quantities of machinery and equipment had to be ordered from foreign firms—many of them German. Ultimately, the problem was that Russia lacked the means to create new industries; machine tools, hydraulic presses, fine instruments—all had to be ordered abroad. Thus Russian wartime submarine construction was severely constrained by the lack of domestically produced diesel engines (engines for some boats had to be taken from the gunboats of the Amur River Flotilla); turbines had to be ordered in Britain for the Black Sea dreadnoughts; and the spherical bearings used to support the 14-inch turrets of the *Izmail*-class battle cruisers, ordered in Germany, were never delivered, and replacements proved impossible to find. (See tables 6.2, 6.3, and 6.4.)

Shipping

Russia's merchant marine was miniscule—less than 6 percent that of Great Britain. However, this does not mean that Russia's volume of trade was small, just that it was carried in foreign bottoms. In fact, Russia's trade was growing as the empire rapidly industrialized, and the imports of manufactured goods that flowed into the empire through the Baltic were paid for by the export of Black Sea grain. This explains the interest of both the Naval Ministry and the Ministry of Foreign Affairs in keeping the Turkish Straits open to Russian trade, as well as the fact that one of Russia's most important wartime political goals was control over these straits.

During the war the navy commandeered many merchant ships, both Russian and foreign, trapped in the Baltic and Black Sea. Hundreds of vessels, from fishing trawlers to large steamers, were pressed into naval service and made vital contributions to Russia's naval war. (See table 6.5.)

Personnel

Demographics

The Russo-Japanese War had a profound effect on the naval officer corps. The most useless officers were weeded out, and the number of admirals was reduced through retirement. Nevertheless, there remained too many officers of indifferent quality. Although reforms opened the officer corps to "Persons of all classes, of the Christian religion" possessing a higher education, it remained a largely aristocratic body—93 percent of entrants to the Naval Corps between 1910 and 1915 were from gentry families.

Russia was a multinational empire, and the officer corps reflected this fact. Although the majority of officers were Russians (a term also used for Ukrainians—"Little Russians"—and White Russians), there were also ethnic Swedes from Finland, Poles, and many others. The largest non-Russian group—about 20 percent—were ethnic Germans (*ostzeiskie*) from the southern Baltic coast, often referred to as the "Baltic barons." There seems to have been little if any discrimination against non-Russian officers; for example, there were navy-sponsored churches for Catholics and Lutherans at Kronshtadt, and at the outbreak of war the Baltic Fleet was commanded by an ethnic German and the Black Sea Fleet by an ethnic Swede. In 1914 there were 4,123 officers serving in all branches; by early 1917 this number had grown to 6,089, including 173 admirals and generals. (See table 6.6.)

Table 6.4 Major Shipyards Engaged in Warship Construction, 1906–17

	Location	Ownership	Ship types	Numbers of workers			
				1906	1910	1914	1917
Admiralty	St. Petersburg	State	BB, CB	1,800	2,324	3,200	4,600
Baltic	St. Petersburg	State	BB, CB, SS	4,205	4,383	7,055	7,645
Metallicheskii (a)	St. Petersburg	Private	DD	NA	NA	4,450	NA
Nevskii	St. Petersburg	Private	DD, SS	NA	3,200	5,500	12,000
Putilovskaia (b)	St. Petersburg	Private	CL, DD	NA	NA	3,700	4,500
Noblessner	Revel	Private	SS	NA	NA	2,700	3,100
Revel Shipbldg (c)	Revel	Private	DD	NA	NA	2,000	7,500
Russo-Baltic (d)	Revel	Private	CL, DD, SS	NA	NA	3,000	5,300
Miulgrabenskaia (e)	Riga	Private	DD	NA	NA	NA	NA
ONZiV (Naval) (f)	Nikolaev	Private	BB, DD, SS	NA	2,100	10,600	13,500
Russud (g)	Nikolaev	Private	BB, CL, SS	NA	NA	2,900	4,000

a. Supported by A.G. Vulcan (Hamburg).
b. Supported by Blohm & Voss.
c. Supported by Normand and Schichau.
d. Supported by Schneider-Creusot.
e. Supported by Schichau.
f. French financial backing, technical support from Vickers.
g. Technical assistance from John Brown.

Sources: Beskrovnyi, *Armiia i flot Rossii v nachale XX V.*, 198–99; *Istoriia otechestvennogo sudostroeniia*, vol. 3, 175–215.

Table 6.5 The Russian Mercantile Marine as of 1 January 1914

	Steamers		Motorships		Sailing vessels		Totals	
	Number	Tonnage	Number	Tonnage	Number	Tonnage	Number	Tonnage
White Sea	62	12,212	9	207	405	22,496	476	34,915
Baltic	227	110,744	4	228	726	75,115	957	186,087
Black Sea	410	222,620	12	404	827	46,447	1,249	269,471
Pacific	33	22,712	1	52	4	185	38	22,949
Caspian	244	108,134	13	11,159	554	110,087	811	229,380
Totals	976	476,422	39	12,050	2,516	254,330	3,531	742,802

Source: Stateman's Year-Book, 1915, 1299.

Table 6.6 Number of Officers, by Assignments, 1914

	Baltic Fleet	Black Sea Fleet	Caspian Flotilla	Pacific	Shore assignments	Total
Number	1,704	658	40	316	1,405	4,123
As % of total	41.33%	15.96%	0.97%	7.66%	34.08%	

There was less ethnic diversity among the enlisted personnel; this was in part a result of the conscription laws, which exempted not only individuals for various reasons but also entire regions of the empire—for example, Finland was excluded from conscription, thus depriving the navy of a potential source of seafaring men. But the navy also sought to ensure a majority of Russians (again including Ukrainians and White Russians) in every ship or unit; Jews and national minorities from the empire's borderlands were deliberately excluded. The Baltic Fleet generally received conscripts from northwestern Russia and the provinces bordering on the Baltic, whereas the Black Sea Fleet's crews generally came from the nine provinces bordering that sea. As a result, the majority of the men of the Baltic Fleet (75–80 percent) were Russians, while in the Black Sea Ukrainians predominated (circa 65 percent).

For obvious reasons, the navy wanted conscripts with some experience of the sea or boat handling, or men who were familiar with machinery. The latter tended to be workers from the urban areas, who were generally better educated than the rural peasants, who still made up the bulk of the army (the literacy rate in the navy was better than 80 percent, while in the infantry it hovered around 50 percent). This conscription policy had a major drawback—urban workers usually had been exposed to some form of socialist propaganda or had even participated in revolutionary activities.

The navy was unpopular with conscripts, primarily because the peacetime term of service was five years, compared to only three years in the army. The draftees were inducted in October and trained ashore until March. At this point the bulk of the men would be distributed to their posts, on board ship or ashore, while the brighter men would be selected for additional training as petty officers. The reenlistment rate of petty officers was very low, which meant that they usually had less shipboard experience than the men they led. As a result, petty officers identified with the enlisted men, not with the service. Warrant officers—*konduktory*—were specialist enlisted men who had decided to remain in the navy. Their small numbers (about 1.6 percent of the crews) and the fact that they were much disliked by the enlisted men meant that they could hardly form a bridge between the officers and the lower deck. After the February Revolution in 1917 there were proposals to eliminate them altogether, and this had in fact been done by December 1917.

The navy's personnel strength peaked in early 1917, when there were more than 137,000 enlisted men on the books. After the February Revolution it declined sharply, and by 1 June 1918 the number had plummeted to 48,216, due to a combination of desertions and the siphoning off of sailors to the land fronts of the accelerating civil war. (See table 6.7.)

Training

Most line officers entered the navy through the Naval Cadet Corps (renamed the Naval Corps in 1906). After the war with Japan the educational emphasis shifted from general and theoretical subjects to naval professional topics (especially naval strategy and tactics). Another postwar change was an increase in the total number of cadets, from 600 to 750, in an effort to replace wartime losses.

The Naval Corps accepted applicants between the ages of fourteen to sixteen; for the first three years of its six-year program a cadet was rated as a *gardemarin* (midshipman) and in addition to classroom studies would go on summer cruises. After passing an examination, he would be promoted to *korabelnyi gardemarin* (shipboard midshipman) and embark on a long cruise, usually to the Mediterranean; upon completion of this and passing another examination, he would be promoted to *michman* (ensign, or sublieutenant).

The Nicholas Naval Academy was the equivalent of a war college, offering a two-year program in the study of naval strategy, tactics, and other advanced topics. The top graduates would be selected for a third year of study, intended to train officers for the Naval General Staff.

Compared to the army, wartime attrition of naval personnel was low, but the numerous auxiliary vessels taken over from commercial service dramatically increased the number of officers and men required. After the outbreak of war the senior classes of midshipmen were given early promotions to *michmany*, which provided an additional 259 officers. In 1916 a special three-month class was established for volunteers, who were intended strictly for duties ashore, thereby liberating other officers for service afloat. The classes were organized at Oranienbaum, near Petrograd. Candidates had to have high school educations and be less than twenty years old. The first group of 150 men was graduated in the late summer of 1916. (See table 6.8.)

Table 6.7 Sailors in Service, All Fleets and Flotillas (not including officers)

Year	Total	Baltic Fleet	Black Sea Fleet	Siberian Flotilla	Caspian Flotilla	Amur Flotilla	Northern Flotilla
1914 (a)	52,011	31,370	14,486	4,207	476	1,472	—
1914 (b)	89,366	54,451	28,037	4,972	533	1,373	—
1915	110,181	68,461	34,583	5,028	660	1,449	—
1916	115,698	67,694	36,036	5,280	747	1,564	4,377
1917	137,215	83,870	41,914	6,055	1,170	993	3,213

a. Premobilization figure.
b. Postmobilization figure.

Note: The figures for 1914 do not include *konduktory*.

Source: Beskrovnyi, *Armiia i flot Rossii v nachale XX v.*, 211.

Table 6.8 Russian Naval Ranks

Rank	Translation	British/American equivalent
Admiral	Admiral	Admiral
Vitse-admiral	Vice admiral	Vice admiral
Kontr-admiral	Rear admiral	Rear admiral
Kapitan pervogo ranga	Captain 1st rank	Captain
Kapitan vtorogo ranga	Captain 2nd rank	Commander
Kapitan-leitenant (1909–11)	Captain-lieutenant	Lieutenant commander
Starshii leitenant	Senior lieutenant	Lieutenant commander
Leitenant	Lieutenant	Lieutenant
Michman		Sublieutenant/ensign
Korabelnyi gardemarin*	Shipboard midshipman	Midshipman
Gardemarin*	Midshipman	Naval cadet

* From the French term *garde de marine*.

Culture

Relations between officers and enlisted men were notoriously poor; discipline was frequently harsh, and although striking subordinates was illegal, it was not unknown. Enlisted men were not allowed in certain parks; they could not smoke in the street or ride on the inside of trolleys. They had to address junior officers as *Vashe Blagorodie* (Your Honor) and senior officers as *Vashe Vysokoblagorodie* (Your High Honor), while officers used the familiar "thou" (*ty*) in addressing enlisted men—the same form of address used for children.

But these grievances should not be overemphasized. Relations between Russia's social elites on the one hand and the rural peasantry and urban proletariat on the other were poor to start with; naval service and wartime conditions merely exacerbated this schism. Against this background, the inactivity of much of the fleet, combined with the growing influence of revolutionary propaganda, made for an explosive situation. Also, paradoxically, strict discipline was often combined with lax oversight, which made it easier for revolutionary parties to infiltrate naval bases and, on occasion, to organize large gatherings. One result of this became evident in 1912 when a plot for a fleetwide revolt in the Black Sea was exposed and several sailors were executed.

The lax supervision exercised by officers probably owed a good deal to a phenomenon noted by one volunteer officer, Konstantin Benkendorf. Having served in the Russo-Japanese War, he was recalled to duty in August 1914 and noted that a change had come over officer-enlisted relations between the wars: "I felt that both sides, officers and men, had withdrawn from each other and, what is more, this fact was not only accepted, especially by the younger officers, but even fostered among them."[4] Perhaps Benkendorf's lapse in service allowed him to see something missed by others—that the officers were as estranged from the men as much as the men were from their officers. It was perhaps something that was easier to ignore than address, and many officers probably felt more comfortable immersing themselves in professional matters than trying to grapple with issues fraught with enormous social implications for both the navy and the empire. Whatever its root causes, the rift between officers and men would have terrible consequences when revolution broke out in early 1917.

THE WAYS OF WAR

Surface Warfare

Doctrine

In a fleet action, the Russian navy intended to fight at long ranges—in 1912 the Baltic Fleet was conducting gunnery practice at an average range of 12,400 yards for big guns, and by 1914 the Black Sea Fleet staff expected to engage at ranges of 16,000–20,000 yards. A form of divisional tactics would be employed, in which the individual brigades would maneuver independently while adhering to an overall battle plan; this would allow each brigade to make full use of its advantages in action, without being hindered by slower or weaker ships. The primary function of destroyers, in either a fleet action or defense of a mine barrier, would be to launch salvos of torpedoes at the enemy—hence the extraordinarily heavy torpedo batteries of the *Novik*-type destroyers.

Ships/Weapons

In August 1914 the only modern surface combatant in the Russian navy was the destroyer *Novik,* and for the war's first year it was the older ships, the survivors of the Russo-Japanese War and the ones built in its immediate aftermath, that would bear the brunt of the fighting at sea. Predreadnought battleships formed the core of the Baltic and Black Sea Fleets. In the Baltic, the most powerful units were the *Andrei Pervozvannyi* and *Imperator Pavel I,* which had entered service in 1911 after eight years under construction. Their design had been much altered as a result of the experience of the Russo-Japanese War; their hulls had been armored overall against high-explosive shells, 120-mm guns had replaced the 75-mm antidestroyer guns of the original design, their superstructures had been much reduced, and cage masts had been fitted. They were effective, if outdated, units.

The other predreadnoughts in both the Baltic (two ships) and Black Sea (five ships) had been refitted to one degree or another before the war. Their superstructures had been cut down, turret machinery improved to increase the rate of fire, gun elevations increased, and modern range finders and sights fitted. None were of outstanding design, but they would give good service during the war.

The four Baltic dreadnoughts of the *Sevastopol* class were rushed into service in late 1914, although they were not ready for combat until the summer of 1915. They featured a powerful armament of twelve 12-inch guns and could make twenty-four knots, but they were relatively weakly protected with a 9-inch belt. Their Black Sea cousins of the *Imperatritsa Mariia* class featured the same armament but a slower (twenty-one-knot) speed and 10.3-inch belts; three of these ships entered service during the war. A fourth ship, *Imperator Nikolai I,* was larger and more stoutly protected, but she was never completed. All Russian dreadnoughts shared a dangerously weak underwater protection scheme that lacked a protective bulkhead; this was a deliberate choice made in order to devote the maximum possible weight to offensive features. The Baltic dreadnoughts saw little action, but the Black Sea ships had several brief encounters with the enemy.

As for cruisers, none of the turbine-driven ships laid down in 1913–14 were destined to be completed by the imperial navy. Of the older ships, by far the most impressive was the Vickers-built *Riurik,* a handsome ship that to all intents and purposes was the equivalent of a predreadnought battle cruiser. She frequently served as Admiral Essen's flagship. All the other cruisers were of pre-1905 design, and all of them underwent extensive rearming either shortly before or during the First World War, as shown in table 6.9.

Photo 6.2. The armored cruiser *Riurik* in 1917. Built by the British firm of Vickers in 1905–1908, she was one of the last and most powerful armored cruisers. She frequently served as the flagship of the Baltic Fleet before the First World War and during the conflict's first year. She participated in the action off Gotland with German cruisers on 2 July 1915. Her foremast was modified to a tripod mast while in dockyard for repairs following mine damage to her bow in November 1916. She was scrapped in the early 1920s. (Boris Lemachko collection)

Table 6.9 Rearming of Cruisers, 1914–17

Name	Type	Fleet	Rearmed	As designed (a)	As rearmed (a)
Rossiia	AC	Baltic	1915	4 (2) x 8-in. 16 (8) x 6-in.	8 (6) x 8-in. 14 (7) x 6-in.
Gromoboi	AC	Baltic	1915	4 (2) x 8-in. 16 (8) x 6-in.	6 (4) x 8-in. 22 (11) x 6-in.
Baian, Admiral Makarov	AC	Baltic	1916	2 (2) x 8-in. 8 (4) x 6-in.	3 (3) x 8-in. 12 (6) x 6-in.
Oleg, Bogatyr	C	Baltic	1916	12 (8) x 6-in.	16 (10) x 130-mm
Diana	C	Baltic	1915	8 (5) x 6-in.	10 (6) x 130-mm
Avrora	C	Baltic	1916/17	8 (5) x 6-in.	14 (8) x 6-in.
Pamiat Merkuriia	C	Black Sea	1914	12 (8) x 6-in.	16 (?) x 6-in.
Kagul	C	Black Sea	1916	12 (8) x 6-in.	14 (8) x 130-mm
Prut (b)	C	Black Sea	1915	2 (2) x 6-in. 8 (4) x 120-mm	10 (6) x 130-mm
Askold	C	Siberian Flotilla		12 (7) x 6-in.	No change
Variag	C	Arctic Flotilla	1916	12 (6) x 6-in.	12 (8) x 6-in.

Note: Pallada of the Baltic Fleet and *Zhemchug* of the Siberian Flotilla were sunk before they could be rearmed.

(a) Figures in parentheses indicate the number of guns that could train on one broadside.

(b) Ex-Turkish *Mecidiye;* struck a mine and sank in shallow water off Odessa on 3 April 1915 and subsequently raised by the Russians.

In terms of destroyers, the Baltic Fleet was much indebted to the "Special Commission for Strengthening the Fleet by Voluntary Contributions," which funded the construction of eighteen destroyers in 1904–1906. Built by both foreign and Russian shipyards, all these ships were essentially similar: 570–640 tons, twenty-five to twenty-six knots, armed with a pair of 75-mm guns and two or three 18-inch torpedo tubes (prior to the war, the 75-mm guns were replaced by 4-inch guns). Destroyers of similar armament but of smaller size were built by government funds, with the result that by 1914 the Baltic Fleet had a relatively uniform force of thirty-nine. The Black Sea Fleet had thirteen similar ships, and in both fleets there were considerable numbers of older and smaller units.

The prototype of the new generation of destroyers was the German-designed *Novik;* she formed the basis for seven subsequent classes, built to varying designs by different shipyards. Thirty of these fine ships were completed during the war, seventeen for the Baltic and thirteen for the Black Sea. Fast and well armed, these ships were among the best destroyers in the world; their worst fault noted in service was that some of the Black Sea hulls suffered from poor stability, which meant that they had to retain a certain amount of oil fuel as ballast, reducing their range.

A considerable number of older torpedo boats remained in service; some were used as dispatch vessels, some were converted to minesweepers. Also deserving mention were the gunboats, a type much favored by the Russian navy (seven in the Baltic, three in the Black Sea). Most were of older construction, but all gave good service by giving fire support to troops ashore. Numerous auxiliaries were acquired or built during the war, ranging from large vessels used as seaplane carriers to small motor minesweepers and antisubmarine launches.

As for the guns arming Russia's surface ships, they generally proved very effective, thanks to a thorough overhaul of shipboard gunnery carried out after the war with Japan. Rate of fire was increased, and shells were much improved; heavy shells with TNT as the bursting charge were introduced in 1908, and by 1914 Russian armor-piercing shells may have been the best in the world. Postwar British tests showed that in terms of penetrative power at oblique angles (twenty degrees) Russian 12-inch shells were only slightly inferior to the British post-Jutland Greenboy shells.

Fire control was explored in experiments conducted by the Black Sea Fleet after the war with Japan. Gunnery doctrine called for frequent and dense salvos—hence the demand for exceptionally high rates of fire in new gunnery systems and the twelve-gun broadsides of all dreadnought designs. The 1911 Geisler fire-control system included a range clock and a device to

Table 6.10 Major Russian Guns, 1914–17

Bore (in./mm)	Cal.	Shell (lbs.)	MV (f/s)	Range (yds.) @ elevation (m)	F/C (sec.)	Ship or classes
14/356	52	1648.8	2400	25,373 @ 25	20 (design)	*Izmail* class
12/305	52	1038.3	2500	25,403 @ 25	36–45	*Sevastopol, Imp. Mariia*
12/305	40	731.4	2600	16,000 @ 15	40	Older battleships
10/254	50	496.5	2950	20,250 @ 21	~30	*Riurik*
8/203	50	247.4	2650	15,800 @ 20	20	*Riurik*, semidreadnoughts
6/152	45	91.4	2600	13,600 @ 25	9	Numerous
5.1/130	55	81.3	2700	16,803 @ 20	10–12	Numerous
4.7/120	50	66	2700	15,200 @ 20	?	Numerous
4/102	60	38.5	2700	16,800 @ 30	12–15	Destroyers

Note: Russian practice measured caliber length from the muzzle to the rear face of the breech end (excluding the breech block and its fixtures).

Source: Aleksandr Shirokad, *Entsiklopediia otechestvennoi artillerii* (Minsk: Kharvest, 2000).

Table 6.11 Russian Torpedoes

Year	Model	Diameter	Length	Total weight	Warhead	Range @ speed
1908	M.1908	450 mm	5.2 m	650 kg	95 kg TNT	1,000 m @ 38 kts 2,000 m @ 27 kts. 3,000 m @ 23 kts.
1912	45-12	450 mm	5.58	810 kg	100 kg TNT	2,000 m @ 43 kts. 5,000 m @ 30 kts. 6,000 m @ 28 kts.
1915	45-15	450 mm	Probably similar to the 45-12			
1917	M.1917	533 mm	?	?	215 kg	3,000 m @ 45 kts. 10,000 m @ 30 kts.

Source: Iu.L. Korshunov and G.V. Uspenskii, *Torpedy rossiiskogo flota* (Morskoe oruzhie 1; St. Petersburg: Gangut/Neptun, 1993), 26–27.

correct for the effects of bore erosion. Immediately before the war five of Arthur Pollen's Argo clocks were purchased; four of these, delivered after the start of the war, were installed on the *Sevastopol*-class dreadnoughts. Ships were equipped with a variety of range finders, all of long baseline—five-meter Zeiss instruments were in the dreadnoughts as completed.

A unique feature of Russian gunnery was a highly developed system for concentration of fire. Three ships would be linked by special shortwave radio sets; the middle ship would take on the role of the "master" ship, relaying fire-control data to her consorts, who would make corrections based on their positions relative to the master. Although in action the Russian system seems to have been overly complex and subject to error, it foreshadowed methods adopted by the Royal Navy after Jutland. (See table 6.10.)

Russian guns were of excellent quality, but Russian torpedoes displayed a number of persistent problems, including erratic running, failure to detonate, and most disturbing of all, circling. Such problems were by no means unique to Russia, however. By 1914 the principle suppliers of torpedoes were the Obukhovskii and Lessner Works, although Whitehead's Fiume Works continued to provide limited numbers as well as designs. The Model 1908 torpedo introduced both a TNT warhead (instead of wet guncotton) and dry-heater propulsion. The Model 45-12 torpedo was the first to employ wet-heater propulsion; just before the war 250 of these were ordered from Fiume, but only twenty-four had been delivered by August 1914. As a result, the Model 45-15, a Russian-made variant of the 45-12, was designed.

All these torpedoes were 450-mm (nominally 18-inch) in diameter. The Russian navy began development of a 533-mm (21-inch) torpedo only in 1917. Prototypes were ordered from the Lessner Works, but none were ever delivered.

In addition to conventional torpedo tubes, the Russian navy developed the Dzhevetskii gear, a trainable, externally mounted launcher for submarines (also adopted in French submarines). Also unusual were the M.1913 triple tube mountings of the post-*Novik* destroyers. These were designed by the Putilovskii Works and allowed the two outer tubes to be trained up to seven degrees separately from the central tube, thus facilitating the launching of spreads. (See table 6.11.)

Submarine Warfare

Offensive

Doctrine

Initially, submarines were regarded as a harbor defense weapon, but after the Russo-Japanese War the need was seen for larger boats that could attack the enemy at sea. As in most other navies, however, no thought was given to using submarines as commerce raiders. There was also some interest in "fleet" submarines, capable of operating tactically with the surface fleet, but the large boats ordered under the 1915 program to meet this requirement were never laid down.

Boats/Weapons

By 1914 the Russian navy had collected a submarine force that was impressive in numerical terms but possessed little combat value. Many of the boats had been hurriedly acquired during or after the Russo-Japanese War; most were small, and all were obsolete by 1914. Nevertheless, early in the war several of these craft were brought by railroad from Vladivostok in the Far East to serve in the European theaters.

For the first year of the war, all the effective boats in service were in the Baltic Fleet—four *Kaiman*-class (1905–11, 409 tons on the surface, 482 tons submerged), based on the designs of the American inventor Simon Lake, and the *Akula* (1906–11, 370/475 tons), designed by the Russian naval constructor I. G. Bubnov. The Black Sea Fleet did not have a single useful submarine. However, there were no less than eighteen boats under construction in Baltic shipyards, and another six were building for the Black Sea Fleet in August 1914. Despite the fact that these submarines had been laid down under the programs of 1911 and 1912, not one of them would be ready for service before 1915.

The majority of submarines under construction were designed by Bubnov, who had the support of the Naval Technical Committee. Taking his *Akula* as a prototype, he designed the three *Nerpa* boats for the Black Sea Fleet (1911–15, 630/773 tons) and the eighteen of the *Bars* class (1913–17, 650/780 tons) for the Baltic Fleet. Their long building times probably played a role in the persistent flaws that plagued his designs. Their hull forms were poor, which reduced their speed; diving times were slow, on the order of three minutes, although at the time this was by no means unique to Bubnov's boats. They also tended to produce thirty-foot "fountains" while diving as the main ballast tanks flooded, often revealing their presence just as they were getting ready to attack.

Other problems were not Bubnov's fault. Among these was the weakness of Russia's diesel-engine industry. This led to many engines being ordered from German firms, leaving most of the *Nerpa*- and *Bars*-class boats without engines once war began. Some engines were taken from the new gunboats of the Amur River Flotilla, and others were ordered from the New London Ship & Engine Company of Groton, Connecticut, but these were far less powerful than the intended units, greatly reducing the surface speed of the boats and increasing the time required to recharge batteries.

Bubnov's main competition came from an American firm, the Holland Torpedo Boat Company, whose designs were preferred by the Naval General Staff. In 1911 three *Narval*-class boats (1911–16, 621/994 tons) were laid down for the Black Sea Fleet using a Holland design; they are frequently described by Russian sources as the best submarines in the fleet. During the war, AG (*Amerikanskii Golland,* i.e., American Holland) boats were ordered; this design was an international favorite, and no fewer than seventy-one boats of this general type served in the Russian, British, American, Italian, and Chilean navies. Although of an American design, the Russian boats were prefabricated in Canada to circumvent neutrality laws; they were delivered in railway-transportable sections to Vladivostok and assembled in shipyards in Petrograd and Nikolaev. The Russians ordered seventeen boats, although six were subsequently canceled; of the eleven delivered, six entered service with the imperial navy, five in the Baltic and one in the Black Sea. After 1918 the Soviet regime completed five more of the class.

One boat was neither a Bubnov nor a Holland design—the submarine minelayer *Krab,* built for the Black Sea Fleet to a design of the railroad engineer M. P. Naletov. During her long construction period she was subjected to many alterations, and the resulting boat was so plagued with problems that her crew nicknamed her the "box of surprises."[5] Nevertheless, her ability to lay up to sixty mines unseen by the enemy made her so useful that two of the *Bars*-class boats under construction for the Baltic Fleet, the *Ersh* and *Forel,* were redesigned to carry forty-two mines; only the *Ersh* entered service, but only in December 1917, and consequently took little part in wartime operations.

Antisubmarine

On 11 October 1914 cruiser *Pallada* was lost with all hands after being torpedoed by *U 26;* this tragedy led to a desperate search for effective antisubmarine weapons. As in other navies, consideration was given to a wide, and sometimes bizarre, assortment of expedients, few of which proved to be effective. A great deal of time and money was expended on various types of indicator nets, mine nets, and antisubmarine sweeps, but none seem to have scored any successes (although there is a slim chance that *UC.15* was lost in the Black Sea by fouling a mine net). Diving shells, with flat or hollow noses to prevent ricochets, were used against both submarines and torpedoes, and some successes against the latter were claimed; in October 1916 the battleship *Panteleimon* (ex–*Kniaz Potëmkin Tavricheskii*) apparently destroyed a torpedo launched at her by *UB 7*.

A variety of depth charges were developed using two types of detonators—hydrostatic and float/lanyard. Both types proved problematic, the first because the explosion of one charge tended to set off any others in the water, the second because the charges had a tendency to explode before reaching their preset depths.

Ultimately, Russia's most successful antisubmarine weapon was the mine. Of the nine U-boats probably destroyed by Russian actions, the losses of six are attributed to mines. After his appointment as commander of the Black Sea Fleet in July 1916, Vice Admiral A. V. Kolchak engaged in a particularly aggressive antisubmarine minelaying campaign, which seems to have paid off: mines destroyed three U-boats in November–December 1916. (See table 6.12.)

Mine Warfare

Doctrine

The Russians were early practitioners of mine warfare and by 1914 were acknowledged masters of its techniques. Mining obviously played a key role in Russian defensive strategy, but it was recognized from the start that an unprotected minefield would soon be swept by the enemy. Therefore mines were usually integrated with coast batteries into "mine-artillery positions." As for offensive minelaying operations off an enemy's coasts, stealth was the chief objective. The Baltic Sea's long winter nights were ideal for such operations, and Russian ships would do everything possible to keep their presence secret, even to the point of refusing to open fire on enemy vessels encountered as long as they themselves were unobserved. The results justified the efforts expended: more enemy vessels were lost to mines than to any other weapon in both the Baltic and Black Sea theaters. The most spectacular success was the virtual destruction of the German X Destroyer Flotilla when it attempted to penetrate the "Forward Position" (see below) on the night of 10–11 November 1916. Seven of its eleven modern destroyers—*V 25, S 57, V 72, G 90, S 58, S 59*, and *V 76*—were sunk on Russian mines at the entrance to the Gulf of Finland.

Ships/Weapons

Extensive minefields were used in defense of the Gulf of Finland, for which purpose the *Ladoga, Narova*, and *Onega* were converted from old armor-belted cruisers; between them they could carry more than two thousand

Table 6.12 Russian Depth Charges

Model	Entered service	Charge (kg.)	Destructive radius (m)	Method of launching	Type of detonator	Depth settings (m)
Shchigolev	Early 1916	18–24	3–3.5	By hand	Hydrostatic	10
Schreiber	1916	8	2	By hand	Float/lanyard	Up to 16
Averkiev 4V	Late 1915	8	2	By hand	Hydrostatic	9–11 14–20 18–27 27–58
4V-B	Early 1917	115	7	Mine rails	Float/lanyard	12, 24, 36, 48
4V-M	1917	16	3	By hand	Hydrostatic	12, 14
Large aviation	Late 1915	16	?	By hand	Hydrostatic	?
Small aviation	Late 1915	3	?	By hand	Hydrostatic	?

Note: The large charge of the 4V-B could damage a slow vessel before it could get far enough away, so it was used only from fast ships.
Source: D. Iu. Kozlov, "Pervye otechestvennye glubinnye bomby," *Gangut*, no. 20 [1999], 68–77.

mines. Most cruisers and destroyers were equipped for offensive minelaying missions.

The most numerous type of mine available at the outbreak of war was the M.1908; substantial numbers of the M.1898 were still in service, as well as some M.1906 mines. The M.1909 introduced an inertial detonator in place of Hertz horns, making the mines safer to handle on deck, while the M.1912 had a timing mechanism that delayed the mine's rise from the bottom. During the war antisubmarine mines were also developed, in which a single mine cable supported three or four mines at different depths. (See table 6.13.)

Table 6.13 Russian Mines

Model	Charge (lbs.)	Explosive	Type of detonator	Maximum depth (ft)	Notes
M.1898	125	Wet guncotton	Hertz horns	130	
M.1906	125–140	Wet guncotton	Hertz horns	?	
M.1908	250	TNT	Hertz horns	360	
M.1909	280	TNT	Inertia	?	
M.1912	220	TNT	Inertia	425	
PL-100	220	TNT	Inertia	425	Submarine minelayer *Krab*

Source: Iu. L. Korshunov, Iu. L. D'iakonov, and Iu. P. D'iakonov, *Miny rossiiskogo flota,* Morskoe oruzhie 5 (St. Petersburg: Gangut/Neptun, 1995), 23; Beskrovnyi, *Armiia i flot Rossii v nachale XX v.*, 204.

Amphibious Warfare

Doctrine/Capabilities

In the late nineteenth century the Russian army and navy worked out elaborate plans to seize the Bosporus. These schemes fell into abeyance after the Russo-Japanese War, but during the First World War the Black Sea Fleet did carry out a number of highly successful amphibious operations on a smaller scale. Between February and June 1916, a series of landings along the northern Anatolian coast succeeded in dislodging the Turks from one strong position after another at little cost. These operations were supported by the Black Sea Fleet's Batumi group, usually consisting of the battleship *Rostislav* plus gunboats and torpedo boats, sometimes assisted by the battleship *Panteleimon*. Techniques were developed for controlling naval gunfire from observation posts ashore.

Two special types of craft were used in these landings. One, the Elpidifors, was a group of small cargo vessels (circa one thousand tons) widely used in the Sea of Azov; a number of them were taken over by the navy, and their shallow drafts and large holds made them ideal for use as landing ships. The type proved so successful that the navy ordered thirty of them in early 1917. Also employed in the landings from May 1916 onward were 255-ton landing barges; these were based on the British X Lighters used in the Dardanelles but were somewhat larger. Like their prototypes, they featured bow ramps, lowered by means of booms. Nicknamed "bolinders," after the Swedish firm that supplied most of the diesel engines that propelled them, fifty of the craft were ordered in December 1915 from the Russud yard in Nikolaev. The first of these became available in March 1916; due to shortages, thirty of them were delivered without engines and were used as barges.

Photo 6.3. The Russian navy's most active battleship during the war was the Baltic Fleet's predreadnought *Slava,* seen here wintering at Helsingfors. Completed too late to take part in the Russo-Japanese War, *Slava* was the only one of the five ships in her class to avoid destruction or capture at Tsushima. During World War I she helped defend the Gulf of Riga in August 1915 and October 1917, exchanging fire with German dreadnoughts on both occasions. Severely damaged in action with the *König* on 17 October 1917, she was scuttled in an effort to block the Moonsund channel. (Stephen McLaughlin collection)

From 1916 onward plans were revived for an assault on the Bosporus, and in July 1916 the emperor personally ordered the new fleet commander, Vice Admiral Kolchak, to make preparations for such a landing. However, in August 1916 Romania joined the allies and promptly collapsed, forcing the Russian command to use the troops intended for the landing to shore up its new ally. In March 1917 the idea of a Bosporus assault was revived, the Turkish defenses having been considerably weakened by the dispatch of troops to other fronts, leaving only two divisions to guard the strait. The new proposal called for a surprise assault using only three divisions, but this was aborted by the turmoil that followed the February Revolution of 1917.

There was far less interest in amphibious operations in the Baltic. Only one small operation was carried out, when 536 men were landed on 22 October 1915 at Petragge, in the Gulf of Riga; this was little more than a diversionary raid behind German lines, and the troops were reembarked later the same day. In July 1916 the navy proposed a much larger landing at Domesnäs, well behind German lines. If successful, the operation might have forced the Germans to withdraw from a large segment of the Baltic coast, but the army rejected the plan.

Coastal Defense

The maritime approaches to St. Petersburg had long been guarded by the fortress of Kronshtadt, which throughout the nineteenth century was regarded as one of the strongest fortified places in the world. But by 1905 Kronshtadt's forts were obsolete, and when work was begun in 1909 on modernizing the capital's defenses, a new position was established about forty miles west of Petersburg, where the Gulf of Finland suddenly narrows like the neck of a wine bottle to a width of about twelve miles. On the northern coast was Fort Ino, on the southern side Krasnaia Gorka; their armament was virtually identical, each with eight 10-inch long guns and eight high-angle 11-inch howitzers, plus a variety of smaller weapons. In 1911 it was decided to add 12-inch/52-caliber guns to their armament. Initially, four guns were installed at each fort in open batteries; another four guns, in two twin turrets, were mounted during the war.

At the same time work was begun on the fortifications farther to the west, at the entrance to the Gulf of Finland. Initially under army control, this complex was turned over to the navy in 1912 and named the Maritime Fortress of the Emperor Peter the Great. This was to be the main line of defense, with powerful coastal batteries flanking deep minefields that would span the thirty-mile-wide reach between the Finnish Porkkala Peninsula and Revel on the Estonian side. The complex would thus protect not only the Gulf of Finland itself but the navy's new main base at Revel.

The start of the war found the Peter the Great fortress far from completion, and during the war the defenses were gradually strengthened using whatever artillery was available. By 1917 guns ranging in caliber from 12-inch to 57-mm had been installed in numerous batteries, creating a formidable defensive position.

The war also led to the extension of the defenses to include the Gulf of Riga, in particular its southern entrance, the Irben Strait. Although after the spring of 1915 the southern coast of the strait was in German hands, on the southern tip of Ösel Island's Tserel (Zerel) Peninsula four 12-inch/52 guns were installed on open mountings, with numerous smaller batteries at other sites throughout the Moonsund Islands.

Coast defenses in the Black Sea were on a considerably smaller scale. The most important fortifications, which included 280-mm and 243-mm guns, guarded Sevastopol. Odessa and other ports had more modest defenses. During the war, 10-inch guns were installed at Batumi, to defend this forward base and the ships sheltering there against any sudden attack by the *Goeben*. A few coastal batteries were also established in north Russia during the war to fend off any raids by German auxiliary cruisers.

Aviation

Although the Russian navy had began experimenting with balloons and man-lifting kites well before the Russo-Japanese War, interest in heavier-than-air craft seems to have been slow in developing. A naval air service was established in the Black Sea Fleet only in the autumn of 1911, with the Baltic Fleet following suit in March 1912. Since aircraft were seen primarily as reconnaissance tools, naval aviation was subordinated to the Service of Observation and Communications in both seas. In November 1916, however, aviation was reorganized and transferred to the direct control of the fleet commanders.

Russian naval aviation fought two very different wars. In the Baltic, the task was to support the fixed defenses of the Gulfs of Finland and Riga; reconnaissance was the primary focus. Major naval air stations were established at Kilkond (on Ösel Island) and Abo, in Finland; smaller stations were set up to act as forward operating bases. When she joined the fleet in February 1915, the Baltic Fleet's sole aviation vessel, the *Orlitsa,* acted as a mobile base, operating her aircraft from harbors and bays.

In the Black Sea, on the other hand, aviation was used offensively, in raids against Turkish and Bulgarian ports—especially the coal port of

Zonguldak and the U-boat base at Varna. The aviation vessels went to sea with the fleet, bombing the enemy and spotting gunfire. The Black Sea fleet had formed what amounted to the world's first "carrier-battleship task force."[6] It was a force used with a considerable degree of imagination and aggressiveness.

Seaplanes—either floatplanes or flying boats—were seen as the best type for naval service. In the first year of the war the Baltic Fleet used Sikorskii S-10 floatplanes and French-designed F.B.A. Type C flying boats (thirty acquired from France, with a further thirty-four manufactured under license by the Lebedev Works). The Black Sea Fleet used the generally similar American Curtiss Type F; the subsequent Curtiss K-type flying boats proved to be a failure due to flawed design and manufacture. By mid-1915 the M.5, designed by D. P. Grigorovich and manufactured by the Shchetinin Works in Petrograd, was entering service with the Black Sea Fleet. The M.5 was not used by the Baltic Fleet, but its successor, the M.9, which appeared in mid-1916, became the most widely used aircraft in both fleets. By November 1916 there were no less than 121 Shchetinin (Grigorovich) machines of all types serving in naval aviation. Most of these aircraft were powered by foreign-made engines, since Russian industry could manufacture only small numbers of aero engines.

As the war continued fighters became necessary, and in response Grigorovich developed the M.11, an attempt at a flying-boat fighter, but it was outclassed by increasing numbers of German high-performance land planes, especially in the Baltic. This led the navy to acquire small numbers of land-plane fighters for the defense of its bases; in 1917 there were eight naval fighters in the Baltic and two in the Black Sea. By this time the total number of aircraft in service was 269, with eighty-eight in the Baltic Fleet, 152 in the Black Sea Fleet, and twenty-nine in the Naval Aviation School. The revolutions of 1917 and the outbreak of civil war in 1918 led to a rapid deterioration, and by October 1918 the Bolshevik naval air service could muster only sixty-one aircraft.

Mention should also be made of the biggest seaplane of the day—a four-engine aircraft, *Ilia Muromets*, designed by Igor Sikorskii and fitted with floats. Unfortunately, this machine was destroyed by accident in the first days of the war. Had it survived it might have proved its value in long-range reconnaissance, but for reasons that are unclear the navy ordered no more of these advanced machines, although the wheeled version saw extensive service with the army's air force.

There was also a short-lived experiment with lighter-than-air aviation: four British Coastal-type nonrigid airships, intended for antisubmarine

Table 6.14 Principle Aircraft Types of the Russian Navy, 1914–18

Type	In service	Weight loaded (lbs)	Length	Wingspan	Engine (hp)	Speed (mph)	Range
Sikorskii S-10 Gidro	1914	1,928	?	45 ft.	100	?	?
F.B.A. Type C	1914	2,072	28 ft. 10 in.	45 ft.	130	68	186 miles
Curtiss F Boat	1914	2,460	27 ft. 4 in.	41 ft. 8 in.	100	69	5 hrs. 30 mins.
Grigorovich M-5	Mid-1915	2,120	28 ft. 2 in.	44 ft. 6 in.	100	65	4 hrs.
Grigorovich M-9	June 1916	3,550	29 ft.	52 ft.	150	65	5 hrs.
Grigorovich M-11	Late 1916?	2,040	25 ft.	29 ft.	110	92	2 hrs.

patrolling, arrived in disassembled form at Sevastopol in late 1916. However, a series of accidents, due both to mishandling and weather, led to the abandonment of this type of aircraft after a short time. (See table 6.14.)

WAR EXPERIENCE AND EVOLUTION

Wartime Evolution

The Baltic

In essence, the war in the Baltic was a question of position. Thanks to geography, Germany was able to block maritime communications between the Baltic and the North Sea, except for the passage of a few British submarines. Although the Germans regarded the Baltic as a secondary theater, they could still bring overwhelming force to bear by shuttling ships from the North Sea via the Kaiser Wilhelm (Kiel) Canal. On the other hand, and again thanks to geography, the Russians were able to establish strong defensive positions at the entrances to the Gulf of Finland and the Gulf of Riga. The latter in particular became an object of at least intermittent German interest.

Positional warfare meant minefields, and over the course of the war the Baltic Fleet would lay about 35,000 mines in defensive barriers. The process began on 31 July 1914—the day before Germany declared war—when 2,129 mines were laid to block the entrance to the Gulf of Finland. This was the first installment of the "Central Position," where any German thrust into the gulf would be met. The German plan, on the other hand, was basically a bluff—active use would be made of second-rank vessels to hold the Russians at bay. However, the bluff was revealed when the light cruiser *Magdeburg* ran aground on Odensholm Island on 26 August 1914 and documents captured on board the ship revealed the weakness of the German forces in the Baltic. This gave Admiral N. O. Essen, the Baltic Fleet commander, the ammunition he needed to gain approval for a more active policy. From late October 1914 to mid-January 1915 (when ice conditions forced a halt) the Baltic Fleet undertook thirteen offensive minelaying operations, laying a total of 1,538 mines off Germany's Baltic ports. One of these mines sank the armored cruiser *Friedrich Carl* on 17 November 1914.

The treasure trove of documents captured on board the *Magdeburg* included her codebooks; sending one copy to the British, the Russians retained a second copy and made arrangements to exploit it. The resulting decryption of German radio messages allowed the Russians to avoid losses that might otherwise have been crippling. Thus when patrols to the west of the Central Position were halted after the armored cruiser *Pallada* was sunk by *U 26* on 11 October 1914, the fleet relied entirely on radio intelligence for warning of a German approach. By 1916 aircraft were also playing an important role in reconnaissance.

The connection between the war on land and the war at sea was clearly shown in the summer of 1915, when the Central Powers overran most of Russian Poland. By July the Germans were at the gates of Riga; if the hastily constructed front there collapsed, Russian control of the Gulf of Riga would be lost, opening the back door to the Gulf of Finland. Russian naval intelligence learned of German plans to seize control of the gulf, and the local defenses were strengthened: minefields were laid in the Irben Strait (the southern entrance to the Gulf of Riga), and the predreadnought *Slava* was sent there to assist in protecting the fields. Thus when the German assault came in August 1915, the Russians could offer strong resistance. Although the Germans did briefly penetrate into the gulf, they were eventually forced to withdraw. Henceforth the navy would render strong support to the army's Riga front, which may well have been the decisive factor in keeping that area stable for more than two years.

By the time of the Riga offensive Admiral Essen was dead of pneumonia, and Vice Admiral V. A. Kanin commanded the Baltic Fleet. He intensified the war against Germany's trade with Sweden, both by submarines and surface ships, although these efforts never posed a serious threat to that trade. Another development during his tenure was the Forward Position, a new mine-artillery position to the west of the Central Position that deepened the Russian defensive system.

In September 1916 Kanin had been replaced by Vice Admiral A. I. Nepenin, who had previously commanded the SNIS. Nepenin planned a more active role for the fleet in the 1917 campaign; in the meantime, he tried to restore discipline, which had lapsed during Kanin's tenure. Unfortunately, the crews saw his efforts as persecution, and this added to the resentment building on the lower deck. Throughout the war there had been minor incidents of indiscipline, most notably on board the dreadnought *Gangut* on 1 November 1915, when the crew rioted after being denied its expected meal of meat and macaroni after coaling ship. By the winter of 1916/17 the situation, not only in the fleet but throughout Russia, was moving toward a crisis. Under the influence of the mystic Grigory Efimovich Rasputin, Empress Alexandra urged her husband to replace one minister after another. Nicholas, at Stavka, usually agreed; the disorganization in government spread to the transportation system, which began to break down under the stress of war. In early March 1917 (late February, by the Russian calendar) riots over a lack of bread in Petrograd turned into a revolution as troops joined the protests. Within days the monarchy collapsed, replaced by competing authorities—the liberal Provisional Government and the radical Petrograd Soviet of Workers' and Soldiers' Deputies.

News of the revolution ignited mutinies at most of the Baltic Fleet's bases; at Helsingfors forty-five officers were murdered, among them Admiral Nepenin; at Kronshtadt twenty-four officers perished; at Revel, where the more active destroyers and submarines were based, only five were killed. Many more officers were forced off their ships. Almost overnight sailor committees took charge of running the ships, and although the remaining officers were theoretically in charge of military activities, their authority was continually undermined. By the autumn of 1917 the fleet had lost much of its combat effectiveness. It did, however, manage to fight one last battle. On 11 October 1917 the Germans launched Operation Albion, the invasion of the Moonsund Islands, which guarded the Gulf of Riga. Within hours the army units ashore had started to collapse, but the navy continued to resist until forced to abandon the gulf on 19 October.

The Bolsheviks seized power in November 1917 (the October Revolution, again according to the Russian calendar), and on 15 December 1917 they signed an armistice with the Central Powers at Brest-Litovsk. However, the ensuing peace negotiations soon deadlocked in the face of Germany's severe demands; therefore, on 18 February, the Central Powers launched an offensive that compelled the Bolsheviks to submit to the German terms. The Treaty of Brest-Litovsk (3 March 1918) was harsh; its naval terms obligated Russia either to keep its ships in Russian ports until the end of the war or, if this was impossible, disarm them immediately. This placed the bulk of the Baltic Fleet, locked in the ice at Helsingfors, under an immediate threat, since the "White" Finns, supported by the Germans, were fast approaching. This led to the famous "Ice Passage," a series of evacuations assisted by icebreakers, that brought all the big ships and most of the smaller ones to Kronshtadt between 12 March and 11 April 1918. The Baltic Fleet's ships thereafter did nothing of note, aside from laying defensive minefields to the west of Kronshtadt in August 1918; these were meant to deter the Germans, if they were tempted by Russian weakness to seize the ships or Petrograd itself. With that, the naval war in the Baltic came to an end—at least until the arrival of British forces in 1919.

The Black Sea

When the First World War erupted, Turkey initially remained neutral, despite the arrival of the German battle cruiser *Goeben*, which, along with her consort, the light cruiser *Breslau*, entered the Dardanelles on 10 August 1914 to escape their British pursuers. Tension in the Black Sea mounted over the next several months, and on 29 October 1914, without a prior declaration of war, Turco-German naval forces launched a series of attacks on Russian ports—Odessa, Novorossiisk, Feodosiia, and Sevastopol, where *Goeben* briefly bombarded the harbor before being driven off by the accurate fire of the coast-defense batteries.

Although the Russians had been caught napping, their loses were small. If the war in the Baltic was one of positions, the Black Sea offered scope for the classic concept of command of the sea, and the outbreak of war placed the Germans and their Turkish allies in a very exposed position. Although the *Goeben* was the most powerful ship in the Black Sea and faster than any Russian ship, these were only temporary advantages, for the Russian dreadnoughts building in Nikolaev would outgun her, and the new *Novik*-type destroyers could outrun her. Moreover, the Ottoman Empire had few railways or paved roads, so Constantinople was dependent to a considerable degree on seaborne supplies, especially coal, most of which came from Zunguldak, about 150 miles east of the Bosporus on the northern Anatolian coast. Moreover, Enver Pasha, the Turkish minister of war, had launched an ill-advised offensive into the Caucasus, which could be supplied only by sea. These maritime lines of communication were open to attack by the Black Sea Fleet.

Photo 6.4. The Red Navy destroyer *Trotskii* sometime in the 1920s, virtually unchanged from when she entered service in 1916 as *Leitenant Ilin*. One of the numerous variations on the basic *Novik* design, *Leitenant Ilin* was armed with four 4-inch guns and nine 18-inch torpedo tubes, making her one of the most powerful destroyers in the world. (Boris Lemachko collection)

Until the Black Sea Fleet's new ships entered service, however, the *Goeben* was more powerful than any of its ships and faster than all save for the new destroyers that were just entering service. Only the united force of the predreadnoughts could survive an encounter with the German battle cruiser. This was shown clearly when the *Goeben* intercepted the main force of the Black Sea Fleet off the southern Crimea on 18 November 1914. Although the German ship scored four hits on the Russian flagship, she was forced to retire when a Russian shell hit her secondary battery, starting a fire that nearly spread to a magazine. The battle cruiser would in future avoid confrontations with the united Russian squadron.

Immediately after the outbreak of war, the Black Sea Fleet started laying defensive minefields. As for offensive minelaying, the first operation off the Bosporus was badly botched, but subsequent efforts proved more successful; on 25 December 1914 the *Goeben* fouled two mines and had to limp back to Constantinople, where she was under repair for several months. The Russians meanwhile undertook a series of raids, on the coal facilities at Zunguldak and at the Bosporus itself. The big new Russian destroyers began making sweeps along the Anatolian coast, sinking or capturing any Turkish vessels they encountered, leading one German officer to complain that the "Russian destroyers with their artillery and speed are the real masters of the sea and need fear no one."[7] In April a Turco-German bombardment of Odessa went seriously awry when the cruiser *Mecidiye* sank in shallow water after straying into a Russian minefield; she was later raised and incorporated into the Russian fleet under the name *Prut*. In July the *Breslau* was damaged on a Russian mine, putting her out of action for several months.

The year 1915 also saw the start of submarine warfare in the Black Sea. The Russians received their first effective submarine in March 1915, when the *Nerpa* entered service; she was soon joined by others. The boats were for the most part employed off the Bosporus, but they proved less effective than the destroyers in blockade duty—their range of vision was too small, and their speed was too low. On the Turco-German side, the first U-boat, *UB 7*, arrived in July from the Mediterranean, and more followed. The threat of the U-boats had a marked impact on Russian operations, the big ships being used more cautiously.

On 6 October 1915 Bulgaria joined the Central Powers. Although its navy was insignificant, the port of Varna soon became an important U-boat base, which provoked the Russian fleet to bombard it several times. In these and other operations the Russians made use of their seaplane carriers, with the aircraft carrying out bombing attacks as well as spotting naval gunfire.

By this time the first of the Black Sea dreadnoughts, *Imperatritsa Mariia,* had joined the fleet. Her sister *Imperatritsa Ekaterina Velikaia* entered service in December and on 8 January 1916 had a brief encounter with the *Goeben,* which managed to escape the more powerful Russian ship thanks to superior speed. But the Russians could now field three maneuvering groups each more powerful than *Goeben*—one built around *Mariia,* another centered on *Ekaterina,* and a third with the fleet's three most modern predreadnoughts, *Evstafii, Ioann Zlatoust,* and *Panteleimon*. Moreover, the Russian blockade of the Bosporus was increasingly effective, and coal was in short supply in Constantinople; the *Goeben*'s sorties into the Black Sea became less frequent.

Throughout the spring and summer of 1916 the Russian army advanced into Anatolia, supported along the coast by a series of amphibious landings. These repeatedly turned the Turks' flank, forcing them to abandon otherwise strong positions. The Russians were also able to reinforce and supply their army by sea, a luxury denied the Turks.

But *Goeben* was by no means out of the war, and in early July 1916 she managed to evade a Russian trap, thanks again to her speed. For the Russian high command this was the last straw; Admiral Ebergard, who was increasingly at odds with the naval staff at Stavka, was replaced by the energetic Vice Admiral Kolchak. The new commander initiated an aggressive offensive minelaying campaign, which by the end of the year had crippled U-boat operations in the Black Sea; he also undertook preparations for a landing at the Bosporus.

By this time the Russians had both the means and the expertise for a large-scale amphibious assault. But it was not to be. On 27 August 1916, after a protracted wooing by both sides, Romania entered the war as an allied power. But most of the country was soon overrun by a German invasion, and the Russians were forced to rush all available troops to the Romanian front, including the units earmarked for the Bosporus operation.

On 20 October 1916 the Black Sea Fleet suffered its greatest loss, when the dreadnought *Imperatritsa Mariia* sank in Sevastopol harbor after an explosion in her forward magazine. Although many believed this to be an act of sabotage by the enemy, in all probability it was the result of an accident. Despite this loss, by the end of 1916 the Black Sea Fleet's prospects seemed bright: its blockade of Turkish coal shipments was crippling Constantinople, more and more ships were due from the builders' yards to reinforce its already considerable superiority over the enemy, and the U-boat threat was well in hand. But all these advantages were negated by the February Revolution of 1917. Although there was no immediate massacre of officers, as there had been in the Baltic Fleet, the same system of shipboard committees was established, and soon the authority of the officers was being increasingly circumscribed by the sailors. On 19 June Admiral Kolchak resigned, frustrated by the recalcitrance of the crews, who saw reactionary conspiracies behind every order. The situation was exemplified when in early November the *Svobodnaia Rossiia* ("Free Russia," ex–*Imperatritsa Ekaterina Velikaia*) refused to take part in a sortie against the *Breslau*.

A few days later the Bolsheviks seized power in Petrograd and sought an armistice with the Germans. The Cossack general A. M. Kaledin thereupon declared the Don region, north of the Caucasus, independent of Bolshevik power. This increased tension between officers and men of the Black Sea Fleet, and by December matters had gotten out of hand, when several officers were arrested, and a few were shot. The real nightmare came in February 1918, when more than sixty officers were rounded up and shot at the Malakhov Redoubt.

By this time the Germans had launched their offensive to convince the Bolshevik authorities to make peace, and they continued their drive deep into southern Russia even after the Brest-Litovsk Treaty was signed. On 13 March they captured Odessa, and within weeks they were threatening the Crimea. In Sevastopol the situation was soon approaching panic, and fissures began to appear between the ethnic Russians and Ukrainians among the ships' crews. In February Germany had recognized an independent Ukrainian state, and there were disagreements over whether the fleet should stay (as the Germans and many Ukrainians wanted) or leave for Novorossiisk (as many Russians wanted). On 29 April the fleet hoisted the Ukrainian flag, but this failed to slow the German advance, and on 14 May 1918, as the Germans entered Sevastopol, the battleships *Volia* ("Liberty," ex–*Imperator Aleksandr III*) and *Svobodnaia Rossiia*, along with four destroyers, sailed for Novorossiisk. There the fleet was joined by several more destroyers. This was no safe haven. Civil war was already raging near the city, and the Germans were demanding the return of the fleet to Sevastopol; Moscow ordered it to scuttle itself rather than give in to the German demands. Debates over what to do raged among the crews, and in the end things were settled along national lines: *Volia* and five destroyers, manned mostly by Ukrainians, returned to Sevastopol, while *Svobodnaia Rossiia* was sunk at Novorossiisk, as were several destroyers.

The German authorities hoped to place *Volia* as well as some of the destroyers and submarines into service under the German flag, but personnel shortages proved almost insuperable. Only on 15 October 1918 did *Volia* enter service, and by this time Germany's allies were falling in rapid succession—the Bulgarians had signed an armistice on 29 September, Turkey followed on 30 October, and Austria on 3 November. The Germans stopped working on the Russian ships on 11 November and handed them over to the allies when they arrived in mid-December 1918. Many of these ships would see service in the civil war, and most would leave Russia forever when General P. N. Wrangel evacuated his White forces from the Crimea in November 1920.

The Arctic

This maritime theater had been completely overlooked by prewar planners, and the sole naval vessel in the Russian north in August 1914 was the fishery-protection ship *Bakan*. The generally accepted short-war scenario did not require ongoing support from abroad, but as the war dragged on and Russia's industry proved unequal to the task of meeting the needs of the armed services the Russian government placed huge orders for weapons, ammunition, aircraft, and other items with foreign firms. These materials could come only through Vladivostok in the Far East or Arkhangelsk on the White Sea; the former was six thousand miles by rail from the theater of war, while the latter was usually frozen from November to May and was connected to the Russian railway net by a single narrow-gauge line. After the start of the war, the port facilities at Arkhangelsk were greatly expanded, and in 1915 work was started on a new, ice-free port in the Kola Inlet, officially named Romanov-na-Murmane in 1916 (in 1917 it was renamed Murmansk). However, the rail link to the latter was completed only in December 1916; it was built primarily by Austrian prisoners of war and Chinese laborers, who were forced to work under barbaric conditions.

In September 1914 the post of chief of Arkhangelsk Sea Region was established, but at first he had little to do; the first German incursion in the Arctic came only in June 1915, when the raider *Meteor* laid 285 mines at the entrance to the White Sea. Russia was suddenly confronted with the need for some form of naval force in the far north. In that same month the post of commander in chief of the Northern Territory was established, to be held by an army general with an admiral as his assistant. At Russian request eight British minesweepers arrived in July 1915, while the Russians themselves began converting local fishing trawlers into minesweepers. They also started searching far and wide for suitable ships, eventually purchasing vessels from Norway, Britain, Spain, Canada, and even Argentina. On 19 July 1916 the motley collection of vessels was dignified with the designation "Flotilla of the Arctic Ocean." In addition to minesweepers, destroyers and small submarines were transferred from the Siberian Flotilla to the Arctic. On 2 November 1916 one of these destroyers, the *Grozovoi*, became the only Russian ship to sink a U-boat when she winged *U 56* with a shell as the boat was diving.

Larger warships were also seen as necessary, to counter any German surface raiders that might try to penetrate into the Arctic—thus the purchase in March 1916 of three ships that had been captured by the Japanese in the Russo-Japanese war, the battleships *Chesma* (ex-*Poltava*, ex-*Tango*), *Peresvet* (ex-*Peresvet*, ex-*Sagami*) and the cruiser *Variag* (*ex-Variag*, ex-*Soya*). *Peresvet* never made it to the Arctic, being sunk by a mine near Port Said. The cruiser *Askold* also joined the Arctic Flotilla.

The increasing disorganization of the country after February 1917 led to the piling up of masses of supplies at Murmansk and Arkhangelsk. With the outbreak of civil war in neighboring Finland—where the Germans were giving strong support to the White Finns against the Reds—the allies became concerned that the northern Russian coast might fall into German hands, especially after the Bolsheviks left the war in March 1918. In July allied forces occupied Murmansk, and by August they had seized Arkhangelsk. Winter forced a cessation of hostilities, but in the spring the action would resume—a story that is beyond the scope of this chapter.

Summary and Assessment

By August 1914 the Russian imperial fleet was a competent force provided for the most part with effective equipment; its gunnery was good, its mine warfare was perhaps the best in the world, and it would soon demonstrate an outstanding capability to take advantage of the windfall of the *Magdeburg*'s codebook. But at the same time its officer corps, especially its senior officers, were of uneven quality, and the chasm between officers and men was a fundamental defect that many officers seemed all too willing to ignore. Yet the imperial naval officer corps was by no means as deeply reactionary as Soviet historians were later to portray it. The fact was that few officers shed any tears when Nicholas II abdicated; the tsar's conduct of the war, his appointment of incompetent nonentities to positions of authority, and the scandalous antics of Rasputin all undermined support for the emperor among the officer corps. Most officers willingly transferred their allegiance to the Provisional Government, and many would remain, more or less willingly, in Red service.

Despite the service of many officers from the imperial navy in the Soviet navy, however, many of the lessons of the First World War would be lost or undermined by the ideological inanities of the new regime. As a result, the Red Navy that fought in the Second World War would not be even a pale shadow of its imperial predecessor.

7

UNITED STATES

The U.S. Navy

Trent Hone

BACKSTORY

Pre-1914 History

Victory over Spain in 1898 made the United States a global power and brought with it an increasing influence over world affairs. Naval power was a critical component of the victory; Spain had been defeated by a new steel navy of modern ships employing the latest technologies. However, the U.S. Navy remained quite modest. Only five battleships and an assortment of cruisers were in commission at the end of the Spanish-American War; the navy was far better prepared for showing the flag on distant stations than it was for fleet action.

With the dawn of the new century, the fleet began to expand rapidly. Several factors contributed to its growth. The navy was a vital instrument for defending American political interests around the globe; as these grew, so did the fleet. Popular histories illustrating the importance of naval power argued for a powerful navy to protect commercial interests. The navy also occupied a special place in the country's defensive plans; it was the first line of defense in war. When couched in defensive terms, arguments for a larger fleet could be embraced by even isolationist politicians.

Defense of the Monroe Doctrine occupied the navy's attention in the Western Hemisphere. The American position in the Caribbean, more powerful with the acquisition of Puerto Rico and the establishment of a protectorate over Cuba, became stronger still in 1901, when improving relations with Great Britain led to the passage of the Hay-Pauncefote Treaty. This agreement freed the United States to proceed with the development of the Panama Canal and implicitly recognized the primacy of American naval power in the Western Hemisphere, a step not all European powers were ready to take.

In the Pacific, naval strategy focused on the maintenance of the Open Door Policy toward China in the face of the growing power and influence of Japan. After victories over China in 1895 and Russia in 1905, Japan was poised to dominate the western Pacific region. Apprehension that Chinese markets would be closed to American commerce fed arguments for the maintenance of a credible naval force in the Pacific Ocean to offset Japan's growing power.

However, the idea of dividing the fleet was rejected. Concentration was a root principle of the navy's doctrine. The battle fleet would remain together, moving as a unit to whichever ocean was most likely to see conflict. This requirement made the Panama Canal a vital part of the American strategic framework. Once it was complete, ships would be able to move rapidly from one coast to the other, concentrating quickly in times of potential hostilities. Without it, a move of ships from one coast to the other demanded a long journey around Cape Horn. From New York to San Francisco via Cape Horn was 19,000 miles; through the canal, it was only five thousand.

The navy's dogmatic emphasis on concentration derived from the writing of Rear Admiral Alfred Thayer Mahan, the most influential naval strategist of his time. Mahan was a powerful advocate for the construction of a modern battle fleet. He had graduated from the U.S. Naval Academy in 1859 and had witnessed the influence naval power had on the land campaigns of the American Civil War. He stressed numerous historical lessons in his seminal work, *The Influence of Sea Power upon History, 1660–1783*, to illustrate the critical importance of sea power. To Mahan, the nation that could control the seas had a decisive political and military advantage; sea power was a prerequisite for strategic power and commercial growth. Supporters of increasing naval strength readily embraced these ideas.

President Theodore Roosevelt was among these supporters; he championed the increase in naval power, linking it to a newly developed brand of American imperialism. In December 1907 a milestone was reached: the fleet had grown to twenty-two modern battleships. Roosevelt sent sixteen of them, the core of the new Atlantic Fleet, on a cruise around the world. This was the voyage of the Great White Fleet, and it was a dramatic demonstration of the power and reach of the new American navy.

Mission/Function

The voyage of the Great White Fleet ended on 22 February 1909. The journey had been an effective test of the fleet and its new ships. It was also a demonstration of their strategic mobility. The ill-fated voyage of the Russian Baltic Fleet had shown what could become of a poorly prepared battle fleet when it sought battle far away from its home bases. The U.S. Navy was determined to be more successful, and the cruise was valuable preparation for that goal.

Strategic mobility was particularly important to the navy; the two conflicts that it considered most likely would both require operations far from established bases. The first was a possible incursion by a European power into the Western Hemisphere. The second was a war in the Pacific against Japan. The navy developed plans for two main strategic areas, the western Atlantic and the western Pacific.

In the western Atlantic, there were two important objectives. The first was to thwart any European power that sought to challenge the Monroe Doctrine; the second was to police the Caribbean region and ensure the stability of its republics. The latter grew in importance after the completion of the Panama Canal in 1914. These two objectives were linked. Any unrest was expected to provide an excuse and opportunity for a foreign power to seize a position in the Western Hemisphere.

Of the European powers, Germany was regarded as the most likely threat. Like the United States, Germany had entered the global stage relatively late; it did not have many colonies or overseas possessions, and it aggressively sought to expand. The navy anticipated that Germany might attempt to force its way into the Caribbean or Central America.

War Plan Black, as it was code-named, was the Navy's plan for a war with Germany. It was initially developed at the Naval War College, in Newport, Rhode Island, and extensively studied there; Germany was the hypothetical opponent in the college's problems of every alternate year beginning in 1900. These exercises showed that a German attack upon the east coast of the United States was impractical; the Germans were expected instead to initiate operations by seizing a base in the Caribbean. To counter this move, the navy would concentrate the battle fleet and dispatch it to Guantanamo Bay. From there, the force would adopt an active defense, seeking out the approaching German fleet, subjecting it to attrition if possible, and ultimately bringing it to action. The war was expected be decided by a major fleet engagement in the western Atlantic. The German view was much the same; Operations Plan III, a plan for war with the United States, called for the rapid seizure of a Caribbean base as an initial step for operations in the Western Hemisphere.

In the Pacific, Japan was the most probable enemy. The navy started work on the first version of War Plan Orange—that is, for a war against "Orange," or Japan—in 1910. In contrast to Plan Black, Plan Orange emphasized the offensive; the navy would move across the Pacific, make use of faraway bases in the Philippines and Guam, and eventually defeat the Japanese battle fleet somewhere in the western Pacific. The task of moving the fleet across the Pacific was daunting, and strategic problems at the Naval War College challenged officers to develop potential solutions.

Plans Orange and Black presented the navy with opposite challenges. Against Germany, a defensive campaign would be fought, while in the Pacific the navy would assume the offensive. This led to the development of exercises that modeled both potential conflicts simultaneously. One part of the fleet would be the aggressor, steaming into enemy territory, seeking to seize an advanced base. The other would be the defender, attempting to locate the approaching enemy, engage his main body, and defeat it. Valuable training was provided to all participants, and the lessons from these exercises were fed back into both war plans.

The navy diligently prepared for the missions involved in these plans. Both Plan Orange and Plan Black assumed that the war would be decided by a clash of battle lines. To secure victory, the navy had to be able to locate the enemy, maneuver into position, and bring the entire battle fleet into combat. The guns of the battleships would be the primary weapon, and critical supporting roles would be performed by scouts and torpedo craft. This was a consequence of Mahan's theories, which emphasized sea control through capital ships.

Unfortunately, these assumptions did not reflect the challenges the navy actually faced upon entry into World War I. By 1917 Germany was using its battle fleet as a fleet-in-being, tying down large elements of the Royal Navy, while it waged a crippling campaign against commerce with its submarines. The U.S. Navy was unprepared for this kind of war and had to make rapid adjustments. Plans for an overseas campaign culminating in a climactic sea battle were set aside. The navy became an effective coalition partner, shepherding the movement of troops and supplies to Europe, augmenting the Royal Navy's Grand Fleet with a battle squadron, and hunting submarines in the Atlantic and Mediterranean with aircraft and small ships.

ORGANIZATION

Command Structure

Administration

The early years of the twentieth century saw several significant changes in the administration of the Navy Department. During this time, the department struggled with the challenges of evolving from a traditional organization to one based on modern organizational concepts; the quest for greater efficiency had to be constantly balanced against calls for economy and the influence of tradition. The majority of these changes were led by the office of the secretary of the navy, a civilian appointed by the president.

Beneath the secretary, the navy was divided into eight different bureaus: Yards and Docks, Equipment and Recruiting, Navigation, Ordnance, Construction and Repair, Steam Engineering, Provisions and Clothing, and Medicine and Surgery. Each of these was responsible for procuring all items in its sphere of responsibility and keeping abreast of technical developments in its field.

The bureau organization had worked well for decades, but the navy lacked sufficient means for effective planning and coordination. "Because the bureau chiefs were immersed in those areas over which they had cognizance, the bureau system was ill suited to provide professional direction to plan and control naval operations."[1] Aside from the secretary, there was no centralized planning authority, and because the terms of the navy secretaries were relatively short, there was no continuity. The Spanish-American War exposed the navy's poor ability to plan and coordinate operations.

Secretary John D. Long created the temporary Naval War Board during the Spanish-American war to help address these shortcomings. It worked well, and in March 1900 he created a more permanent advisory board. The resulting General Board brought an increased focus to war planning and preparation. It influenced ship designs, tactics, and war plans and was extremely important in helping to integrate strategic plans and tactical thought.

In 1909, Secretary George von Lengerke Meyer attempted to further enhance the coordination of planning and operations by creating four separate divisions: Operations of the Fleet, Personnel, Material, and Inspections. Each division was assigned an "aide," a senior officer who could provide the secretary with direct advice and coordinate activities within his area of responsibility. Like the General Board, the Naval Aides were advisors and possessed no executive authority. Their positions would not last long but were part of an inevitable move toward a more permanent naval staff structure.

This was the situation when President Woodrow Wilson took office in March 1913. Wilson would serve two terms; for his entire tenure, Josephus Daniels would be his navy secretary, and the future president Franklin Delano Roosevelt would occupy the post of assistant secretary. Daniels was a populist newspaperman from North Carolina and firmly believed in civilian authority over the military. Daniels's firm convictions about civilian control did not stem from passivity or timidity. He was quite willing to support and promote American interests: in 1914 he approved the use of force in Vera Cruz, Mexico; in 1915, he had the navy intervene to restore order in Haiti; the following year a similar intervention was made in the Dominican Republic. In 1917 Daniels supported the purchase of the Danish West Indies, which became the U.S. Virgin Islands, to prevent their being acquired by a hostile European power.

The aide system had been in place for several years, but Daniels disapproved of it. He let two of the aides rotate out of their positions without appointing replacements. However, he retained Rear Admiral Bradley A. Fiske, the Aide for Operations. Fiske argued vehemently for a more powerful position, one that had the authority to plan for war and command the fleet. His arguments were not restricted to the department; Fiske actively lobbied Congress. Congressman Richard P. Hobson agreed with these assessments and introduced "a Chief of Naval Operations . . . responsible for the readiness of the Navy for war and . . . charged with its general direction" in the Naval Appropriations Bill of 1915.[2]

Command Organization

Daniels did not want a Chief of Naval Operations (CNO), and he certainly did not want one with so much power. He feared that Hobson's provision would unacceptably compromise civilian authority. Daniels insisted upon revisions but could not stop the creation of the office. In the end, although the CNO was "charged with the operations of the fleet and with the preparation and readiness of plans for its use in war," it lacked sufficient authority to do so. Real authority remained with Daniels.[3]

He reinforced this outcome by choosing Captain William S. Benson as the first CNO. In doing so Daniels passed over a number of well-qualified senior officers, including Fiske, whose tenure as Aide for Operations ended with Benson's appointment. Daniels hoped to select a talented individual who would respect civilian authority. He chose wisely; Benson was skilled and got along well with Daniels. Despite the office's limited authority, Benson performed well.

Greater authority for the CNO came sooner than expected. By the middle of 1916 it had become apparent that the United States might be drawn into the war or face a hostile coalition after its end. This spurred an increase in military preparedness, despite the country's neutral stance. The resulting 1916 Naval Appropriations Bill called for construction that would make the navy the world's largest. It also provided a number of organizational improvements, including additional power and authority for the CNO.

Photo 7.1. Secretary of the Navy Josephus Daniels and Admiral William S. Benson, the first Chief of Naval Operations, in Paris for the peace conference. Daniels chose well in selecting Benson. The two got along well, and when war came Daniels was able to leave the coordination of operations to Benson, as Congress had intended. (Naval History and Heritage Command)

Fleet Organization and Order of Battle

The main fighting strength of the navy was concentrated in the Atlantic Fleet, which contained all the battleships and the most modern cruisers and destroyers. During the war, the Atlantic Fleet was commanded by Admiral

Henry T. Mayo. His predecessor, Admiral Frank Friday Fletcher, had published a set of battle instructions that brought fleet doctrine into line with the latest tactical principles.

The Pacific Fleet was made up of armored cruisers, coastal torpedo boats, and submarines that operated in defense of vital areas. During the war, the fleet was commanded by Admiral William Banks Caperton.

Table 7.1 U.S. Navy Order of Battle, April 1917

Atlantic Fleet (Mayo)	
Battleships:	
First-line:	12
Second-line:	19
Armored cruisers:	4
Second-class cruisers:	4
Third-class cruisers:	6
Monitors:	3 (operating as submarine tenders)
Destroyers:	50
Coastal torpedo boats:	2
Submarines:	23
Gunboats:	10
Pacific Fleet (Caperton)	
Armored cruisers:	6
First-class cruisers:	4
Third-class cruisers:	7
Monitors:	1 (operating as submarine tender)
Coastal torpedo boats:	9
Submarines:	9
Gunboats:	3
Asiatic Fleet (Winterhalter)	
First-class cruisers:	1
Third-class cruisers:	2
Monitors:	2
Coastal torpedo boats:	5
Submarines:	9
Gunboats:	10

The Asiatic Fleet was much smaller, with old torpedo boats, small submarines, some very old cruisers, and a pair of ancient monitors. Many of the Asiatic Fleet's most active units were gunboats patrolling in the Philippines and China. Admiral Albert G. Winterhalter commanded the Asiatic Fleet when America entered the war. He was replaced in May 1917 by Admiral Austin M. Knight. Knight also directed American naval operations at Vladivostok during the allied intervention in the Russian Civil War.

Anticipating the American entry into the war, in late March 1917 Wilson authorized the navy to establish contact with the British. Rear Admiral William Snowden Sims, then president of the Naval War College, was sent to England to develop plans for the coordination of the naval war. Sims's background was an important factor. He was Canadian-born and had developed close relationships with British officers; these friendships made Sims the logical choice to become commander of American naval forces operating in Europe.

Eventually, two battleship divisions were sent to operate from the British Isles under Sims. Rear Admiral Hugh Rodman's Battleship Division 9 operated with the Royal Navy's Grand Fleet, becoming its 6th Battle Squadron. Battleship Division 6, commanded by Rear Admiral Thomas. S. Rodgers, operated from Berehaven on the coast of Ireland, ready to confront any German raids into the Atlantic. (See table 7.1.)

Communications

In the years before World War I, the navy began to transition away from the use of purely visual signaling systems, such as flags and lights, and started to experiment with radio. Early experience showed the value of the technology, but determining how best to integrate it into the tactical operations of the fleet was challenging; several technological advancements were required before the navy fully embraced radio. Early radio had distinct disadvantages. The most serious was the limited range of frequencies available. This made it impossible for more than one ship to transmit at once; if two or more transmitted simultaneously, both transmissions would be garbled. The limited frequency range also made radio extremely susceptible to enemy jamming. Experiments with radio during the cruise of the Great White Fleet pointed out the need for specifically naval solutions to problems presented by the technology. This led to the creation in 1908 of the Naval Radio-Telegraphic Laboratory, which would ultimately become the Naval Research Laboratory. The laboratory quickly proved its worth.

By 1911 the navy had issued its first official frequency plan, a milestone in the tactical employment of radio. The next year, Lieutenant Stanford C.

Hooper became the Atlantic Fleet's first radio officer, charged with developing methods for the tactical use of radio and enhancing the fleet's proficiency. Radio officers for each ship soon followed. "By the eve of the First World War, the U.S. Navy earnestly had committed to integrating wireless telegraphy into fleet operations."[4]

However, problems remained. Although it was possible to tune radios to different frequencies, the process was difficult and imprecise. Transmissions on similar frequencies still overwhelmed each other. The risk of jamming remained, and there was no effective counter. Procedures for encoding messages lacked sophistication and were time-consuming, delaying transmissions and reducing their value. Despite these issues, radio was one of the most important elements of the 1916 Battle Instructions. It had become a weapon of war.

Radio would be used for fleet operations and sighting reports. To make sighting reports easier to transmit and understand, they were broken into a series of short messages. The initial report might include the enemy bearing, a second the speed of the enemy vessels, and a third the composition of the enemy formation. The challenges of piecing this information back together in a flagship are obvious. With no reliable way to link disparate messages together or guarantee receipt, it is apparent that in a real battle the situation would have quickly become confused and reliable plots of the enemy almost impossible to obtain.

Further improvements were necessary to make radio more effective for tactical coordination. They arrived with the introduction of the CW 936 radiotelephone equipment in March 1917. This device allowed reliable transmissions on five different frequencies and, for the first time, enabled effective voice communications between ships, overcoming the challenges associated with the kind of encoding and decoding that had been adopted to reduce message lengths. It greatly enhanced the effectiveness of the navy's antisubmarine campaign, allowing ships to rapidly coordinate their activities in real time. Aircraft also began to be integrated into fleet communications, and by the end of the war large navy aircraft could send and receive wireless radio signals fairly reliably.

Intelligence

The navy's intelligence service, the Office of Naval Intelligence (ONI), maintained a series of naval attachés at foreign capitals, managed communication with foreign naval attachés in the United States, and collected information that might have a bearing on naval warfare. Prior to World War I, ONI was small—with only eight officers and eight civilians—and much of its information came from publicly available sources. It would also grow as a result of the 1916 appropriations bill and continue to increase in size during the war.

Before the war, ONI focused on the technical evaluation of foreign capabilities and generally ignored the broader context—the operational intelligence—that could have illustrated how those capabilities were intended to be used. This narrow view led to a poor understanding of enemy strategic intentions and often reinforced existing suspicions, the most prominent being that Germany and Japan had hostile intentions toward the United States. The fact that the two had been at war with each other since 1914 did not change this assessment. This meant that although the technical capabilities of enemy ships were fairly well understood, there was little understanding of how potential enemies would employ their naval forces to further strategic objectives. Poor preparation for an antisubmarine campaign was the most visible result.

Before U.S. entry into the war, important changes were made. In 1915, when the office of the CNO was created, ONI became part of it. In the 1916 appropriation, significantly more funding for ONI was provided, and by the end of the war ONI had grown to employ 306 officers and eighteen civilians.

Additional funding led to the creation of the War Information Service, an undercover operation designed to prevent sabotage of naval and other military industries. A parallel undercover operation, the Naval Information Service, operated overseas. Agents on the ONI payroll scoured lonely Caribbean and South American coastlines, looking fruitlessly for secret German U-boat anchorages.

Infrastructure, Logistics, and Commerce

Bases

Prior to the Wilson administration, the navy's network of facilities was relatively neglected. There were eleven navy yards in 1913. In total numbers this compared favorably with Germany's three and Great Britain's six, but the American facilities were outdated and quite limited; the entire dry-dock capacity of all eleven yards was less than that of the single largest British facility. This limited the navy's strength, despite the growing size of the battle fleet.

Investment in the yards increased during the Wilson administration. West Coast facilities, including Bremerton, San Francisco, Los Angeles, and San Diego, were expanded; the new dry docks in San Francisco became some of the largest in the world. Improved facilities permitted the yards in

Philadelphia and Brooklyn to build battleships while other yards began to build smaller ships. New management techniques, borrowed from the civilian sector, reduced the cost of construction in the navy yards, making them more competitive.

Of the specific improvements, none was more important than the increase in dry docks. By 1916 there were plans to have six of the largest in the world for the fleet's use. Two were authorized for Norfolk and Philadelphia; a third for the East Coast was planned to be built in Boston.

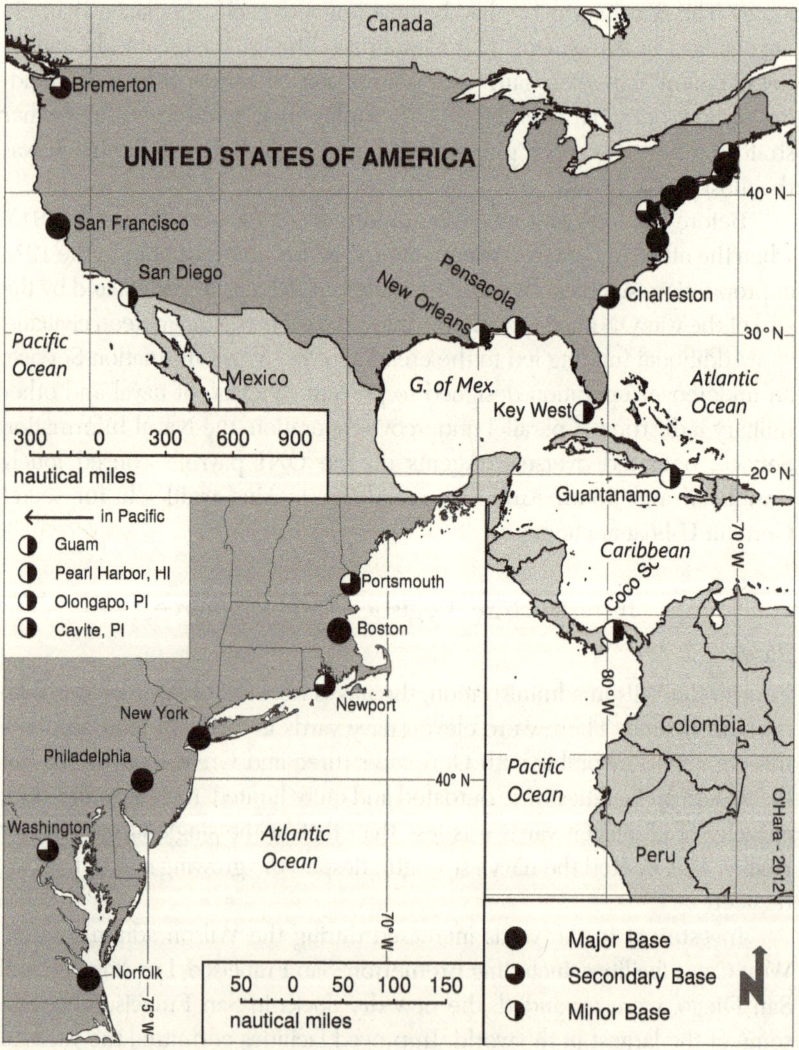

Map 7.1. U.S. Naval Bases

One was at Balboa in the Panama Canal Zone, another was planned for San Francisco, and the last was under construction at Pearl Harbor.

Overseas bases were improved as well. Facilities were developed in the Pacific at Guam, as well as Olongapo and Cavite in the Philippines. In the Caribbean, the focus was on the Panama Canal, which finally opened in August 1914. Guantanamo Bay was selected for future development, and in the meantime it provided a sheltered anchorage from which the fleet could guard the eastern entrance to the Caribbean Basin. (See map 7.1.)

Industry

Secretary Daniels emphasized an increasing level of partnership with private enterprise in arrangements that spanned multiple industries, including manufacturing, research and technology, and shipping. Increased cooperation was necessary to produce essential war materials in quantity, such as armor, guns, smokeless powder, and fuel. Daniels worked to foster improved relationships with industries in these areas, so that the navy could benefit from the latest technological developments and employ their expertise in wartime.

The use of private manufacturers proved essential to meet the unprecedented demands of war. The manufacture of the Mark (Mk) 6 mine, developed for the Northern Barrage, is an excellent example. It was designed to be built in quantity by a variety of manufactures. In total, more than 125,000 of them were manufactured, and peak production reached a thousand a day. There were 140 principal contractors and over four hundred subcontractors participating, including firms, such as in the automotive industry, that were new to navy contracts. Equally impressive efforts were put forth in the manufacture of ammunition, guns, and ships, including destroyers, submarines, subchasers, and Eagle boats.

Daniels also hoped to harness the talents of the nation's brightest minds to give the navy a technological edge. In July 1915, he wrote the inventor Thomas Edison to request his assistance in organizing an advisory board containing the best technical minds in the nation. The result was the Naval Consulting Board, which, although "not particularly effective," did make contributions to the antisubmarine campaign and the development of wireless communications.[5]

Logistics

The navy's approach to logistics was driven by the assumption that the decisive battle would be fought and won far from established bases. This prospect led the navy toward a unique emphasis on strategic mobility that was reflected in nearly all aspects of plans and doctrine. While other navies planned cruiser warfare in remote oceans or sent fleets on long voyages when compelled by strategic necessity, the United States was alone in planning for serious operations by the entire fleet far away from major bases.

In order to operate in remote locations, the fleet had to be capable of performing regular maintenance organically, without significant reliance on fixed bases. The voyage of the Great White Fleet tested this approach, and from it the navy derived important lessons. Work continued in the following years to make the fleet even more capable. Auxiliaries were constructed to help service and maintain the fleet. An increasing number of colliers gave the fleet great range. Tenders and depot ships provided maintenance facilities. As much as possible, the fleet became responsible for its own upkeep.

During the occupation of Vera Cruz, the repair ship *Vestal* demonstrated what had become possible. She and her crew rebuilt the boilers of the cruiser *Nashville* and made extensive repairs to the scout cruiser *Salem*. All this work was performed in the inner harbor at Vera Cruz; the ships never left the forward zone.

Individual ships were made as self-sufficient as possible, to ensure the fleet's mobility. Commander Joseph K. Taussig's 8th Destroyer Division showed what the navy hoped to achieve. When his ships arrived at Queenstown on the west coast of Ireland, Taussig was asked by Vice Admiral Sir Lewis Bayly, Commander of the Coast of Ireland, when the American destroyers would be ready for sea. Although some maintenance was needed, the ships were capable of operations, and without hesitation Taussig answered, "We are ready now, sir, that is as soon as we finish refueling."[6] His Royal Navy superiors were impressed by Taussig and his six modest "thousand-tonners."

Shipping and Trade Protection

To improve the capability of the American merchant marine and ensure the effective mobilization of merchant shipping in the event of war, the U.S. Shipping Board was established on 7 September 1916. Although its initial goals were rather broad, when America entered the war the board's focus shifted to a distinct and narrow goal, the maintenance of lines of communication with Europe. To meet this need, it created the Emergency Fleet Corporation on 16 April 1917. This organization oversaw the acquisition, maintenance, and operation of merchant shipping, providing centralized coordination of this vital asset during the conflict.

Offensive measures were believed to be the most effective approach to commerce protection. This belief led to several important decisions that influenced the navy's conduct of the war. Merchant ships were armed, to protect them from enemy raiders and submarines; offensive patrols by destroyers, subchasers, and submarines were initiated to seek out and hunt down U-boats; and the fleet would remain concentrated, ready to engage the enemy in decisive battle. Although the navy ultimately retreated from the last of these points and accepted a division of the battle fleet to aid the fight in the decisive theater, the other two remained a fundamental part of the navy's approach to the war.

On 13 March 1917, Daniels issued regulations allowing the arming of merchant vessels. When the decision was made, however, only 376 guns were available; hundreds more were needed. More than four hundred guns were removed from old battleships and cruisers. New production remained insufficient to meet demand until October 1918, an indication of the relatively poor preparedness of the American industrial base.

In any case, the effort expended to arm these ships could have been more profitably invested elsewhere. German submarines, which could remain submerged and sink their targets, were not deterred by armed merchantmen. The threat of surface raiders, inflated by the well-publicized exploits of a few vessels, proved largely irrelevant, particularly once convoying began.

Passive measures, not active ones, were the key to success in the U-boat campaign. The decision to move to a convoy system made all the difference. Previously the allies had expended significant effort scouring the ocean for U-boats to hunt and kill, distributing their efforts broadly. With convoys, they could focus their efforts on defending the merchant ships, waiting for U-boats to come to them. The move to convoys reduced the rate of losses dramatically and ensured the security of communications to Europe.

Personnel

At the start of the twentieth century, the navy's mechanisms for promotion and advancement relied on traditional approaches that rewarded seniority over skill. Although President Roosevelt had attempted to introduce a system of promotion based on merit, little progress was made. Under Secretary Daniels, this would change. Daniels faced two interrelated problems. First, the promotion of officers was based on seniority, not ability. Second, there were too few officers to meet the needs of the rapidly expanding fleet. Although Congress had authorized larger class sizes for the Naval Academy, this change threatened to make the problem even worse. It was impossible to promote officers until senior positions for them opened up; those positions were limited by law. When they did open, age limits forced officers to move through the most advanced grades so rapidly they had very little time to learn their new responsibilities. The navy faced a glut of aging ensigns and lieutenants, with no legal way to promote them.

Daniels worked to solve both of these issues. In July 1914, he appointed a Personnel Board to increase the visibility of the problem and explain its complexity to congressional leaders. Two years later these efforts finally produced results. The large appropriations bill of 1916 introduced promotion by selection; the most qualified officers would now be chosen to advance to the next grade, regardless of seniority.

Demographics

In 1915, enlistment in the navy was about 52,000 men, but the Bureau of Navigation projected that 7,500 more would be needed by 1917; an increase of that amount was requested in 1916, but Congress provided even more. To man all the additional ships authorized in the 1916 bill, Congress increased the navy to 74,700 men. The number of officers was correspondingly increased, from 2,122 to 2,988.

Although significant, these increases were insufficient to meet the needs of a war emergency. Reserve fleets for both the Atlantic and Pacific had been established in 1912, but these did little more than provide a structure to maintain older vessels. A framework was needed that could quickly draw on the civilian talent of the country. After extensive lobbying, Congress moved to create a naval reserve in 1915 and with the 1916 appropriation expanded it into an organization that was more comprehensive. It included former officers and men of the navy, officers and men of the merchant marine, and civilians whose professions allowed them to render valuable service in time of war, such as aviators and radiomen.

Training

Personnel

Secretary Daniels believed that the navy had an obligation to educate servicemen and prepare them for careers outside the service. A shipboard system of instruction was established to provide academic, vocational, and technical education. Daniels credited it with reducing the desertion rate and improving morale. He also placed increased emphasis on the navy's technical schools, like the Torpedo and Seaman Gunners' School at Newport, the Electricians' Schools at New York and at Mare Island, California, and the Machinists' School at Charleston, South Carolina.

Officer education was broadened and strengthened. An increased emphasis at the Naval Academy was placed on arts and literature. Postgraduate educational programs included technical subjects as well as strategy and the art of command. The Naval War College was a vital element of this system. Daniels directed that attendance to the college be considered when selecting officers for promotion, a policy that led to increased attendance and greater prestige for the institution.

Fleet

Fleet training comprised a regular series of exercises and maneuvers. Some of these tested new tactics and techniques, while others reinforced existing practices. The concentration of the most modern and powerful ships in the Atlantic Fleet starting in 1906 allowed the navy to study complex tactics and maneuvers on a large scale for the first time. While the Asiatic and Pacific Fleets patrolled distant stations, the Atlantic Fleet became a laboratory for modern fleet operations.

Large-scale annual maneuvers were held in the Atlantic and Caribbean. Strategic Maneuver Number 3, conducted from 20 to 31 August 1916, was a good example. It simulated an effort by a European power to seize a base on the East Coast. The exercises helped to improve fleet tactics, but they were more effective at pointing out deficiencies, such as the lack of effective scouting vessels and the difficulty of coordinating the movements of dispersed forces.

THE WAYS OF WAR
Surface Warfare

Doctrine

The navy's combat doctrine rested on a set of principles, and one of the most important of these was concentration. To divide was to invite defeat in detail. In tactical exercises, both at sea and on war-game boards at the Naval War College, divided formations generally met with defeat. Battle-line speed was a complicating factor. In general, because they had been designed for great endurance, the navy's battleships sacrificed speed for radius of action and were slower than their potential opponents. Slower speeds and the principle of concentration led to the development of Battle Plan No. 1 in 1906.

Despite its name, Battle Plan No. 1 was not a plan for battle. It was a plan of maneuver, designed to ensure that an enemy battle line could be kept from achieving an advantageous position even if it was superior in speed. Under Battle Plan No. 1, the lead ship of the line would adjust course so that the lead ship of the enemy formation would always remain abreast; the remaining ships of the line would follow the motions of the leader. By turning inside a faster enemy, the line would gracefully bend but not break. When tested on the game board, this approach was found to be effective.

In early 1907, the plan was tested at sea. As long as the two fleets steamed roughly parallel courses, the slower was able to turn gradually and keep the faster on its beam. However, if the fleets steamed in opposite directions, the faster fleet could close and overwhelm the rear of the slower. To mitigate this danger, doctrine came to stress the importance of forcing the enemy to deploy first.

Battle Plan No. 2 was introduced in 1911. It followed the same general outline but allowed for maneuver of the battle line by squadrons rather than as one uniform line, a natural consequence of the growing size of the fleet. Each squadron would turn independently to keep the enemy abreast. Cohesion would be maintained without the need for rigid centralized control.

The influence of these plans can be found in the Atlantic Fleet's Battle Instructions of May 1916, issued by Admiral Fletcher. These focused on the operation of the fleet as a cohesive unit in battle; sections were devoted to destroyers, submarines, and aircraft, as well as to the handling of the battle line. Although some sections, like those on aircraft and submarines, were very brief, they all emphasized the operation of the fleet as an entire unit.

Battle-line tactics evolved directly from Battle Plans No. 1 and No. 2: "It matters not in what formation the enemy may be, whether in line, column, echelon, or whether he is in pursuit, or in retreat, or on a parallel course. Your line should be kept normal to the bearing of the enemy. Neither does it matter in what formation your line of ships may be. . . . This principle applies to all conditions of battle."[7]

Relatively simple maneuvers were expected to be able to keep the battle line normal to the bearing of the enemy. Maneuvers were kept simple to ensure cohesion of the battleship formation. For the same reason, speed changes were to be avoided; in battle, the speed of the line would be sixteen knots.

Concentration remained a fundamental principle. The comments of the Battle Instructions on dividing the line are worth quoting at length:

> Battleships will be kept in one line as long as the enemy's battleships are kept in one formation. No advantage can be gained by dividing our battle line to attack the enemy's line from different points. If, however, the enemy divides his force with a view to attacking either one or both of our flanks a detachment of suitable force from our flanks must operate against his detached forces. Our detached forces, however, will operate only at such distances from our flank as will insure correct maneuvering for gunfire. This disposition maintains our forces on interior lines and enables them to concentrate and take advantage of any tactical errors of the enemy.[8]

Maneuver, then, was acceptable, but division of the battle line was not. Tactical exercises had reinforced the lessons learned at the Naval War College and illustrated the danger of distributed formations. There were two possible formations. One placed the strongest battle squadron in the van and the weakest at the rear; this was ideal if the enemy could be maintained on a parallel course throughout the battle. If not, the alternative formation would be superior; it placed the two strongest squadrons on the wings and the weakest ships in the center.

By observing the initial battles of the war as actually fought, however, the navy learned that opening ranges would be much greater than anticipated and that ships would open fire at the maximum reach of their weapons. Experimental firings in 1916 to determine maximum effective range showed that the limit of the navy's 12-inch gunfire was about 16,000 yards. It was expected that this could be increased to 20,000 yards with additional practice, and the navy strove to reach this goal.

Because accurate gunfire relied on visibility, the effects of weather conditions, which could limit the effectiveness of spotting and range finding, were very important. A choice of deployment course could make the difference between accurate fire and wild shooting. The wind and its influence on funnel exhaust and hot gasses from the guns, the direction of the sea and its effect on the motion of the ship, and the position of the sun and its impact on visibility—all had to be considered.

Fire distribution would be simple; each ship would fire at her opposite in the enemy line. If there were fewer enemy battleships, double concentrations would be employed, starting from the enemy's van. If the enemy had more ships, divided fire would be employed, starting from the enemy's rear. Provision was made in the Battle Instructions for temporary concentrations on vulnerable portions of the enemy line, should opportunity arise.

Battleships were the supreme weapon in battle, but destroyers were considered a close second. In action, they would take station at van and rear of the battle line. They had two important tactical roles. Their primary mission was to attack enemy battleships with torpedoes. Even if unsuccessful, an attack could force the enemy formation to maneuver and thereby throw off the accuracy of its fire or force it into a disadvantageous position. Destroyers were also responsible for breaking up similar attacks on their own battle line.

Before a general action, destroyers would screen the battle fleet and act as scouts. Destroyers were pressed into the scouting role because the navy lacked enough light cruisers to perform the task. This was a problem, as destroyers were often inadequate for the purpose, particularly in rough North Atlantic conditions. Small, high-speed cruisers that could operate with the battle fleet were urgently needed. Although requested by the General Board many times, the necessary ships were not authorized until 1916, and they would not be completed before the war ended. In the meantime, destroyers became larger and more capable; they also developed new tactics.

As scouts, destroyers had one major advantage: they had a potentially lethal armament of torpedoes. This allowed them to transition from scouting to attacking immediately after making contact with the enemy. These tactics were particularly effective at night, leading to the development of "night search and attack" tactics. In a March 1915 exercise, destroyers attacked through a screen and launched dud torpedoes against a formation of battleships from close range. Eighteen torpedoes were fired; eleven certain hits were scored, with another two highly likely. This impressive hit percentage illustrated just what a determined group of destroyer captains could accomplish; the night search and attack was a staple of navy destroyer doctrine for the next thirty years.

Battle Instructions devoted considerable attention to avoiding such enemy attacks. The navy did not expect to seek a general action at night; the goal was the preservation of the battle fleet for a daylight action. When cruising at night, destroyers would be separated from the battle line. Cruisers would screen it. This separation was intended to prevent friendly fire and ease identification of the enemy; if the cruisers or battleships saw a destroyer, they could assume it was hostile and open fire. Searchlights and, later, star shells (a wartime invention) would help separate friend from foe in the darkness.

Ships

In 1903 the General Board recommended a fleet of forty-eight battleships, divided into six battle squadrons, each supported by a number of other vessels, including armored cruisers, scout cruisers, and destroyers. The number of supporting vessels varied over the years as the board reacted to the latest technological and tactical developments. Plans for a forty-eight-battleship fleet survived only until 1916, but the concept of a balanced fleet remained an important part of the board's thinking and the navy's building programs for many years to come.

Battleships

Battleships were the cornerstone of the navy's combat power. Starting in 1912, they were built to a revolutionary new design. The *Nevada* class introduced the "all or nothing" armor scheme, a protective arrangement that placed the heaviest armor over the most vital areas and left the rest of the ship unarmored. The arrangement was developed in part from an analysis of the damage to *San Marcos,* formerly battleship *Texas,* which was used as a target in March 1911.

The "all or nothing" approach anticipated the increasing ranges at which battleships could fight. *Nevada* was the first battleship consciously designed to resist armor-piercing shells fired from over 10,000 yards, the expected battle range in 1912. At these ranges it would be impossible to aim at specific parts of a target ship. The existing practice of using high-explosive shells to selectively destroy secondary batteries or bridges had to be discarded; they would explode with little effect if they struck heavy armor. Instead, armor-piercing shells would be fired exclusively, so that the maximum potential damage could be guaranteed.

To protect the ship against such fire, only the heaviest possible armor was used, and it was arranged to cover only the most important areas. Contemporary ships in foreign navies were still being armored with "incremental" schemes, including upper-belt armor to protect secondary batteries, and lacked the substantial deck armor of the U.S. Navy's designs. *Nevada* and the battleships that followed her were revolutionary and far in advance of contemporary foreign designs.

This was a direct result of the work of the General Board. In 1908, dissatisfaction with the navy's most recent battleship design, the *Delaware* class, triggered a conference at the Naval War College. The three bureaus responsible for warship design—Construction and Repair, Steam Engineering, and Ordnance—were not coordinating their efforts effectively, and insufficient attention was being paid to the overall design. To solve the problem the General Board was made responsible for detailed characteristics of new ship designs, ensuring that they fit into strategic plans and reflected the latest tactical developments.

Nevada was the first battleship design to go completely through the new process. She introduced triple turrets and oil fuel. Firepower was equivalent to prior classes, but triple turrets meant ten guns could be carried in four turrets instead of five; that meant less weight, offsetting the increase in armor. Oil fuel gave greater range, but *Nevada* and her sister had different power plants as well. *Oklahoma* was the last navy battleship with reciprocating engines; *Nevada* introduced geared turbines. Both could make just under twenty-one knots.

Following classes provided incremental improvements. *Pennsylvania* and her sister *Arizona* added two more 14-inch guns. *New Mexico* and her two sisters had an improved hull design, additional armor, larger turrets, and more powerful, 50-caliber 14-inch guns. The most radical change introduced by *New Mexico* was not outwardly visible—an entirely new propulsion system. Turbines were retained, but rather than being connected to the propeller shafts mechanically through a series of reduction gears as in her sisters, the turbines drove a set of generators that were wired to electric motors. These motors drove the propellers. Although heavier than conventional installations, this turbo-electric drive was significantly more fuel efficient, providing longer ranges and greater strategic mobility. Removing the physical linkage between the turbines and propeller shafts also allowed greater subdivision of the engineering spaces and more protection from underwater attack.

Older battleships designed before *Nevada* fit into three broad categories. The most modern were "all-big-gun" battleships, with maximum speeds close to twenty-one knots. A number of slower predreadnought ships remained on active service but were not considered "first line"; they made up the second group. The third category were the oldest battleships; they were in reserve and unfit for combat but still useful as training vessels.

The "all-big-gun" ships included the eight ships of the *Delaware, Florida, Wyoming,* and *Texas* classes. These ships were all built in rapid succession, with little time to incorporate lessons from prior construction; all were coal-fired. The *Delaware* and *Florida* designs were very similar, with nearly identical layouts; *Delaware* had reciprocating engines, but her sister *North Dakota* had direct-drive turbines, as did *Florida* and *Utah*.

The *Wyoming* and *Texas* classes were much larger and marked a significant increase in fighting strength. These were the navy's first battleships to incorporate lessons from the cruise of the Great White Fleet, and they were dryer as a result. *Wyoming* had twelve 12-inch/50-caliber guns and direct-drive turbines; *Texas* introduced 14-inch guns and reverted to reciprocating engines to provide greater fuel economy. All four ships of this group served with the Grand Fleet during the war.

Second-line ships included the *South Carolina, Vermont, Connecticut, Virginia, Maine,* and *Illinois* classes, nineteen ships in total. Although *South Carolina* and her sister were the navy's first "all-big-gun" battleships, they were designed to operate tactically with their predecessors and not the more modern ships. They were relegated to the second line after 1914. The predreadnought ships had mixed batteries of 12-inch, 8-inch, and 7-inch or 6-inch guns. Top speeds varied between sixteen and eighteen knots.

The oldest battleships, in reserve, were the six ships of the *Indiana, Iowa,* and *Kearsarge* classes. They were of limited military value, with low-velocity guns and speeds of sixteen knots or less.

Cruisers and Scouts

In the years after the Spanish-American War, the navy augmented its battle fleet with the "Big Ten," a group of large armored cruisers comparable to contemporary battleships in size and cost; accordingly, they were named after states. The first six, the *Pennsylvania* class, served primarily in the Pacific Fleet; they had main batteries of four 8-inch guns. The *Tennessee* class of four vessels rounded out the group. With their 10-inch main batteries, the *Tennessees* were effectively small battleships; they served with the battle fleet in the Atlantic. All ten were capable of twenty-two knots. They were rapidly outclassed by the introduction of the battle cruiser. As their relative fighting strength declined, the ships were renamed for cities; *Colorado,* for example, became *Pueblo.*

The predecessors to the "Big Ten" were categorized as first-class cruisers; they were a mix of obsolete designs with limited military value. The three cruisers of the *St. Louis* class could make twenty-two knots and were armed with 6-inch guns. *Rochester,* formerly named *Saratoga* and called *New York* before that, was the navy's first armored cruiser; rebuilt between 1905 and 1909, she was armed with modern weapons and had a top speed of twenty knots. *Brooklyn* had been Commodore Winfield Scott Schley's flagship at the battle of Santiago; she was armed with old 8-inch guns and could also make twenty knots.

The navy's four second-class cruisers were similarly obsolete. *Chicago* had been serving as a training ship since 1908, but she became flagship of the Atlantic Submarine Force in 1917. *Columbia* and her sister *Minneapolis* were twenty years old when the war started but could make good speed and so escorted convoys. *Olympia,* the famous flagship of Commodore George Dewey at Manila Bay, had been relegated to accommodation duty at Charleston but was pressed back into service during the war.

Third-class cruisers were designed to show the flag on remote stations, not to operate with a modern battle fleet. The six ships of the *Denver* class had more in common with gunboats than cruisers, and ultimately they were redesignated as such. Their speed was less than seventeen knots, but they were armed with 5-inch guns and could carry a significant number of troops to police distant stations. *Cincinnati* and *Raleigh* were similar but older. *New Orleans* and *Albany* had been purchased in March 1898 to augment the navy in the war with Spain; they were rearmed with modern weapons in 1910.

Although the General Board's long-range building program called for a large number of scouting cruisers to support the battle fleet, only three such ships were built before the war. These constituted the *Chester* class; they were test beds for new propulsion technologies. *Birmingham* had triple-expansion reciprocating engines, *Salem* had Curtiss turbines, and *Chester* had turbines from Parsons. The Curtiss installation proved unsatisfactory, and *Salem*'s turbines were replaced with General Electric models in 1917. All could make twenty-four knots and operated with the Atlantic Fleet.

Destroyers

In 1904, President Roosevelt ordered the navy to convene a temporary board to make recommendations on the appropriate types and characteristics of future destroyers. The board's report emphasized the need for destroyers to be capable of operating with the battle fleet at great distances from American shores. This meant high endurance and the ability to make good speed in rough weather, something existing destroyers could not do.

New designs were produced to meet the need, leading to larger and more capable ships. The first group of oceangoing destroyers was *Smith* class of five ships, authorized in 1906 and 1907. Armed with three—later increased to six—18-inch torpedo tubes, these ships were powered by turbines and displaced around seven hundred tons. On trial, *Flusser* achieved over thirty knots. *Smith* was two knots slower.

The ten ships of the *Paulding* class followed. They were slightly larger, displaced about 750 tons, had more power, and introduced oil fuel. *Paulding* made nearly thirty-three knots on trial. These ships introduced twin torpedo tubes; six 18-inch tubes were arranged in three twin mounts. Eleven more ships repeated the same basic design. These twenty-six early destroyers were known collectively as the "flivvers," a slang term for lightweights. Future designs would be larger and more capable.

As the range and striking power of torpedoes increased, the influence of destroyer tactics grew. A determined attack could damage a battle fleet, disrupt its gunnery, or force it to maneuver into a disadvantageous position; destroyers became an essential element of battle-line tactics. They also became important as scouts. When scouting, destroyers had to steam at high speeds of twenty knots or more for long periods of time. This taxed the machinery of the small vessels and led to frequent maintenance and repairs. However, it encouraged the development of even larger destroyers. The result was the *Cassin* class of 1911, the first of the "thousand tonners."

The *Cassin* class had a more powerful, 4-inch, gun battery and four twin 18-inch torpedo tubes. The *Cassins* were followed by three more classes of "thousand tonners." The *O'Brien* class introduced 21-inch torpedo tubes; the *Tucker* class repeated their design. The *Sampson* class, the final variant of the type, increased torpedo armament to twelve 21-inch tubes in four triple mounts. These three classes totaled twenty-six ships; all had maximum speeds of about twenty-nine knots. Although slower than their predecessors, they had greater range and better sea-keeping abilities.

Photo 7.2. The crew of a 4-inch/50 stands by its weapon on the foredeck of a "thousand tonner." Larger and more capable than earlier destroyers, these ships were more specifically designed to operate with the battle fleet and support it in distant oceans. (Hone collection)

Incremental improvement followed. The *Caldwell* class introduced a flush-decked hull, which provided still better sea-keeping and simplified the overall design. Armament was similar to the previous class, and maximum speed was thirty knots. These ships were the prototypes of the navy's wartime destroyer program.

Wartime construction was dominated by the "flush-deckers," the ships of the *Wickes* and *Clemson* classes. With few exceptions, they were armed like the *Caldwell* class. An improved hull form and more powerful turbines increased speed to thirty-five knots. They were produced in great numbers; a total of 273 "flush-deckers" were authorized, and of these a remarkable 266 were completed. However, only thirty-nine were in commission when the war ended.

Sixteen older ships, originally considered destroyers, had by 1916 been redesignated as coastal torpedo boats. The five ships of the *Bainbridge* class, the oldest, were good representatives of the basic type. They mounted just two 18-inch torpedo tubes. The remainder varied only in size and layout. Most were in the Pacific or Asiatic Fleet when America entered the war. *Bainbridge* and her sisters would serve in the Mediterranean; the three ships of the *Truxton* class operated from Brest.

In addition to the massive destroyer building program, industrial resources were also focused on subchasers and Eagle boats. The subchasers were nimble boats with internal-combustion engines and displacements of about 75 tons. They mounted light guns and depth charges. Almost all were wooden-hulled; over four hundred were commissioned during the war. The Eagle boats, antisubmarine (ASW) vessels of six hundred tons, were built by the Ford Motor Company. Use of the automaker relieved existing shipbuilding facilities from being taken up by their construction, a novel approach. Only two Eagle boats had entered service by the time the war ended.

Auxiliaries and Gunboats

Although the navy's tactical thought emphasized the supremacy of the battle line, strategic thinking focused on the ability to project naval power. The fleet had to be able to move to distant locations, fight from undeveloped anchorages, and win battles in the open sea. This required a strong logistical base organic to the fleet; modern auxiliaries were essential. Accordingly, the General Board made colliers and tankers, repair ships, and other supporting ships part of its annual recommendations.

Not all of these recommendations were approved, but the result was a steady, if relatively slow, growth in the logistical capability of the fleet and a corresponding increase in its ability to fight from remote anchorages. No fewer than twenty fuel ships were in commission by 1916, with another two under construction. Of these, thirteen had been authorized in the previous eight years. Construction of supply ships and transports lagged behind. There were five transports and four supply ships in commission in 1916; one of each type was under construction.

Numerous tenders served as mobile supports for the smaller ships of the fleet. Three destroyer tenders served with the Atlantic Fleet—*Dixie, Melville,* and *Panther. Iris* tendered the Pacific Fleet's destroyers, and *Pompey* helped maintain those in the Philippines. Submarine tenders *Bushnell* and *Fulton* operated with the Atlantic Fleet and *Alert* with the Pacific. They were supported by the old monitors of the *Ozark* class, which had been converted to submarine tenders. *Black Hawk* was the flagship of the Mine Force as well as its repair ship.

Although not as auxiliaries, the navy also employed a large number of gunboats. There were twenty-nine of these in the three fleets, although many of them were old and no longer operational. They policed American interests on distant stations, such as the Philippines, the Caribbean, and the Yangtze River in China.

Gunnery

Surface

The navy placed great emphasis on gunnery, which it considered the primary weapon of naval warfare. As technological advancements allowed accurate fire to be delivered at longer ranges, more sophisticated procedures were introduced to make the most of these advances. The result was a feedback loop, with technical and procedural enhancements developing together. These included the introduction of the all-big-gun ship, salvo firing, mechanical computers, gun directors, centralized control, and competitive target practice.

Fire control—determining where to aim the guns to hit the target—was the central problem in gunnery. Sophisticated procedures, orchestrating the activities of many individuals, had to be developed and refined to maximize the chances of hitting. The range to the target ship was determined by long-base range finders. In older battleships these were mounted in the open, atop the turrets; starting with *Texas* they were mounted inside, at the rear of the turrets.

Directors, high aloft in the navy's distinctive cage masts, tracked the motion of the target. Their crews made initial estimates of the target's course and speed, providing a preliminary solution to the fire-control problem. Directors gave significantly better results at long range. The first mounting was on *Texas* in 1915; other battleships followed, and by 1916 the navy was using them to practice at ranges up to 20,000 yards.

The plotting room, the brains of the fire-control system, made final determinations of enemy course, speed, and range, with the aid of a Ford range-keeper. The range-keeper was a sophisticated mechanical computer that could predict the range to the target at a future time based on observations of the target and information about the firing ship's course and speed. The future bearing to the target was derived from a plot maintained by the plotting room's crew. The two were combined to determine where to aim the ship's guns.

The range-keeper was similar to the Argo Clock, developed by British inventor Arthur Pollen, but there were some important differences. The most significant of these was the fact that the range-keeper was more reliant on manual inputs. "Manual input made it easier to integrate the range-keeper into the existing fire-control system. It was also easier to smooth or

Table 7.2 U.S. Navy Large- and Medium-Caliber Guns

Name	Mounted on	MV (feet/sec)	Shell weight (pounds)	Range/elevation
14-inch/45 Mk 1, 2, 3, 5	Battleships—*New York, Nevada, Pennsylvania*	2,600	1,400	23,000 yards/15°
14-inch/50 Mk 4, 6	Battleships—*New Mexico*	2,800	1,400	24,000 yards/15°
13-inch/35 Mk 1, 2	Battleships—*Indiana, Kearsarge, Illinois*	2,000	1130	12,100 yards/15°
12-inch/35 Mk 1, 2	Battleships—*Iowa* Monitors—*Monterey*	2,100	850	12,500 yards/15°
12-inch/40 Mk 3, 4	Battleships—*Maine* and *Virginia* Monitors—*Arkansas* class	2,400	870	19,000 yards/15°
12-inch/45 Mk 5, 6	Battleships—*Connecticut, Vermont, Mississippi, South Carolina, Delaware, North Dakota* classes	2,700	870	20,000 yards/15° (*Connecticut* and *Mississippi* classes elevation was 20°)
12-inch/50 Mk 7	Battleships—*Arkansas* class	2,900	870	23,500 yards/15°
10-inch/30 and 34 Mk 1, 2	Monitors—*Amphitrite* class and *Monterey*	2,000	500	11,500 yards/15°
10-inch/40 Mk 3	Cruisers—*Tennessee* class	2,700	510	20,000 yards/15°
8-inch/35 Mk 3, 4	Battleships—*Indiana, Iowa, Kearsarge* classes Cruisers—*Brooklyn, New York* (until 1909) Early cruisers	2,080	250	10,500 yards/20°
8-inch/40 Mk 5	Cruisers—*Pennsylvania* class (until 1909), *Colombia* class	2,500	260	20,000 yards/20°

8-inch/45 Mk 6	Battleships—*Virginia, Connecticut, Vermont, Mississippi* classes Cruisers—*Pennsylvania* class (from 1909), *New York* (from 1909)	2,750	260	22,500 yards/20°
7-inch/45 Mk 1	Battleships—*Connecticut, Vermont, Mississippi* classes	2,700	165	16,500 yards/15°
6-inch/30 (40 in Mk 3, Mod 2) Mk 2, 3	Battleships, cruisers, and gunboats	1,950	105	9,000 yards/15°
6-inch/40 Mk 4	Battleships, cruisers, and gunboats	2,150	105	10,000 yards/15°
6-inch/50 Mk 5	Cruisers *New Orleans* and *Albany*	2,536	100	16,500 yards/15°
6-inch/46 Mk 6, 8	Battleships, cruisers	2,800	105	15,000 yards/15°
6-inch/40 Mk 7	Cruiser *Baltimore*	2,400	100	8,600 yards/15°
6-inch/44 Mk 9	Cruisers *Columbia* and *Minneapolis*, auxiliaries	2,250	105	10,000 yards/15°
5-inch/40 Mk 2, 4	Battleships, cruisers	2,500	50	8,500 yards/15°
5-inch/40 Mk 3	Battleships, cruisers	2,300	50	8,500 yards/15°
5-inch/50 Mk 5	Cruisers	2,700	60	13,500 yards/15°
5-inch/50 Mk 6	Battleships, cruisers	3,000	50	14,000 yards/15°
5-inch/51 Mk 7, 8	Battleships, destroyers	3,150	50	14,050 yards/15° 15,850 yards/20°
4-inch/40 Mk 1–6	Battleships, cruisers, gunboats	2,000	33	11,500 yards/31°
4-inch/50 Mk 7, 8, 9, 10	Destroyers	2,500–2,900	33	15,920 yards/20° 20,940 yards/45°

filter data before inserting it."[9] This meant that the range-keeper required skilled personnel to operate it effectively.

Once future range and bearing of the target were determined, a fire-control "solution" had been obtained. The proper train and elevation orders were transmitted from the plotting room to the turrets. When the turret crews had trained and elevated the guns accordingly, the director operator closely watched the horizon and closed the firing circuit at the proper point in the ship's roll; then the guns fired. Once the initial salvo landed, it became the spotter's responsibility to bring the guns onto the target.

Spotters, high up in the masts, were the final link in the fire-control system; they closed the feedback loop and fed corrections into the fire-control solution. The move to salvo firing and the emphasis on firing all a battleship's guns in a single salvo derived from an effort to simplify the spotting problem and make battleship gunfire more accurate. The factors influencing the flight of a large-caliber shell over many miles are numerous, and the exact point at which a shell will land is best expressed by a probability curve. In practice this meant that the more splashes that could be observed in a single salvo, the more likely a spotter would to be able to estimate the type of correction that might score hits.

In his annual report for 1916, Secretary Daniels praised the effectiveness of the fleet's gunnery, stating that "the American Navy has not only equaled, but in battle target practice has actually excelled the best records believed to have been made in recent European naval battles."[10] Unfortunately, this assessment was inaccurate. After they joined the Grand Fleet in 1917, it quickly became apparent that Admiral Rodman's battleships could not shoot as well as their British counterparts.

The inferior gunnery of the American ships was due to several causes, the most important of which was training. The manual processes in the fire-control system made it heavily dependent on the experience and skill of the men involved. The wartime expansion had been so rapid that it had been impossible to train personnel adequately; on some ships as many as three-quarters of those in the gunnery division had less than a year's experience.

The navy's practices were also inadequate. They were conducted under favorable conditions and failed to tax crewmen. In the Royal Navy it was far different; exercises and drills were more realistic and were performed in much more challenging conditions. In frank communications to Daniels, Rodman criticized the navy's approach to gunnery practice. He also was quick to adopt British methods, and as a result the firing of his ships began to improve. By July 1918 Rodman was receiving praise for the squadron's accuracy and considered his ships "at least equal if not superior to the British."[11] The rest of the fleet soon followed, introducing techniques modeled on British practice. (See table 7.2.)

Antiaircraft

Antiaircraft guns, like the planes they were designed to counter, were relatively unsophisticated. The navy's first purpose-built antiaircraft gun was the 3-inch Mk 10, a 50-caliber weapon derived from an antidestroyer gun. It fired a 13-pound shell at a muzzle velocity of 2,700 feet per second. A prototype of this model was mounted on *Texas* in 1916; four of them became the standard battleship battery.

For smaller vessels, a lighter 3-inch antiaircraft gun, the Mk 14, was developed from a landing gun. It was a 23.5-caliber weapon and also fired a 13-pound shell. This gun equipped wartime destroyers, submarines, and other small craft.

Light antiaircraft guns were adapted from existing one-pounder "pom-pom" guns. The earliest of these had entered service before the Spanish-American War; antiaircraft versions were in service by 1916. They equipped destroyers of the *Sampson* class, as well as those "flush-deckers" that did not receive a 3-inch gun. The navy also used 0.30-caliber machine guns as antiaircraft armament.

Torpedoes

The navy developed larger and more capable torpedoes as it sought ways to integrate them and the ships carrying them into the operations of the fleet. After the introduction of gyroscopes that allowed torpedoes to maintain a straight course, the navy realized that more complex gyroscopes could also force a torpedo to take up a new course after emerging from its tube.

From 1910 on, the navy designed its torpedoes for this kind of curved fire. This allowed destroyers to launch their entire battery of torpedoes in one salvo, even with tubes mounted on both beams. They did not have to reverse course to launch torpedoes from one side and then the other. This meant that a group of ships could approach at high speed, launch, and turn only when they wanted to escape; it made their attacks stealthier, because they could maintain a less-visible end-on relationship to the target until after their torpedoes were in the water. (See table 7.3.)

Table 7.3 U.S. Navy Torpedoes

Name	Year	Mounted on	Dimensions	Warhead	Range
Type A (Whitehead Mk III)	1898	Submarines: *A* through *D* classes	18-in. x 11 ft., 8 in.	140-lb.	800 yards/26.5 knots
Type B (Whitehead Mk I)	~1898	Torpedo boats	18-in. x 16 ft., 5 in.	212-lb.	1,000 yards/27.5 knots
Type C (Whitehead Mk II)	~1898	Battleships	18-in. x 16 ft., 5 in.	131-lb.	1,500 yards/28 knots
Mk 1 (Bliss-Leavitt)	1905	Battleships	21-in. x 16 ft., 5 in.	199-lb.	4,000 yards/26 knots
Mk 2 (Bliss-Leavitt)	1905	Battleships, cruisers	21-in. x 17 feet	207-lb.	3,500 yards/26 knots
Mk 3 (Bliss-Leavitt)	1909	Battleships, cruisers	21-in. x 17 feet	218-lb.	4,000 yards/26.5 knots
Mk 4–1 (Bliss-Leavitt)	1904	Submarines	18-in. x 16 ft., 5 in.	199-lb.	3,000 yards/29 knots
Mk 4 (Bliss-Leavitt Mk IV)	1908	Submarines: D class (from 1912)	18-in. x 16 ft., 5 in.	200-lb.	2,000 yards/30 knots
Mk 5 (Whitehead)	1908	Submarines, destroyers, and cruisers	18-in. x 17 ft.	200-lb. (206-lb. TNT for Mod 1)	4,000 yards/29 knots 3,500 yards/26 knots 2,000 yards/36 knots 1,000 yards/40 knots
Mk 6 (Bliss-Leavitt)	1909	Submarines: E through H classes; destroyers and cruisers	18-in. x 17 ft.	200-lb.	2,000 yards/35 knots
Mk 7 (Bliss-Leavitt)	1912	Submarines: K, L, M, N, O, R classes; destroyers, cruisers; aircraft	18-in. x 17 ft.	205-lb. TNT	4,000 yards/32 knots
Mk 8	1911	Battleships, cruisers, destroyers	21-in. x 21 ft., 4.3 in.	321-lb.	12,500 yards/27 knots
Mk 9	1915	Battleships, submarines	21-in. x 17 ft.	210-lb.	7,000 yards/27 knots
Mk 10	1915	Submarines: R and S classes	21-in. x 16 ft., 3 in.	497-lb. TNT	3,500 yards/36 knots

Submarine Warfare

Offensive

Submarine Doctrine

Submarine doctrine, like the submarines built to carry it out, initially focused on coastal and harbor defense. With the battle fleet concentrated in the Atlantic, the Pacific coast was vulnerable. Submarines were stationed at vital harbors and other critical locations as part of an integrated coastal-defense scheme, operating, collectively, very much like an intelligent and mobile minefield. They were stationed in the Philippines, the Panama Canal Zone, and on both coasts of the United States.

However, the navy, and in particular the General Board, did not want submarines restricted to defensive roles. As with other new weapons, there was a strong desire to integrate submarines with the offensive operations of the fleet. This led to the development of the "fleet submarine" concept, envisioning a larger, oceangoing boat that could keep up with the battle fleet and operate with it tactically. The 1916 Battle Instructions anticipated the development of larger fleet boats with "sufficient speed and seagoing qualities" to operate with the fleet but acknowledged that none yet existed. This meant that submarines would need to operate independently. If in the same general area as the fleet, a group of boats would be employed as a mobile minefield, waiting in a location where the enemy was likely to be encountered. Otherwise, submarines would congregate at critical choke points, such as strait or channels, through which the enemy had to pass. Their primary targets would be enemy capital ships. During the war they operated this way in their patrols, although their targets were U-boats instead of battleships.

Boats/Weapons

The navy's submarines fit into three broad categories. The earliest vessels were harbor-defense types with limited endurance and capabilities. From these evolved a series of coastal designs that were capable of defending regional areas. The final variants were oceangoing submarines capable of operating over much greater distances. Throughout the development process, the General Board sought a "fleet submarine" that could operate with the battle fleet.

Harbor-defense vessels included the A and B classes, derived from the design of *Holland*. A-class boats were very small and had single 18-inch torpedo tubes. The B-class boats were an incremental improvement, with two torpedo tubes. Both types had relatively high underwater speeds, but their gasoline engines were dangerous because of the risk of combustible fumes. They served in the Philippines during the war.

The majority of the navy's submarines were coastal-defense types. *Octopus* was the initial prototype; authorized along with the boats of the B class in 1904, she was almost twice the size of earlier submarines, with a displacement of 240 tons. Four similar boats followed, and together they made the C class. During the war they guarded the approaches to the Panama Canal.

The D, E, and F classes were even larger, all around three hundred tons. Armament was doubled to four 18-inch torpedo tubes; four tubes became standard, because four torpedo hits were considered necessary to disable or sink a battleship. The E and F classes introduced diesel engines, but the original engines proved to be unreliable; new engines were installed in 1915.

The four ships grouped together as the G class were largely experimental. Three of them—*Seal, Tuna,* and *Turbot*—were from the firm of Simon Lake. *Thresher* was built to a design from Cesare Laurenti, an Italian naval constructor. These were all unusual designs, but they were useful training boats during the war and helped to fine-tune hydrophone designs and improve the skills of new recruits. None led to further development.

Evolution of the F design resulted in a series of boats of increasing capability. These submarines retained the same torpedo armament but had more effective diesel engines. The H class was the first iteration. The K class increased displacement to almost four hundred tons; the L class was larger still, at 450 tons, and introduced a 3-inch deck gun. *M-1* was a parallel design to the L class, but with a double-hull. She had stability problems and was largely unsuccessful. The O class continued the trend toward large and more capable designs, reaching 520 tons. Finally, the N class reverted to more moderate dimensions and discarded the deck gun.

Because they were the newest boats in commission at the outbreak of war, boats of the K and L classes were sent overseas; the K boats of Submarine Division 4 operated from the Azores and the L boats of Submarine Division 5 from Ireland. The L boats were renamed "AL" to distinguish them from the Royal Navy's L class.

The R class was the final evolution of the navy's coastal-defense submarine. An improvement of the O-class design, the R boats increased displacement slightly and moved to 21-inch torpedo tubes; a larger, more powerful 3-inch deck gun was also provided. These were the most modern of the navy's submarines to serve in the war.

In the meantime, the General Board continued to press for a fleet submarine. Simulations at the Naval War College had shown their value in a fleet action, and with the T class, the type finally arrived. However, and though much larger than anything before, these boats proved disappointing;

they were too slow for fleet operations, and their complex power plants were unreliable. They only served for a short time, and none were ready before the armistice.

The navy's submariners disliked the distinction the General Board made between fleet submarines and coastal types. They argued for a design between the two sizes that they believed would be capable of fulfilling both roles. The German eight-hundred-ton U-boat was cited as an example of what could be done; *U 53,* a boat of this type, visited Newport in 1916 and was cited to reinforce these arguments.

The S class was developed to meet this need. Scaled up from the R class, S boats displaced 850 tons, had four 21-inch torpedo tubes, and mounted a 4-inch deck gun. This was the standard design in place when the United States entered the war, and like the "flush deckers," the S boats were built in large quantities. However, none were completed before the end of hostilities.

Antisubmarine

Submarines were particularly difficult to attack. Once underwater, they were invulnerable to conventional shipboard weapons, the gun and the torpedo. Depth charges were the only effective weapon. Following the lead of the Royal Navy, the U.S. Navy introduced its first depth charge in February 1917. Cooperation with the British after the American entry into the war brought more effective designs, and by the end of 1917 American ingenuity had coupled the depth charge to the Y-gun, a specialized mortar, increasing the spread and lethality of depth-charge attacks.

Although depth charges worked, submarines had to be located fairly precisely in order to be attacked successfully. When operating at periscope depth or below, submarines were extremely difficult to detect from surface ships. However, they could still be heard. The acoustic properties of water gave attacking ships a potential advantage; if they could hear a submarine, they might be able to direct an attack even if the target was underwater.

Hydrophones were invented with this idea in mind. They picked up sounds in the water and relayed them to an operator inside the ship. Unlike sonar installations developed between the wars, hydrophones were passive; the idea of beaming acoustic waves into the water and listening for a return was only starting to be developed by the time the war ended. The navy installed hydrophones on surface ships and submarines. Several different hydrophone installations were developed during the war in an effort to increase accuracy and performance. The C-tube was the initial model, followed by increasingly sophisticated variants—the SC, K, Y, and MV.

Effective range varied a great deal depending on conditions and the skill of the operator; hydrophones were very difficult to use in convoy conditions, for example, because the noise from the ships generally drowned out any hint of submarines. When used by skilled operators in good conditions, they proved to be accurate and effective. The British noted that American hydrophones were far more effective than their own equipment, which was so ineffective it was almost never used. An L-class boat of Submarine Division 5, for example, used her SC-tube to accurately determine the bearing, number, and type of approaching vessels before they came into visual range.

Hydrophones were most effective on submarines and subchasers, both of which could stop their internal-combustion engines to listen and then restart them rapidly to pursue a submarine. Destroyers, with turbine power plants, could not turn their engines off and then on again so quickly. Because the hydrophone could give only a bearing, not a range, subchasers generally operated in groups of three so they could triangulate the correct position for an attack.

Signals intelligence, another passive form of listening, was also effective. The navy had begun experimenting with radio direction-finders in 1912 and knew they could be used to locate transmitting ships. By listening to German radio messages and occasionally decoding their contents, commands could predict the movements of U-boats and route antisubmarine craft to the appropriate location to hunt them and, if not kill them, at least keep them below the surface.

Offensive antisubmarine patrols appeared to be effective during the war. Subchasers were frequently involved in these efforts, and they claimed to have sunk numerous U-boats. However, after the armistice it became clear that their claims were exaggerated; none of the kills could be confirmed. Submarine Division 5 was no more successful, but it made numerous sightings and had several near successes. *L-1* and *L-11* each made one unsuccessful attack. *L-4* attacked U-boats on two occasions without success. One of her encounters was at close range, and she had a narrow escape—after crash diving to periscope depth the crew heard the whine of a German torpedo pass through the water overhead. Q-ships operating along the U.S. coast were also unsuccessful.

There were only two confirmed sinkings of enemy submarines by navy vessels during the war. On 17 November 1917, the destroyer *Fanning*, in corporation with destroyer *Nicholson*, forced *U 58* to the surface after a depth-charge attack. The Germans surrendered and then scuttled their boat. The converted yacht *Lydonia*, in concert with the British destroyer

Basilisk, sank *UB 70* on 8 May 1918 while escorting a convoy from Bizerte to Gibraltar. *Lydonia* was one of a number of yachts acquired by the navy to operate as ASW escorts, reflecting the shortage of purpose-built ASW craft upon entry into the war.

Offensive ASW patrols, with destroyers, subchasers, or submarines, did not have to sink U-boats to be successful. They could reduce the effectiveness of enemy submarines by forcing them to spend more time submerged and therefore to move through the patrol area more slowly. U-boat endurance was limited; the more time boats spent getting to their patrol areas, the less time they could spend hunting for targets. After the war, it was estimated that a U-boat's average daily advance had been reduced from two hundred miles to five miles in areas where ASW patrols were active.

Aircraft also played an essential part in the antisubmarine effort. Large, long-range flying boats operating from bases in the United States and Europe patrolled the shipping lanes, watching for U-boats and attacking them with bombs and machine guns. Lighter-than-air craft were also employed. These could stay aloft for many hours, shepherding several convoys into and out of vital harbors during each sortie.

ASW Weapons

A variety of ASW weapons were developed and employed. The most effective of these was the depth charge. The initial model, the Mark 1, was introduced in February 1917. It was a small and unsophisticated weapon, with a charge of only fifty pounds of explosive. The Mk 1 was triggered by a surface float and a line that extended as the charge sank; when the charge reached the set depth, the line between the charge and the surface float would become taut, triggering the charge.

The Mk 2 followed, entering service in the fall of 1917. It borrowed heavily from a British design but employed an American hydrostatic fuse, which made it more reliable. The Mk 2 had a charge of three hundred pounds and maximum depth of two hundred feet. As U-boats increased their effective operating depths, the Mk 3 was introduced to compensate; it could reach a depth of three hundred feet and used the same warhead as the Mk 2. The final wartime model was the monster Mk 4, with a warhead of six hundred pounds; Mk 4 models were first issued in September 1918.

Depth charges were rolled off racks and fired from depth-charge mortars called Y-guns. In combination, racks and Y-guns produced a pattern of explosions intended to ring the submarine and account for any maneuvers it might have made since last being seen or heard.

The Y-gun was so named because its two barrels were at an angle of forty-five degrees from the vertical; viewed together, they made the shape of the letter *Y*. Different charges gave Y-guns ranges of fifty, sixty-six, or eighty yards, with Mk 2 or Mk 3 depth charges. They entered service very quickly; the first deliveries of Y-guns were made in December 1917, the same month the initial contract to produce them was signed.

In addition to these underwater weapons, in 1917 the navy introduced flat-nosed shells that would not ricochet upon striking the water. They were intended specifically to penetrate the water and strike the hull of surfaced boats; they were produced for calibers from eight to three inches.

Amphibious Warfare

The navy was quite adept at landing sailors and marines on hostile shores but not against prepared defenses manned by trained troops. Interventions in the Caribbean and Central America provided many opportunities to practice such landings. These operations were made easier by the assumption that the Marine Corps, operating as the navy's organic infantry, would move with the fleet in wartime, securing and defending advanced bases as required. There was, therefore, a readily available source of manpower with which to secure foreign territory.

Before American entry into the war, landings were made in Haiti, the Dominican Republic, and at Vera Cruz, Mexico. In general, these landings were made by men from the crews and marine detachments of ships, not a separate, dedicated force. Of the men landed at Vera Cruz in April 1914, more than three hundred were from the battleships *Florida* and *Utah*. On this occasion a dedicated marine unit also participated, but that was a rare occurrence.

These landings were almost never opposed, although guns stood ready to support the landing parties as they rowed their whaleboats ashore. The intimidating sight of warships was generally sufficient to prevent resistance to a landing. When the fleet appeared off Vera Cruz, for example, Mexican general Gustavo Maass withdrew his forces and allowed the Americans to land unopposed. However, not all landings were so easy. In June 1916, marines and sailors from gunboat *Sacramento* landed at the Dominican coastal town of Puerto Plata; they came under fire from about five hundred irregulars as they approached the beach. *Sacramento* fired shells into the enemy trenches to suppress this fire but "refrained from using devastating firepower" in order to prevent civilian casualties.[12]

Mine Warfare

Prior to 1905 mines had been the province of the U.S. Army and its coast-defense plans. The Russo-Japanese War, however, showed the potential of mines in modern fleet operations, and soon thereafter the navy sought a mine-depot ship for operations with the fleet. No specialized ship was authorized, but in 1912 the elderly cruiser *San Francisco* became a mine carrier. She was soon joined by the cruiser *Baltimore* and the old gunboat *Dubuque*. These ships began to work out how to integrate mine warfare with the fleet.

Practice in sweeping and laying mines at Pensacola and Culebra demonstrated the potential of mine warfare. Before long, all battleships had been fitted for minesweeping, and plans were being made to operate mine vessels with the battle fleet; this led to the creation of a fleet Mine Division. Although high-speed minelayers were lacking, there were plenty of destroyers. Many of these were fitted with mine racks and pressed into service as minelayers. Destroyers were well suited because they were fast enough to lay mines in the path of an opposing battle line in action.

Photo 7.3. A Mark 6 mine ready for deployment. These mines were rapidly produced for the Northern Barrage, an extensive mining operation designed to prevent U-boats from using the northern exit of the North Sea. The "K Device" fuse mechanism, a long wire attached to a float, is readily visible. (Hone collection)

The navy's early mines were based on foreign designs. The Mk 2 was a French Sauter-Harlé type. Both the Mk 3 and Mk 4 employed a cork float fuse derived from a Vickers design. These models proved ineffective during the war. They were replaced by the Mk 5, a "horned" type that resembled a sea urchin. It was derived from a German design.

Soon after entering the war, the Bureau of Ordnance suggested that a mine barrage extending from the east coast of Scotland to the west coast of Norway could prevent U-boats from exiting the North Sea and reaching the shipping lanes to the west. This was called the "Northern Barrage." After an evaluation of existing alternatives, the bureau concluded that a new mine would be needed, one that could be triggered by a submarine passing close by as well as upon contact. Development work on the new mine began in May 1917. Trials were performed in June and July; the results convinced the bureau that the new approach was sound.

The Mk 6 mine was triggered by the "K device," a copper antenna extending upward from the mine toward the surface. Connected to a copper plate on the mine, the antenna formed a relay. The surrounding sea water was used as a battery. When the steel hull of an approaching ship touched the wire, it triggered a current, and the mine went off. The apparatus was very successful in tests. Because a single mine could cover multiple depths, by virtue of the wire, the Bureau of Ordnance concluded that the number of mines required for the barrage could be reduced by two-thirds.

Table 7.4 U.S. Navy Mines

Name	Type	Trigger mechanism	Warhead	Year
Mk 1	spherical moored	inertia pistol	136 pounds	Before 1909
Mk 2	Sauter-Harle (French)	contact-inertia	175 pounds	~1909
Mk 3	Vickers type	protruding float inertia	150 pounds	1915
Mk 4	Vickers type	protruding float inertia	250 pounds	1916
Mk 5	Moored Hertz horn mine	acid trigger	500 pounds	1917
Mk 6	spherical moored	"K device"	300 pounds	1917

The Northern Barrage began to be put in place in the spring of 1918; a variety of vessels participated. *San Francisco* and *Baltimore* were augmented by numerous cargo vessels, many originally designed for service on the Great Lakes. Eventually, the force had ten ships, including the flagship

Black Hawk. By 29 July 1918 the barrier in the American sector was complete; additional sorties augmented it until October. Ultimately, 70,263 mines were laid, of which 56,611 were the Mk 6 type.

For all this effort, there was relatively little return. The barrage "probably accounted for no more than six or seven U-boats" throughout its career, and this is an optimistic number. While the effort illustrated the capabilities of American industry and the technological expertise of the Bureau of Ordnance, the effort could have been more profitably invested elsewhere. (See table 7.4.)

Aviation

Doctrine

By the time the 1916 Battle Instructions were written it was apparent that airplanes had potential utility, but the fleet was not prepared to integrate aircraft into its tactical plans; more experience was needed to determine how best to operate them with the fleet in battle. However, significant experience had already been gained using aircraft as scouts.

Airplanes had first operated with the fleet in the annual exercises of 1913. They performed well, and Daniels, convinced of their value, established a Board of Aeronautics later that year. Battleship *Mississippi* became an experimental ship, tasked with working out how best to integrate airplanes with the fleet. In 1914 both she and the cruiser *Birmingham* operated Curtiss Model F flying boats during the occupation of Vera Cruz. The planes scouted for mines and located enemy troop concentrations.

Several of the large armored cruisers, which were already operating as scouts, began to carry aircraft. *North Carolina* was fitted with a prototype catapult in 1915, and she launched her first flying boat on 5 November. A standardized version was fitted in June 1916. Both *Seattle* and *Huntington* were equipped with similar catapults in 1917. In addition to seaplanes, these cruisers also operated kite balloons. Experiments with the armored cruisers ended once America entered the war; the cruiser catapults were mounted over the after turrets in a fixed position, making it impossible to use the turrets and effectively cutting the firepower of the cruisers in half. When war was declared, the catapults were removed to free the cruisers to operate as convoy escorts.

Ironically, although the navy's prewar emphasis focused on determining how best to operate aircraft with the fleet, those operating from land bases would prove to be most important during the war. Long-range, land-based planes and airships became vital components of the campaign against the U-boats, screening convoys and helping to secure the supply lines to

Europe. The bulk of the growth in naval aviation during the war was to support this component of the U-boat war.

Aircraft

At the dawn of the war, naval aviation capabilities were extremely limited. Although interest in the arm was developing, in 1913 Congress appropriated only $20,000 for naval aviation. In that same year, the navy ranked fourteenth in the world in terms of aviation expenditures. There were only fourteen aviators in the service and just four flying boats.

Wilson's administration increased the emphasis on naval aviation. Daniels not only set up a Board of Aeronautics but approved the use of the Pensacola Navy Yard for the Naval Aeronautical School, to develop new doctrine and train aviators. Experiments with the fleet began, to determine how best to integrate aircraft with fleet operations.

Ship-Based

The navy employed a variety of Curtiss aircraft, both on shore and at sea, starting in 1910 with the Model D, the first airplane to take off and land from a ship. The Model D was a pusher biplane with a tricycle undercarriage and relatively limited performance. Curtiss followed this with the Model E, a true flying boat, with a hull. The navy began purchasing planes of this type in 1911. Derived from the Model D, the Model E was small and cramped for its crew of two.

The Model F followed soon thereafter, first flying in January 1912. With a larger and more seaworthy hull, the Model F began to demonstrate naval aviation's potential. These planes participated in the occupation of Vera Cruz and were used for continued experimentation before American entry into the war, proving the concept of a catapult launch and testing approaches to automatic remote control.

As planes increased in size and capabilities, the navy experimented with aircraft from a wider variety of manufacturers, including Wright, Burgess, Martin, Thomas, and Gallaudet. The armored cruiser *Huntington* carried a large Burgess model. The majority of these types were seaplanes, reflecting the navy's interest in operating aircraft with the fleet.

Experiments with ship-based aviation largely came to a stop during the war. The armored cruisers that had become the focus of experimentation after the sale of *Mississippi* were employed as convoy escorts, and their planes were removed. Although there was limited experimentation with flying-off platforms, as used in the Royal Navy, wartime attention would focus more on land-based patrol planes and airships. (See table 7.5.)

Table 7.5 U.S. Navy Aircraft

Designation	Manufacturer	Year	Description	Notes
Model F	Curtiss	1912	single-engine flying boat	Prewar experimental type. Used for training during the war.
H-12	Curtiss	1916	twin-engine flying boat	Large flying boat. Used for ASW patrol.
HS-1	Curtiss	1917	single-engine flying boat	Used for ASW patrol.
HS-2	Curtiss	1918	single-engine flying boat	Development of HS-1. 25% more wing area for greater ordnance loads. Also used for ASW patrol.
H-16	Curtiss	1918	twin-engine flying boat	Evolution of the H-12. First aircraft built at the Naval Aircraft Factory. Also used for ASW patrol.
F-5L	Naval Aircraft Factory	1918	twin-engine flying boat	Evolution of the H-16. Adapted for more rapid manufacture. Also used for ASW patrol.
NC	Curtiss	1918	multi-engine flying boat	Variants had three and four engines. Largest flying boats of their time. First flight was made in October 1918. Largely experimental.
R Series	Curtiss	1915	single-engine seaplane	Operated from cruisers, performed submarine patrols, and were used as experimental torpedo bombers.
Model S	Burgess	1916	single-engine seaplane	Operated from cruisers. Not produced in quantity.
N-9	Curtiss	1916	single-engine seaplane	Naval variant of the Curtiss Jenny. Used as a trainer in the war.
JN Series	Curtiss	1917	single-engine seaplane and land plane	Jenny produced for the Navy. Used as advanced trainers.
DH-4	Dayton-Wright	1918	single-engine land plane	Primarily used by marines. Employed in their Northern Bombing Group squadrons.
N-1	Naval Aircraft Factory	1918	experimental single-engine seaplane	Designed to use the recoilless Davis Gun, an ASW weapon in experimental development when the war ended. Not produced in quantity.
Ca-44	Caproni	1918	twin-engine bomber	Employed in the Navy Northern Bombing Group squadrons. Engines proved very unreliable.

Shore-Based

With the start of the war, the Curtiss Model F began to be produced in quantity; it became the navy's standard flying-boat trainer in 1917. Training would be necessary—in the years since the Model F first flew, Curtiss had developed larger and more powerful flying boats, leading to the Model H.

The Model H was originally built in response to a prize offered by the London *Daily Mail* for the first nonstop aerial crossing of the Atlantic. The war erupted before Curtiss could make an attempt at the prize, but the firm modified its design into a series of effective patrol aircraft. The first of these was the H-12. Adopted initially by the Royal Navy, the H-12 entered service with the U.S. Navy in July 1917. It was a twin-engine design that could carry two 230-pound ASW bombs.

The single-engine HS-1 was a smaller variant. These entered service in February 1918. The HS-1 could carry two 180-pound bombs, but these proved too small to be effective. A series of modifications led to the H-2; with a larger wingspan, the H-2 had the carrying capacity for two 230-pound bombs. Range was 517 miles.

Evolution of the H-12 design led to the H-16. Deliveries of this model started in February 1918; the H-16 had a crew of four and could carry four 230-pound bombs. Range was 452 miles. The need for rapid production led to detailed refinements, resulting in the F-5L design, which entered service in July 1918. Like the H-16, the F-5L could carry four 230-pound bombs; endurance with a combat load was eight and one-half hours, and maximum range was 765 miles. Both of these types were built at the newly constructed Naval Aircraft Factory in Philadelphia in 1917 and 1918.

These were supplemented by lighter-than-air craft. The navy's interest in airships began in 1915, when a contract was placed for a nonrigid airship, the experimental *DN-1*. Delivered in April 1917, she was unique because she was provided with a floating hangar, to test her ability to operate as a unit of the fleet. Overall, she was a disappointment, but experiments continued. The B-class airships followed; the first of a class of sixteen was delivered in July 1917. They were used for training and shore patrol. Many of the pilots trained on the B ships went on to pilot airships from bases in Europe.

The most significant of these bases was Paimboeuf, near the mouth of the Loire River in France. Here the navy operated a variety of airships loaned from the French, including *AT-1*, *VZ-3*, and *AT-13*. On 27 April 1918, Lieutenant F. P. Culbert's *AT-1* spent twenty-five hours and forty-three minutes on patrol, shepherding three separate convoys through a mined area. Additional air bases in Europe operated similar craft, patrolling coastal waters and keeping convoys safe.

WAR EXPERIENCE AND EVOLUTION

Wartime Evolution

There were two central themes to the navy's wartime development. The first and most visible was the incredible expansion that started with the 1916 naval appropriations bill and accelerated once America entered the war. The second was the fact that the navy was forced to fight a war significantly different from those it had planned; visions of a decisive battle in the Pacific and Caribbean evaporated when confronted by the necessity of maintaining lines of communication to Europe in the face of the German submarine campaign.

The growth of the navy during the war was massive. In July 1916 the navy had 4,293 officers and 54,234 enlisted men. By November 1918 these figures had grown to 32,474 and 497,030. In specific areas, the relative increases were even larger; naval aviation was one of them. At the time America entered the war there were just 201 officers and men in the navy's fledgling aviation division; by the time of the armistice there were 37,409.

The seeds of expansion were planted in 1915. The war and the hostile international situation began to illustrate just how weak America was in the face of more aggressive powers. Germany's first unrestricted submarine campaign, highlighted by the sinking of *Lusitania,* underscored the difficulty America would have maintaining a neutral stance while simultaneously protecting American lives and property. Japan's increasingly hostile attitude toward China, manifest in the notorious "Twenty-One Demands," demonstrated the vulnerability of American interests in East Asia. Wilson, Daniels, and other leaders began to consider increasing the level of military spending to protect America from foreign aggression.

Although the war was a catalyst for greater preparedness, the intention was not to join the conflict itself. Wilson and others in his administration firmly believed in neutrality. The greatest threat appeared to be from a postwar coalition, most likely of Germany and Japan. The Zimmerman Telegram, which proposed a three-way alliance of Germany, Japan, and Mexico against the United States, provided tangible evidence reinforcing these fears.

Wilson asked Daniels and his counterpart in the War Department for estimates on 21 July 1915. Departing from the usual approach, the president requested a plan spanning several years, one that would provide for "consistent and progressive development." This was a watershed event; it was the first time that Wilson had asked for "full and frank opinions" from his military advisors; there were no limitations on the request. The General Board drafted the navy's response and for 1916 recommended a five-year building program with ten battleships, six battle cruisers, and a large number of supporting vessels.

Congress remained to be convinced. The House Naval Affairs Committee supported a much more modest appropriation and called for "balanced fighting efficiency," a creative way of describing a limited amount of spending. The full House followed the committee's lead. Before the Senate could take up the bill, however, the world appeared to become much more threatening.

News of the battle of Jutland arrived the day after the House vote, dramatically illustrating the need for a modern battle fleet. On 22 June, American soldiers exchanged fire with their Mexican counterparts while hunting Pancho Villa. On 3 July, news of a diplomatic arrangement between Russia and Japan arrived; this agreement appeared to align both nations against American interests in the Far East. Each of these events supported the call for greater preparedness and increased naval spending. The Senate Naval Affairs Committee reflected on the increasingly threatening global situation and, in a "display of bipartisanship then unprecedented in service legislation," adopted the basic outline of the General Board's plan but stipulated that the ships of the five-year program were to be completed in three. In this form the bill passed the Senate. The House, encouraged by Wilson, soon followed.

The resulting appropriation was massive, but many of the ships planned would never be completed. Construction of the largest ships was delayed to make way for lighter craft that could fight the U-boats, and most of the battleships and battle cruisers were ultimately canceled by the naval limitation treaty of 1922. The shift to smaller ships reflected the fact that the navy was unprepared for the type of war it entered in 1917.

Friction occurred in the development of a strategy for this unanticipated conflict. Sims, in London and fully aware of the crippling effectiveness of the German submarines, advocated diverting resources to focus on what he correctly believed to be the critical effort. Benson, supported by Daniels and the General Board, opposed this view. They remained focused on a longer-term outlook designed to husband the navy's resources and preserve them for a possible postwar conflict. The debate went on for months.

Captain William V. Pratt, a loyal assistant to Benson but also a friend of Sims, found himself in the middle. Recognizing the accuracy of Sims' perspective, Pratt worked to change the Navy Department's view. Although he did not represent the majority opinion in the office of the CNO, Pratt's effective arguments helped convince Daniels and Benson that victory in the current war had to be their first priority.

This led to more than just a change in construction priorities. The battle fleet, in a step that ran counter to all existing strategic thought, was now divided, with two divisions separated from the main fleet and sent overseas to help with the effort in the decisive theater. This not only strengthened the Allied position in European waters but allowed the Royal Navy to decommission a number of old battleships and use their officers and men to crew antisubmarine vessels.

Battleship Division 9 arrived in Scapa Flow on 7 December 1917, under the command of Admiral Rodman. The battleships *New York, Delaware, Wyoming,* and *Florida* became the 6th Battle Squadron of the Royal Navy's Grand Fleet; *Texas* joined them in February 1918. In July, *Arkansas* replaced *Delaware.* All these ships were coal-burning, by the Royal Navy's request, because coal was more readily available than oil in the British Isles.

Photo 7.4. Battleship *Nevada* running trials in 1916. Her design introduced a new approach to protection, one far ahead of its time. Note the bare and uncluttered superstructure, typical of prewar USN dreadnoughts, and the distinctive cage masts. She was part of Battleship Division 6 and was stationed at Berehaven, Ireland, in 1918. (Hone collection)

Admiral Rodgers's Battleship Division 6, with *Utah, Nevada,* and *Oklahoma,* was stationed at Berehaven, Ireland, beginning in August 1918; its mission was to cover troop convoys and protect them from potential German surface raiders. Because *Nevada* and *Oklahoma* burned oil, a tanker went with them to keep them supplied.

Despite increased focus on winning the current war, an undercurrent of suspicion remained, particularly toward Japan. Increased cooperation became possible once an agreement was reached between Secretary of State Robert Lansing and Viscount Ishii Kikujiro, who headed a special congratulatory mission sent to the United States after the American entry into the war. This agreement committed both countries to supporting the Open Door Policy and the territorial integrity of China, a significant diplomatic victory. With peace in the Pacific assured by the promise of Japanese partnership, Benson was free to use the ships of the Pacific Fleet in the Atlantic and the Mediterranean; they assisted with convoy protection and other necessary activities.

A large number of ships and men were stationed overseas during the war. Many of these were focused on protecting the sea-lanes and approaches to Europe, ensuring the safe delivery of the troops of the American Expeditionary Force (AEF) to France. By August 1918, 1.4 million American troops had been safely delivered to France; none had been lost to enemy U-boats—a notable achievement, given the success German submarines had been enjoying in the spring of 1917.

By October 1918 there were 338 navy vessels in European waters, and they operated from a variety of locations. Submarine Division 5, with several L-class boats, operated from Bantry Bay and patrolled the Irish Sea. Submarine Division 4 was stationed at the Azores; monitor *Tonopah* and her guns provided local defense for their anchorage. A group of destroyers and a subchaser detachment was based at Queenstown. Additional destroyers were based at Brest.

The three cruisers of the *Salem* class operated from Gibraltar, along with the coastal torpedo boats of the *Bainbridge* class, which had sailed west from the Philippines to arrive on station. Subchasers operated from bases at Plymouth, Queenstown, Brest, Gibraltar, and Corfu. The chasers at Corfu participated in the Otranto Barrage, a patrol of the strait designed to prevent German and Austro-Hungarian submarines from leaving the Adriatic. The chasers on the barrage conducted thirty-seven hunts and claimed nineteen kills. None of these could be confirmed.

German U-boats were more successful. The largest of the navy's warships lost during the war was the armored cruiser *San Diego,* which struck a German mine off Fire Island, Maine, on 19 July 1918 and sank within half an hour. Destroyer *Jacob Jones* was torpedoed and sunk off the Scillies by *U 53* on 6 December 1917. On 15 October 1917, the destroyer *Cassin* lost her stern to a torpedo but was towed into Queenstown and repaired. A few transports, including *Antilles, President Lincoln,* and *Covington,* were torpedoed and sunk.

On 2 October 1918 the navy participated in its only major tactical operation of the war, the bombardment of Durazzo, an Austro-Hungarian base on the Albanian coast. Triggered by the defeat of Bulgaria, the bombardment was an attempt to diminish the ability of the Germans and Austrians to resupply their forces in the Balkans. The bombardment was conducted by a multinational force led by Italian vice admiral Paolo Thaon di Revel in battleship *Dante Alighieri*.

There were two bombardment waves. The first was composed of three Italian *Pisa*-class armored cruisers, eight British destroyers, and eight Italian torpedo boats. The second had three British light cruisers and four British destroyers. *Dante Alighieri,* along with additional cruisers and destroyers, operated as a distant covering force. The U.S. Navy's contribution was twelve subchasers that attempted to screen the bombardment area and prevent submarine attacks. Austro-Hungarian submarines *U 31* and *U 29* penetrated this screen; *U 31* torpedoed the cruiser *Weymouth,* blowing off her stern. The subchasers retaliated and claimed to have sunk her. *U 29* was sighted by subchaser *No. 129* as she attempted to get into firing position and was vigorously attacked. The subchasers also claimed her as a kill. Both submarines survived.

Naval aviation during the war focused primarily on the campaign against the U-boats. Patrol stations were added all along the eastern seaboard, from Halifax, Nova Scotia, to Key West, Florida. Additional stations were added at San Diego and in the Panama Canal Zone. Lighter-than-air training was performed in Akron, Ohio. Several overseas stations were created; there were four in Ireland, at Whiddy Island, Queenstown, Wexford, and Lough Foyle. A kite-balloon station was established at Berehaven. There were six additional seaplane stations in France and two in the Adriatic.

In England, a seaplane station at Killingholme, near the mouth of the Humber, was handed over to American forces in 1918. Operating under the Royal Navy's East Coast Command, planes from this base escorted coastal convoys and covered minelaying operations, as well as performing reconnaissance toward the Dutch coast. The northern bombing group fell under the Royal Navy's Dover command and had a distinctly offensive role, the bombing of German submarine bases at Zeebrugge, Ostend, and Bruges. Day-bombing squadrons were manned by marines, the night-bombing squadrons by naval personnel.

Sailors also became directly involved in the land war. Five 14-inch, 50-caliber guns were mounted on railway cars and shipped to France. Daniels considered this "one of the greatest achievements of the Navy." The mounts were designed, built, and delivered in less than four months, providing the United States with some of the "largest and most high-powered mobile land artillery in the world."[13] They fired at railway junctions and other vital locations behind German lines in the last months of the war.

In addition to guns, the navy also provided two regiments of marines for the fighting on the western front. The 5th and 6th Regiments formed the 4th Marine Brigade, part of the army's 2nd Infantry Division; they became two of the most celebrated American units of the war. These marine regiments fought at Chateau Thierry, Belleau Wood, and St. Mihiel, helping to blunt the final German offensives.

Summary and Assessment

The navy matured during World War I. In the years before the war the battle fleet grew large enough to be ranked as one of the most powerful in the world, but the supporting mechanisms behind it—the infrastructure and network of bases, the system of officer promotion, the approach to planning and coordinating military operations, and the development of tactics—lagged behind. During the war, many changes were made that addressed these deficiencies; the effectiveness of the navy's administration and organization increased in stages, with dramatic improvements coming in 1916. The final missing element was wartime experience.

Tactical thought and the development of battle doctrine suffered from a lack of practical experience. Although the 1916 Battle Instructions were thorough and reflected a good deal of analysis, they had evolved largely from tabletop simulations at the Naval War College. They had numerous shortcomings, particularly with respect to command, control, and communications. The navy's gunnery exercises were similarly inadequate, as illustrated by the experience of Rodman's battleships with the Grand Fleet. Wartime experience exposed these deficiencies and provided the opportunity to improve. The navy focused greater attention on these areas in its postwar development.

Although strategic planning had been much more thorough and detailed before the war, it was nonetheless inadequate and displayed a lack of imagination. As a result, the navy was unprepared for the war it was compelled to wage. It clung doggedly to Plans Black and Orange even when the hypothetical conflicts these plans envisioned became less and less likely the longer the war in Europe went on. Even after entering the war, Benson and Daniels were slow to abandon these plans and realize the importance of focusing their efforts against the U-boats.

The fact that ultimately they could do so, and could do so effectively in such a short period of time, was due to changes made in prior years. None of these was more important than the introduction of the Chief of Naval Operations. In the CNO's office the navy had an effective staff organization that could, in the name of the secretary, coordinate global activities among all the fleets. This development was a vital part of the effectiveness the navy enjoyed during the war.

The General Board was another effective staff. It had been in place for over a decade by the time the war began and had exercised a positive influence on ship designs, war plans, and the development of strategic mobility. The board was the driving influence behind the navy's global reach. The ability to send so many ships and men overseas, and their ability in turn to operate effectively so soon after arrival, was a testament to the positive influence of the board.

Daniels was responsible for a number of other changes that made the navy more efficient and effective. Under his tenure, a modern system of officer promotion based on skill and capability was finally introduced. Contemporary industrial-management practices were brought to the navy yards, transforming their operations. Their size, capability, and efficiency all increased, providing a solid foundation for future construction and maintenance of the fleet.

These important changes married with wartime experience to transform the navy. Through the effort exerted hunting for U-boats, escorting convoys, laying mines on the Northern Barrage, and steaming in company with the Grand Fleet, the navy became familiar with the demands and rigors of war. Lingering bureaucratic and organizational deficiencies had been corrected prior to entering the conflict, but the exposure to warfare was the missing ingredient that gave the navy the experience necessary to begin to transform itself fully into a modern institution.

The navy emerged from the war with all the necessary ingredients to become "second to none." The foundations had been laid. The necessary infrastructure, organization, and ships were in place. The next generation of officers had gained the required experience. They would spend the ensuing two decades of peace developing the plans and doctrine that would allow the navy to occupy the supreme position it would achieve at the end of the next war.

8

OTHER NAVIES

Vincent P. O'Hara and Richard Worth

Beyond the fleets of the major belligerents, others navies had the potential to significantly contribute to war operations but for one reason or the other did not.

As a result of South America's regional arms race, Brazil initiated a major building program in 1904 and ordered two dreadnoughts from British yards. While this gave the appearance of a burgeoning naval power, Brazil then suffered a remarkable reversal of economic fortune. A third battleship ordered from Britain had to be sold while building, and the completed ships suffered utter neglect. An advisor dispatched by the United States learned that battleships *Minas Gerais* and *São Paulo* had not fired their guns at all since their delivery in 1910, nor had their boiler tubes ever been cleaned.[1] Boiler problems associated with disuse hamstrung nearly the entire surface fleet. Not surprisingly, when Brazil declared war against Germany in 1917 in response to U-boat attacks, the navy had little to contribute. A cruiser-destroyer detachment operated out of Dakar for the final three months of the war.

Greece too had some naval potential, having just bested the Ottoman fleet in the First Balkan War and displaying enough ambition to buy two used battleships from the United States. However, the country found itself caught between its king's pro-German inclinations and pressure from the allies. The French effectively settled the matter by seizing the Greek navy in October 1916. The largest Greek units were demilitarized, while the French took over the most important light units. Thus it was Greece's ports that made the nation's largest contribution to the naval war.

There were two countries, however, that warrant attention: one whose vast fleet was little utilized and one whose outnumbered navy could only hope to manage the challenges it faced. These were the navies of Japan and the Ottoman Empire.

JAPAN

By the start of the First World War, Japan had completed a fifty-year transformation from a preindustrial hermit kingdom to an international power. The fleet had played a major role in this process, scoring key victories in the successful wars against Japan's two principal and theoretically stronger regional foes, China (1894–95) and Russia (1904–1905). In contrast, the Japanese Imperial Navy saw limited participation in the Great War but nevertheless obtained valuable operational experience and impressed its allies with the quality of its ships and men.

Pre-1914 History

The Japanese Imperial Navy was formed in the 1870s as the threat of European imperialism forced Japan's leaders to modernize the nation's industry and military and make self-defense the immediate priority. The incipient navy took its cues from France's Jeune École doctrine, which focused on trade war and coast defense with cruisers supported by swarms of expendable torpedo boats. The Japanese ordered one armored and six protected cruisers from British and French shipyards during the 1880s. By 1885, plans called for forty-six torpedo boats, and though finances restricted construction to only twenty-five, Japanese yards themselves completed a handful of these boats.

The 1890s brought dramatic change. Tension with China and concern over Russia's expansionist policies prompted the navy to develop a fleet capable of intervening overseas. This process coincided with the publication of *The Influence of Sea Power upon History,* Alfred Mahan's treatise on naval philosophy that influenced planning in all major navies. Mahan stressed the primacy of the battleship fleet and taught that this fleet should defeat its enemy counterpart to establish command of the sea. The Japanese found much here that applied to their situation as an island nation dependent upon overseas commerce, and they became convinced that the "aim of a naval engagement was the total annihilation of the enemy fleet in a decisive battle."[2] The decisive-battle concept crystallized as a permanent fixture in Japan's naval planning and dictated construction plans for decades to come.

Japan's first battleships, of the *Fuji* class, were laid down in British yards in 1894. That same year war erupted with China. A force of Japanese cruisers and gunboats trounced the Qing fleet at the battle of the Yalu River on 17 September 1894. This and the subsequent naval blockade of China's main harbor at Weihai guaranteed victory. However, after the war, Germany, Russia, and France prevented Japan from retaining Port Arthur and the Liaotung Peninsula, the principal reward Tokyo had expected from its triumph. This humiliating intervention accelerated Japan's naval expansion. Russia's subsequent lease of Port Arthur and its muscle-flexing in Korea confirmed Japan's perception that it needed to control the seas of East Asia for its own security.

In 1902 Japan negotiated a treaty with the world's premier power, the United Kingdom. The two signatories agreed to respect each other's special interests in China and Korea, to remain neutral if either signatory went to war with one enemy and to support the other if either became involved in war with multiple enemies. This treaty certified Japan's status as a great naval power and guaranteed that no coalition of European powers would steal the fruits of its next victory.

War with Russia came two years later. Instead of a mélange of cruisers and gunboats, the Japanese navy deployed an elite battle line: six battleships and eight armored cruisers supported by ten modern protected and unprotected cruisers, sixteen older cruisers, six gunboats, twenty destroyers, and fifty-seven torpedo boats. On 27–28 May 1905 this fleet defeated the Russian navy in the landmark battle of the Tsushima Straits, one of the most decisive naval victories in modern history.

Victory over the two greatest foreign threats did nothing to forestall another war from taking place at home. Japan's national constitution granted cabinet posts to the army and navy, each having the power to bring down a government; the savagery of their political and budgetary rivalry ensured that each service would endlessly seek pretexts to trumpet its own importance. Remarkably, the 1907 Imperial National Defense Policy, rather than correcting this duality, formalized it by designating two different countries as the primary threat to Japan: Russia (according to the army) and the United States (according to the navy).

The oceanic expanse separating Japan from the United States represented not a buffer but the only direction for Japanese expansion that granted the navy top billing. Hostility with America had simmered since the Hawaiian crisis of 1893, and American policy toward Japanese emigrants caused considerable offense. Both countries jealously guarded their interests in China. Even Mahan, so instrumental in the formation of Japanese naval policy, presented a problem; the popularity of his views in America gave a menacing hint of naval aspirations there. Japanese planners calculated that a proper defense necessitated a fleet equaling 70 percent of U.S. strength, and this gave birth to an "Eight-Eight-Eight Fleet" policy—eight new battleships and eight new battle cruisers built every eight years.

The 1911 renewal of the Anglo-Japanese alliance came with a hitch, as London insisted on a new clause removing any obligation for either country to fight the United States. The treaty thus lost much of its value for the Japanese, though it ensured continued Japanese access to some British technology. The Royal Navy had, in fact, already classified Japan as a future threat and stopped sharing secret information, like advanced fire-control methods and mechanisms, since 1909.[3]

Of course, the ultimate goal was freedom from reliance on any other fleet, and the Mahan-inspired "big ships, big guns" policy took hold in domestic warship construction, within the limits of that industry's capabilities. Two units of the *Satsuma* class (19,372 tons normal displacement; four 12-inch/45-caliber guns; twelve 10-inch/45; 18.25 knots) began construction in 1905 and were sources of great national pride, as the largest battleships in the world—at least until the British rushed their battleship *Dreadnought* into service, with its firepower concentrated in a battery of ten 12-inch guns, which became the pattern for all modern battleships. In fact, an early draft of the *Satsuma* design featured a uniform main battery like *Dreadnought*'s, but the technical challenge proved too intimidating for the Japanese. Likewise, Japan laid down a mighty foursome of armored cruisers, the *Tsukuba* and *Kurama* classes, armed with the same four 12-inch guns that a battleship would carry, only to see Britain commission *Invincible* with *eight* 12-inch guns. This was such a revolutionary step in cruiser development that *Invincible* and her sisters received a new rating as "battle cruisers," a label the Japanese quickly pinned onto the *Tsukuba*s and *Kurama*s despite their obvious inferiority to *Invincible*.

Japan finally commissioned its first dreadnoughts in 1912—more than five years after *Dreadnought* herself—completing *Kawachi* and *Settsu* (21,443 tons; twelve 12-inch guns; twenty knots) with 12-inch guns at a time when the British already had ships with 13.5-inch and the Americans 14-inch guns. The larger calibers completely derailed Japan's battle-cruiser program, and Tokyo accepted the humbling but pragmatic solution of importing from Britain not only a new ship but also shipbuilding expertise. *Kongo*, the last Japanese capital ship built overseas, reached completion in 1913—the largest warship in the world, mounting the largest guns. Thereafter the Japanese were able to complete her three sister ships in domestic yards.

This acquisition advanced Japanese naval technology in other ways: domestically constructed fire-control directors and range clocks of Vickers design appeared in 1915. Nonetheless, the Japanese remained well behind British standards of fire control throughout this period.

Japan went on to launch two *Fuso*-class battleships, even larger than *Kongo,* in 1914–15 and then two *Ise*-class ships in 1916–17. By 1917, when the Japanese laid down *Nagato,* which would become the first dreadnought with 16-inch guns (actually 410-mm), they were completely independent of British tutelage

Japan at War

Geography dictated that Japan's participation in the Great War at sea would not be commensurate with the size of its navy, even admitting the artificial inflation of its fleet list with old Russian vessels. (See table 8.1.)

Table 8.1 Japanese Navy, August 1914 and August 1918

Type	1914	1918
Dreadnought battleship	2	6
Predreadnought	11 (6 ex-Russian)	8 (3 ex-Russian)
Battle cruiser	6*	8*
Coastal-defense ship	3 (2 ex-Russian)	3 (1 ex-Russian)
Armored cruiser	12	11
Light cruiser	6	6
Protected cruiser	9	7
Destroyer	52	74
Torpedo boat	28	19
Gunboat	4	4
Minelayer	2	13

* Including the *Tsukubas* and *Kuramas*.

After declaring war on the Hohenzollern and Habsburg empires, the United Kingdom called upon Japan to honor the 1911 naval agreement. Japan saw a golden opportunity to advance its position in East Asia and on 15 August 1914 demanded that Germany surrender its holdings on China's Shandong Peninsula and in the Caroline, Mariana, and Marshall Islands, and also order all warships to evacuate the Pacific. Germany predictably failed to comply, and Japan declared war on 23 August.

Supported by a small British contingent, the Japanese navy landed 30,000 men on the Shandong Peninsula, besieged the Germans at Qingdao, and ultimately captured the city on 7 November 1914. Three naval squadrons—the 1st, Southern, and American Expeditionary—were formed ostensibly to hunt for Admiral Maximilian Spee's German force. The first two squadrons also occupied Germany's island possessions north of the equator. The latter formation patrolled the Pacific coast of South America until March 1915, when a British squadron sank the light cruiser *Dresden* off Chile.

When the German light cruiser *Emden* appeared in the Indian Ocean, the cruiser *Chikuma* sailed there. The battle cruiser *Ibuki* escorted the thirty-eight transport "Anzac Convoy" across the Indian Ocean to Aden. The Japanese 3rd Squadron, consisting of several cruisers, operated from Singapore; at the request of the Royal Navy, it patrolled the waters of Australia and New Zealand in late 1914 and again between March 1916 and December 1917. Its biggest action came in February 1915, when a landing party assisted in suppressing a mutiny of Indian troops at Singapore. After December 1917 the 1st Special Squadron assumed responsibility for Indian Ocean shipping lanes.

Though the Japanese sent personnel to serve with the Royal Navy (some of them dying at Jutland), they firmly resisted requests for ships in European waters. The desperate British then tried to buy two of the *Kongo*s, even sweetening the offer with two Royal Navy battleships in exchange. The Japanese were unmoved. Only when the British pledged postwar support for Japan's claims on its captured German territories was an agreement reached. In April 1917, two cruisers transferred to Cape Town and the 2nd Special Squadron deployed to Malta. The Mediterranean formation (one cruiser and eight new destroyers, eventually growing to two cruisers and fourteen destroyers, including two transferred British H-class units) escorted 788 allied ships in 348 missions. Its ships worked closely with the British and earned an excellent reputation.

Other Japanese vessels served in Europe but under foreign command. Japanese yards exported a dozen 665-ton destroyers to France, and the Italians and French purchased for patrol duties forty-seven and thirty-four former fishing vessels, respectively.

Japan's warship losses were insignificant. The Qingdao operation cost the torpedo boat *Shirotae* (grounded then shelled, 3 September) and the old protected cruiser *Naniwa* (torpedoed and sunk by German *T 90*, 17 October). The new destroyer *Sakaki* survived a torpedo hit from the Austro-Hungarian submarine *U 27* on 11 June 1917 off Corfu but lost sixty-eight men, including her captain.

The war provided little experience in combat but much in long-range escort and overseas deployment. The 2nd Special Squadron practiced the most modern techniques of antisubmarine warfare—lessons largely overlooked by the high command, which persisted with its fixation on "big ships, big guns." The June 1918 review of the Imperial National Defense Policy retained the United States as the navy's chief hypothetical foe, despite the fact the two powers were allies, and the navy determined that only an Eight-Eight-Eight construction program would provide sufficient strength to deal with this potential foe.

Japan's economy precluded the realization of such plans, but the 1922 Washington Conference transformed all strategic scenarios in any case. While it avoided another naval race like the one preceding World War I, the Washington Treaty galled many in the Japanese navy who saw national security only through unfettered growth in armament. This faction longed for an armed confrontation with the United States, and Japan's planning for a naval war became a self-fulfilling prophecy.

THE OTTOMAN NAVY

Pre-1914 History

The nineteenth century saw the once-formidable Ottoman navy decline into irrelevance, reflecting not only the fading status of the empire itself but its rulers' attitudes—the latter ranging from childlike extravagance to active hostility toward the maritime service. In 1890, after defeat in the Russo-Turkish War, Sultan Abdul Hamid II eased his distrust of the navy long enough to approve construction of an 8,100-ton battleship, larger than any previous domestic project; nineteen years later, the still-incomplete hull was cleared from the slip. Perhaps this was not surprising. In 1905 this same sultan explained to the British naval attaché that he preferred submarines over surface ships because they could not aim their guns at his palace.

The 1897 war with Greece revealed the fleet's impotence, and humiliation prompted the leadership to undertake genuine reform. Momentum increased with rise of the Young Turks and restoration of the constitution in 1908, but stable leadership did not return—the post of navy minister changed hands nine times over the next three years—and other fundamental problems remained.

The national treasury was exhausted. Plans for new construction repeatedly failed because finances could not cover refits of existing units. One ironclad waited in a foreign yard for six years while the navy scrounged for funds. A flotilla of old warships heading for modernization in Germany found itself stuck in Genoa for months pending settlement of Ottoman debts in Italy. The government resorted to public subscription for the purchase of warships in Germany; when that sum proved inadequate, the deal went through only because the sellers noticed that the deposed sultan's German bank account bridged the gap.

Even worse than the lack of modern ships was the lack of skilled personnel. Decades of naval decline had created shortages at all levels: commanders, enlisted men, strategic planners, and shipbuilders. Administrators often proved more attentive to self-interest than to duty. Crewmen who had brought a ship to Germany for reconstruction were abandoned on board a transport that sat at Kiel for over a year before anyone paid for their return trip. Officers' commissions, handed out like candy, provided personal income but not necessarily personal responsibilities. A yacht serving as stationary guard ship at Vathi had a crew of thirty-five men, along with thirteen officers—most of whom had never been on board.

As it turned out, those no-show officers were especially fortunate. The yacht became the recipient of battleship gunfire during the 1911–12 war against Italy—only the first losing campaign entangling the Ottomans on the eve of World War I. The subsequent Balkan Wars offered a more winnable naval scenario, which in the end simply made defeat more embarrassing. The Greek victors relied heavily on a single armored cruiser that repeatedly outmaneuvered and frustrated the Turkish Battle Division and its three capital ships.

Despite the navy's modern history of disorganization, indifference, and wartime disaster, the fleet did manage to acquire some respectable warships, due largely to eager businessmen who hoped that accommodations now might lead to lucrative deals later. Thanks to the efforts of banks in Britain and Turkey, as well as favorable terms from the Vickers yard, the Ottomans ordered a dreadnought, *Reşadiye*. Optimism rose so high that the fleet formulated a building program including six such ships—without specifics as to their financing or manning. The government duly rejected the plan. Other possibilities arose. A third party tried to procure Brazil's two dreadnoughts for Turkey in exchange for oil rights in Mesopotamia. This proposal fell through, but Brazil's antibattleship fervor made available a battleship under construction in Britain. Dealing with the builder Armstrong regarding port privileges in Turkey, the Ottomans managed to buy their second battleship, *Sultan Osman-i Evvel*. With the navy now enjoying great public support—Greek dreadnought ambitions were well known—policy solidified. The contract for a third dreadnought, *Fatih*, was signed with Vickers. Work on the ship began less than three weeks before Franz Ferdinand's assassination.

Table 8.2 Ottoman Navy, August 1914 and August 1918

Type	1914	1918
Dreadnought battleship	0*	0
Predreadnought	2	1
Battle cruiser	1**	1
Coastal-defense ship	2	2
Armored cruiser	1	0
Light cruiser	1***	1
Torpedo cruiser	2	2
Sloop/armed yacht	6	4
Destroyer	9	6
Torpedo boat	9	5
Gunboat	19	9
Minelayer	2	2

* *Sultan Osman I* (ex-*Rio de Janeiro*) seized 2 August 1914, the day before being handed over to Turkish control.
** Ex-German *Goeben*.
*** Ex-German *Breslau*.

By July 1914 Turkey had numerous foreign orders in place—unfortunately, in countries soon to be enemies. These included six 1,040-ton destroyers and two submarines from France; four 700-ton destroyers from Italy; and from Britain, three battleships, two 3,550-ton protected cruisers, four 1,100-ton destroyers, and two submarines.

In the event, Britain delayed construction of *Reşadiye* and *Sultan Osman-ı Evvel*, formally seizing the ships before either country was a combatant. This understandably caused great offense. The British did offer some compensation, but this was hardly sufficient to undo the diplomatic damage. In fact, Constantinople's lost fleet represented a force far stronger than the one the Ottomans actually operated during the war. Domestic yards had some capability but no longer met modern naval standards. As war nullified plans for British-led shipyard renovation, the Germans eagerly sought to take up the slack, but wartime efforts simply could not negate decades of neglect. In general, local shipyards sufficed only for basic maintenance, repairs, and conversion of merchant craft. Destiny, though, intervened to provide Turkey with a naval upgrade, and it was a game changer.

In 1910 the Ottomans opened discussions with Germany regarding used ships. The armored cruiser *Blücher*, just entering service with the

Germans at the time, earned consideration before ambitions escalated. The new battle cruiser *Von der Tann,* the newer battle cruiser *Moltke,* and even a battle cruiser so new it was known only as *"H"* were all contemplated. But when finances had the final word, the deal settled at two antique battleships and a set of new destroyers. No one could have imagined at the time that *"H"* would indeed go to Turkey, under her commissioned name *Goeben.* Commanded by Admiral Wilhelm Souchon and accompanied by the light cruiser *Breslau, Goeben* reached the Dardanelles on 10 August 1914 ahead of a superior British squadron seeking to bring her to battle. The two ships became *Yavuz Sultan Selim* and *Midilli,* respectively, and Souchon became the commander of the Ottoman fleet on 3 September 1914.

The Ottoman Navy at War

Germans would head the navy almost through the end of the war. Hubert von Rebeur-Paschwitz relieved Souchon on 24 August 1917 and served until 3 November 1918, when Arif Ahmet Paşa assumed command. Given Germany's experience with the complexities of fleet operations, the prominence of German personnel was reasonable, though they experienced some distaste at finding so many of the best-trained Turkish officers to be Anglophiles, a result of the British naval mission that had worked strenuously (though, for the most part, futilely) in Turkey from 1907 to 1910. German officers commanded many Ottoman ships, often with mixed crews.

It was the Turkish government's pro-German leanings prewar that facilitated wartime cooperation. *Goeben* had already visited Turkey in 1913, the same year that the Turks invited Germany to send a military mission to the straits. In August 1914, Admiral Guido von Usedom led a group of coast-defense personnel to serve in the Dardanelles and Bosporus installations. German technicians who came to inspect the fleet found the ships in shocking disrepair, even uninhabitable. Turks received technical training in Germany.

As organized in October 1914, the Ottoman navy concentrated its largest vessels in the I Squadron. In addition to *Yavuz,* this included the three capital ships bested by the Greeks—the armored vessel *Mesudiye* (9,190 tons) and the two ex-German battleships *Torgud Reis* and *Barbaros Hayredin* (10,013 tons). *Yavuz* completely outclassed her squadron mates, which the Germans considered unfit for sea, but the haste that had sent her to Turkey left her in need of boiler servicing. She lacked the latest fire-control equipment, shells, or propellant, which helps explain how Russian gunfire so easily outranged her. All these problems persisted into 1918 before correction. Active only intermittently and subject to neglect, *Yavuz's* greatest importance lay in her merely existing and forcing the Russians to account for her in their plans.

The II Squadron comprised the fleet's cruiser force. *Midilli* mostly shared in *Yavuz*'s fortunes, and like the battle cruiser she far excelled her squadron mates, which included a pair of German-built torpedo-cruisers (775 tons), soundly built but of no decisive merit. The British-built protected cruiser *Hamidiye* (3,904 tons) enjoyed a fine reputation based on her successful raiding operations in the Balkan War, when she had had only the Greeks to fight. The American-built *Mecidiye* (3,485 tons) resembled *Hamidiye* in specifications but suffered from faulty construction that severely compromised her seaworthiness. Coastal raids by the cruisers and *Yavuz* constituted the only appreciable naval offensive action by the Ottomans during the war.

The I Destroyer Squadron consisted of four new 765-ton German destroyers, the II Destroyer Squadron of four 284-ton French-built destroyers dating to 1907. Humbler still, the I and II Torpedo Boat Squadrons each had four vessels of 97–165 tons. All these units saw extensive service in escort and patrol duty, and the German-built destroyer *Muavenet-i Milliye* torpedoed and sank an old British battleship. On the other hand, one torpedo boat became a loss when its engines gave out during a pursuit by British destroyers.

The Mine Group included four disparate craft, including one that ranked second only to *Yavuz* in wartime impact, the 365-ton, German-built minelayer *Nusret*. On 8 March 1915 she laid some of Turkey's last remaining mines in the Dardanelles. Ten days later allied battleships tried to force their way through, and the mines sank three predreadnoughts. By securing the Dardanelles and the Bosporus, minelayers achieved the Ottoman navy's most important strategic success.

The fleet had no submarines operational when war began, though a pair of craft remained from the 1880s; not even the Germans found a way to make them useful. A damaged French submarine (ironically, the *Turquoise*), captured in 1915, took the name *Müstecip Ombaşı* but served only as a platform for propaganda and battery charging for German boats. The operation of German submarines from Turkish bases, however, combined with the threat of *Yavuz,* gave the Russians something more than a nuisance to manage.

For combat against submarines, the Turks eventually received depth charges, but at no time did their efforts accomplish much. Surface craft presented more deterrent than threat. Mines and nets had some value, but coastal guns were the most effective measure in the narrow waters.

Turkey's miscellany of small craft and auxiliaries worked tirelessly and incurred heavy losses. A collection of vessels on the Tigris and Euphrates, headed by the 422-ton gunboat *Marmaris,* had little impact on developments there.

Thanks largely to French assistance starting in 1913, the Turkish fleet had an air arm and a seaplane station at the outbreak of the war. In time, both the training and the operational arm acquired German commanders. Though units often transferred to duty with the army, the naval arm maintained its independence. It operated jointly with army fliers in Palestine and performed useful reconnaissance over the straits and the Sea of Marmara, suffering operational losses but none in combat.

Prewar events had evicted the Ottoman navy from the Aegean and Mediterranean. Wartime developments eliminated it as a factor in the Black Sea. Attrition and a lack of maintenance reduced the merchant fleet to near extinction and left allied submarines with a paucity of worthwhile targets. Caught in the pincer of strong allied fleets, the navy could hope only to defend its coasts, and in this limited task it managed heavily qualified success.

CONCLUSION

In August 1914, only a seer could have anticipated the events of the upcoming war at sea—its vast geographical scope or its long, grisly calendar. The relative scarcity of naval actions and an abundance of new technology developed over the preceding fifty years had left admiralties with tidy theories on how sea power should be exerted but no reliable template for its real-world application.

When war finally came it disregarded theory and lacked the knockout blow that the battles of the Yalu River, Santiago, or Tsushima had seemed to foretell. Although—amid much public anguish—Britain's battleships failed to win at Jutland the anticipated second Trafalgar, they imposed a distant blockade and kept Germany's capital ships confined to port. The Germans in turn innovated and attempted a counter-quarantine by striking from beneath the waves. In the end, the British blockade persisted while a revival of the discarded practice of convoying overcame the German effort, with war-winning implications.

In the Mediterranean, after Italy's switch to the Allied camp, two dreadnought navies faced one another across a much too narrow sea. A hit and run naval war ensured as the dreadnoughts swung at anchor, although even there they were not safe. The Italians pioneered the motor torpedo boat and special weapons while the Austrians proved equally crafty practitioners of littoral warfare—all to no avail as blockage and defeat on land led to the extinction of the Kaiserliche und Königliche Kriegsmarine.

The Russians, unfortunate students of the most recent naval lessons delivered by Japan a decade before, lacked a world-class fleet to implement what they had learned. Nonetheless, they made the most of mines and safeguarded their coastlines until a whirlwind of revolution brought defeat from an unexpected direction. Japan, their former foe, had witnessed the consequences of sending a powerful fleet to fight on the other side of the world and remained little more than a spectator throughout World War I. The U.S. Navy, on the other hand, jumped into the European conflict enthusiastically. Although American ideas like the North Sea mine barrier proved extravagant and ineffective, the exposure to war accelerated reforms already under way and laid the foundation for success in the next world war. France also absorbed the lessons from 1914 to 1918 to create a new and better navy, one that saw limited action but nonetheless would turn out to be the nation's best asset after defeat by Germany in 1940.

A remarkable feature of World War I's naval war was the rapid, often awkward, and sometimes different ways in which navies integrated new weapons and tools. Mass-produced motorboats and huge minelaying efforts made coastal operations more perilous. Wireless signals revolutionized command and control and gave intelligence innovative and sometimes decisive ways to discern enemy intentions. The age-old practice of commerce warfare was complicated by new airborne and submerged threats. These in turn engendered countermeasures, some effective and others desperate. Aircraft and submarines themselves promised to revolutionize naval warfare, although that promise remained unrealized in 1918. The battleship proved too expensive for routine use. Dreadnoughts nonetheless emerged from the war as the incumbent arbitrators of sea power, at least in the minds of most admirals, although others harbored doubts.

Junior officers in 1914 were to be admirals in 1939. Much of what they had learned in the first war they applied in the second. By 1945 MTBs and special weapons had ceased to be novelties; destroyers maintained their status as the workhorses of the fleet. Germany again attempted a subsurface naval blockade—unrestricted from near the start—with ultimately less success than in the first war, while the Royal Navy's continental quarantine lacked the impact of 1918. Only the U.S. Navy's subsurface force enjoyed success in this regard, against Japan. But once again advances in technology meant that lessons were not always reliable. Amphibious operations had mixed results in the first war but in the second they constituted a decisive instrument of naval power. Aircraft sank dozens of ships at sea in the first war and thousands in the second. Finally, the mighty dreadnoughts that were the measure of naval strength in 1914 and so remained in 1939 finished the latter war as artillery platforms to support landing forces and as aircraft-carrier escorts. Today, a century later, weapons pioneered in the Great War—the submarine and airplane—are the arbiters of sea power, while battleships survive only as museums. Yet the lesson of World War I is that peacetime evolution is followed by wartime revolution. New weapons—satellites, drones, lasers, magnetic guns—exist. The template is that future naval wars will be different in unexpected ways.

APPENDIX: CONVERSIONS AND ABBREVIATIONS

Conversions

1 nautical mile = 2,205 yards, 1,852 meters, or 1.151 statute miles
1 knot = 1.852 km/hour or 1.151 statute mile/hour
1 meter = 1.094 yards
1 yard = .9144 meters
1 centimeter = .3937 inches
1 inch = 2.54 centimeters
1 kilogram = 2.205 pounds
1 pound = 0.4536 kilograms
1 tonne = .9842 long tons
1 long ton = 1.016 tonnes

Abbreviations

General

AA	antiaircraft
ACNS	Assistant Chief of Naval Staff
AEF	American Expeditionary Force
AH	Austro-Hungarian
AP	armor-piercing
APC	armor-piercing capped
ASW	antisubmarine warfare
BEF	British Expeditionary Force
BL	breechloading
Cal.	caliber
CNO	Chief of Naval Operations
CNS	Chief of Naval Staff
DC	depth charge
DCNS	Deputy Chief of Naval Staff
D/F	direction finding
DP	dual-purpose
EOC	Elswick Ordnance Company
F/C	firing cycle
GRT	gross registered tons

HE	high-explosive (or high effect)
KM	Kaiserliche Marine
k.u.k.	Kaiserliche und Königliche
LDF	Local Defence Flotilla
Mk	mark
MV	muzzle velocity
NCO	noncommissioned officer
NGS	Naval General Staff
NID	Naval Intelligence Division
ONI	Office of Naval Intelligence
QF	quick-firing
RAF	Royal Air Force
RAN	Royal Australian Navy
RCN	Royal Canadian Navy
RFA	Royal Fleet Auxiliary
RFC	Royal Flying Corps
RN	Royal Navy
RNAS	Royal Naval Air Service
RNCF	Royal Navy Cordite Factory
RNR	Royal Navy Reserve
RNR(T)	Royal Navy Reserve (Trawler)
RNVR	Royal Navy Volunteer Reserve
SIGINT	signals intelligence
Sk	*Schnellfeuergeschütz* (rapid fire)
SNIS	Service of Observation and Communications (Sluzhba nabliudeniia i sviazi)
U.S.	United States
USN	U.S. Navy
VSM	Vickers Sons and Maxim
W/T	wireless [telegraphy]

Ship Types

AC	armored cruiser
AMC	armed merchant cruiser
Aux	Auxiliary
BB	dreadnought battleship
BC	battle cruiser
BM	monitor
C	protected cruiser
CB	coastal battleship (obsolete)
CD	coastal defense armored ship
CL	light cruiser
CMB	coastal motorboat

CV	aircraft carrier
DD	destroyer
DS	sloop/escort
DC	corvette
GB	gunboat
MAS	Italian motor torpedo boat (*motoscafi armati siluranti* or *motoscafi anti sommergibili*)
ML	minelayer
MTB	motor torpedo boat
O	old
OBB	predreadnought battleship
PB	patrol boat
SC	submarine chaser
SS	submarine
TB	torpedo boat
U-boat	*unterseeboot* (German or Austro-Hungarian submarine)

NOTES

Chapter 1. Austria-Hungary

1. P. Handel-Mazzetti, "Hermann Freiherr von Spaun," *Neue Österreichische Biographie ab 1918* 15, 113–18.
2. For the STT shipyard at Trieste it was important to start building both dreadnoughts immediately after the completion of the last *Radetzky*-class unit. To wait a year for the financial approval would require giving notice to the hundreds of workers, endangering the existence of STT and delaying construction even more. A solution was found by arranging a loan from the mighty Creditanstalt bank to STT and declaring the ships to be built on speculation and sold abroad if not bought by the navy. In fact the shipyard, together with the Skoda and Witkowitz factories (where guns and triple turrets were ordered), belonged to the same bank. Everybody of importance knew the real situation, but no one could give any official guarantee before the parliaments gave their approval. See E. Sieche, "SMS *Szent István*, Hungaria's Only and Ill-Fated Dreadnought," *Warship International*, no. 2 (1991), 112–46.

Chapter 2. France

1. The classification of French cruisers often varied between 1874 and 1897 and even beyond. Documents, official and unofficial, were not always consistent in their terminology, and some warships changed classification several times. By 1914 the categories had finally become armored cruisers, protected cruisers (officially first- or second-class), and third-class cruisers. Typical of the persistent confusion, one can cite the example of *Surcouf, Cosmao, Lavoisier,* and *D'Estrées,* presented as sloops in the book *Flottes de combat* 1914, even though contemporary fleet lists from 1892 on classified them as third-class cruisers.

Chapter 6. Russia

1. P. E. Stogov, "Vospominaniia o Morskom General'nom Shtabe," in S. V. Gladkii and Iu. K. Dvorzhitskii, eds., *S beregov Ameriki: Iubileinyi istoricheskii sbornik o-va russkikh morskikh ofitserov v Amerikie 1923–1938* (New York: Association of Former Russian Naval Officers in America, 1939), 260.
2. V. V. Romanov, "Radiorazviedka," *Zapiski Voenno-Morskogo Istoricheskago imeni Admirala Kolchaka Kruzhka,* no. 7 (January 1937), 28.

3. Telegram dated 28 February [1917?], ADM 137/4695, National Archives, Kew, London.
4. Constantine Benckendorff [Benkendorf], *Half a Life: The Reminiscences of a Russian Gentleman* (London: Richards, 1954), 155.
5. I. V. Zav'ialov, "Podvodnyi flot v kanun Pervoi mirovoi voiny," *Gangut,* no. 51 (2009), 98.
6. R. D. Layman and Boris V. Drashpil, "Early Russian Shipboard Aviation," U.S. Naval Institute *Proceedings* 97, no. 4 (April 1971), 56.
7. Quoted in Paul G. Halpern, *A Naval History of World War I* (Annapolis, Md.: Naval Institute Press, 1994), 235.

Chapter 7. United States

1. Paolo E. Coletta, ed., *American Secretaries of the Navy,* vol. 2, *1913–1972* (Annapolis, Md.: Naval Institute Press, 1980), xiv.
2. Julius Augustus Furer, *Administration of the Navy Department in World War Two* (Washington, D.C.: Department of the Navy, 1959), 109.
3. Ibid.
4. Timothy S. Wolters, *Managing a Sea of Information: Shipboard Command and Control in the United States Navy, 1899–1945* (Doctor of Philosophy thesis, Massachusetts Institute of Technology, 2003), 84.
5. Ibid., 100–101.
6. Paul G. Halpern, *A Naval History of World War I* (Annapolis, Md.: Naval Institute Press, 1994), 359.
7. *Description of Maneuver Board, Appliances, and Rules, Section 18, Admiral Fletcher's Tactics of the Battle Line*, Naval War College, Newport, R.I., 1916, 2.
8. *Battle Instructions, United States Atlantic Fleet,* 27 May 1916.
9. Norman Friedman, *Naval Firepower* (Annapolis, Md.: Naval Institute Press, 2010), 184.
10. *Annual Reports of the Navy Department for the Fiscal Year 1916* (Washington, D.C.: Government Printing Office, 1917), 22.
11. Jerry W. Jones, *U.S. Battleship Operations in World War I* (Annapolis, Md.: Naval Institute Press, 1998), 87.
12. Donald A Yerxa, *Admirals and Empire: The United States Navy and the Caribbean, 1898–1945* (Columbia: University of South Carolina Press, 1991), 47.
13. *Annual Report of the Secretary of the Navy for the Fiscal Year 1918* (Washington, D.C.: Government Printing Office, 1918), 47–48.

Chapter 8. Other Navies

1. David Healy, "Admiral William B. Caperton and United States Naval Diplomacy in South America, 1917–1919," *Journal of Latin American Studies* 8, no. 2 (November 1976), 316–17.
2. Sadao Asada, *From Mahan to Pearl Harbor* (Annapolis, Md.: Naval Institute Press, 2006), 8.
3. Friedman, *Naval Firepower,* 228.

BIBLIOGRAPHY

The historiography of the First World War is immense. This essay identifies important works the authors used in composing their chapters. Some recent works in English are also included to guide the interested reader.

AUSTRIA HUNGARY

Austro-Hungarian Warships

Aichelburg, Wladimir. *K.u.k. Unterseeboote*. Graz: Weishaupt, 1981.

———. *Register der k.(u.)k. Kriegsschiffe*. Vienna: Neuer Wissenschaftlicher Verlag, 2002.

Aichelburg, W., et al. *Die Tegetthoff-Klasse*. Munich: Bernard & Graefe, 1981.

Bilzer, Franz Ferdinand. *Die Torpedoschiffe und Zerstörer der k.u.k. Kriegsmarine*. Graz: Weishaupt, 1990.

———. *Die Torpedoboote der k.u.k. Kriegsmarine*. Graz: Weishaupt, 1996.

Baumgartner, Lothar, and E. Sieche. *Die Schiffe der k.(u.)k. Kriegsmarine im Bild*. Vol. 1, *1848–1895*. Vienna: Stöhr, 1999.

———. *Die Schiffe der k.(u.)k. Kriegsmarine im Bild*. Vol. 2, *1896–1918*. Vienna: Stöhr, 2001.

Greger, René. *Austro-Hungarian Warships of World War I*. London: Ian Allan, 1976.

Gogg, Karl. *Österreichs Kriegsmarine 1440–1848*. Salzburg: Bergland Buch, 1967.

———. *Österreichs Kriegsmarine 1848–1918*. Salzburg: Bergland Buch, 1972.

Sieche, Erwin. *Die Kreuzer der k.u.k. Marine*. Friedberg: Podzun-Pallas-Verlag, 1996.

———. *Die Schlachtschiffe der k.u.k. Marine*. Friedberg: Podzun-Pallas-Verlag, 1991.

———. *Die Zerstörer der k.u.k Marine*. Friedberg: Podzun-Pallas-Verlag, 1999.

———. *Kreuzer und Kreuzerprojekte der k.u.k. Kriegsmarine 1889–1918*. Vienna: Neuer Wissenschaftlicher Verlag, 2002.

Austro-Hungarian Operations

Gruber, Karl. *Seemacht unter rot weiss roter Flagge*. Salzburg: Milizverlag, 2005/2006.

Halpern, Paul G. *Anton Haus: Österreich-Ungarns Grossadmiral*. Graz: Styria, 1998.

Sokol, Hans Hugo. *Des Kaisers Seemacht*. Vienna: Amalthea, 1980.

———. *Österreich-Ungarns Seekrieg 1914–18*. Zürich: Amalthea, 1933.

Austro-Hungarian Naval Weapons and Aircraft

Schupita, Peter. *Die K.u.k. Seeflieger.* Koblenz: Bernard & Graefe, 1983.

———. *Die Waffen der k.(u.)k. Kriegsmarine in Bild, 1860–1918.* Vienna: Stöhr, 2006.

For communications:

Sifferlinger, Nikolaus A. *Auslaufen verspricht Erfolg—Die Radiotelegraphie der k.u.k. Kriegsmarine.* Vienna: Verlag Österreich, 2000.

For intelligence:

Baumgartner, Lothar, and Nikolaus Sifferlinger. *Österreichische Militärgeschichte, Sonderband 2002-1 & 2002-2.* Vienna: Stöhr, 1993.

———. *"Abgelauscht"—Die Funkaufklärung der k.u.k. Kriegsmarine.* Vienna: Stöhr, 2002.

FRANCE

Garier, Gérard. *L'odyssée technique et humaine du sous-marin en Francen time 3, à l'épreuve de la Grande Guerre.* Nantes: Marines éditions, 2002.

Labayle-Couhat, Jean. *French Warships of World War I.* London: Ian Allan, 1974.

Laurens, Adolphe, et al. *Précis d'histoire de la guerre navale 1914–1918.* Paris: Payot, 1929.

Le Masson, Henri, *Propos maritimes.* Paris: Editions Maritimes et d'Outre-Mer, 1970.

Masson, Philippe. *Histoire de la Marine,* tome 2, *de la vapeur à l'atome.* Paris: Lavauzelle, 1983.

Morareau, Lucien, et al. *L'aviation maritime française pendant la Grande guerre.* Paris: Ardhan, 1999.

Moulin, Jean. *Les navires de guerre français 1914–1918 en images.* Nantes: Marines éditions, 2008.

Salaun, Henri. *La Marine française.* Paris: Les éditions de France, 1934.

Union des grandes associations françaises contre la propaganda ennemie. *Les marins de France.* Paris: UGAFCPE, 1919[?].

GERMANY

General

Granier, Gerhard. *Die deutsche Seekriegsleitung im Ersten Weltkrieg.* Koblenz: Bundesarchiv, 1999.

Herwig, Holger H. *Luxury Fleet: The Imperial German Navy 1888–1918.* London: George Allen & Unwin, 1980.

Scheer, Reinhard. *Germany's High Sea Fleet in the World War.* London: Cassell, 1920.

Spindler, Arno. *Der Krieg zur See 1914–1918.* Berlin: Mittler & Sohn, 1964.

Warships

Bürkner, Hans. *Erinnerungen und Gedanken eines alten Kriegsschiffbauers*. Dresden: Literatur-Vert. 1940.

Grießmer, Axel. *Große Kreuzer der Kaiserlichen Marine 1906–1918*. Bonn: Bernard & Graefe, 1996.

———. *Linienschiffe der Kaiserlichen Marine 1906–1918*. Bonn: Bernard & Graefe, 1999.

Gröner, Erich. *Die deutschen Kriegsschiffe 1815–1945*. 5 vols. Munich: Lehmann, 1982–1999.

Koop, Gerhard, and Klaus-Peter Schmolke. *Die Großen Kreuzer Von der Tann bis Hindenburg*. Bonn: Bernard & Graefe, 1998.

———. *Die Linienschiffe der Bayern-Klasse*. Bonn: Bernard & Graefe, 1996.

———. *Die Linienschiffe der Brandenburg-bis Deutschland*-Klasse. Bonn: Bernard & Graefe, 2001.

———. *Kleine Kreuzer 1903–1918 Bremen-bis Cöln-Klasse*. Bonn: Bernard & Graefe, 2004.

———. *Von der Nassau- zur König-Klasse*. Bonn: Bernard & Graefe, 1999.

Weyer, B. *Taschenbuch der Kriegsflotten 1918*. Bonn: Bernard & Graefe, 1997.

Surface Warfare

Fock, Harald. *Schwarze Gesellen: Torpedobotte bis 1914*. Vol. 1. Herford: Koehlers, 1979.

———. *Schwarze Gesellen: Torpedobotte bis 1914*. Vol. 2. Herford: Koehlers, 1981.

———. *Z-vor!*. Vol. 1. Herford: Koehlers, 1989.

Submarines

Bauer, Hermann. *Als Führer der U-Boote im Weltkriege*. Leipzig: Koehler & Amelang, 1942.

Herzog, Bodo. *60 Jahre deutsche U-Boote 1906–1966*. Munich: Lehmann, 1968.

Michelsen, Andreas. *Der U-Bootkrieg 1914–1918*. Leipzig: Hase & Koehler, 1925.

Rössler, Eberhard. *Deutsche U-Boote 1898–1918*. Hamburg: Mittler, 2011.

———. *Die deutschen U-Kreuzer und Transport-U-Boote*. Bonn: Bernard & Graefe, 2003.

———. *Die Torpedos der deutschen U-Boote*. Hamburg: Mittler, 2005.

———. *Die Unterseeboote der Kaiserlichen Marine*. Bonn: Bernard & Graefe, 1997.

Spindler, Arno. *Der Handelskrieg mit U-Booten*. Berlin: Mittler & Sohn, 1932.

Intelligence

Giessler, Helmuth. *Der Marine Nachrichten- und Ortungsdienst*. Munich: J. F. Lehmann, 1971.

Logistics

Karlsch, Rainer, and Raymond Stokes. *Faktor Öl: die Mineralölwirtschaft in Deutschland 1859–1974*. Munich: Beck, 2003.

Weapons

Ledebur, von Gerhard. *Die Seemine*. Munich: Lehmann, 1977.

Schmalenbach, Paul. *Die Geschichte der deutschen Schiffsartillerie*. Herford: Koehlers, 1968.

Schubert, Peter, et al. *Die deutschen Marinen im Minenkrieg, Bd 1*. Rostock: Norderstedt, 2006.

Personnel

Scheerer, Thomas E. *Die Marineoffiziere der Kaiserlichen Marine*. Bochum: Winkler, 2002.

GREAT BRITAIN

Beesley, Patrick. *Room 40: British Naval Intelligence 1914–18*. London: Hamish Hamilton, 1982.

Black, Nicholas. *The British Naval Staff in the First World War*. Rochester, N.Y.: Boydell, 2009.

Brooks, John. *Dreadnought Gunnery and the Battle of Jutland: The Question of Fire Control*. Abingdon, England: Routledge, 2005.

Brown, D. K. *The Grand Fleet: Warship Design and Development 1906–1922*. London: Chatham, 1999.

Corbett, Sir Julian, and Henry Newbolt. *Naval Operations*. 5 vols. London: Longmans, Green, 1920–31.

Dittmar, F. J., and J. J. Colledge. *British Warships 1914–1919*. London: Ian Allen, 1972.

Goldrick, James. *The King's Ships Were at Sea: The War in the North Sea August 1914–February 1915*. Annapolis, Md.: Naval Institute Press, 1984.

Grainger, John, ed. *The Maritime Blockade of Germany in the Great War*. Aldershot, England: Ashgate for the Naval Records Society, 2003.

Marder, Arthur J. *From the Dreadnought to Scapa Flow*. 5 vols. Oxford, England: Oxford University Press, 1961–1970.

Ranft, Brian, ed. *The Beatty Papers*. Vol. 1, *1902–1918*. Aldershot, England: Scolar Press for the Naval Records Society, 1989.

———. *The Beatty Papers*. Vol. 2, *1916–1927*. Aldershot, England: Scolar Press for the Naval Records Society, 1993.

ITALY

The most important study of the Italian navy during World War I is the Ufficio Storico della Marina Militare [hereafter USMM], Cronistoria documentata della Guerra marittima italo-austriaca 1915–1918, Rome, 1919–1933, in eighteen volumes. It is available at the Ufficio Storico's Archives in Rome. An eight-volume version is:

Almagià, Guido, Silvio Salza, and Zoli Achille. *La Marina italiana nella Grande Guerra.* Florence: Vallecchi, 1935–1942.

Warships

Bagnasco. Erminio, and Rastelli Achille. *Navi e marinai italiani nella Grande Guerra.* Parma: Albertelli, 1997.

Fraccaroli, Aldo. *Italian Warships of World War One.* London: Ian Allan, 1970.

Politics and Naval Development

Baratelli, Franco Micali. *La Marina italiana nella vità nazionale (1860–1914).* Milan: Mursia, 1983.

Gabriele, Mariano. *Le convenzioni navali della Triplice.* Rome: USMM, 1969.

Giuliano, Friz, and Gabriele Mariano. *La politica navale italiana dal 1885 al 1915.* Rome: USMM, 1982.

Operations

Bravetta, Ettore. *La Grande Guerra sul mare.* Milan: Mondadori, 1925.

Ferrante, Ezio. *La Grande Guerra in Adriatico.* Rome: USMM, 1987.

Manfroni, Camillo. *I nostri alleati navali.* Milan: Mondadori, 1927.

———. *Storia della Marina italiana durante la Guerra mondiale.* Bologna: Zanichelli, 1925.

Po, Guido. *La guerra marittima dell'Italia.* Milan: Corbaccio, 1934.

Rastelli, Achille, and Alessandro Massignani, eds. *La guerra navale 1914–1918.* Valdagno: Gino Rossato, 2002.

Personnel

Ferrante, Ezio. *Il Grande Ammiraglio Paolo Thaon di Revel.* Supplemento della Rivista Marittima, August/September 1989.

Turrini Alessandro, *L'opera di Cesare Laurenti.* Rome: USMM, 2002.

Air

Ferrari, Paolo, ed. *La Grande Guerra aerea 1915–1918.* Valdagno: Gino Rossato, 1994.

RUSSIAN NAVY

Many excellent monographs are available; however, there is as yet no post-glasnost work that covers the Russian navy throughout the war. In addition to the works cited in the endnotes and source notes to the tables, the following provide valuable coverage of the First World War era.

Graf, H. *The Russian Navy in War and Revolution from 1914 up to 1918.* Munich: R. Oldenbourg, 1923.

Greger, René. *The Russian Fleet 1914–1917.* Translated by Jill Gearing. London: Ian Allan, 1972.

Mawdsley, Evan. *The Russian Revolution and the Baltic Fleet: War and Politics, February 1917–April 1918*. London: Macmillan, 1978.

Pavlovich, N. B. *The Fleet in the First World War.* Vol. 1, *Operations of the Russian Fleet*. New Delhi: Amerind, 1979.

Saul, Norman E. *Sailors in Revolt: The Russian Baltic Fleet in 1917.* Lawrence: Regents Press of Kansas, 1978.

For those with a knowledge of Russian:

Ships

Apal'kov, Iu. V. *Boevye korabli russkogo flota 8.1914g–10.1917g: Spravochnik.* St. Petersburg: Intek, 1996.

Tsvetkov, I. F. *Istoriia otechestvennogo sudostroeniia.* Vol. 3, *Sudostroenie v nachale XX vv.* St. Petersburg: Sudostroenie, 1995. [This is an indispensable source for ships, programs, and the shipbuilding industry.]

Politics and Naval Development

Grigorovich, I. K. *Vospominaniia vyvshego morskogo ministra.* St. Petersburg: Deva, 1993.

Finally, the journal *Gangut* is a rich source of articles on many aspects of the Russian navy, while the website www.sistematima.narod.ru provides access to scans of many handbooks, manuals, and other publications from the First World War era.

U.S. NAVY

Beach, Edward L. *From Annapolis to Scapa Flow.* Annapolis, Md.: Naval Institute Press, 2003.

Braisted, William Reynolds. *The United States Navy in the Pacific, 1909–1922.* Austin: University of Texas Press, 1971.

Chisholm, Donald. *Waiting for Dead Men's Shoes: Origins and Development of the U.S. Navy's Officer Personnel System, 1793–1941.* Stanford, Calif.: Stanford University Press, 2001.

Coletta, Paolo E., ed. *American Secretaries of the Navy.* Vol. 2, *1913–1972.* Annapolis, Md.: Naval Institute Press, 1980.

Jones, Jerry W. *U.S. Battleship Operations in World War I.* Annapolis, Md.: Naval Institute Press, 1998.

Packard, Wyman H. *A Century of U.S. Naval Intelligence.* Washington, D.C.: Department of the Navy, 1996.

Still, William N., Jr. *Crisis at Sea: The United States Navy in European Waters in World War I.* Gainesville: University Press of Florida, 2006.

Wolters, Timothy S. *Managing a Sea of Information: Shipboard Command and Control in the United States Navy, 1899–1945.* Doctor of Philosophy thesis, Massachusetts Institute of Technology, 2003.

Yerxa, Donald A. *Admirals and Empire: The United States Navy and the Caribbean, 1898–1945.* Columbia: University of South Carolina Press, 1991.

OTHER NAVIES

Evans, David C., and Mark R. Peattie. *Kaigun: Strategy, Tactics, and Technology in the Imperial Japanese Navy 1887–1941.* Annapolis, Md.: Naval Institute Press, 1997.

Konstantinos, Varfis. "Naval Actions during the First Balkan War, 1912–1913." In *New Interpretations in Naval History,* edited by William R. Roberts and Jack Sweetman. Annapolis, Md.: Naval Institute Press, 1991.

Langensiepen, Bernd, and Ahmet Güleryüz. *Ottoman Steam Navy 1828–1923.* Annapolis, Md.: Naval Institute Press, 1995.

Yaner, Emir, ed. *Osmanli Donanmasinin Seyir Defteri: Gemiler, Efsaneler, Denizciler/Logbook of the Ottoman Navy: Ships, Legends, Sailors.* Istanbul: Pera Museum, 2009.

GENERAL WORKS

Friedman, Norman. *Naval Weapons of World War One.* Annapolis, Md.: Naval Institute Press, 2011.

Gardiner, Robert, ed. *Conway's All the World's Fighting Ships 1906–1921.* Annapolis, Md.: Naval Institute Press, 1985.

Halpern, Paul G. *The Naval War in the Mediterranean 1914–18.* Annapolis, Md.: Naval Institute Press, 1987.

———. *A Naval History of World War I.* Annapolis, Md.: Naval Institute Press, 1994. [This is the best one-volume history.]

Hough, Richard. *The Great War at Sea 1914–1918.* Oxford, England: Oxford University Press, 1983.

Massie, Robert K. *Castles of Steel: Britain, Germany, and the Winning of the Great War at Sea.* New York: Random House, 2003.

———. *Dreadnought: Britain, Germany, and the Coming of the Great War.* New York: Random House, 1991.

Tucker, Spencer C. *The Encyclopedia of World War I: A Political, Social, and Military History.* Santa Barbara, Calif.: ABC CLIO, 2005.

BATTLES

Barrett, Michael B. *Operation Albion: The German Conquest of the Baltic Islands.* Bloomsdale, IN: Indiana University Press, 2008.

Campbell, John. *Jutland: An Analysis of the Fighting.* London: Conway Maritime Press, 1986.

Costello, J. and T. Hughes. *Jutland 1916.* New York: Holt, Reinhart, Winston, 1976.

Gordon, Andrew. *The Rules of the Game: Jutland and British Naval Command.* London: John Murray, 1996.

Halpern, Paul G. *The Battle of the Otranto Straits*. Bloomington: Indiana University Press, 2004.
Macintyre, Donald. *Jutland*. New York: Norton, 1958.
Osborne, Eric W. *The Battle of Heligoland Bight*. Bloomington: Indiana University Press, 2006.

INDEX

N

The Naval Institute Press is the book-publishing arm of the U.S. Naval Institute, a private, nonprofit, membership society for sea service professionals and others who share an interest in naval and maritime affairs. Established in 1873 at the U.S. Naval Academy in Annapolis, Maryland, where its offices remain today, the Naval Institute has members worldwide.

Members of the Naval Institute support the education programs of the society and receive the influential monthly magazine *Proceedings* or the colorful bimonthly magazine *Naval History* and discounts on fine nautical prints and on ship and aircraft photos. They also have access to the transcripts of the Institute's Oral History Program and get discounted admission to any of the Institute-sponsored seminars offered around the country.

The Naval Institute's book-publishing program, begun in 1898 with basic guides to naval practices, has broadened its scope to include books of more general interest. Now the Naval Institute Press publishes about seventy titles each year, ranging from how-to books on boating and navigation to battle histories, biographies, ship and aircraft guides, and novels. Institute members receive significant discounts on the Press's more than eight hundred books in print.

Full-time students are eligible for special half-price membership rates. Life memberships are also available.

For a free catalog describing Naval Institute Press books currently available, and for further information about joining the U.S. Naval Institute, please write to:

Member Services
U.S. Naval Institute
291 Wood Road
Annapolis, MD 21402-5034
Telephone: (800) 233-8764
Fax: (410) 571-1703
Web address: www.usni.org